MW00453262

Provincial Passages

Provincial Passages

Culture, Space, and the Origins
of Chinese Communism

WEN-HSIN YEH

University of California Press

BERKELEY   LOS ANGELES   LONDON

An earlier version of Chapter 8 was originally published as "Middle
County Radicalism: The May Fourth Movement in Hangzhou,"
China Quarterly 140 (December 1994): 903–25.

University of California Press
Berkeley and Los Angeles, California

University of California Press, Ltd.
London, England

Library of Congress Cataloging-in-Publication Data
Yeh, Wen-hsin.
    Provincial passages : culture, space, and the origins of Chinese
communism / Wen-hsin Yeh.
        p.   cm.
    Includes bibliographical references and index.
    ISBN 0-520-20068-3
    1. Chekiang Province (China)—History.   2. Intellectuals—
China—Chekiang Province.   3. Communism—China—Chekiang
Province.   4. China—History—May Fourth Movement, 1919.
I. Title.
    DS793.C3Y44   1996
    306'.0951'242—dc20   95-38179
                                                          CIP

Printed in the United States of America
9 8 7 6 5 4 3 2 1

The paper used in this publication meets the minimum requirements
of American National Standard for Information Sciences—Permanence
of Paper for Printed Library Materials, ANSI Z39.48-1984.⊚

To the memory of my grandmother, Yen Lin Mulan
(1893–1992)

Contents

Acknowledgments

Support for the research and writing of this book was provided by the Committee on Scholarly Communication with the People's Republic of China, and by the President's Humanities Fellowship, the Chancellor's Humanities Fellowship, the Committee on Research, the Center for Chinese Studies, and the Institute of East Asian Studies, of the University of California at Berkeley.

Research for this project was launched in the summer of 1990 in Hangzhou. I am grateful for the assistance of the many archivists, researchers, and librarians at the Archives of the Historical Commission of the Chinese Nationalist Party, Taipei; East Asiatic Library, the Center for Chinese Studies Library, University of California at Berkeley; the East Asian Collection, Hoover Institution, Stanford, California; the Museum of the First Party Congress of the Chinese Communist Party, Shanghai; the Shanghai Municipal Library; the Shanghai Academy of Social Sciences; the Zhejiang Academy of Social Sciences and the Zhejiang Provincial Archives, Hangzhou.

I send thanks to Professor Wang Xi, Director, Center for American Studies, Fudan University, for helping with the arrangement of a field trip to Yecun, Jinhua, in the summer of 1992.

Earlier versions of parts of this study were presented to a Fudan University conference, "China's Quest for Modernization," Shanghai, June 1992; at the Annual Meeting of the Association of Asian Studies, Los Angeles, March 1993; and at the International Symposium on the Urban History of Shanghai at the Shanghai Academy of Social Sciences in August 1993. I gratefully acknowledge the comments and suggestions received on those occasions.

Susan Glosser and Guo Qitao helped to assemble the maps and the bibliography of this book. Timothy Weston offered research assistance at an earlier stage. Susan Stone gave indispensable advice on UNIX commands. Elinor Levine not only provided assistance with the maps and the bibliography but also coordinated communication during the stage of production. I owe her an especially great debt for making this such a reasonably painless process.

Scholarly comments and helpful suggestions were offered by Professors Marie-Claire Bergère, Prasenjit Duara, Joshua Fogel, Lü Fang-shang, Paul Pickowicz, and Xiong Yuezhi. I am particularly grateful to James Clark, David Keightley, Robert Middlekauff, Elizabeth Perry, Don Price, Mary Backus Rankin, Nicholas Riasanovsky, Irwin Scheiner, and Frederic Wakeman, Sr., for their careful reading of earlier versions of this manuscript. This book has gone through several transformations between inception and completion. I wish to thank Frederic Wakeman, Jr., for the numerous hours of discussion and the myriad thoughts that were shared.

Last but not least, my thanks to Jim and Irvin for their sense of humor and steady support.

Maps

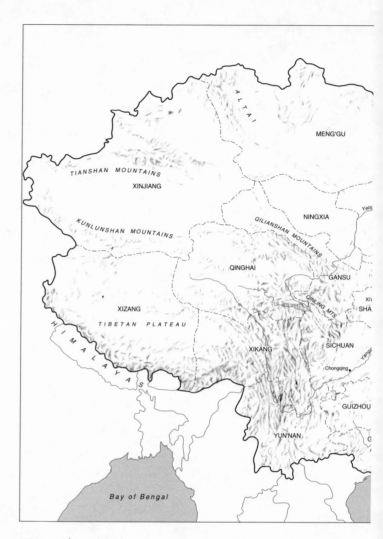

Map 1. China

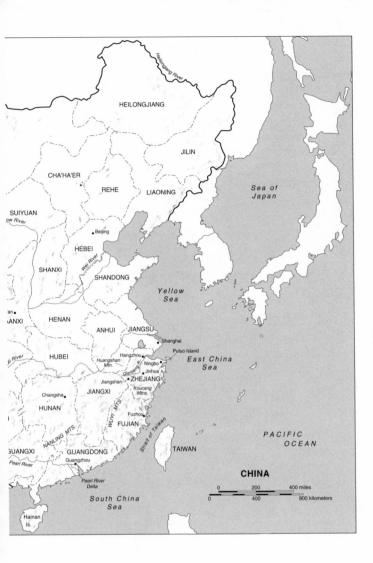

HEILONGJIANG

Heilongjiang River

JILIN

CHA'HA'ER

REHE   LIAONING

SUIYUAN
ow River

• Beijing

HEBEI

SHANXI
Wei River

SHANDONG

SHAANXI

HENAN

ANHUI   JIANGSU

HUBEI   Hangzhou•   Putuo Island
Huangshan   •Ningbo
Mtn.   *Qiantang R.*   •Jinhua
Jiangshan~   •ZHEJIANG
Changsha•   JIANGXI   *Koucang*
Mtns.

HUNAN   *WUYI MTS.*

Fuzhou•

FUJIAN

NANLING MTS.

GUANGXI   GUANGDONG   TAIWAN
Pearl River   Guangzhou•

Pearl River
Delta

South China
Sea

Hainan
Is.

Sea of
Japan

Yellow
Sea

Shanghai

East China
Sea

PACIFIC
OCEAN

CHINA

0	200	400 miles
0	400	800 kilometers

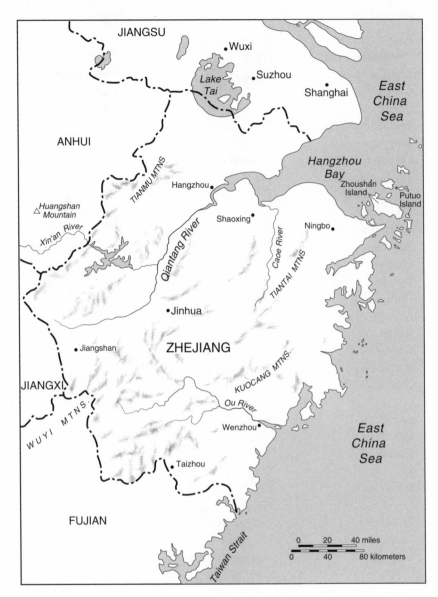

Map 2. Zhejiang

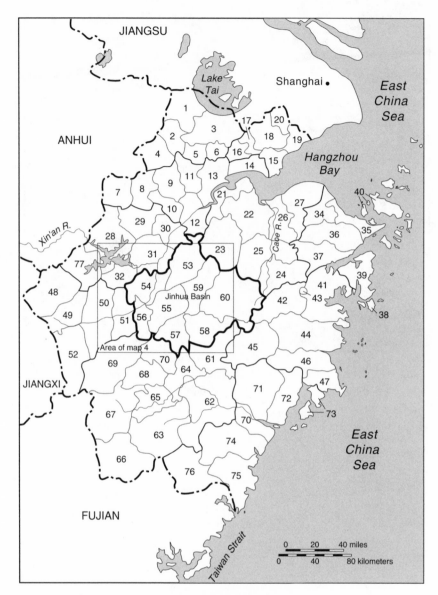

Map 3. Administrative Counties in Zhejiang

NOTE: See Map 4 for elevations of Jinhua and environs (rectangular inset). See Map 5 for Jinhua Basin (bold outline).

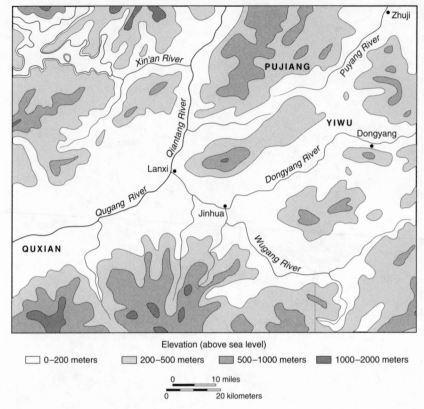

Map 4. Jinhua and Environs

Map 5.   Jinhua Basin

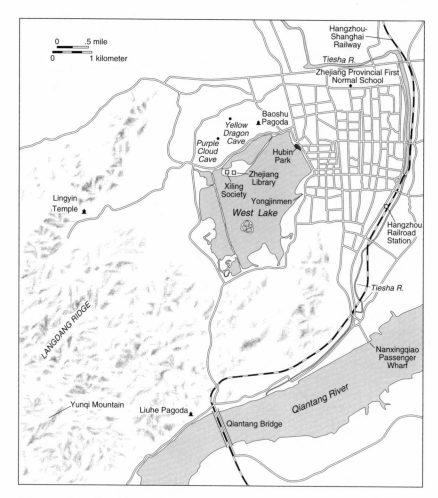

Map 6.   Hangzhou, ca. 1910–1920

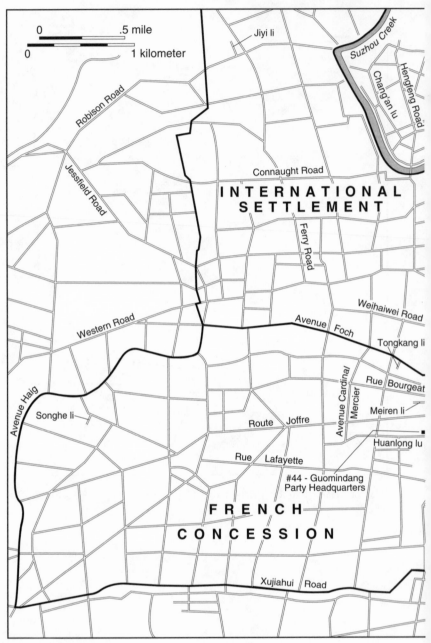

Map 7. Shanghai

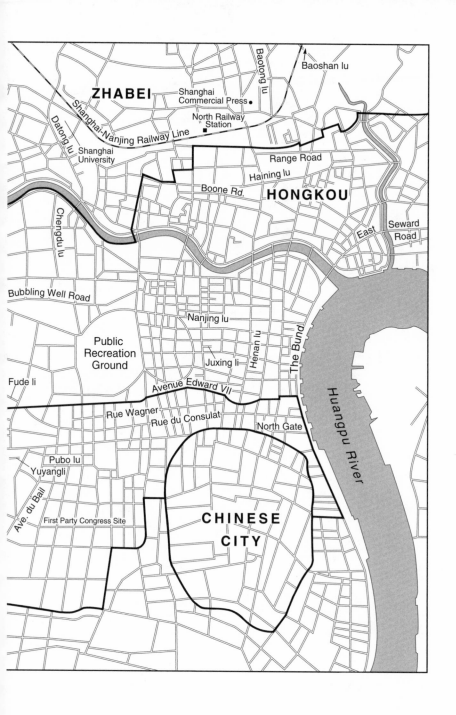

Introduction

The May Fourth Movement of 1919, like the democracy movement of 1989 that it inspired seventy years later, is one of the pivotal events in modern Chinese history that ushered in decades of change with profound consequences. It was named after the incident of May 4, 1919, when more than three thousand students from Beijing University and other institutions held a mass demonstration provoked by news that the peacemakers at Versailles had decided to leave in Japanese hands the former German concessions in Shandong. The demonstrators burned the house of a pro-Japanese cabinet minister and beat the Chinese minister to Japan. They confronted the police, who turned parts of Beijing University campus into a temporary prison. In the subsequent weeks the demonstrators formed work teams to lecture the population and sent telegrams to mobilize students elsewhere. Similar demonstrations spread to Shanghai, Tianjin, Guangzhou, Wuhan, and other major cities. The intellectuals and students who led the demonstrations soon won the sympathy of urban merchants and industrial workers. The protests evolved into a broadly based patriotic alliance that closed down schools and shops and brought out citizens in mass rallies in city after city. The alliance inundated government offices with petitions and launched a national campaign to boycott Japanese goods. The government in Beijing backed down. It called off the police surrounding Beijing University campus and recalled its diplomats at Versailles. It also removed the pro-Japanese officials from their posts.

These events were remarkable not only because they were led by intellectuals and students who, like their successors of the democracy movement of the 1980s, had been experimenting with a new culture that was meant to be drastically different from the old, but also because speeches, statements, slogans, and rallies seemed politically effective, and newspapers and telegrams, for the first time in Chinese history, became instruments of mass mobilization. Although the May Fourth Movement toppled no established regime, the revolutionary potential of the moment did not go unrecognized. It has since inspired competing explanations about its nature, and occupies a special position in our thinking about modern China as the point of convergence for two sets of historical constructions.

In China, according to official textbooks explaining the rise of the People's Republic that were disseminated in the 1950s by the new socialist state, 1919 was identified as the precise moment of origin when cultural iconoclasm was joined with a political activism devoted to anti-imperialist and antifeudal struggle: the watershed of proletarian inevitability down which all subsequent revolutionary history must flow. In the West, however, as presented in Chow Tse-tsung's highly influential 1960 volume, May Fourth was singled out as the moment of patriotic awakening springing from Chinese intellectual exposure to such Western liberal values as science, democracy, liberty, and individualism.[1] The May Fourth Movement has since been characterized variously as a response to Western liberal influence; as a product of education abroad in Japan, Europe, or the United States; as an awakening to the call of international Bolshevism; and as an evaluative rejection of traditional Confucianism as the primary source of authority. Whether deemed liberal or revolutionary, these intellectual developments were then seen as the inspiration for a unified national political movement that spread outward from Beijing and Shanghai into the provinces.

These divergent constructions of the May Fourth Movement, although informed by major differences in ideological orientation, in fact share certain basic assumptions. Modernity in China, for instance, is associated with a sweeping intellectual conversion to Western political ideas that presumably dictate values diametrically opposed to what the Chinese past is thought to represent. Modernity, furthermore, is regarded not only as the result of a recent encounter with the West, but also as a process centered on the active construction of the modern Chinese nation as its unquestionable subject.

Because of the strategic importance of the May Fourth Movement in narrative conventions of modern Chinese history, the events of 1919 have been repeatedly reexamined each time new sets of issues arise. Scholars and commentators frustrated by China's seeming inability to become modern in the twentieth century return time and again to the questions: What was the nature of the May Fourth Movement? Did it usher in a new era characterized by a clean break with China's past? These issues have come under serious reconsideration most recently in the writings of Chinese thinkers driven by their reflections on the Cultural Revolution and, of late, by the events of 1989.[2]

The approach of the present study, unlike many others, does not place emphasis on temporal issues of continuity and disruption. It seeks, instead, to examine the spatial dimensions of center versus periphery in the construction of the May Fourth Movement as a national phenomenon, and it does so by recognizing, first of all, the many threads of activism that went into the making of the moment.

The deep division within the ranks of the New Culture intellectuals over the issue of political activism was well publicized even before the events of 1919 had run their full course. There were those activists who considered cultural enlightenment as the primary task of the intellectuals; others defined their goals in terms of social revitalization. Among the latter, which included political activists who espoused the early Chinese Communist movement, several distinct strands of thoughts and deeds coexisted at various points, and not all of them were plaited into the thought of Mao Zedong and the future orthodoxy of the People's Republic of China. There was, in short, a multiplicity of subjects that shared the historical moment of the May Fourth Movement, each of them informed by the pursuit of distinct projects within its own social space.

Among the actors in the May Fourth Movement was a group of Hangzhou radicals who in 1920 became majority members of the Shanghai Marxism Study Society, an organization that melded into the First Congress of the Chinese Communist Party in the summer of 1921. Although some of these youths appear in canonized historical writings as revolutionary martyrs, after 1949 many were expunged from the commemorative texts or relegated to footnotes as alleged Trotskyists and backsliders of dubious ideological sympathy. Altogether, in the master narrative of the revolution produced after the founding of the People's Republic, the lives and memories of Hangzhou radicals, truncated and heavily edited, have simply been used to supply regional variations to the triumphant national tune orchestrated in Beijing.

A centralized political score, understandably, serves a necessary didactic function in the consolidated People's Republic. Its effective suppression of contending regional diversities, however, also deflects attention from the very historical moment it seeks to explain. When we examine the events in Hangzhou without the editorial mediation that emphasizes the ascendancy of the Maoist center, the May Fourth Movement in Zhejiang reveals a dimension of radicalization that differs significantly from what has often been held up as the national norm.

Because Zhejiang was one of the most culturally sophisticated and commercially advanced regions during the late imperial period, the radicalization of its youth during the early Republican years (1911–27) draws our attention to the paradoxical relationship between a strong commitment to Confucian values on the one hand, and an ardent espousal of progressive politics on the other. The most important and radical contingent of May Fourth students came from Zhejiang's middle counties in the agrarian backwaters along the Qiantang River Valley. At the turn of the century, these districts were considered the province's most solidly conservative counties. Yet the youths who hailed from Zhejiang's middle counties constituted a generation which, on arrival in Hangzhou, moved from a profound cultural conservatism to a vehemently radical attack on all forms of traditional authority.

As radicals, these middle-county youths embraced anarchocommunism fervently. They did so, however, out of a fundamentalist ardor to salvage the ethical intent of the Confucianism they had imbibed in their family and village schools. The self-understanding of the student leaders of the May Fourth Movement in Hangzhou was thus far from the worldview of the Beijing and Shanghai educated elite, who envisioned a brighter future for China along thoroughly Western lines and who were more readily able to part with their Confucian past. The Hangzhou students' iconoclasm, in contrast, was the product of an intense moral outrage that acquired force not so much as these youths learned about the wonders of the new world but as they were deeply disappointed by the decay of the old.

Standard accounts of the May Fourth Movement, intent on pinpointing the dawning moment of Chinese modernity in a temporally linear sense, present its iconoclastic spirit as the inevitable outcome of systemic clashes between two incompatible ways of life: those of the old and the new. The prime targets of the iconoclasts, from this perspective, were the salient features of Chinese tradition. Whether referred to as feudal or traditional, "culture" was understood as a body of doctrines and norms with a particular internal coherence. Traditional culture—whether this meant the expression of a certain stage of Chinese development or the quintessential state of Chineseness over time—was understood in terms of coded texts rather than evolving practices, a pejorative rather than a positive view.

Consideration of the May Fourth Movement in the distinct environment of Hangzhou forces us to pay attention to the specific historical circumstances that abetted cultural iconoclasm in the first place. To place Hangzhou in context, we see, for example, that there was a significant reconfiguration of Zhejiang's political economy after Shanghai was opened as a treaty port in 1843. We recognize also that the impact of the disastrous Taiping Uprising—which took tens of millions of lives throughout China—was distinctly different in the north and south of the province during the late 1800s. By the turn of the century, the northern plains and coastal regions had emerged as modernized centers of new-style wealth, while the middle counties in the Qiantang Valley were increasingly isolated into provincial backwaters. Modernity in the case of Zhejiang was not merely a function of time, but also a question of space, cultural as well as geographical. The northern region of the province, in the course of its urbanization, became home to Zhejiang's progressive but gradualist reformers. The southern middle counties, by contrast, produced Zhejiang's most determined radicals.

Structural changes in Zhejiang's socioeconomic conditions did not in themselves engender cultural iconoclasm. As the history of the May Fourth Movement in Hangzhou shows, iconoclasm arose from the active thinking and questioning among a group of youths rooted in the declining middle counties. Radical outbursts during the May Fourth Movement in Hangzhou were thus not produced by the forces of modernization or of tradition in mutual isolation. They occurred when these youths crossed cultural spaces, so to speak, causing the dissonance between the two worlds to be more sharply felt. Modernizing ideologies trickling down from metropolitan centers into provincial towns did not in themselves promote iconoclasm, nor was provincial radicalism the necessary expression of hinterland frustration. Cultural iconoclasm in the May Fourth Movement in Hangzhou was, rather, a consequence of the dialectical interaction between the quickening pace of modernization and the petrifying weight of traditionalism. At the provincial capital, earnest upriver students suddenly found themselves straddling an ever-widening abyss between home and school, personal past and present. The result was a shift of cultural allegiance from one space to another and a profound erosion of faith in the integrity of established ways of life at home. May Fourth cultural iconoclasm in Hangzhou was more than a sweeping attack against the past on behalf of the future. It was a quest for new self-understanding by the generation poised at a transformative juncture in the province's life.

Yet the students' very embeddedness in their home communities prevented them from renouncing their cultural ideals in a detached, totalistic way. Instead, they were engaged enough by traditional values to be shocked by the disjuncture between the community's professed norms and its actual practices. They consequently attacked the latter in defense of the former, accusing others of perfidy with all the zeal of self-styled protectors of those Confucian values from which they drew sustenance for their own angry rebelliousness. Zhejiang radicalism, which played such a large part in the foundation of the Chinese Communist Party, was a far cry from the informed cultural choices we generally associate with accounts of the intellectual elites of the May Fourth Movement in Beijing and Shanghai. It attracted young minds departing from spaces where time seemed to stand still, who were made to see this sorry state of hometown stagnancy by exposure to an emerging order in which life moved at perilous speeds.

The intention behind this book is to deepen our understanding of modern Chinese history not only by introducing a spatial dimension into the discussion of China's quest for modernity, but also by placing the historical observer on the margin of the conventional core-periphery dichotomy familiar to geographers and anthropologists alike. Instead of standing at the center core of Zhejiang in order to observe the forces behind modern China's iconoclastic drive, we will begin by positioning ourselves at the outer limits of the region and looking inward: from the mountainous borders of the province, as it were, down the Qiantang River toward the capital of Hangzhou below.[3]

The organization of the book reflects that decision. Part 1 begins with an examination of the creation of provincial backwaters at the turn of the century in Zhejiang's Qiantang Valley, and especially in the district of Jinhua, which, in an earlier time, had been idealized as a self-contained and self-sufficient middle county. Part 2 follows the movement of middle-county youths who had to go down the river to the provincial capital to continue their education, and offers an analysis of the May Fourth Movement in Hangzhou during a ten-month period in 1919–20. In Hangzhou, middle-county youths raised on conservative Confucian practices were exposed to the liberal teaching of progressive gentry educators as well as to radical ideas emanating out of Shanghai and Beijing through the printed media. The subsequent radicalization of these youths resulted in their expulsion from the province altogether. Part 3 examines their transient lives as uprooted provincials in Shanghai's foreign concessions, concluding with an analysis of the rise of particular variants of urban Chinese Communism within that milieu.

These landscapes—the middle county, the provincial capital, and the metropolis—are presented as separated from each other by uneven paces of change as well as by critical differences in orientation. One thread that runs through them all, from Jinhua to Hangzhou to Shanghai, is the life story of Shi Cuntong (1899–1970), one of the most intensely radical figures to emerge from rural Zhejiang and become a determined revolutionary known throughout the nation. Shi's biography, like those of many of his contemporaries, was intelligible more in terms of life's twists and turns, disjunctions, disruptures, unintended consequences, and unfulfilled wishes than in terms of development and continuity. A man of intelligence, passion, integrity, and commitment, Shi Cuntong was nonetheless best known for his radical departure from observed norms at critical junctures. In 1920, at the age of twenty-one, he renounced his father. In 1927, following the purge of the Communists by the Nationalists, he renounced the Communist Party. In 1937, when the Communists and the Nationalists announced their Second United Front, he renounced some of his own long-held beliefs in favor of a "centrist position" that was critical of both parties. This disjointed quality of Shi Cuntong's life complements the fragmented landscape across which he moved. It was his sensitivity toward such discrepancies that made a journey through geographical space a crossing of cultural boundaries.

In the passage between geographic and cultural spaces, Zhejiang's middle-county youths radicalized into Shanghai's early Communists. The May Fourth Movement in Hangzhou, as elsewhere, ushered in the birth of the Chinese Communist movement. As we trace the career trajectory of Zhejiang radicals in Shanghai in the 1920s, however, we see how their life stories joined with and then diverged from the development of the Chinese Communist Party. The Zhejiang case shows that the history of socialist revolution in twentieth-century China may not be coterminous with the process that led to the triumphant march of the People's Liberation Army under the banners of the Chinese Communist Party. One of the most significant phenomena about urban Chinese Communism in the 1920s, indeed, was the story of how, for many of the lower Yangzi radicals, the early Communists and their organized party grew apart. In the aftermath of 1927 these men became neither Bolsheviks nor anarchists, but Marxists and social democrats of divergent sorts. No longer active as party organizers and labor agitators, they made their living as authors, journalists, translators, editors, and professors in Shanghai, and gave birth to a new kind of urban radical culture that powerfully shaped the intellectual climate on college campuses in the 1930s and 1940s.[4]

What, then, were the dynamics between ideas and mobilization, culture and revolution in modern Chinese intellectual attempts to change China, of which the May Fourth Movement was such a watershed? Although a hodgepodge of Western ideas from Kropotkin to Marx, from Rousseau to Darwin, had been imported into the Chinese world via translation, it was up to the Chinese intellectuals themselves, often products of concrete indigenous social environments, to construct the meanings and relevance of these ideas in practice. The changes that these men (and a few women) introduced rarely took the form of a linear progression, in distinct phases, from tradition to modernity; they almost always involved negotiations between disparate attributes distributed across geographic and cultural space. To gain a better sense of that space and the divisions within which lay the ground for the rise of modern Chinese radicalism, let us turn to an examination of the many constructions of Zhejiang.

1

1 Zhejiang

It remains for us to explain this diversity—the breaks and
contrasts, extreme and not so extreme, and the chronic
fragmentation of the whole.
—Fernand Braudel, *The Identity of France*

Zhejiang province was named after a crooked waterway that was locally
much better known as the Qiantang.[1] A winding river of more than eight
hundred miles, the Qiantang traverses a landscape of "thousands of lush
peaks and rolling hills" through a region of over twenty thousand square
miles.[2] Together with the mountain ranges that contour its flow, this river
defines the topographical features of Zhejiang.

Zhejiang is located at the point where the southeastern mountain ranges
of China meet the East China Sea. Different geologists advance different
hypotheses, but by one theory, Zhejiang's mountains were formed tens of
millions of years ago, when the Pacific plate thrust itself under the Asian
plate at a wide angle along China's southeastern corner. The result is a
pattern of mountains arching from southwest to northeast—the great
"Cathaysian geosyncline" that created, among other things, strings of
islands off the coast, leaving a mere 15 percent of coastal China at less than
fifteen hundred feet above sea level.

By the same tectonic theory, the Indian continent, riding on a north-
ward-drifting plate, collided with Asia some forty million years ago. This
"Himalayan Frontal Thrust" created, in China's southwest, the world's
steepest mountain ranges and highest plateaus, resulting in a distinct
pattern of mountain blocks, inter-mountain plateaus, and basins that follow
a northwest-southeast strike.[3]

One chain of hills links these two mountain systems: the Nanling
(Southern Ridges), which run eastward from the Tibetan Plateau toward
the South China Sea, forming the watershed between the drainage systems
of central and south China. Nanling's easterly thrust toward the sea is
altered when the ridges run into what geographers term the southwest-
northeast "strike" of the Fujian-Zhejiang hills and particularly the higher

ranges of the Wuyi and the Huangshan mountains—part of the Cathaysian geosyncline that arcs to embrace sea, not land.

Where the Nanling mountains run into the Wuyi and Huangshan ranges, the ridges intertwine to form the watershed that separates the drainage system of the Yangzi from that of the Fujian-Zhejiang hills. This knot of mountains, which traditionally forms part of Zhejiang's provincial borders with Anhui and Jiangxi, is also Zhejiang's area of highest elevation. Administratively this area, where the Wuyi range begins its descent from above six thousand feet into the province, is divided into the counties of Jiangshan, Changshan, and Kaihua. As the mountains move northeasterly, they shape the topography of Yanzhou Prefecture, dividing its western districts into hill counties such as Sui'an, Chun'an, Yuqian, and Lin'an. The western slopes of these ridges often spill across Zhejiang's border with Anhui, where they join the nationally famous scenic peaks of Huangshan. On their northern reach, the hills come to a somewhat abrupt stop on the edges of the Lake Tai basin of Zhexi (western Zhejiang), where the twin peaks of Mount Tianmu, literally "heaven's eyes," look down from a height of five thousand feet on a fertile region of five thousand square miles that stretches from the southern shores of China's largest clear-water lake to the coast of the East China Sea.

The elevated southwestern corner of Zhejiang is also where another range of mountains extends eastward, descending from five thousand feet to link up with the northeastern-running coastal hills of Donggongshan from Fujian. These hills of southeastern Zhejiang, at an elevation of three thousand feet, stand a whole level below the southwestern mountains on the provincial topographical staircase, cresting at such scenic peaks as Yandang, Kuocang, and Tiantai, the sacred mountain in Buddhism. From Mount Tiantai to the mouth of the Qiantang River in the counties of Shaoxing and Ningbo, the coastal region is defined by a chain of undulating hills that, according to one geographer, contains no fewer than 280 peaks.[4] Beyond the coast of Ningbo these hills run into the sea and rise from its floor, breaking the surface of the water with large and small islands that include the Zhoushan Archipelago, famed for its fishing villages, and Mount Putuo, a busy Buddhist pilgrimage site centered on the worship of Guanyin.

The two chains of mountains that descend from the high plateau of Jiangshan in southwestern Zhejiang thus form boundaries for two distinct subregions in the province: the Qiantang Valley bounded by the ranges, and the patches of coastal plains fertilized by mountain streams flowing easterly into the sea. These two subregions, the river valley and the coast, together constitute Zhedong (eastern Zhejiang), the bulk of the province south of the Qiantang Estuary. Northward across the Qiantang, meanwhile, lie the open plains of Zhexi (western Zhejiang), bounded on the north by Lake Tai and on the west by the Tianmu Mountains—the provincial border with Anhui. Zhejiang in this sense straddles two larger and geographically distinct terrains that include contiguous portions of its provincial neighbors: the southeastern coastal hills of Fujian-Zhedong, and the lower Yangzi alluvial plains of Jiangnan-Zhexi. While Zhedong became noted for its spectacular mountain scenery, its ground fog, and its green tea, much of Zhexi was envied for its wealth gained in rice and silk. Between the carving and crossing of the mountain ranges, Zhedong and Zhexi together give the province its three distinct constituents: the plains, the hills, and the coast.

To the extent that the province lacks sharp definition as a coherent region, it has also been correspondingly open to trade and traffic in many areas beyond the provincial boundaries. While Hangzhou, the leading city in Zhexi and the provincial capital at the terminal point of the Grand Canal, had been for centuries a center for the collection and distribution of goods throughout the region, Jiangshan, the county seat on the southwestern periphery of the province, was no less important strategically both as a conduit of goods into neighboring Fujian and Jiangxi and as a military outpost, though far less significant as an economic center in itself.[5] The porousness of Zhejiang's borders overland was matched by its openness along the coast. Although maritime trade setting out from the ports of Ningbo and Wenzhou under the Ming (1368–1644) and the Qing (1644–1911) was primarily coastal, much earlier in the twelfth century these cities had served as extremely active points of contact in a trading network that included Japan, Korea, and Southeast Asia.[6] Far from being dominated by a single central place at the top of its urban hierarchy, the trading system of Zhejiang was sustained by multiple points of contact with the outside world. This in turn meant that instead of prospering and suffering in tandem as a provincial unit in response to the same sets of socioeconomic factors, each of Zhejiang's subregions rose and fell in accordance with its own exclusive dynamics.

THE PLAINS

The Zhexi plains were crisscrossed by hundreds of navigable canals and irrigated by thousands of fish-producing ponds. Administratively, the plains came under the jurisdiction of twenty counties belonging to three prefectures: Hangzhou, Jiaxing, and Huzhou (Hang-Jia-Hu), which, together with the southern Jiangsu prefectures of Suzhou, Songjiang, and Taicang (Su-Song-Tai), constituted the most affluent areas of the Chinese empire under the Qing. It was a region of long history, great refinement, and extraordinary political influence.[7] For the purpose of the present study, two features deserve special attention: its highly sophisticated commercial economy and well-differentiated society since the sixteenth century, and its extensive ties with the neighboring prefectures in Jiangsu.

"Above there is Heaven; on earth there are Suzhou and Hangzhou"—so runs a sixteenth-century paean to the two leading cities of the region, Hangzhou in Zhejiang and Suzhou in Jiangsu.[8] Connected by the Grand Canal along which constantly flowed huge quantities of tax grain, official salt, merchant goods, traveling bureaucrats, itinerant craftsmen, and so forth, both cities had since the sixteenth century ranked among China's most populous urban centers and the largest cities in the world.[9] Situated on China's leading silk-producing plains, both cities developed from the fourteenth century into industrial weaving centers, featuring an elaborate system of purchasing, financing, manufacturing, and distributing that linked the acres of mulberry leaves to the sheets of silkworms in the hands of peasant women and children through the hundreds of cocoon collectors on the streets to the thousands of weaving looms in a highly leveraged production system that generated a tremendous amount of mercantile wealth.[10] Silk craftsmanship in the area was of such quality that Emperor Kangxi sent his trusted bondservants Cao Yin and Li Xu to supervise the two Imperial Silk Works in Suzhou and Hangzhou in the designing and weaving of ceremonial court robes. Operating with capital drawn from the imperial privy purse, the two manufactories profited handsomely not only from the fine silk they produced, but also from the highly lucrative side-line credit operations that fueled the frenzy of the region's high-stake monetary market.[11]

Where the Grand Canal came to an end outside the eastern gates of Hangzhou, a thriving commercial district developed with hostels, teahouses, restaurants, theaters, markets, and shops to serve the needs of traveling merchants and sailors. Like Shanghai, Hankou, and Tianjin, Hangzhou was a city with a significant sojourning mercantile population. Its importance as a financial and commercial center was reflected in the hundreds of *qianzhuang* (old-style Chinese "native banks") in the city and the prominent presence of the "Six Trades"—raw silk, silk fabric, rice, tea, lumber, and cotton cloth—that were dominated by the merchant associations of Shaoxing, Ningbo, Jinhua, and Huizhou.[12] The Gongchenqiao area declined only in the 1910s, when railroads were built to link Hangzhou with Shanghai to the north and with Ningbo to the south, causing travelers to shift to the train station inside the city.[13] In its heyday this area, where thousands of porters and boatmen daily passed through its gates, was also the site of many Buddhist vegetarian halls and a secretive sectarian congregation commonly known as the Luo Sect, which appealed to the practical as well as spiritual needs of aging and ailing Grand Canal boatmen, most of whom hailed from Shandong. The authorities consequently regarded the commercial district as a breeding ground of heterodox doctrines and subversive rites that required the constant vigilance of the Confucian state.[14]

Zhexi's documented historical association with the Jiangnan region went back to the sixth century B.C., when the two areas together formed the flourishing Wu State, which, under its ruler Fuchai, proved its superior organized prowess by first (in 506 B.C.) defeating the kingdom of Chu in central Yangzi, and then (in 494 B.C.) crushing the men of Yue from the hills of Zhedong.[15] The region began its rise in socioeconomic importance during the Six Dynasties (A.D. 229–589) when large numbers of northerners left the central plains for the south. The construction of the Grand Canal (605–8) facilitated the regional integration of north China and the Yangzi region, laying the economic foundation of the imperial order under the Tang Empire (618–907).[16] Zhexi Prefecture, which in its Tang jurisdiction encompassed the entire natural terrain of the Lake Tai basin, experienced rapid growth during this time. The growth continued through the Northern Song (960–1127). In 1128 the Song moved its capital to Hangzhou. During the following century the region, referred to as the Western Region of Liangzhe (Liangzhe xilu) or Zhexi, as opposed to the Eastern Region of Liangzhe (Liangzhe donglu) or Zhedong, developed into the empire's wealthiest and most populous area. Under the jurisdiction of Zhexi were nine administrative units large and small that geographically enclosed Suzhou as well as Hangzhou. When provinces were created as higher-level administrative units under the Yuan (1279–1367), the two regions of Zhedong and Zhexi were joined to form the province of Liangzhe (the Two Zhe), which included present-day Zhejiang as well as southern Jiangsu.

The founding Ming emperor, Zhu Yuanzhang (reigned 1368–98), radically redrew Zhexi's administrative boundaries. Shortly after the new dynasty established its imperial capital in Nanjing in 1368, the emperor split the Lake Tai basin area, which had given strong support earlier to his rival imperial contender Zhang Shicheng (1321–67), in half.[17] Each half was linked up with the poorer hill country and coastal regions to its respective north and south to constitute the new provinces of Jiangsu and Zhejiang. Other measures that the new emperor took to reduce the established wealth and weaken the local influence in the region included the forced dispersal of hundreds of eminent lineages from Zhexi to distant parts of the empire, and the introduction of a control system headed by the *liangzhang,* or tax captain, to serve as resident agent of the state.[18] By drawing the lines as he did, the Ming founder superimposed his administrative divisions on the natural boundaries of the plains around Lake Tai—bounded by the Yangzi to the north, the Qiantang to the south, the sea to the east, and the hills to the west—thereby doubling the presence of the imperial state bureaucracy in an area of considerable urban wealth and strong local gentry initiatives.

Even before the fall of the Ming in 1644, criticisms were heard against such divisions: "On the borders separating Suzhou and Songjiang (in Jiangsu) from Hangzhou, Jiaxing, and Huzhou (in Zhejiang) there were neither the barriers of hills nor that of waters. There were neither mountain passes nor military fortresses, and yet a line was drawn right across the plains. This is like having a live person cut up right across his waist, and dividing him up into two halves. How does anyone expect either half to survive, let alone prosper?"[19] The administrative division was viewed not only as a detriment to the region's overall economic growth and cultural life, but also as creating problems for the state in the effective policing of the area: "Between Jiaxing and Huzhou there lie vast areas of lakes and swamps. There are also major bandit chiefs, who assemble under their command thousands of followers. These men routinely pillage wealthy households in the Jiangsu counties, and then flee across provincial lines into Zhejiang to seek refuge. Little has been done by the officials and the gentry of the two provinces to stop this. All they do is to fix blame on each other. Countless bureaucratic papers have been exchanged between provincial authorities, and yet not a single bandit has ever been caught."[20]

The first Ming emperor had in mind goals other than the social order and economic benefit of the region, however, when he rearranged the administrative boundaries. By cutting up the economically most advanced region of China into separate administrative units, the dynasty channeled the region's elites into separate bargaining sessions with their respective provincial authorities over vital concerns such as land tax privileges and county civil service examination quotas. Provincial elites clustered under the respective provincial authorities of Jiangsu and Zhejiang in the two capital cities of Suzhou and Hangzhou. Administrative divisions thus served to weaken rather than strengthen the potential for elite political formation in this culturally sophisticated and socially fluid region.[21]

As a constituent component of Zhejiang, Zhexi was nonetheless oriented more toward Jiangnan across its provincial borders than toward Zhedong. Together with Jiangnan it emerged in the sixteenth century as one of the most highly urbanized and commercialized areas in China. The growth of its silk-weaving industry empirically supports the thesis espoused by twentieth-century Chinese Marxist historians that there were "sprouts of capitalism" in China well before the coming of the West. Gu Yanwu (1613–82), the classical scholar and a native of the area, observed that Zhexi, with its flat country of swamps and lakes, had customs that were "extravagant and refined," much like that of neighboring Suzhou and Changzhou, while Zhedong shared the "simple and straightforward" customs of Fujian.[22] Differences between the plains of Zhexi and the hills of Zhedong extended even into cultural and academic traditions that respectively distinguished the two areas under the Qing. Zhexi, together with Jiangnan, was the center of philological studies of the Confucian classics: the Han School of Learning that traced its founding to Gu Yanwu's vision and inspiration. Zhedong, in contrast, was home to a scholarly tradition that stressed historical writings and criticisms opposing the autocratic nature of the imperial system, a spirit that was firmly associated with the seventeenth-century master Huang Zongxi (1610–95).[23]

THE COAST

In Zhedong, the coastal strip on the eastern slope of the ridges is divided into several discrete river systems that all empty into the East China Sea. Each of these rivers is contained within its own chain of hills and ridges, creating fertile but narrow valleys rich in the production of rice and grains. There are no easy ways to leave these valleys except via the seafaring junks that ply the water between coastal harbors, sailing from port to port through narrow passages defined by the thousands of offshore islands that dot the coastal line. Yongjia at the mouth of the Ou River in the southeastern prefecture of Wenzhou is thus connected to Haining, Dinghai, and Zhenhai (all parts of Ningbo Prefecture on the northern coast) via the ports of Taizhou in the middle section of the littoral.

One exception to this description was the Ning-Shao plain on the northern end of the Zhedong coast, immediately south of the Qiantang Estuary. Relatively spacious by the standard of Zhedong's coastal plains and conveniently located with easy access to the Zhexi plains, this region was home to a distinct form of civilization as early as some seven thousand years ago. Modern archaeologists now hypothesize that the way of life that prevailed in this area—such as that associated with the findings at Hemudu—was qualitatively different from yet no less advanced than that on the north China plains, traditionally regarded as the cradle of Chinese civilization. These early inhabitants left behind signs of rice cultivation and lineage organizations. They were also makers and users of a large number of jade instruments, glazed potteries, ivory pieces, and artistic objects for a variety of purposes.[24] New discoveries made since the 1960s of dozens of Neolithic sites in Zhejiang gave strong support to the thesis that there were multiple origins instead of a singular one (traditionally located in the Yellow River plains) to the civilization that came to be known as Chinese.[25]

When northern elites arrived in this area in the declining years of the Eastern Han dynasty (25–220), some of them did not conceal their disdain for the customs, language, and habits of the local society. A growing number of modern scholars, drawing from an expanding body of knowledge about the indigenous culture and society of the Ning-Shao region, are inclined to treat such utterances as expressions of cultural differences instead of authentic superiority over the south. The contrastive features of the two civilizations, one continental and the other coastal, do help to underscore a few key themes in the long history of Zhedong. Coastal Zhedong tended to receive major stimulus for growth not in periods of political unity but in times of disunity, when northern dynasties were compelled to relocate political centers to the south, bringing along northern elites fleeing from the turmoils of their homeland. The rise of Zhedong, furthermore, often entailed significant development in maritime trade along the southeastern coast—a regional orientation with its own cultural expression, which set these coastal strips quite apart from the continental empires of the north China plains.

By the third century the Ning-Shao plain had developed a solid economic foundation in the manufacturing of porcelain, copper mirrors, and paper. It also showed strength in several handicrafts industries. The area's population increased significantly in the fourth century, when tens of thousands of northerners arrived after the fall of the Western Jin imperial capital to an army of northern nomads. Known as Guiji County, the Ning-Shao plain served as the administrative and military headquarters of the entire area of present-day Zhedong during the Eastern Jin period

(318–420). It also produced enough rice to supply the southern imperial capital in Nanjing. Great lineages with exalted connections and hereditary eminence set up estates in this area. They eventually turned the hillsides into their ancestral burial grounds as well.[26] The wealth and population of the Ning-Shao plains grew steadily throughout the Six Dynasties, while Ningbo itself began to flourish no later than the fifth century as the home port for seafaring junks bound for Southeast Asia.[27]

Maritime trade along the China coast began to pick up momentum in the centuries after the Six Dynasties. By the eighth century, Ningbo, known as Mingzhou under the Tang, had developed into a major East Asian port, central in an active network of trade among Korea, Japan, and China. By the eleventh century the many Chinese, Arabian, and other sea vessels going through its port—typically laden with silk, porcelain, gold, aluminum, lacquer, and copper coins on their way out, and South Sea spices, ivory, animal horns, coral, amber, crystal, and gems on their way in—had grown to such a significant proportion that Ningbo became the site of an imperial maritime trade commissioner's office (*shibo si*).[28] It was a cosmopolitan city where shipping as well as shipbuilding industries were concentrated. Wenzhou, farther south on the Zhedong coast, and Taizhou, the midpoint between the two, were also among the busiest ports in the world of the twelfth century. In these three ports an estimated two hundred thousand individuals made their living in the water transport business either year-round or on a seasonal basis.[29] Far from being an isolated strip of land sealed off from the continental heartland of Chinese cultural and political power, Zhedong coastal cities were strategically positioned at the center of an extensive maritime network that, through direct as well as indirect trade, reached from the ports of the East China Sea to places as far away as the Persian Gulf.[30]

American scholars have recently stressed that under Mongol rule (1279–1368) China was drawn into a cosmopolitan empire of intercontinental scope.[31] This was no doubt true for the Eurasian caravan routes, often dominated by Iranian merchants, that Marco Polo traversed all the way to Hangzhou.[32] But Ningbo (known as Qingyuan under the Yuan), quite separately, continued a maritime cosmopolitanism of its own making as Zhedong's leading trading port in the fourteenth century. It developed especially strong economic ties with the ports of Japan.[33] However, its fortune—and that of the tens of thousands of private traders along the southeastern China coast—underwent a sharp downturn in the late fourteenth century after the founding of the Ming dynasty.

Coastal Zhedong, much like Zhexi, gave its support to one of the Ming founder's rival imperial contenders in the last years leading up to the fall of the Yuan dynasty.[34] The Ming victory on the land prompted many of the region's local notables to resort to their well-established maritime network and seek refuge overseas. To establish firm control of China's coastline, the new emperor forcefully placed a ban on private maritime trade and threatened to put to death anyone caught smuggling able-bodied males and military hardware overseas. He also placed severe restrictions on the construction of large seafaring vessels.[35] This policy, which was repeatedly upheld by later Ming rulers, called on the power of the continental bureaucracy to attack the robust energy of private enterprises that had fueled the growth of an expanding maritime trade for centuries.[36] At its best, the Ming government "gave foreign trade no support but taxed and regulated it without any policy of encouragement."[37] Those who traded and traveled overseas ran the risk of being punished by the state as "pirates," especially in the mid-sixteenth century.[38] Although the Ming state was far from able to assert effective control on the sea and the coast, bureaucratic intervention nonetheless functioned as a powerful force that vitiated the coastal trade.[39]

Without the economic stimulation of an overseas network, Zhedong's coastal cities were deprived of their stimulus for continuing growth.[40] Although the ban on maritime trade was lifted briefly toward the end of the sixteenth century, it was reimposed by the new rulers of the Qing in a similar effort to consolidate the dynasty's rule of the southeastern coast. In 1683 the Qing took Taiwan and defeated the last Ming loyalists, thereby removing a principal threat to its position in the East China Sea.[41] The following year the court lifted the ban on coastal trade, although overseas trade that went beyond the framework of the tributary relations continued to be restricted to the one port of Guangzhou.[42]

Ningbo in the eighteenth century became, once again, the center of a busy coastal network of trade. Its merchants developed close business ties in shipping and finance with Shanghai, and from there they wove a network of connections up the Yangzi River.[43] They also obtained soy beans from Manchuria, and carried on tribute trade with the island kingdom of Liuqiu (Ryukyu) which "masked a Chinese exchange with Japan." Activities like this "bespoke a Chinese entrepreneurship in sea trade that was largely beyond bureaucratic regulation."[44] Despite the sizable presence of overseas Chinese communities in Southeast Asia, Chinese merchants could expect little protection from the state, and trading dynamics in East Asian waters shifted steadily to the disadvantage of the Chinese. Instead of the large trading vessels of earlier centuries that made Ningbo and Wenzhou home ports to fleets of export ships loaded with silk and spices, junks plied the coastal water in the nineteenth century as part of a network of opium trade.[45]

To the extent that maritime activites constituted a "minor tradition" that was peripheral to the continental orientations of the late imperial Chinese state, nineteenth-century coastal Zhedong was perceived as peripheral in relation to major centers of wealth and power, such as Suzhou and Hangzhou, of the Qing empire.[46] Until the arrival of Western steamships, which dramatically altered not so much the reality as the power dynamics and perceptions of coastal China, the littoral of eastern Zhejiang south of Ningbo seemed eternally encapsulated in a string of fisheries and rocky salterns. Coastal Zhedong's orientation, compared with that of Zhexi's alluvial plains and Zhedong's inland hills, was unmistakably toward the sea. But without overseas trading networks the riverine valleys of coastal Zhedong became self-contained and self-sufficient, enclosed within the boundaries of their rugged hills and hemmed in by the tall waves of the open sea.

THE HILLS

South of the Zhexi plains and bounded by the western (Wuyi) and eastern (Donggong) mountain chains of Zhejiang stretches the Qiantang River Valley—twelve thousand square miles of land that represents over twofifths the area of the province. Of lesser importance in commerce and economy than Zhexi and Ning-Shao, this provincial heartland is largely defined by the changing characteristics of the river as it descends from the mountains and traverses northeasterly into the sea. At midstream, where the two chains of mountains stand apart to make room for a broadening valley, the Qiantang is joined by two more streams coming down the eastern and western hills from the subtropical woods of central Zhejiang and eastern Anhui. This central valley, more or less encircled by hills on all sides except for an opening to the north, is the Jin-Qu Basin, which, in late imperial times, came under the jurisdiction of Jinhua and Quzhou prefectures. Densely populated and intensively cultivated, these fertile plains and carefully terraced hills are self-sufficient in rice cultivation and rich in farm as well as mountain products. The main roads that run through the valley were constantly traveled by the merchants of Zhejiang and also those of Anhui, Jiangxi, Fujian, and Guangdong. The Jin-Qu Basin at the midstream of the Qiantang is, in other words, the agricultural mainstay of the province and a world in itself at the hub of a multiprovincial trading network that traveled and shipped by carts and boats.

At its point of origin the Qiantang collects its water from dozens of streams that flow each spring down the slopes of the Wuyi and Huang-shan ranges. Its primary source, which remains a subject of scientific dispute, is equally traceable to the rapids and falls that descend from the high mountains in the tea and bamboo country of southwestern Zhe-jiang and eastern Anhui, and to the hillside torrents and creeks of the hill counties standing at about three thousand feet in elevation in central Zhejiang.[47]

Above Quzhou the river retains the character of a mountain creek. It runs through narrow valleys lined by villages with peasant dwellings carved out from the hillside, backed up against rising slopes. The subtropical climate of the region brings plentiful rainfall throughout the year. The endless mountains, often densely covered with woods, have long provided a habitat to monkeys, deer, wild goats, jackals, birds, an occasional bear, and a variety of snakes—most of which the locals did not hesitate to serve as major delicacies of local cuisine, along with mountain frogs, river turtles, chili peppers, and pure distilled liquor.[48]

Below Quzhou, where the Qiantang cuts across the Jin-Qu Basin, the river broadens and deepens after taking in the water of several more hillside tributaries.[49] This is the scenic stretch of the river punctuated by gorges and cliffs that rise up sharply with surfaces as smooth as if cut by a knife. Local pride supports the claim that the Qilitan Gorge (Seven-Mile Gorge) above Tonglu, which an Eastern Han hermit allegedly once used as his fishing ground, matches the Three Gorges of the Yangzi in sweep and beauty. The area was once famed both for a rich tapestry of natural pines, cypresses, and bamboos that covered the hills and for wild flowers, espe-cially orchids, that filled the valleys.[50] To this day Quzhou still boasts of the unmatched quality of its orange and tangerine groves: with all fifteen of its communes and four hundred of its production brigades devoting themselves to the task, Quzhou proudly expanded its orange acreage fivefold in the forty years after 1949.[51]

Left to nature, the Qiantang was unreliable through this section. Early twentieth-century travelers up the stream often had to abandon their boats for the back of a mule on the cliffsides in order to cross the rapids.[52] It was only with the massive hydraulic engineering intervention under the People's Republic that the river—especially the tributary Xin'an Jiang—became suitable for upstream navigation. The midstream stretch of the Xin'an Jiang became, in the 1950s, the site for the first major power plant of eastern China. To build the dam and the reservoir, two counties had to be permanently submerged, and 180,000 people were relocated away from their homeland.

Below Tonglu the river widens, but the waterway commonly referred to as the Qiantang does not begin until the river reaches the outskirts of Hangzhou. The river in its lower reach is commonly associated with networks of canals, powerful pounding tides, and gigantic stone dikes. In Hangzhou the river connects to the channels of the Grand Canal. Beyond Hangzhou it is further joined by the Caoe, the principal stream that comes down the boundary hills of the Ning-Shao plain. After this intersection, the Qiantang is joined by hundreds of watercourses that are parts of the system of navigable canals crisscrossing the alluvial plains linking Zhexi to the mouth of the Yangzi, the combined length of which represents one-third of all such waterways in China.[53] Those who sing praises of the river no longer focus on the mere abundance of fish in the water. Instead they celebrate the coming and going of junks and boats that give birth to an active commercial economy on the plains.

Between Haining and Shaoxing, two counties on opposite sides of the Qiantang, the river enters the East China Sea. Because the mouth of the river is shaped like a wide trumpet blowing out toward the sea, it funnels in raging tides that pound the shores along the estuary. The tidal bores in mid-autumn carry enough force to roll over twenty-six-foot dikes and move eight-thousand-pound metal columns from their anchorage.[54]

Dikes of stone have been repeatedly built since the early settlement of the area. It is little wonder that the mythical kings of this region tend to be associated with titanic battles against the raging tides. Legend has it that King Qian Liu of the sixth century mustered an army of ten thousand men to fight the capricious God of the Tide, deploying his men to attack the towering figure of the deity when it emerged roaring from the sea to celebrate its birthday on the eighteenth day of the eighth lunar month. In the ensuing battle thousands of warriors lost their lives charging into the sea. Finally King Qian Liu quelled the currents by personally piercing the God of the Tide with a gigantic arrow shot from his royal bow.[55]

During the three centuries of Qing rule, the Qiantang dikes underwent no fewer than fifteen rounds of major reconstruction, involving over ten thousand repair projects. The result was a huge "fish-scale stone dike" system of more than 250 miles on both sides of the river's mouth, built of iron chains, concrete, and slabs of stone. These dikes were sometimes referred to as the "great wall against the sea."[56] Just as the Great Wall in the north was rather ineffectual in keeping out invading armies, however, these dikes traditionally offered less than certain protection to lives and property ashore.

Under the People's Republic the state took in stride the challenge posed by nature. Gathering the technological and organizational resources at its disposal, the government stabilized its victory over the Qiantang tides by lengthening the dikes to 375 miles and by building multiple layers of concrete barriers to divert and head off the bore. To the extent that these bureaucratically managed engineering projects have been effective, they have also put an end to a scenic spectacle of nature's unbridled energy much eulogized by poets in the past, as well as to a colorful and highly reputed autumn festival celebrated locally since the tenth century that once used to attract throngs of visitors to its food fairs, handicrafts displays, and boating contests.[57]

Before the use of steamships and the rise of competing sea routes, the Qiantang waterway was the prime artery of trade and travel for the province, connecting the mountains of the southwest to the plains of its delta. Each end of the artery was connected to external trading systems, though in markedly asymmetric ways. Jiangshan, where part of the river began, was a jumping-off point for travelers from downstream to set off on the three hundred li uphill trek through the mountains into Pucheng in Fujian. Hangzhou, as has already been suggested, was where the river richly realized its commercial potential beyond the confines of the Zhedong hills.

In between the two lay a half dozen county seats along the Qiantang that marked the various points where new tributaries came down from the hills to join the main course, and where cargoes and passengers were passed on from one form of water transportation to the next. The largest and most important of these county seats was Lanxi, at the center of the Jin-Qu Basin, 360 li above Hangzhou and nearly three days' voyage upstream by the mode of navigation available at the turn of the century. A central point where the rafts and junks coming down the rapids of the high mountains of eastern Anhui and southwestern Zhejiang converged with the large and small inner-water steamboats bound for the wider river down below, Lanxi, with "hundreds of ships at its docks and thousands of small shops teeming on the shore" in the 1910s, was the "Little Shanghai" of middle Zhejiang.[58]

At the confluence of two rivers (Wugang and Qugang) and strategically located where the mountain counties accessed the broadening river, Lanxi embodied the full economic potential of the Qiantang in its middle reaches.

This was represented, on the one hand, by a highly commercialized strip of ten li (three and a half miles) along the water with boatloads of prostitutes and scores of eateries catering to a transient population speaking a wide variety of regional dialects. It was expressed, on the other hand, in the 451,300 mou (approximately 68,500 acres) of terraced fields—representing 70 percent of the arable land—covering the narrow valleys and undulating hills. While the county seat, with its walls and gates, sat atop a central plateau that overlooked the waterfront to its south, it also looked up toward chains of rising peaks to the north.[59] Within the bounds drawn up by the ever extending hills, the hundreds of boats, with their comings and goings, and the endless fields, with their seasonal ripening and withering, summed up the centuries of life that had endured and prospered in the middle counties of Zhejiang.

Trading and tilling interwove to sustain a remarkably stable way of life in the Jin-Qu Basin around Lanxi. Signs of trade were evident along the main roads as well as the river, in county seats as well as in major towns. The intensive labor that had been steadily devoted to the tilling of the fields, meanwhile, quietly tamed the landscape from the bottom of the valleys to the slopes of the hills. While trading sustained a community of sojourners, farming was the way of life for the peasants and tenant farmers who for generations spent their entire lives in the valley. Although the land gave the area a unique sense of itself, it was the river that defined its place in relation to the larger world outside.

Social stratifications developed as a result of both commercial enterprises and land ownership. Major lineages and landlords of large estates occupied hereditary mansions in the city, while their poor relatives and permanent tenants found shelter in simple dwellings in faraway villages. Lanxi's mercantile sector similarly contained two tiers. The area's long-distance trade in transit goods originating from half a dozen other provinces—Fujian, Jiangxi, Guandong, Anhui, and so on—was in the hands of the tightly knit merchant associations of sojourning natives of Huizhou and Ning-Shao. The retail and handicrafts operations that catered directly to consumers on the street, however, were small businesses that employed no less than 20 percent of Lanxi's 50,000 households (260,000 population) in the 1920s. Not that the two tiers were strictly segregated: Huizhou and Ning-Shao merchants certainly operated their own local outlets. Nor were the landed unfamiliar with commercial wealth, and vice versa. The majority of the shops and restaurants that lined the main streets in the county seat were nonetheless typically functioning with no more than a handful of members of the immediate family—a far cry from the regional merchants who set the seasonal price in tea and rice via their easy access to the resources of pawnshops and native banks.

Trading and farming, indeed, were intertwined: the bulk of the trade consisted of agricultural products from the fields as well as from the hills. Of the roughly two thousand stores operating in Lanxi in the late 1920s, at least several hundred dealt in the distribution of rice, charcoal, firewood, fruit, mushrooms, fungus, dried seafood, cooking oil, preserved meat, and fresh meat. Another couple of hundred shops served food, noodles, tea, and wine, catering to local businesspeople as well as to a large traveling clientele.[60]

Lanxi's multiprovincial transit trade also shared this basically agrarian character. The freighters, reloaded at Lanxi to go back down the Qiantang, carried the cloth and porcelain of Jiangxi, tea and tobacco from Fujian, lacquers of Anhui, herbs and medicines from Sichuan and Guangdong, and the wines of Shaoxing and Yiwu. More important, the Jin-Qu Basin itself produced enough to satisfy local consumption and to export a variety of products that ranged from rice, ham, and dates to timber and bamboo.[61] Even in a bad year for exports the basin was confident in its self-sufficiency.[62] Although it had never soared to such heights of commercial development and maritime activity as enjoyed by Hangzhou and Ningbo, the middle reaches of the Qiantang Valley constituted a world unto itself where the climate was mild and the rain plentiful, the soil was fertile, and the people had for centuries been frugal and industrious. It was blessed, above all, with many waterways navigable enough to permit the realization of all the riches that nature had deposited in between the hills of the valley basin.

Tang Long, a Ming poet native to Lanxi, was once inspired to eulogize the beauty of his homeland in a collection of poems celebrating exceptional sights: "wild orchids in the spring," "peach blossoms along the stream," "diving swallows over the sand dune," "giant rainbows dipping into the water," "shimmering moonlight reflected on the river," "sunset ablaze in the mountains," "flickering lights aboard fishermen's boats afloat in midstream," and "wood-cutters and their singing voices in the southern hills."[63] Tang's "Eight Odes" (*Ba yong*) were taken quite seriously. The texts were carved into the walls of the main literary hall of the prefecture, which was accordingly renamed, and they became part of the local gentry-literati tradition of celebrating the tranquility, leisurely pace, and closeness to nature that seemed so central a way of life to the people dwelling in the hills and the rivers of the middle counties.

In their serene sense of contentment, the self-contained inhabitants of the Qiantang's seemingly timeless middle reach enjoyed a style of life that contrasted sharply with both the sericultural commercial capitalism within the plains of Zhexi and the maritime mercantilism along the coast of Zhedong. This style of life found expression in the valley basin's economy as well as in its culture and society. The middle counties of Zhejiang did not simply occupy a strategically central location in the province; they sustained a whole way of life with special values and traditions kept alive from generation to generation.

2 The Idea of a Middle County

A setting is not just a spatial parameter, and physical
environment, in which interaction "occurs": it is these
elements mobilized as part of the interaction.
         —Anthony Giddens, *Central Problems*
         in Social Theory

Few spots shone brighter on the map of Neo-Confucian cultural geography
than the Jin-Qu Basin in Song-Yuan times.[1] Between the twelfth and
fifteenth centuries this region produced hundreds of Neo-Confucian scholars and philosophers of lasting influence. At least 150 of these luminaries
hailed from Jinhua County itself, which by the early eighteenth century
enjoyed the rare distinction of having four of its fellow natives immor-
talized in the Temple of Confucius. Referred to sometimes as the "Little
Zou-Lu" (*xiao Zou Lu*), Jinhua was idealized as a place of perfect ritual
propriety and social harmony, analogous to the states of Zou and Lu, the
birthplaces of Confucius and Mencius, in the classical period.

Meanwhile, with the region's mild climate and industrious peasants,
Jinhua natives could boast of living in one of the most prosperous and
populous counties of late imperial China.[2] Its fields produced three crops
of rice and wheat. Its women and children harvested enough oranges and
chicken eggs to supply the entire basin in the time frame of a single day's
journey to the county seat. To average people outside of Zhejiang, in fact,
Jinhua's national reputation rested not so much on its scholars as on the
quality of its smoked hams, preserved dates, and refined sugar. These farm
exports represented a supplementary income of thousands of taels of silver
to Jinhua's village households, enabling many residents to send their sons
to school while motivating others to aspire toward higher levels of Confucian respectability.

Jinhua, in short, was the idyllic embodiment of the Confucian way of
life that combined agrarian self-sufficiency with moral self-cultivation.
This idealization was so firmly established that it became a fundamental
part of local self-regard: Jinhua had long been the proud center of its own
universe. Even its modern-day iconoclastic detractors conceded that they

had been born in a "good place." At their zenith, the academies lured students from north China as well as from Jiangxi, Fujian, and Guangdong; and even in their declining years, Jinhua's Confucian schools continued to attract students from all parts of southern Zhejiang. Much as the old empire saw itself as the Middle Kingdom to its tributary states, Jinhua, in its own microcosmos, was the middle county to all who sought to enter its gates.[3]

Because of its location, Jinhua's geographic catchment was circumscribed, especially when compared to that of cities on the higher rung of the urban hierarchy, such as Hangzhou. But it was precisely this compactness that contributed to a denseness in the clustering of social ties in the county over the centuries, which gave rise to a strong sense of its own uniqueness. Sustained by stable kinship organizations rooted in landed interests, distinguished from neighboring communities by a regional dialect with its own popular opera, Jinhua at the end of the nineteenth century had a well-developed sense of its own values and tradition.

This chapter explores this sense of middle-county self-sufficiency as it evolved over the ages, before it was eclipsed by the forces of change at the turn of the twentieth century. Jinhua's nativist construction of its own past, through the selective use of monuments and gazetteers, and encapsulated in a handful of icons and images, was almost bound to be different from the sort of description and analysis that a modern scholar—say an American social historian schooled in structural analysis of Chinese lineages— was likely to produce.[4] As insufficiently "critical" or "objective" as this self-construction (which amounted at times to a certain degree of self-absorption) was bound to be, still it was an awareness in the very air, so to speak, that Jinhua's native sons breathed, and it informed their perception of themselves as historical actors.[5]

THE GARDEN

According to the local gazetteer, Heaven had destined Jinhua to be the site where the riches of China's southeast were to be realized. Strategically placed between the mountains of Fujian and Zhejiang, "this is an area of vital importance, far superior to others in the back country and off the main roads."[6] The North Mountains (Beishan), which defined the northern boundaries of the basin,[7] entered and stretched across the landscape of the county "like the body of a winding dragon."[8] The shape of the mountains, the locals believed, was a clear sign of Heaven's wish to bestow special favor on the land. It accounted for Jinhua's centuries of extraordinary fortune in producing more than its share of eminent scholars. The disturbance of this environment in the late sixteenth century by the construction of main roads—"the virtual decapitation of the dragon through drilling and tunneling by the foolish and greedy"—also accounted for the steady decline of Jinhua's fortune thereafter.[9]

Even so, that Heaven had willed the very creation of Jinhua was evident in the lone peak rising six hundred feet above the North Mountains. Here, Xuanyuan, the mythical first ruler of prehistoric China, was believed to have stopped his carriage once upon a time. The rut left by his carriage caught enough water from the sky to form a pond, on which a water lily grew. One day a petal fell from this golden blossom to the plains down below. Where the petal had fallen, a whole county eventually came into being. Jinhua, literally "golden blossom," was the unhurried fruition of this heavenly inception.[10]

Once created, the county was blessed by the Supreme Goddess of the Ninth Heaven, who chose to take up residence in Jinhua's Purple Pine Temple, where she spent her days preparing a magical potion as an offering to heaven and earth. Before leaving the temple, the goddess buried away in Jinhua's hills and valleys her utensils and products, thereby enchanting the land for millennia to come. During the twelfth century, it is said, a Daoist priest saw his chicken peck loose from underneath a bamboo bush a brilliant pill, which conferred magical powers and longevity that only a goddess could bestow. Every direct and indirect contact with the divine hidden treasure of the land proved to be a source of much happiness. The priest lived to his nineties in full vigor and vitality, and even his chicken survived for thirty years after the discovery.[11] Jinhua, by its own mythical imagination, was a land blessed by a perfect blending of the mystical with the ordinary, the celestial Daoist with the mundane barnyard fowl, where every square inch of its soil promised to yield exceptional heaven-sent rewards to inhabitants merely going about their ordinary business.

This sense of bliss found ready expression in the Jinhua literati's much cultivated admiration for the beauty of their homeland. Over the centuries, the dozens of peaks of the North Mountains have been repeatedly eulogized in poetry and prose as the site of hundreds of scenic spots: creeks, springs, wells, waterfalls, and, above all, deep dark caverns with tortuous passages and dramatic crystal formations that open up acres of underground space. Lotus Peak, which rises above the county seat, for example, contains a chain of three vertically connected caves: the Morning Purity, the Ice Jar, and the Twin Dragons. These were magical spots where Song officials prayed for rain and delivered their messages to the mystics. These stalactite-studded caves were also believed to have been the dwellings of many Daoist immortals who took up residence there.[12]

As these immortals made their presence felt, the local legends claimed, the slopes of the North Mountains and the villages of their foothills turned into gardens of jasmine, orchids, and cymbidia. The immortals gave the blossoms an exquisite scent by watering them with the streams that flowed down through the mouth of the Twin Dragons. The streams and the flowers in turn gave birth to scores of villages named with words such as *dragon, lotus, plum, bamboo, maple, rock, crane, cave, bridge, pond,* and *creek.* Although none of the cave-dwelling Daoist immortals was ever spotted again after the fifteenth century, one local shepherd boy was said to have joined their ranks as an immortal himself one day in a cave at the foot of the North Mountains, thereby fostering a cult of his own down into present times.[13] Herds of deer and an occasional rare bird, with crimson feathers in its crown, could still be seen in the foothill villages centuries after the Daoist masters were gone.[14] Elite aestheticism and village oral traditions complemented each other to weave together an idyllic image of Jinhua's bliss and beauty, where the mystical benevolence of nature enabled people to find sustenance and tranquility.

THE HAVEN

While the creation myth of Jinhua linked the origin of the county to the prehistoric birth of Chinese civilization, those who peopled Jinhua and dominated its local society—those who were largely responsible for the generation and perpetuation of Jinhua's mythical origin—did not, however, arrive on the scene until the twelfth century. These "Jinhua natives" who turned their association with the locale into such bliss were, in fact, Song-period migrants into the area from their homes on the north China plains (Hebei and Henan in particular).[15] Although the local mythology of Jinhua's origin was devised by twelfth-century immigrants seeking refuge from turmoil farther north, the actual beginning of civilization there occurred much earlier.

Recent archaeological findings made by Chinese scholars in the 1980s show that around 1100 B.C., the Jinhua-Quzhou Basin area was at the center of a well-developed southern culture characterized by the production and distribution of a fine, blue-glazed porcelain that distinguished its creators from the pottery makers of the north China plains.[16] Jinhua, by that token, had its own antiquity, albeit parallel to the history of the dynastic cycle as it unfolded on the Yellow River plains. Nonetheless, during much of the ancient and medieval periods, Jinhua in the eyes of northerners had been a peripheral patch of wilderness on the frontier of the continental empire; "history" and "civilization," from their perspective, did not begin in Jinhua until the twelfth century, when settlers from the north migrated into this area.

This abrupt beginning in Jinhua was directly linked to the Song dynasty's traumatic loss of the north China plains in 1127.[17] That year, Jurchen cavalry units overwhelmed Song military resistance in their sweep across north China. The barbarian invaders captured Kaifeng, the capital, carrying off the ruling emperor along with most of the imperial household and killing many members of the court. Northern notables crossed the Yellow River in huge numbers to flee from the marauding invaders. When a branch of the dynastic house reestablished itself in Hangzhou and filled the city with a revamped Southern Song imperial entourage, many of the uprooted royalists did not stop at the Zhexi plains, but pressed on up the Qiantang River to fill up the riverine heartland in the enclosure of the Jinhua hills. This sudden influx of well-connected northerners marked the beginning of Jinhua as a meaningful space in official dynastic historical narratives. Before 1127, according to the nativist construct, the basin was essentially empty space—a silence that was punctuated by the occasional honk of the wild geese flying over it. Thereafter, it not only offered refuge to distinguished northern gentry clans, but flourished to become home to generations of Neo-Confucian luminaries and eminent bureaucratic lineages whose presence continued to be felt through the early twentieth century.[18]

Many of Jinhua's characteristics as a locale, including its physical landscape, were the constructions of this new landed elite that reestablished itself in Jinhua after the twelfth century.[19] Over the centuries, two distinct styles of elite orientation emerged. Both styles, in their different ways, contributed to Jinhua's sense of its centrality.

Between the twelfth and fourteenth centuries, Jinhua was the center of the Jinhua School of Neo-Confucianism (Jinhua Lixue) with its continuing tradition of classical scholarship and moral philosophy of considerable intellectual vitality. It produced an elite that concerned itself less with political matters than with moral and scholarly ones, and whose members took personal cultivation and the creation of a social order based on Confucian ideals as the main pursuits of their lives.[20] Jinhua, where their lineages were firmly located, was the initial site of their activities. The appropriate setting for this elite was Jinhua's hills and valleys (rather than its walled county seat). There, in the towns and villages at the foot of the

North Mountains, this moral elite devoted itself to the construction of a social order that was based on the realization of Confucian norms governing personal and familial relationships.[21]

A second major orientation of the Jinhua elite was classical learning directed toward bureaucratic statesmanship.[22] As we shall see, after the fourteenth century classical scholarship of the Jinhua School merged with and became part of the orthodox state Confucianism associated with the name of Zhu Xi (1130–1200), the leading Neo-Confucian master of the premodern period.[23] A tradition previously embedded in Jinhua was expanded to encompass the empire as a whole while correspondingly distanced from communal affairs. Jinhua's educated elite leaders were transformed from scholar-moralists at home into powerful gentry-bureaucrats with high lineage connections. These elites no longer sought fulfillment merely in their native place, but pursued power and position at far ends of the empire. The county ceased to be where their most memorable words and deeds were publicly imprinted and enacted. It became, instead, a domestic space where their honors and ranks, achieved elsewhere, were collected and commemorated.

THE MORAL ELITE AND A LIFE IN THE COUNTRY

Few of China's great families of the medieval period had survived with their wealth and social standing intact by the twelfth century. Among those who settled in Jinhua after 1127, however, were scions of eminent northern lineages that had enjoyed power and privilege for generations. Of these, Lü Zuqian (1137–81), who was held in high esteem by his fellow gentry, appeared to have the most illustrious ancestry with a long line of high offices, including a prime ministership, and several noble titles during the Northern Song.[24] By the time of the Southern Song, the family's days of such supreme influence in national politics were apparently over. Its politics diverged from the mainstream of the court, and access to the emperor often seemed blocked by the wrong people at critical moments.

This sense of being somewhat on the political margin, combined with the self-confidence of heredity and education, contributed to the Lüs' readiness to be vocal critics of court affairs from time to time. Lü Zujian, Zuqian's brother, for instance, spoke out against a powerful minister for mourning his stepmother with the rituals prescribed for a dead aunt rather than a dead mother—a major breach in propriety, according to Lü Zujian. Zujian also earned himself a term in exile by accusing Prime Minister Han

Tuozhou of leading the emperor astray.[25] Pan Lianggui, another Jinhua scion, received a similar dismissal from the court for adamantly scolding an imperial favorite one day in the emperor's presence and saying that the minister had occupied imperial attention with matters of triviality rather than importance, thereby contributing to Song weakness in its dealings with the Jin.[26]

This fearlessness in the presence of powerful court figures went hand in hand with a contempt for individual gains, material temptations, and personal connections with the rich but unrefined. A true gentleman of an established line, indeed, disdained marriage alliances with social climbers and parvenus. Pan Lianggui, whose fame as a budding talent was much enhanced by the *jinshi* degree he earned in his early twenties, turned down several marriage proposals made by the newly rich and powerful, including the imperial councillor Zhang Chun.[27] Zhang wished to marry his granddaughter to Pan and offered a dowry of three million strings of copper cash. Pan replied: "I take a wife to perform her filial duties to her in-laws. I do not marry women from families of the rich and haughty." He married instead a woman of the impoverished Fan clan descended from the Northern Song prime minister Fan Zhongyan, the Confucian scholar noted for being among the first to draw up clan rules and create a charity estate. Pan's bride was chosen for her family values as well as for the refined manners by which she had been reared.[28]

Genteel poverty and forced retirement from the court eventually became points of pride rather than embarrassment in the lives of these scions. Pan Lianggui, after the scolding incident in court, was dismissed by the emperor, and retired to Jinhua, where he devoted himself to classical learning. Even the ruler heard about the humble condition of his dwelling, which was barely serviceable as a shelter against the weather. When Pan died, his heirs were left in considerable poverty. He received a decent burial in accordance with Confucian ritual prescriptions only because the emperor contributed to the expenses.[29] Such behavior won the admiration of fellow moralists and scholars, including the Neo-Confucian master Zhu Xi.

In their readiness to take on the powerful, these men drew sustenance from their identification with their lineages, which also functioned as communities of value. Lü Zuqian, sometimes referred to as the "founding father" of the Jinhua School of Neo-Confucianism, had an illustrious lineage to support him. More important, the familial line was also a line of intellectual transmission, both in the teaching of classical scholarship and in the observance of ritual practices within the familial context.[30]

Zuqian's fifth-generation ancestor in the Northern Song, Lü Xizhe, had been taught classical scholarship by his father and brought up following strict rules of proper conduct in accordance with prescriptions in the Confucian classics.[31] Before his tenth birthday, Xizhe had already mastered the *Xiao jing* (Classic of filial piety), the *Analects*, the *Zhongyong*, and the *Daxue* (Great learning). Meanwhile, he was taught to "tirelessly wait upon his parents every day, whether it was in the heat of the summer or the bitter coldness of the winter. He waited upon them in full attention with the greatest respect. Unless ordered to take a seat, he would not have the presumptuousness to do so on his own. Each morning he donned his hat and belt properly in preparation for his audience with his parents and elders. He was taught not to present himself to his parents without his cap, socks, gown, and belt, even on a hot summer day."[32]

This rigorous training in proper ritual conduct as classical learning was accompanied by careful monitoring of the environment in which the child was to move about: "He was told never to enter teahouses or wine shops. He was never to expose himself to impolite talk on the street, nor to lewd tunes in pleasure quarters. He was never to set eyes on indecent publications. Nor should he ever be exposed to immodest scenes." Training was supplemented, at the same time, by opportunities for friendship with scions of comparable background and by further instructions from leading masters of the time.[33]

In this connection, several points deserve special attention. First of all, under the influence of Neo-Confucianism as developed during the Southern Song, a heavy emphasis had been placed on the virtue of filial piety, understood as strict adherence to ritual propriety as laid down in the classics.[34] Many of Jinhua's most distinguished scholars earned high reputations for their filiality, which was a demonstration both of their mastery of ancient treatises on rites and of an ability to turn moral knowledge into practice. For example, Wang Shiyu, a disciple of Zuqian's grandfather Lü Benzhong, became noted as a filial son both for the heart-stricken grief that he expressed on the death of his father and for his insistence on a proper burial in accordance with the ritual prescriptions set forth in the Confucian classics. On the death of his mother, his reputation for filiality was further enhanced by the profound grief that he expressed, "which nearly caused his own death," as literally prescribed in the classics.[35]

Pan Jingxian, a disciple of Lü Zuqian, earned praises from fellow moralists when he turned down a government post of higher rank in favor of a minor teaching position, giving as his explanation, much in the spirit of the *Classic of Filial Piety*, that the latter post would situate him in a county closer to his aging parents. On the death of his father, Pan built a hut nearby the tomb and, as prescribed by the classics, kept vigil for three years. During the mourning period he allowed himself to become so distraught with grief that "his figure was emaciated; he never so much as showed his teeth in smile; his drink and rest were both strictly in accordance with classical ritual prescriptions." Neither did he ever again serve in office.[36]

Filial deeds and ritually appropriate behavior, as hallmarks of gentry lineages of learning and cultivation in this area, were often accompanied by a scholarly mastery of the Confucian classics, which supplied the textual foundation of Confucian moral behavior.[37] Gentry lineages that stressed filial conduct were therefore often vaunted also for producing scores of eminent scholars over multiple generations. The Lü lineage produced seventeen scholars over seven generations who merited biographical entries in the *Song Yuan xuean*, the authoritative text that constructed an intellectual genealogy for Neo-Confucianism from the tenth through the fourteenth centuries.[38] Several other Jinhua lineages—Shi, Wang, Pan, He, Qi, Ni, Ye, Tang—were also able to claim comparable success.[39]

These ritual and textual practices, once lodged within the lineages as a family tradition, had a way of migrating into other lineages through master-disciple relationships. The "Lü Family Rules," exemplifed in Lü Xizhe's early education, became the rules observed during the fourteenth century in the family of Ye Shenyan, because Shenyan's grandfather Ye Gui was a disciple of Lü Zuqian. Like Pan Jingxian a century earlier, Ye Shenyan refused official assignments that would take him away from his elderly mother. He also earned a high reputation for achieving order and harmony among relatives by the influence of his sheer moral presence.[40]

The portraits of outstanding figures of this period are best described not as able statesmen or social activists, but as filial sons and studious scholars.[41] These men were not solitary truth-seekers beyond the bounds of society, but moral practitioners who placed themselves within the intricacies of familial and kinship obligations. The qualities that won greatest admiration were those of moderation, dedication, and self-restraint, as opposed to passion and ambition. A true gentleman did not seek to rise up high in the world. He sought, instead, the equanimity of a man of moral self-sufficiency, content at home in the midst of kith and kin.

HOME OF NEO-CONFUCIANISM

Concomitant with the rise of familial lineages as carriers of intellectual traditions was the constitution of scholarly intellectual lineages in which the filial reverence of disciples for their masters entailed a distinct reluctance to part from the teachings handed down by their philosophical ancestors.

In the intellectual genealogy of the Jinhua School, Lü Zuqian was a pivotal figure who provided the linkage that situated Jinhua in the mainstream of Neo-Confucianism in its development from the eleventh through the fourteenth centuries. This was due, in part, to his ancestry and family. Like his forebears of the previous century, Zuqian was educated in the Confucian classics at home by his father, who had been taught as a child by Zuqian's grandfather. Lü Zuqian's intellectual genealogy could thus be traced ultimately to the early Song Neo-Confucian masters of north China, including such luminaries as Ouyang Xiu and Wang Anshi, as well as Cheng Hao, Cheng Yi, and Zhang Zai, who had either taught or befriended one of his ancestors.[42] Zuqian's presence in Jinhua in the twelfth century signified the perpetuation of a vital line of northern Neo-Confucian philosophical teaching—known as the Central Plains literary tradition (*Zhong yuan wenxian*)—in the south after the traumatic fall of the dynasty in 1127.[43]

Even though he died relatively young at forty-five, Lü Zuqian had been an active scholar and teacher throughout his life. His teaching was characterized by a willingness to accommodate divergent views, an interest in practical affairs of policy, an appreciation of literary knowledge, a love of historical studies, and an attention to institutional arrangements. He combined this wide-ranging coverage with an insistence on the primacy of moral practice, in the sense of both personal self-cultivation and Confucian classical scholarship.[44] He gathered a large number of disciples who came from all parts of Zhejiang to seek his instruction, laying the foundation of the Lize Academy in Jinhua, which became one of the most active centers of Neo-Confucian teaching through the early Ming.[45]

Those who received instructions from Zuqian, while in residence in Jinhua, formed a tightly woven community of scholars among themselves.[46] On returning to their hometowns, these disciples went about their separate ways, teaching family members and lecturing in county academies, thereby contributing to the spread of Jinhua Neo-Confucianism to other parts of Zhejiang. Ye Gui, for instance, was instrumental in the spread of Lü's teaching eastward to the neighboring county of Yiwu. Ye's son, Ye Rongfa, served as the education supervisor of Lanxi and brought the Jinhua School precepts westward to that county.[47] Lü Zuqian was thus the undisputed master of an important thirteenth-century intellectual community centered on Jinhua that spread its influence throughout Zhedong.

More important, because of Lü Zuqian's lasting friendship and philosophical compatability with Zhu Xi, Jinhua became after the twelfth century a critical center in the development of Zhu Xi Neo-Confucianism.

Neo-Confucianism of the Zhu Xi School, by virtue of its eventual ascendancy to state ideology during the Ming and Qing, represented the mainstream of Chinese intellectual life from the thirteenth century onward. This ascendancy, however, was not achieved in the master's own lifetime, but occurred under Mongol rule when Xu Heng (1209–81), a northern Confucian scholar, gained the favor of Khubilai Khan.[48] Mongols, in 1313, became the first rulers to base the civil service examinations on Zhu Xi's interpretations of the Confucian classics, principally the Four Books. This Yuan precedent was readily emulated by subsequent dynasties. In 1415, the Ming court issued an officially endorsed anthology on moral philosophy that was based on the teachings of the Zhu Xi School. The Qing court, in 1715, issued a concise edition of this same compilation.[49] These court-sanctioned editions, three centuries apart, became the basis of the required curriculum for the civil service examinations. Until the abolition of these examinations in 1905, mastery (and memorization) of the Confucian classics along the lines annotated by the Zhu Xi School was the most fundamental preparation for entrance into the imperial bureaucracy.

Neo-Confucianism, according to the intellectual historian Wing-tsit Chan (Chen Rongjie), owed its eminence first of all to the scope and depth of the master's intellectual vision. Beyond that, it owed its uninterrupted line of transmission to a group of dedicated followers who built an extensive network of private academies throughout the counties of southern China, especially during the critical period of the early thirteenth century, when Zhu Xi's teachings were denounced by the Southern Song authorities as false.[50] Even though Zhu Xi spent most of the remaining years of his life in Fujian, his teaching was passed on through a line of outstanding scholars in Jinhua, far to the north. This was due, in no small measure, to Zhu Xi's friendship with Lü Zuqian and the latter's receptiveness to Zhu's ideas, which had much to do with Lü Zuqian's character.

Lü Zuqian was warmly remembered by his friends and disciples as being of mild temperament and gentle manner. Unlike Zhu Xi, he consistently showed a "preference to harmonize differences instead of fostering them, to strive for centrist instead of extreme positions."[51] Among his most memorable deeds were his valiant efforts to reconcile the sharp disagreements dividing Zhu Xi from his arch intellectual detractor Lu Jiuyuan (1139–93), an effort that led to the celebrated Goose Lake Temple debates between the two masters in Jiangxi.[52] Although the meeting failed

to resolve much differences, Lü Zuqian's friendship with Zhu Xi contin-
ued to grow. The two men exchanged several visits during their lifetime.
They also kept up a significant amount of correspondence on the classics.
With their blessing, extensive contacts among their disciples ensued.
These contacts led to the formation not only of personal friendships but
also of marital alliances. Pan Jingxian's daughter, for example, married
Zhu Xi's son. Pan's younger brother Jingliang, meanwhile, was the son-
in-law of Lü Zuqian.[53] The two intellectual communities spawned by the
teachings of Zhu Xi and Lü Zuqian became intimately interrelated from
an early point.

The most critical development in the transmission of the Zhu Xi School
of Neo-Confucianism took place when the Fujianese Huang Gan (Mian-
zhai), the master's most accomplished disciple as well as son-in-law, was
appointed to an official position in Zhejiang. Among his colleagues was He
Boling, a disciple of Lü Zuqian, who presented his two sons to become
Huang's students. He Ji (1188–1268), the younger one of the two, soon
established himself as the leading scholar of the Zhu Xi School on his return
to his hometown, Jinhua. He Ji passed on his Neo-Confucian learning
through a line of intellectual descendants, composed primarily of fellow
Jinhua natives, that included Wang Bo (1197–1274), Jin Lüxiang (1232–
1303), and Xu Qian (1270–1337). Collectively known as the Four Masters
of the North Mountains, these men—He, Wang, Jin, Xu—represented
Jinhua's critical contribution to the development of Neo-Confucianism as
late imperial Chinese state ideology.[54] For that reason the four masters
were posthumously canonized in the Temple of Confucius by the Qing
court. For Jinhua, its elite members' canonization assured the locale a
central place in official narratives about the rise of state Confucianism.

A PLACE FOR ICONS AND RELICS

The attention lavished on Jinhua—the respectful reference to Jinhua as
Little Zou-Lu by outsiders—was a spot of light on the empire's cultural
map that acknowledged the place Jinhua once occupied in the intellectual
geography of Neo-Confucianism. It was a spatial representation that necessarily contained a temporal dimension in the form of the locale's past as
constructed by its elites. Much of the highlighting of Jinhua as a special
region was the product of a strategy that made ample references to the
biographical portraits of those outstanding individuals. Jinhua's claim to
national attention rested so squarely on its native scholars' critical contribution to the rise of Neo-Confucianism that its spatial centrality—its

"middleness," so to speak—was dependent on, and derived from, the biographical characterizations of Jinhua's Neo-Confucian luminaries.

Confucian biographies, as we have learned from Denis Twitchett and Arthur Wright, tended to be commemorative in purpose and didactic in function: "essentially an exploration not of a life but of the performance by its subject of some function or role."[55] Whether official or private, they focused attention on deeds and words that presented the subject's life not as an expression of changing times, but as the embodiment of timeless norms. Given the dependency of local self-representation on collective biographical portraits of its elites, the Confucian construction of space, no less than its construction of biographies, was an exercise at the service of a didactic project. In the case of biographical accounts, essentialist aspects were often accentuated at the expense of historical contingencies. In the case of portraits of the locale, all too often a unitary spatial ordering was imposed at the expense of more variegated descriptions of a landscape replete with tension and diversity.

The physical landscape of Jinhua had been presented, first of all, as a repository for the historical relics of its great men. The structure behind the old county academy, for instance, was the former home of Lü Zuqian. Two burial mounds at the foot of the hills were the tombs of He Ji and Wang Bo.[56] The North Mountains contained "the cave to which Wu Lai had withdrawn."[57] In the foothills there were not just simple village huts but "the hut in which He Ji spread his books." These scenes and relics were commemorative reminders of lives that had been compressed into icons and paragons. Huang Gan, in his eulogy of Zhu Xi, described a man who "lived the frugal and disciplined life of a sage." The historian Conrad Schirokauer paraphrases Huang's portrait of Zhu Xi as follows:

> His demeanor was grave; his movements relaxed but respectful. He sat up straight and when tired rested by closing his eyes without changing his posture. We are told that he arose before daylight, put on his long robe, hat, and square shoes, and began the day by worshipping his ancestors. . . . His physical wants were few: enough cloth to cover his body, enough food to still his hunger, a house to keep out wind and rain. He is said to have been content in surroundings that other people could not have borne. . . . He is presented as a model of filial piety. Punctilious in his attention to the details of ritual observances, whether in offering sacrifices or in celebrating a birthday or wedding, Zhu Xi carried concern for precise order into the routine of his daily life.[58]

Schirokauer goes on to dismiss the value of such eulogistic accounts for historical information. But eulogies of this sort, which repeatedly deployed a handful of tropes, dominated the pages of successive editions of Jinhua's local gazetteer. He Ji, for instance, was lauded as a "filial son," a "studious scholar," a man "without a harsh word ever to families and kinsfolk," and "punctilious in attention to details of ritual propriety."[59] Xu Qian, similarly, was a "filial son" and "studious scholar" who "spent his entire life in the caves of the North Mountains" with "little regard for rank and fame." Like Zhu Xi, "his physical wants were few," and he took delight in the company of fellow scholars equally devoted to the quest for the Confucian Way.[60] Numerous others were repeatedly noted for their "filiality," "dedication to classical scholarship," "mild demeanor," "harmonizing effect upon kinsmen and relatives through their moral presence," "integrity while serving as officials," "refusal to bend to the wishes of the powerful," "frugality," "simplicity in style of life," "readiness to endure hardship," "caring for the average people," "reverence," "sincerity," and "punctilious attention to the details of ritual propriety."[61] A constant refrain that ran through many of the Jinhua hagiographies was the image of a moral elite discovering amid the hills and valleys of their hometown a perfect sense of fulfillment: an unhurried life of cultivation that combined tilling, scholarship, and the perpetuation of the family line.

In addition to the local gazetteer's hagiographical output, there were shrines and statues that affirmed the locale's special claim on its native-born elites of national fame. In the courtyard of the Lize Academy where Lü Zuqian once gathered his disciples, the Shrine of Three Worthies honored the memory of Lü Zuqian, Zhu Xi, and Zhang Shi. In the Chongzheng Academy, the Shrine of Four Worthies was maintained for the worship of He Ji, Wang Bo, Jin Lüxiang, and Xu Qian. The subjects of these commemorative acts, in the final analysis, were not individuals in the totality of their lives, but exemplary figures embodying timeless norms. As moral icons instead of historical characters, the presence of these luminaries was never a matter of the past; rather, even in printed and carved images their presence was an assertion of moral authority that compelled emulation on the part of those who entered their moral space.

Even though the physical landscape of Jinhua was densely littered with relics of past masters, the county, by the Confucian conception of space, was not a museum for chapters in an intellectual history, but a living spot of inspiration that compelled constant reenactment of its timeless norms.[62] In the words of Chen Tingmo of the early Qing, Jinhua as a locale was of such unique quality that it was able to engender "exemplary cases of loyalty, filiality, chastity, and integrity with the passing of each generation."[63] For those who lived in this highly moralized space created by the eternal presence of canonized Confucianists, however, the normative imperatives present in the locale could become so compelling that the past threatened to subordinate the present: the forebears in relation to their descendants, and the icons in relation to men and women of flesh and blood.

While the Song and Yuan masters were men of tolerance and persuasion who relied on personal practices and pragmatic implementation to spread their teaching, the Ming elites of Jinhua, by contrast, had become high-ranking gentry-bureaucrats as well as large landowners.[64] These elites commanded both the ideological authority of the state and the organizational power of the lineage, and regarded it as their duty to regulate societal norms. The articulation of Confucian values under the Ming, compared with the Song, was no longer a matter left to the lectures and readings of private scholars and local gentry in the country, but fell under the institutional mediation of the imperial bureaucracy as well as of the incorporated lineages.[65] The ethical became joined to the political to form the foundation of the legal, and became firmly embedded in an institutional infrastructure that assured its perpetuation. Much of Jinhua's pride about itself thereafter rested on its serene confidence in this seamless union between the ethical and the political.

BUREAUCRATIC ELITES AND THE COUNTY SEAT
OF MANSIONS AND ARCHWAYS

In the summer of 1933, when two young economists, neither a native of Zhedong, entered the county seat of Dongyang of the former Jinhua Prefecture on their mission of rural investigation, they were immediately impressed by the abundance of signs of the county's high bureaucratic connections under the imperial rule of the Ming and Qing and by the strength of its gentry lineages. Their journal entry described a "very small, walled city that contained a large number of ancestral halls, and lots of large compounds of houses that flew banners high above, declaring that the compounds were formerly homes of men of high standing—either as state ministers of some sorts or as jinshi, holders of the highest civil service examinations degree. Readily visible in the public areas of the county were many archways painted with coiled dragons—a symbol of an imperial decree. Dozens of such archways could be found crowding the marketplace just in the one tiny corner near the west gate of the county seat." In Dongyang, the visitors concluded, "one cannot fail to be impressed by the august power and ritual propriety of the Han court [*Han guan wei yi*]!"[66]

When gentry compounds, banners, archways, plaques, and ancestral halls were tallied as physical evidence of elite-bureaucratic connections, Jinhua's county seat was an even more impressive place than Dongyang. As in the case of Dongyang, along Jinhua's narrow, winding streets there were many extensive compounds featuring enclosed courtyards and gardens that flew large banners high above their main gates, many of which dated back to the Ming and the Qing. The titles and honors announced in this case tended to be of the empire's highest offices, such as the grand councillorship and presidency of the censorate, and of the top palace examinations winners, such as the *zhuangyuan, bangyan,* and *tanhua,* won mainly before the decline of Jinhua's fortune with "the decapitation" of the county's dragon spirit in the sixteenth century.

Since Jinhua was the site of the prefectural as well as the county governments, these gentry dwellings existed in close proximity with government buildings that housed the top-ranking bureaucrats of the basin. Besides containing the offices of the prefect, district magistrate, tax collectors, textile manufacturers, postal service, county bookkeepers, and so forth, the county seat was the site for official Confucian instruction and for local military defense, featuring examination halls, county academies, lecture halls, military drill grounds, arsenals, armored gates, and watch towers.[67]

Frequent interaction took place between members of the local gentry and officialdom in this setting under the Ming and the Qing. In addition to their usual responsibilities for tax collection, the judicial docket, and local defense, Jinhua's magistrates—all of whom were by the rule of avoidance outsiders to the region—took care to pay particular homage to the locale's illustrious Neo-Confucian past. Magistrate Li Qi of the Jingtai reign (1450–56), for instance, offered special recognition to Jinhua's filial sons and chaste women.[68] Magistrate Long Yuqi of the Wanli reign (1573–1619) served most self-consciously as a mentor-teacher, directly overseeing local students enrolled in the county's various academies, and Magistrate Gao Zhuo of the early Chongzhen reign (1628–44) tirelessly discussed the fine points of the classics with Jinhua's scholars. Magistrates Zhao Taisheng and Huang Jinsheng, of the Kangxi (1662–1722) and Jiaqing (1796–1820) periods, collaborated with the county's local notables to compile and publish more comprehensive editions of Jinhua's local gazetteer.[69]

The concentration of the gentry's presence in the county seat, along with a growing elite dependence on the state bureaucracy, was, after the fifteenth century, much more a Ming development than that of an earlier time.[70] The erection of hundreds of officially blessed archways, which completely redefined the urban landscape in this county seat of no more than fifty or sixty thousand people, attested to the appearance of a new type of alliance between prominent gentry lineages and the imperial bureaucracy. In a most visible departure from the locale's self-centered orientation under the influence of Song-Yuan Neo-Confucianism, most of Jinhua's archways were monuments to high bureaucratic achievements and court honors. One of the several "primus archways" (*zhuang-yuan fang*) for winners of first place in palace examinations, for instance, was built to celebrate Tang Ruji's successful attainment of that distinction.[71] Gentry lineages continued as they had in the Southern Song to carry on the instruction of classical scholarship within the kinship network. Instead of lauding the successful establishment of a familial tradition of scholarship and filiality, however, Ming archways celebrated gentry lineages' ability to perpetuate "generations of exam degree success" (*shideng jiadi; shike*) as well as to garner generations of high offices.[72] Qian Ying and Qian Xuekong, father and son, for example, were commemorated as two generations of jinshi with an archway near the Lize Academy. The families of Xu, Zhao, Hu, Lü, Zhang, Jin, Yu, Tang, and Wang were all honored for the number of "exceptional talents" (*bajun*) that their lineages had produced. The prominent Qi lineage was able to display at least two archways, erected back to back on one of the county seat's busiest streets, that acknowledged their special distinctions for "generations of exam degrees" (Qi Xiong, Qi Ang, Qi Hu, Qi Xi) and "generations of imperial censors" (Qi Xiong, Qi Ang).[73] The Pan lineage, like the Qi, also won recognition for producing more than one imperial censor.[74] Altogether no more than a dozen major surnames—Pan, Qi, Zhang, Ye, Feng, Xu, Tang, Qian—repeatedly shared these honors among themselves during the Ming.[75]

Gentry lineages frequently intermarried, as they had under the Song. While the males of these lineages were praised for their examination success and high office, their women, daughters as well as daughters-in-law, were often lauded as "chaste widows" notable for their filiality.[76] Thus the women of the Ye lineage, which produced a board president with his own archway and more than a dozen high-degree holders in the Ming, married into the Zhang, Shen, Teng, and Ling, and were all awarded "chaste" and "filial" honors. That same Ye lineage also commemorated exemplary daughters-in-law in a late Ming archway dedicated to the chastity of wives of the Ye lineage: Jiang, wife of Ye Chun; Huang, wife of Ye Tingyuan; and Teng, wife of Ye Tingyu.[77] Concomitant with the reorientation of Jinhua lineages toward the imperial bureaucracy was a spatial rearrangement that restructured the relationship between the country and the city. Lineages of major prominence took up residence inside the county seat (the Yes in the Gunxiu Fang behind the Yongfu Temple, the Pans right around the corner in the Xinglian Fang, the Wangs in the Jianzhong Fang next to the Jingxiao Gate), while lesser ones maintained their residence in the countryside.[78] The moral elites of the Song had felt at home in rustic rural settings. Ming bureaucratic elites, however, had become urban dwellers occupying large compounds in the county seat. Archways that commemorated civil service honors and high government positions, attainable only by male members of the lineages, were typically erected in the county seat, whereas those that commemorated chastity and filiality—primarily female deeds in domestic settings—rarely appeared in the county seat where the gentry-bureaucratic presence was so palpable, but were placed instead in towns and villages in the countryside.

Jinhua had produced few "martyrs" for the fallen dynasty in the last years of the Southern Song.[79] The majority of its moral elite had continued to lead their private scholarly lives with kinsmen and disciples through the fourteenth century, retreating even deeper into the hills in some cases in order to detach themselves further from the new dynasty.[80] On the fall of the Ming dynasty, however, Jinhua became the site of fierce fighting and heroic resistance, its gentry-bureaucratic defenders perishing in flames together with the city. As it turned out, the city was attacked not by military units of the Manchus, but by former Ming troops led by the turncoat Ruan Dacheng. The Ming cause by this time was rather hopeless: Nanjing had already fallen, and the Southern Ming defense had collapsed. Jinhua's military defender, Zhu Dadian, nevertheless prepared for the fall of the city by drowning, first of all, his favorite concubines, his younger sons, and his daughter-in-law in a well. He then gathered his four grown sons and other loyal followers, including members of the local gentry lineages, in the Bayong Pavilion (the Pavilion of Eight Odes), where the Jinhua literati used to gather for poetry. Zhu placed explosives around the building, fought the Ming turncoats to the last man, and then set the pavilion on fire when he received news that the enemy had entered the west gate. The center of the county seat went up in flames, with several gentry clans—the Ye, Ni, Feng, and Zhang—

and their women following Zhu Dadian's example.[81] Later during the Kangxi reign, on the order of the Qing court, Zhu Dadian and his fellow gentrymen were commemorated in a shrine of martyrs established in the county seat.[82]

VALLEYS OF SHRINES AND TOMBS

Jinhua's bureaucratic fortune declined after the seventeenth century not only in comparison with the Zhexi prefectures, but also as measured against its own past performances. Despite a steady increase in its population, the county produced only about half as many holders of the jinshi and *juren* (provincial examination) degrees in the two centuries after 1644 as during the roughly two hundred previous years.[83] With its archways, shrines, and proud memories of bureaucratic success, however, Jinhua's powerful families, through their extensive landownership, ancestral halls, and lineage organizations, incised the locale's reified tradition of chaste widows, filial sons, and martyred loyalists deep into the county's village society.

Jinhua's women, like women elsewhere, occupied a secondary and subordinate position to male members of their lineages. But the strength of Jinhua's lineage organizations gave the locale such an inclusive sense of its native-born members that in its hierarchy of categories of people ("worthies," "officials," "scholars," "literary talent," "extraordinary deeds," "martyrs," and so forth)—indexed to each category's relative distance from the center of the concentric circles that encompassed Jinhua— "women" were consciously placed above "sojourners," "Buddhists," and "Daoists." Women deserved to be placed above sojourners, explained the Qing local gazetteer, because the men and women of Jinhua, after all, were linked by their shared affinity to the native place (*tong yi*), whereas a sojourning man, even though he might have spent a good part of his life in Jinhua, was secondary to the local women as a result of his origin.[84] Differentiation by gender, in other words, was of lesser consequence than differentiation by place of origin. Buddhists and Daoists deserved to be placed at the very bottom of this hierarchy (that is, in the outermost sphere of Jinhua's concentric circles) because these men, regardless of where they had been born, had chosen to abandon the Confucian way of life and follow a different system of belief. Differentiation by faith was thus an excluding mechanism of even greater importance, overriding either place of origin or sex.

Within Jinhua's Confucian patriarchy, women primarily occupied a secondary position. In the county's villages, female infanticide had been a common practice that, at least since the high Qing, local officials had repeatedly sought to control without much success. Footbinding was widely practiced in gentry as well as in peasant households.[85] The county's wealthy households, furthermore, were notorious for "the unwholesome custom," in the words of Zhejiang governor Qu Yingguang (1912–14), of locking up their female servants as a way to assure the master's exclusive proprietary claim.[86] Jinhua women, utterly defenseless in the presence of even the most amateur style of banditry, readily committed suicide by slashing their own throats, jumping into wells, and throwing themselves off of cliffs whenever they were threatened with the compromise of their purity.[87] The pages of the local gazetteer were filled with brief entries of such deeds committed by hundreds of nameless women of all ages, identified only by lineage, who found themselves in harm's way and won praise for preserving the honor of their husband's surname by committing suicide. These entries recorded a particularly large number of such incidents around the mid-nineteenth century, when social tremors ran through the area in conjunction with the outbreak of the Taiping Uprising in southern China.

By the late Qing, Jinhua society had become rather bifurcated as a result of the heavy concentration of landownership in the hands of a small number of gentry lineages that had established themselves in the county seat for generations. Researchers in nearby Dongyang found that in the late 1920s, less than 8 percent of the county's households owned nearly 75 percent of all its arable acreage.[88] Within these lineages it was not at all uncommon, furthermore, for residents of entire villages to be tenanted to their wealthier county kins who controlled the incorporated lineages. A "feudal patriarchal ideology," according to modern researchers, permeated Jinhua society. This ideology gave rise, in addition, to a particular form of landholding in the Jinhua Basin that empowered the lineage organizations as agents of the dead ancestors vis-à-vis the living descendants in a struggle over the use of land.

The area's strong emphasis on ancestral worship found expression in a unique social practice on inheritance that had become customary throughout the Jinhua Basin. On inheriting a piece of landed property, the heirs were expected to set aside a certain percentage of the inheritance as permanent communal land (*gong chang tian*), the yields of which were to be used exclusively to maintain rituals of ancestral worship for the deceased. Individual heirs were expected to tend to this particular lot of sacrificial land (*ji tian*), but the lot's ownership belonged to the lineage. This means no individual was able to engage freely in the buying and selling that involved the sacrificial land. The effect of this customary practice was to amass more land under lineage ownership while reducing the total amount of acreage available for transaction in the county from generation to generation. It also reduced the size of the land available for inheritance within familial units. With the multiplication of descendants, the size of the partible inheritance had become so drastically reduced—in some cases as low as 1.2 mu per capita, or 6.7 mu per household, in the 1920s—that the heirs often simply stepped into their forebear's role as a tenant to the lineage. One Republican-period survey in this area showed that of eight villages with a total of 329 households, only 1 household was able to claim ownership of land of its own. The remainder were all tenants and hired hands, many to their own lineages. It was not uncommon, indeed, for whole villages on the periphery of the county to be inhabited by none but tenants and hired hands.[89]

As tenants to their own lineages, many Jinhua peasants tilled their ancestral land, and assumed a share of the expenses incurred in connection with the repair of the lineage ancestral hall, the sacrificial ceremonies in autumn and spring, and the maintenance of seasonal worship of their own direct line of forebears. They often paid a low rent, lived in nucleated villages in proximity to fellow kinspeople, and enjoyed considerable security in holding onto their tenancy. The Cheng lineage of Dongyang, for instance, collectively owned over ten thousand mu of land in the southeastern corner of the county, and its members were the sole occupants in half a dozen villages.[90]

Life in these villages was not without financial turbulence. A Zhejiang University survey of the 1920s showed, for instance, that 58.81 percent of Jinhua households had gone into debt amounting to 31.6 percent of their total assets. Pawnshops and credit associations were extremely active in the area. A variety of agreements, mostly short-term, existed on loans and mortgages secured by crops, grains, and anything of marketable value, carrying interest charges that ranged from 16 to 50 percent depending on the time of the year, the source of the loan, the borrower's sense of desperation, and the nature of the relationships between the creditors and debtors.[91]

Nevertheless, because of the powerful hold of the lineages over the land, outright transactions of land ownership remained rare occurrences. Even as the number of impoverished households multiplied, the pattern of relationship between tenancy, lineage organizations, and the land remained remarkably stable. Beneath the surface of an active financial scene driven by greed and despair was a bedrock of landed stability. The lineages, through corporate landownership, effectively contributed to the ingrown quality of middle-county society. Anyone who attempted to rent from a lineage other than his own was often asked to put down an initial payment several times that asked of a lineage member. The Cheng of Dongyang asked for forty yuan from outsiders, for instance, as opposed to none from a lineage member.[92] Anyone who came from outside of the locale—single men arriving on foot across the provincial borders of Jiangxi and Fujian in search of a job—were rarely offered an opportunity to settle down, but were mainly employed as day laborers and hired hands, if not confined downright to their separate communities as "shed people" (*peng min*) in the hills.[93]

Armed conflicts between lineages were not at all unheard of in this part of Zhedong.[94] Under the influence of the incorporated lineages, death was invested with far greater significance than either birth or marriage. Funerals and burials, along with ancestral worship, contributed so much to the mobilization and rededication of kinship ties that these were among the most rigidly ritualized and solemnly regarded of all occasions. Proper observance of these rites required the investment not only of time and resources, but quite often of good acreage under cultivation, in the selection of auspicious spots for burial. So much of Zhedong's best land had been committed to deceased ancestors as their final resting place (up to 20 percent of all arable land in some counties in the Republican period) that several of the province's Nationalist governors complained loudly about Zhedong's "exceptionally superstitious" frame of mind that yielded precious space needed by the living to the ghosts of the dead.[95] With filial piety, ritual propriety, and ancestral worship so deeply rooted in Zhedong's long history of powerful lineages and Confucian ideology, however, Governor Huang Shaohong's repeated campaigns to simplify funeral rites, to reduce burial costs, and to construct public cemeteries were doomed to failure.

Although the shrines of the Three Worthies and the Four Worthies continued to stand in its county seat, Jinhua at the start of the twentieth century had been transformed from a Daoist garden, with wild orchids covering its valley and limning the caves of enlightened eremites, to a land weighed down by the constructions and monuments of its more recent Neo-Confucian past. As the lineages that put down roots in this area developed over the centuries, they filled up the valley, built mansions and fortunes, won banners and archways, canonized the filial and chaste, and achieved influence and fame. As their relative bureaucratic decline set in after the seventeenth century, they also reified their norms into icons, consolidating the hold of the past over the present, closing the basin off to outside forces, and turning the verdant slopes of the hills into ancestral tombs, the valley into a shrine of ancestral spirits.

With its compact, nucleated villages clustered at the foot of bamboo-covered hills immediately adjacent to lineage rice fields; with its tombs, ancestral halls, schools, and temples dotting the landscape, Jinhua at the turn of the twentieth century was still a world central to itself—a middle kingdom of its own—in the eyes of the cultural conservatives of its day. Governor Qu Yingguang, no doubt remembering the Little Zou-Lu of former days, praised the "diligence, thrift, sincerity, and honesty" of Jinhua's people, "much as in the days of the ancient sages."[96] Underneath the unfathomable silence that hung over the valley lay not the perfect Confucian order of a morally self-sufficient elite with its deferential peasantry, however, but a rigidly ritualized society that had been encapsulated by its own past. The middle county in the Jinhua Basin was long since past its heyday and soon saw its standing deteriorate into a middling society. This was both the result of the inner process of cultural reification of its icons and the result of the larger forces of social and economic change that had come to envelop the province since the middle decades of the nineteenth century.

3 Provincial Backwaters

Home was always like this, and although it has not improved,
still it is not so depressing as I imagine; it is only my mood
that has changed, because I am coming back to the country
this time with no illusions.
—Lu Xun, *The Complete Stories of Lu Xun*

Two developments, the Taiping Uprising and the rise of Shanghai from
a county seat to a major metropolis, set in motion processes of immense
consequence for the social history of Zhejiang during the late nineteenth
century. The Taiping Uprising (1850–64), a peasant rebellion led by Hong
Xiuquan, the self-proclaimed "younger son of Jehovah, brother of Jesus"
and Heavenly King to his Society of God Worshipers, broke out in dozens
of Hakka villages of charcoal burners and unemployed miners in the
mountains of Guangxi in 1850. The uprising spread inexorably, bringing
intense fighting and extensive militarization to local societies in large parts
of southern and central China, including Zhejiang, for the next fourteen
years.[1]

Shanghai, meanwhile, became one of five coastal cities opened to direct
trade with the West in 1843 by the terms set in the Treaty of Nanjing that
concluded the Opium War (1839–42). Within a decade it surpassed
Guangzhou to become China's leading port of direct trade with the West,
the value of goods passing through its port amounting to nearly half of
such trade for all China. During the Taiping years, when cities such as
Hankou and Suzhou fell into the hands of the rebels, Shanghai seized its
opportunity to become the leading financial center of central China,
thanks to the presence of foreign concessions that now functioned as safe
havens for the wealthy fleeing from the Taipings. The steady, spectacular
rise of Shanghai from the mid-nineteenth century onward as a vital economic center of many functions asserted a powerful influence on existing
patterns of trade and credit throughout the Yangzi Valley, rechanneling
trade routes and redirecting the flow of merchant capital in many regions,
including Zhejiang.[2]

Because of Zhejiang's diverse terrain, these larger forces of change had differing repercussions in various parts of the province. Coastal Zhedong, together with the Zhexi plains, underwent a major economic transformation from the mid-1860s onward. Both emerged, by the turn of the century, as areas with enhanced wealth and improved access to Shanghai. In contrast, the agrarian heartland in the Qiantang Valley, with its inland trading network eclipsed by the rise of sea routes between southern and central China, became even more isolated from the economic dynamics visible elsewhere. The Jin-Qu Basin lost its ease with a timeless way of life as well as its sense of cultural centrality. It declined into a middling sector of the province, outpaced and outmoded by the transformation to its north.

THE TAIPING UPRISING IN ZHEJIANG

The first serious Taiping invasion of the province took place in the spring of 1858, when the rebels, though victorious on the battlefield, undercut their own cause by breaking into a fierce leadership struggle in their capital at Nanjing.[3] Shi Dakai, one of the disgruntled leaders, left the Heavenly Capital and headed down to Jiangxi. There he broke through the imperial defense lines in eastern Jiangxi in March, forced his way through the mountain passes at Jiangshan in April, and spread warfare up and down the Qiantang River Valley into the Jin-Qu Basin. Famed for his tactical adroitness, Shi Dakai personally led the attack on the prefectural seat of Quzhou, a strategic point that controlled access to Hangzhou. To secure his right flank, Shi dispatched a division to attack Jinhua. There the Taipings were opposed by local officials and imperial troops; they also encountered the stiff resistance of local militiamen organized by the region's gentry. Some of these militia units were sufficiently well equipped to operate outside of their immediate home territory. The Lanxi militiamen, numbering in the thousands, for instance, fought the Taipings on their march toward the mountain county of Shouchang. Though the Taipings took heavy casualties, they dealt severe damage to the defenders, especially the gentry militia. Notwithstanding this local Taiping victory, the siege of Quzhou was lifted in July because the dynasty's other defenders launched attacks on Shi Dakai's rear units in Jiangxi, thereby forcing the Taipings to reconfigure their overall strategic position in central China.[4]

In February 1860, the Taipings returned to Zhejiang from the other end of the province for a different kind of operation. By then the Qing imperial army had successfully imposed yet another siege on Nanjing. The objective of this new Zhejiang operation, led by Li Xiucheng, one of the most talented

Taiping strategists, was to inflict a swift blow on Hangzhou in order to divert the imperial units away from the rebels' Heavenly Capital at Nanjing. Sometimes disguised as imperial troops to avoid military engagement, Taiping soldiers led by Li and his lieutenant Li Shixian advanced on two fronts toward Hangzhou from the adjoining Anhui hills, taking nearly all the counties on the Zhexi plains north of the Qiantang River and reaching the outskirts of the provincial capital in less than a week. On March 19 Li Xiucheng's sappers blew open a section of Hangzhou's city wall and stormed the provincial capital. Hundreds of Zhejiang's top officials, trapped in the city, perished along with their families when the rebels, six thousand in all, poured through the breach. The Qing, however, promptly mustered over twenty thousand men and dispatched them to the scene, forcing the Taipings to abandon Hangzhou overnight. Although the withdrawal into the Tianmu Mountains was carried out with as much speed as the attack on Hangzhou, the rebels were still able to pack away tens of thousands of silver taels looted from the provincial treasury.[5]

The Taipings mounted their most serious offensive on Zhejiang in the fall of 1861. By then Suzhou and the other major Jiangnan cities had already fallen into their hands. Although the old walled city of Shanghai had been occupied by members of the Small Swords Society since 1853, the new foreign concessions—to which the Qing officials and local gentry had retreated—were successfully defended with the help of the British and the Americans. The Taiping objective in Zhejiang, therefore, was to take the province and deprive the dynasty of its rich resources before mounting another attempt to capture all of Shanghai. Because of developments in Anhui and Jiangxi, the Taiping Loyal Prince, Li Xiucheng, was able to gather a force of seven hundred thousand men, whom he led into Zhejiang through the southern mountain pass of Jiangshan. To reach Hangzhou, the Taipings once again attacked Jinhua, taking nearly the entire Jin-Qu Basin and the southern half of the province. The rebel army then bypassed Quzhou and moved down the Qiantang River. Before crossing the river, Li dispatched his lieutenants to lead attacks on Ningbo and Shaoxing, which they accomplished with ease. These units rejoined him shortly afterward, and the Taiping main force then mounted a massive siege on Hangzhou. The provincial capital fell in less than two months. Tens of thousands perished, including Governor Wang Youling, who took his own life.[6]

The worst years in Zhejiang's experience with civil war lay still ahead, however, when the Taipings became the defenders of their newly acquired territory and fought the Hunan Army under the command of Zuo Zongtang, the new Qing governor of Zhejiang appointed by the imperial court.

Zuo, like the Taipings before him, launched his military campaign from the southwestern mountains of the upper Qiantang Valley. The two sides fought bitterly protracted battles with each other for the next three years, turning the province into a bloody battlefield. The Jin-Qu Basin, where the Hunan Army fought its way into the province, was doubly ravaged because this was also where the Taiping commander Li Shixian set up his head-quarters to oppose the enemy's advance downstream to Hangzhou.[7]

The demographic result of such prolonged devastation was dire. A whole decade after the Taiping Uprising, Zhejiang's population was only about 40 percent of its level ten years prior to the outbreak of the rebellion. In the hills surrounding the Jin-Qu Basin, where villages lay alongside the high-ways of marching marauders, some locales only had two out of every ten people survive the Taiping warfare. In Hangzhou itself, the population was reduced from 810,000 in 1850 to fewer than 50,000 in 1864. In Xiaofeng, a hotly contested area on the outskirts of the provincial capital, only one out of every thirty people lived on.

One obvious consequence of this depopulation in central and northern Zhejiang was regional migration. After the uprising, migrant laborers moved or were brought into parts of the province to help reclaim fields abandoned during the war. Because coastal Zhedong south of Ningbo had by and large been spared during the Taiping invasions, the two prefectures of Wenzhou and Taizhou became major sources of surplus labor for other parts of the province in the late 1860s. Day laborers and hired hands throughout coastal Zhedong responded eagerly to postwar opportunities in the fertile plains of Zhexi. Under policies and programs instituted by Governor Zuo Zongtong, these men were given tenancy rights in perpe-tuity in large parts of Huzhou and Hangzhou. Zuo's measures contributed significantly to the steady economic recovery of the Zhexi plains during the 1870s and 1880s. By evening out the contractual arrangements between landlords and tenants, these measures also helped to ease social tensions in an area where there had been a high level of concentration of wealth in the hands of a landowning minority prior to the Taiping Uprising.[8]

The Jin-Qu Basin and the hills in the Qiantang Valley, although no less devastated than the Zhexi plains by war, were bypassed by the stream of laborers migrating inland from the Zhedong coast.[9] Tens of thousands of acres of arable land lay fallow in the basin as late as 1880. While the northern part of the province was poised to embark on the mechanization of manufacturing, the former agrarian heartland in central Zhejiang was still struggling to regain its earlier level of productivity.[10] This disparity in regional recovery became all the more pronounced when Shanghai rose to become the center of a new economic order, drawing northern Zhejiang into its orbit. As this crucial swing began, the Jin-Qu Basin and the upper Qiantang Valley were simply left out, persisting uncomfortably on the margins of that new concentration of wealth and power.

SHANGHAI AND ZHEJIANG

Shanghai was a busy coastal shipping center well before the outbreak of the Opium War. From the late seventeenth century onward, ships setting sail from its harbor carried tea, cloth, and other goods from the southern provinces of Guangdong and Fujian northbound to Qingdao (Shandong), Tianjin (Zhili), and Dalien (Manchuria). These ships, referred to as sand boats (*sha chuan*) because they used the silt at the mouth of the Yangzi as ballast, carried soy beans and wheat as their return cargo to the south. Many of these shipping ventures were launched by Ningbo natives, who made three to four round-trips a year. Fujian and Guangdong sailors brought southern products such as sugar and lumber into the Shanghai market to trade at the Little East Gate (Xiaodongmen) on the waterfront of the county seat where a major pier stood and where "ocean imports and southern goods were consigned to Shanghai merchants."[11]

These shipping activities stimulated the development of a credit system in the form of Shanghai's native banks,[12] but they did not make Shanghai the preeminent financial or shipping center of the lower Yangzi region, which, until the outbreak of the Taiping Uprising, was economically dominated by Suzhou and Yangzhou. Suzhou, the seat of the governor general's yamen, was where government fiscal activities and gentry landed wealth were concentrated. Located at the heart of the world's leading silk-producing region since the sixteenth century, Suzhou was also a major urban center with a sophisticated monetary economy that sustained its own silk manufacturing industry, producing private fortunes that amounted to millions of taels of silver.[13]

Yangzhou, meanwhile, was the southern hub of inland waterways and the shipping center of the lower Yangzi region. This was due to the imperial government's traditional reliance on the Grand Canal as the principal conduit for the shipment of tributary rice and copper from central China to Beijing, despite the availability of the sea routes. More than four and a half million piculs of rice went through the Grand Canal entrepôt of Yangzhou annually in the mid-nineteenth century.[14] Even though there were over three thousand merchant vessels operating out of Shanghai in

1825, each with tonnage capacities measured by the thousands, this operation was dwarfed in size by that under the management of the shipping bureau of the imperial bureaucracy, which employed nearly a quarter million sailors and porters from Hangzhou to the northern terminus in Tongzhou.[15]

In sum, despite the existence of an active shipping business along the coast, Shanghai prior to the 1850s was not the dominant urban center in the lower Yangzi Valley. It was, instead, part of a web of economic relationships supported by multiple urban nodes with decentralized vital functions such as shipping, finance, long-distance trade, and manufacturing. In addition, before 1843, Shanghai-based coastal shipping involved virtually no direct trade with the West. Foreign trade in the form of silk and tea exports and the import of cotton cloth and opium was restricted to the southern port of Guangzhou. Tea leaves harvested from the hills of Anhui and Zhejiang had to be shipped overland to reach the market in Guangzhou.

The opening of Shanghai as a treaty port in 1843, therefore, was a matter of considerable economic significance. It meant ultimately that silk and tea produced in the lower Yangzi region for export could be traded in Shanghai instead of Guangzhou. Coastal shipping routes between central and south China would be adjusted accordingly, although Guangzhou continued to hold a partial advantage as a long-established commercial center with a well-developed network of trade routes and marketing channels. It was not immediately evident after the signing of the Treaty of Nanjing that Shanghai was going to become China's leading metropolis by the end of the century.

Much of Shanghai's spectacular rise after the 1850s was a consequence of the outbreak of the Taiping Uprising, and the disruption of established patterns of trade and commerce in those years. One after another, cities of critical regional economic importance fell into the hands of the rebel forces. Time and again, the assets held in these cities were transferred to Shanghai, the only major lower Yangzi city that remained under the control of the dynasty throughout the Taiping era. Millions of taels of silver, for instance, poured into Shanghai's financial market in the early 1860s as a result of the fall of Hankou and Suzhou to the Taipings. These included state funds formerly under the management of the Shanxi banks (*piao hao*) in Hankou as well as the personal assets of gentry-officials and wealthy merchants from Suzhou who fled the rebels when eastern Jiangsu was taken.[16]

The fall of Yangzhou to the Taipings also enhanced Shanghai's economic centrality by putting an end to government shipment of tributary grain along the Grand Canal. With the inland waterways blocked, the sea route via Shanghai became the only viable alternative. Except for a brief period from 1853 to 1855, Shanghai served as the southern hub for collecting and transporting rice to Tianjin. At least one and a half million piculs of tributary grain, collected mainly from Jiangsu and Zhejiang, went through its port annually in the 1850s.[17]

The major shift in the regional economy that took place in the lower Yangzi Valley during the second half of the nineteenth century has often been referred to as the rise of Shanghai at the expense of Suzhou, but Shanghai did not simply replace Suzhou as an urban center. It surpassed Guangzhou in maritime trade, absorbed the functions of Yangzhou on inland waterways, overtook Suzhou in wealth, and, with its Western trading firms and banks, also displaced provincial capitals such as Hangzhou by becoming the financial arena where the private secretaries of regional governors brokered deals to underwrite military expenditures and state enterprises. Compared with Suzhou alone, the rise of Shanghai represented the ascent of a new economic order with a sharply defined urban hierarchy, in which many more functions were concentrated at one central place than ever before in Chinese history. This development had as much to do with historical contingencies during the Taiping Uprising as with structural factors in the development of Shanghai. Once this new economic order took shape, Shanghai emerged not only as a large city attracting wealth and investment, but also as a dominant metropolis that projected—via telegraph wires, railways, modern newspapers, and the credit lines extended by a modern banking system—a transformative power on its surrounding hinterland. This was particularly evident in the case of northern Zhejiang.

CHANGES IN ZHEXI

Zhejiang's textile industry was mechanized in the 1880s, when steam-powered cotton gins were introduced in the coastal regions of Ningbo and Shaoxing, and in the Hang-Jia-Hu counties of the Zhexi plains.[18] At about the same time, silk-reeling was mechanized, so that by the turn of the century, some eighty mechanical silk filatures were operating in Zhexi, making Zhejiang's sericulture industry the third largest in China in terms of capital investment.[19]

This process of mechanization was the product of a commercial revolution that had been taking place quietly on the China coast since the opening up of the first treaty ports in 1843.[20] Drawn into the world market, Zhejiang's silk manufacturers quickly became aware of the necessity to improve on their traditional methods of production and distribution.

Gentry-merchant elites of the Zhexi plains assumed leadership in this effort by setting up experimental cocoon farms in the hope of producing higher quality raw silk. Together with the local officials, they also took it upon themselves to educate the peasant-growers. As the trade grew in volume, a host of changes rapidly took place in business practices that affected the entire organization of the silk trade from the purchase of saplings to the finance of the silk firms.[21]

Zhexi merchants, especially those of a handful of Nanxun lineages in Huzhou, had been long established as the leading silk merchants of the empire. In the late nineteenth century, Huzhou silk merchants not only were able to consolidate their position as silk collectors and dealers at home, but further succeeded in capturing the Sino-Western trading network in Shanghai by acting as the purchasing agents for major foreign export firms. The "Huzhou Gang" (Huzhou bang) subsequently accumulated legendary wealth. Contemporaries referred, rather sneeringly in the social columns of Shanghai's newly emergent newspapers, to "the four elephants, the eight cows, and the seventy-two dogs of Nanxun"—using animals of various sizes to refer to individuals and the magnitude of their fortunes.[22]

The financing of the silk trade, along with the financing of Zhexi's equally important export trade in tea and cotton, stimulated an extraordinary growth of financial institutions that were chiefly located in the plains. Hangzhou boasted more than 150 native banks by the turn of the century. The larger ones among them generated average annual revenues of over four hundred thousand silver dollars.[23]

The rise of commercial wealth in Zhexi blurred the social distinctions between gentry and merchants in the area. While traditional gentry leaders had become increasingly active in local affairs, leading to the expansion of a public sphere that lay outside the formal jurisdiction of the bureaucratic state, these newly conjoined gentry-merchant elites formed voluntary associations of their own that assumed some of the functions of local administrative organs.[24] By the turn of the century, in fact, there had emerged on the Zhexi plains a significantly different social formation that saw the balance of local power tilted in favor of the organized gentry-merchants rather than the state bureaucracy.

These civic elites actively sought Zhejiang's economic modernization, and promoted educational reforms designed to bring forth a new citizenship. Their sociopolitical concerns went beyond local issues to address China's problems as a nation-state under imperialist invasion. The chambers of commerce and associations of education became in the first decade of the 1900s the principal organizations that agitated not only for the establishment of a provincial assembly but also for the creation of a constitutional monarchy as a means of enhancing national wealth and power.[25]

These momentous changes in Zhexi at the turn of the twentieth century were part of a larger phenomenon in the Jiangnan area that was intimately connected with the rise of Shanghai as a new kind of metropolis. Telegraph wires were erected between Shanghai and the northern Zhejiang cities of Hangzhou and Ningbo in 1883–84. Railroad lines were laid between Shanghai and Ningbo in 1908, and between Shanghai and Hangzhou by 1909.[26] From the perspectives of the emergence of a new pattern of Sino-Western relationships, these developments had a lot to do with the consolidation of a "sphere of influence" in the lower Yangzi Valley driven by the British interest in Shanghai. Modern means of communication greatly enhanced the circulation of capital, goods, and ideas between Shanghai and northern Zhejiang. The fight over financial control of such facilities also became major rallying points for gentry mobilization and nationalist protests in the hinterland.[27]

New kinds of institutions, Western in origin, also made their appearance at this time, first in Shanghai and then in Hangzhou. The founding in 1907 of the first Chinese private commercial bank, the Zhejiang Industrial Bank, was a prime example of this development. The bank was organized by a gentry-merchant group (the leading silk merchants of Huzhou and the first generation of students trained in Japan) to help finance the construction of the railroad linking Shanghai to Hangzhou and Ningbo. Its initial capitalization, raised by gentry shareholders, was a total of twenty-three million silver dollars. Once they had invested, the shareholders applied pressure on the Qing court, insisting that local interests rather than foreign financial groups own the railroads running through their home province. Using this powerful gambit, they were also able to force the Qing government to withdraw from negotiations with the British Hong Kong and Shanghai Banking Corporation for a loan to build the railroad.[28]

New cultural and political thinking circulated among Zhexi's educated circles as well, fashioned by ideas first championed by Shanghai-based intellectuals publishing in the city's newspapers and journals.[29] Shanghai's rise led to such a fundamental realignment in the socioeconomic dynamics of its extended hinterland that in the 1920s it even found political expression in an unsuccessful but nonetheless significant campaign launched locally by the area's elites to sever Zhexi from its administrative allegiance to Zhejiang and join together with the Jiangsu prefectures of Suzhou,

Shanghai, and Changzhou to create a thoroughly modernized and self-governing province.[30]

Merchants from the two northeastern coastal prefectures of Ningbo and Shaoxing, like their Huizhou counterparts, had traditionally been the mainstay of trading communities flung far and wide throughout the empire, ranging from metropolitan entrepôts such as Hankou to inner valley trading centers such as Lanxi. Ningbo, in particular, was a major center of interport shipping and fishing.[31] Thus the proverb *Wu Hui bu cheng shi* (Without Huizhou merchants there is no market town) was in the late imperial period extended to Ningbo as well: *Wu Ning bu cheng shi* (Without Ningbo merchants there is no market town). From the seventeenth century onward, Ningbo merchants such as the Li and Fang lineages of Zhenhai and the Dong lineage of Cixi dominated the coastal junk trade, particularly between Ningbo and Shanghai, and riverine shipping to the various ports up the Yangzi. At the same time they operated native banks along these routes, creating the largest private credit network in central China.[32]

The ascent of Shanghai after 1842 quickly drew Ningbo into its orbit, knitting a close bond between the two cities that involved a constant flow back and forth of wealth and talent. From the mid-nineteenth century on, the youngest and most innovative Ningbo merchants shifted their attention more exclusively to Shanghai. Like the Huzhou silk merchants, Ningbo merchants built on their dominance of traditional shipping and banking to secure a strategic position in the growing Sino-Western trade, becoming compradores to foreign banks and shipping houses in the city.[33] From Shanghai they went on to dominate hundreds of traditional banks in Jiangnan and Zhexi, and to become founders of new-style Chinese-owned banks.[34]

The formation of the Shanghai Native Bankers' Association in 1917 and, in 1918, the Shanghai Bankers' Association enabled these Ningbo financiers to consolidate their influence on Shanghai's economy during the 1920s. In the 1930s, they and some of their Zhexi counterparts became powerful enough to gain a firm hold over the chairmanship of the Shanghai General Chamber of Commerce as well as the Federation of Shanghai Merchants' Associations.[35] It was thus mainly these Zhejiang entrepreneurs, along with their counterparts from Jiangnan, who comprised the upper crust of the famous "Shanghai bourgeoisie" of the Nanjing decade (1927–37).

Ningbo's poorer neighbors in former Shaoxing Prefecture, up the Caoe River in the hills behind the coast, were no less profoundly affected by the rise of Shanghai. Whereas Ningbo supplied the city with its top-tier bankers and industrialists, Shaoxing was the source of common laborers, industrial workers, women silk workers, female teahouse entertainers, and even pickpockets and organized street robbers.[36] The much disdained Shaoxing Opera, performed often by young woman singers in teahouses in Zhabei, Shanghai's industrial district, for instance, was at the turn of the century a trade monopolized by gangsters and performers from the hills of Shengxian, Shaoxing. In the Republican period Shengxian men and women also made up the bulk of silk workers under modern-style management in Shanghai, whereas Huzhou women tended to dominate the work force in Shanghai's smaller silk filatures of the old style.[37] It was estimated that at least four hundred thousand natives of Ningbo and Shaoxing were employed in Shanghai in the 1920s, engaging in all walks of life and encompassing a broad spectrum of the city's highly differentiated society.

LINKAGES

The drastic reorientation of both the Zhexi plains and the Zhedong littoral toward the opportunities represented by the rise of Shanghai signaled major changes in the political economy of the region. Zhejiang ceased to be a unit by and large contained within the administratively delineated boundaries of the old imperial province. It became more than ever a hinterland drawn into Shanghai's commercial dynamics, with a deepened economic dependence on the global import-export trade centered on China's greatest port city. The impact of this dependence has long been the subject of a powerful but now dated body of left-wing literature that saw Shanghai as the rathole through which much of China's wealth was drained to the outside world.[38] This left-wing literature linked the bankruptcy of rural China in the twentieth century to the impact of economic imperialism.[39] In this construct, members of the Shanghai bourgeoisie were seen as principal collaborators of foreign business interests' attempts to dominate the Chinese economy; they were viewed as "compradore capitalists" who had betrayed the sovereign rights of the Chinese people for the sake of their own fortune.[40]

The Zhexi plains and the Zhedong coast also became much more closely linked than ever before thanks to the use of steamships to convey quantities of goods and passengers in relative safety from the southern coast of

Wenzhou via Ningbo to Shanghai. Early-twentieth-century Wenzhou was among the fastest growing cities in Zhejiang. By 1920 it had been transformed from a sleepy regional port serving Fujian and Taiwan with transshipments of rice and sugar to one of the largest and most bustling population centers in the province, on a par with northern cities such as Hangzhou, Ningbo, and Jiaxing.[41]

Northern Zhejiang and Shanghai were also linked by an emerging business in resorts and tourism. During the Nanjing decade it was not uncommon for the very wealthy and the politically powerful to escape Shanghai's suffocating summer heat by renting villas in such scenic mountain resorts of southern Zhexi as Tianmu and Mogan. Shanghai artists and writers often found their inspiration by the shore of Hangzhou's West Lake or at the various pilgrimage sites of rocky Putuo Island off the Ningbo coast. It would have been difficult indeed to find a student in Shanghai's expensive private colleges who had not spent at least one spring break on an expedition to either of the two resort spots.

PROVINCIAL BACKWATERS:
THE QIANTANG VALLEY

While Zhejiang's plains and coastal regions grew in wealth through their linkages to Shanghai, the province's inland counties south of the Qiantang River declined economically because of their isolation from the metropolis. The northern cities were increasingly drawn, starting in the 1870s, into a system of native banks centered on Shanghai that permitted the smooth flow of sizable capital throughout the system. Jinhua's credit market, by comparison, remained dominated by large numbers of pawnshops as late as the 1930s—which visibly indexed the immobility of its capital.[42]

For Zhejiang as a whole, the north and south grew increasingly polarized after the turn of the century. While cities like Hangzhou tore down their ancient ramparts to build thoroughfares, parks, and athletic fields, county seats in the south remained immured within their old city walls. Not only were the district centers walled; there were hundreds of walled villages and family compounds protecting neighbors and kin from the social unrest that accompanied economic decline.[43]

The open, fluid nature of the expanding north thus contrasted sharply with the fragmented, walled societies of the contracting south. While the north was linked to Shanghai via telegraphs and railroads, many central and southern counties, including those of the Jin-Qu Basin, were unable even to maintain their primitive dirt roads. It was not until 1928 that electricity was first introduced south of the Qiantang River, and the first sections of railroad tracks were being laid between Hangzhou and Jinhua. By then railroads and electricity had been in use in northern Zhejiang for nearly two decades. Ningbo and Shanghai had daily steamship service. Zhexi cities were linked to Jiangnan by an automobile highway network, and Hangzhou was connected to Shanghai and Nanjing by airplanes.

With the rise of maritime trade centered on Shanghai, the Qiantang hill counties' former overland trading function as a conduit between central and southern China steeply declined. That is, once Ningbo was opened in 1843 as a treaty port, a different pattern of inland trading took shape from east to west. Foreign goods, mainly cotton cloth, entered the Qiantang Valley via Ningbo traveling upriver to Jinhua, from which they were distributed across the provincial border into Anhui and Jiangxi. By the 1870s, this trade had turned southern Zhejiang counties into relatively impoverished markets for cheap Western goods, while traditional native products lost their appeal. During the Republican period, these new trading patterns had a discernibly negative impact on many Jin-Qu Basin counties, including Lanxi, Yiwu, and Jinhua.[44]

Lanxi

While Republican Lanxi, the riverine port of Jinhua Prefecture, had lost a share of the trade that came downstream from Jiangshan, it was still the transit port vital to the mountain counties of Zhejiang's two inland neighbors, Anhui and Jiangxi. To an official visitor such as Governor Qu Yingguang, who made a brief stop in the county in 1915, there was little in the county's appearance to indicate its sliding economic importance.[45] The trade that went through its piers was changing, however: instead of sending lumber and sugar downriver to supply Hangzhou, it was distributing cotton cloth imported through Ningbo upstream into the hills.

Lanxi's increasing backwardness was measured both by comparison with the accelerated pace of economic growth in Hangzhou and Ningbo and by the gradual decay of the city's commercial life. While significant sectors of Hangzhou and Ningbo were becoming industrialized, Lanxi remained predominantly agrarian. When the new Nationalist county government took office in 1928, the largest industrial facility it could find was a match factory employing five hundred workers and valued at only forty thousand yuan in capitalization.[46]

Republican merchant associations in Lanxi, unlike those in Hangzhou, Ningbo, and Shanghai, were small, fragmented, and financially weak. Merchant organizations took few initiatives in local projects. The city slowly took on a decrepit look: by the 1920s even main roads that led up to the city gates had been allowed to fall into disrepair, and the public ferry at the south end of the city, first built in the eighteenth century and destroyed during the Taiping Uprising, was left to crumble in ruins.[47] Not until the new county government of the Nationalists mobilized local philanthropists later in the 1920s was sufficient funding raised to build an orphanage, a women's shelter, and a poorhouse.[48]

Yiwu

Whereas Lanxi was a trading port, Yiwu, to the east of agrarian Jinhua, was the home of the itinerant peddlers of the province. Living in a hill county rich in the production of a green-skinned sugarcane yet poor in grain yields, Yiwu villagers made the best of the high sugar content of their crop to make sweets. Using peanuts, sesame, and dried rice, they produced a variety of candy products that ranged from so-called candy drops, candy cubes, and candy slices, to candy sheets. Each huckster packed these into two wooden barrels kept dry by grain husks. The barrels were attached to a pole that the peddler carried on his shoulder as he set off on foot to peddle the candies in places as far away as Changsha to the west and Xuzhou to the north, where the climate was unsuitable for sugarcane cultivation.[49]

Over the centuries Yiwu natives had developed an elaborate distribution system with their own trading routes, special hostels, remittance mechanisms, and collective security arrangements—all of which enabled tens of thousands of Yiwu villagers to leave home in the company of a few veterans of the trade, carrying no more than a change of underclothing and their candy pole, prepared to journey hundreds of miles on foot for a whole year. Traditionally, these middle-county villagers commenced their annual journey by descending from the Yiwu hills three days after the Lantern Festival in the first lunar month, heading either north into Hangzhou via Shaoxing, or west into Jiangxi via Jinhua and Quzhou.[50]

In the eighteenth century, when the itinerant candyman trade was at its peak, Yiwu peddlers went up and down major streets and stood outside temple fairs in towns throughout central China, enticing children with the distinctive lilt of their chanting, accompanied by the sound of a small drum.[51] No matter how far they might have traveled, it was imperative that the Yiwu candymen return home by the eve of the Chinese New Year. Before entering their own villages, these men, in small groups, took time to wash up and rest. The next day they put on brand new suits of clothing and filled up their candy barrels with gifts before filing into their villages with their group leaders. The entire village came out to welcome them with elaborate manifestations of joy, and the march into the village was as triumphant as if they had just returned victorious from the battlefield.[52]

For Yiwu's itinerant candymen, the Taiping years marked the turning point in the practice of their trade. Prior to the Taipings the candymen of the middle county followed routes that took them down the hills into towns and large markets on the plains, where they sold candies to children and were paid in copper cash. After the Taipings the peddlers found themselves increasingly forced to choose routes that took them farther up the hills into remote villages high in the mountains. In these mountain villages peasant women preferred sewing accessories and trinkets to candies, bartering with old pieces of furniture and used household articles instead of paying in cash. To cater to the needs of their newly found clientele, the Yiwu candymen consequently transformed themselves into dealers of assorted used goods, though they persisted in taking their candies along each time.[53]

Sometime around the turn of the century this scenario shifted from bad to worse. In the late 1910s Yiwu became noted for the armed conflicts that broke out between its own villages as well as for the large number of able-bodied single men that it supplied upstream to Jiangshan, where they became the toughest and most ruthless of Qiantang River pirates. The countryside of Yiwu continued to feature religious processions and opera contests, but this kind of harmless revelry was gradually replaced by feverish nighttime *huahui* gambling that fueled superstitious fears of the spirits and permitted women to mix freely with men from dusk till dawn. These social evils drew sharp criticism from Governor Qu Yingguang when he inspected the county in 1915.[54]

Jinhua

Jinhua villages during the early 1900s were sizable communities with hundreds and even thousands of households. Large villages, such as Yuanxi and Yanping (120 square li) that bordered Lanxi County, registered 1,149 and 1,362 households each, with 5,091 and 6,315 individuals respectively.[55] Such sizes and population density, attained decades after the Taiping Uprising, were significant for purposes of comparison with villages in the lower Yangzi Delta, China's most prosperous and commercialized region since the sixteenth century. Of the twenty-two townships, administrative villages, and natural villages in the eight Yangzi Delta counties surveyed by the Land Reform Committee of the East China Commission for Military Administration in 1949, only three villages showed a total number of households exceeding one thousand and a population of more than five thousand. The 1949 figures no doubt reflected the casualties sustained from years of war. Under normal circumstances, therefore, Jinhua villages quite possibly averaged about half the size of those in the lower Yangzi "inner core."[56]

By its own standards, however, Jinhua was slipping. A good harvest would normally enable Jinhua to feed its people for up to two years, but the first Republican decade had seen more than its usual share of droughts. Lack of rainwater seriously reduced both the county's grain yields and its reserves. Jinhua's ponds and canals, on which the county had relied for irrigation, had clogged up because of tardy maintenance. Worse yet, the marshes and swamps had been steadily enclosed by the poor for cultivation, drastically reducing the reservoir of water for irrigation.[57]

Evil customs had crept in, meanwhile, from the eastern countryside, where Jinhua bordered Yiwu. Gang fighting and armed feuds between neighboring villages became frequent occurrences in these parts by the middle teens of the twentieth century.[58] Huahui gambling was also spreading, along with more extravagant contests. Since Jinhua villagers were substantial peasants, at least compared with their neighbors, the county was able to afford a diversion unique to the region: bull or ox fights, with villagers laying down bets and shouting raucously as one beast gored the other. To contemporary moralists these signs of social decay were particularly alarming, precisely because Jinhua, in their idealized view, had been distinguished by none but a long tradition of Song-style Neo-Confucian learning. In their pious rhetoric against evil customs of the present day, they drew attention to the many sacred episodes in the transmission of the Confucian Way. If such a fundamentally orthodox community could fall on morally hard times, indeed, how would less upright locales fare during a period of revolutionary change?[59]

When the Qing dynasty was overthrown in 1911, political events in Zhexi and Zhedong reflected the striking social and economic differences between the northern and southern parts of the province. In Hangzhou, the October 27 uprising was largely the undertaking of urban elites from the core zone of Jiaxing, Hangzhou, Shaoxing, and Ningbo. These elites, participants in the modern sector of the economy, were "in close communication with the elite groups of Shanghai, who were also involved in the revolutionary movement." In the middle counties up the Qiantang River, on the other hand, the uprisings were of a traditional nature, "controlled by the gentry, secret societies and local garrisons acting on their own account," and interested not in liberating but in containing emergent social forces. The middle-county uprisings in 1911 were inspired by neither reform projects nor revolutionary ideology. Instead, precisely because so many parts of central and southern Zhejiang fell into social chaos, the 1911 Revolution gave rise to "a concomitant reinforcement of the traditional oligarchies, activated by a reflex of self-preservation."[60]

During the years between the fall of the empire and the outbreak of the May Fourth Movement, little took place to close the gap between the politically progressive north and the culturally conservative south. If anything, the south appeared to have retreated into a "counterrevolutionary" backlash. In contrast, northern Zhejiang, as part of Shanghai's immediate neighboring territory, was transformed by the tremendous industrial and financial boom of World War I. Between 1914 and 1919, the average profit made by Shanghai's cotton mills rose by 267 percent per bale of yarn, while the profits of the city's native banks rose on the average by 80 percent.[61] Many of Shanghai's most innovative industrialists and financiers came from the prefectures of northern Zhejiang, but the hill districts of central and southern Zhejiang, still in the hands of conservative landlords, remained tradition-bound and economically stagnant: middling counties whose youth had no choice, once they had finished secondary school, but to go down to Hangzhou to continue their education. Once there, confronted by the economic expansiveness of northern Zhejiang during the wartime boom of 1914–19, they could not but have lamented the backwardness of their hinterland homes—provincial backwaters marginalized by modern times.

2

4 First Normal

When the May Fourth Movement broke out in Beijing in 1919, the responses in Zhejiang were geographically quite distinct. Zhejiang's northern cities reacted strongly: merchant associations backed the initiative to boycott Japanese goods with great enthusiasm; gentry reformers responded by calling civic meetings and printing newspaper declarations to announce their support for the students against the Beijing government. In county after county, students staged street demonstrations to shout slogans against foreign imperialists and Chinese warlords. To the great alarm of Zhejiang's conservative government, the northern cities of the province seemed swept away in an unprecedented outpouring of patriotic sentiments. The south, however, remained silent: a small group of Jinhua's elementary school students put on an orderly march one day waving national flags. The rest of the Qiantang Valley gave no sign of being affected.[1]

Hangzhou's students were clearly among the most active of the province's May Fourth demonstrators. The city was the scene, on May 12, of a large demonstration that brought out to the street three thousand secondary and normal school students, including a handful of women. These students demanded that the Beijing government reject the Versailles Peace Treaty. They also demanded that the government punish those Chinese officials, including the minister of foreign affairs, who were responsible for the negotiations. Within days students elsewhere acted to follow the lead of Hangzhou students. In Jiaxing, Huzhou, and Ningbo, as well as in Wenzhou, students assembled to shout demands outside of government offices. They also conducted raids on stores that carried Japanese goods.

The provincial government, which was dominated by southern military men and gentry leaders, was not about to permit these student activities to continue. Through the provincial bureau of education, it announced abruptly on May 30 that summer vacation for all Zhejiang schools was to begin immediately, closing the schools weeks before the term ended. To the disappointment of a small group of local student organizers, the flurry of protest activities died down swiftly. Within days school dormitories were emptied. By the time student leaders representing the national movement arrived at Hangzhou from Beijing and Shanghai, they discovered that it was no longer possible to bring a Zhejiang protest movement out on the street.

As a moment of patriotic mobilization and of student demonstrations, the May Fourth Movement was short-lived in Zhejiang, but as the political expression of the New Culture Movement centered on the publication of the *Xin qingnian* (New youth) magazine in Beijing in 1917—as China's first "cultural revolution," according to Mao Zedong—it fared quite differently in Zhejiang. In April 1919, well before there were any signs about the street demonstrations of the following months, Zhejiang students were already busily engaged in discussions over issues raised in the pages of *New Youth*. They formed study societies and published journals of their own, in which they voiced support for the iconoclastic spirit that informed the New Culture Movement in Beijing. These activities continued through the months of protest in the late spring of 1919. Thereafter, despite government displeasure, student publishing became even more active than before. Such activities tapered off only in January 1921, after the provincial authorities cracked down on a group of Hangzhou radicals. Altogether, twenty-six journals were published during this time, with sixteen of them appearing in Hangzhou.[2]

The most active publishing period fell between October 1919 and March 1920, when ten different journals were brought out within six months.[3] In terms of issuance, the concentration in time and space was even more impressive. An estimated total of 134 to 150 issues of student journals were published in Zhejiang in association with the May Fourth Movement. Of these, two-thirds, or 83 to 100 issues, appeared during that half-year span. Hangzhou was clearly the intellectual center of the development: more than 80 percent, or 127 issues, of these iconoclastic publications appeared in the provincial capital, leaving only a couple of dozen to be printed elsewhere in the province. During the peak period of activity immediately after the May Fourth incident in Beijing, Hangzhou students were thus exposed to three to four issues of the new journals each week. By comparison, few students in other parts of the province took an active part in the cultural and political debates that such journals helped to generate.[4]

In Hangzhou, the school that emerged as the leading radical institution in this regard was the Zhejiang Provincial First Normal School. Over half of Hangzhou's student publishing was done by First Normal students.[5] They earned distinction, however, not only because they were the most active, but also because their fervor pushed the anti-Confucian iconoclasm of the May Fourth Movement to a new height. Their rejection of the Confucian rites in provincial state ceremonies and their critique of filial piety, the cardinal Confucian ethical imperative, drew national attention at the time. These were also recognized as high watermarks of May Fourth iconoclasm in subsequent textbook accounts. Their open defiance of the authority of the Confucian political tradition eventually prompted the provincial government to single out First Normal for a crackdown. In its aftermath the leading radicals were compelled to leave the province altogether, and sought refuge in the foreign concessions in Shanghai. There the radicalization continued on. In a much less publicized development, these Zhejiang students took part in the development of early Chinese Communism. Of the original seven members of the Shanghai Marxism Study Society led by Chen Duxiu, five were former teachers and students of the Zhejiang First Normal School.

There was clearly something unique about First Normal that lent itself to such an extraordinary political development. As we shall see in the next chapter, many of its most radical students came from the middle counties of the Qiantang Valley, not the busy seaports and commercial centers in the north. Their earlier lives in that staid provincial backwater, coupled with their exciting school experience in the dynamic environment of Hangzhou, resulted in an exceptional dimension in their cultural messages of the May Fourth Movement, quite unlike all the other voices of protest. This development, an interactive process in itself, defined the character of radical social thinking in Zhejiang.

For the faculty and administration of First Normal, the May Fourth Movement in Zhejiang held a different kind of meaning. The school's principal, Jing Ziyuan, was one of the most influential educational reformers of the early Republican period. In his capacity as the president of the Zhejiang Provincial Educational Association, Jing Ziyuan was a prominent voice in educational affairs not only within the province but also in the nation. Widely viewed in Hangzhou's political circles both as a liberal and a Republican of Guomindang (Nationalist Party) affiliation, Jing had his share of allies as well as antagonists. Both friends and enemies recognized the central place of new-style educators in bringing forth a new kind of political order. Both readily attributed political significance, furthermore, to Jing's pedagogical philosophy at the First Normal. But it was above all Jing's conservative rivals who linked student radicalism to the principal's educational views. As the cultural iconoclasm of Zhejiang's First Normal students ran its course in the context of the May Fourth Movement, provincial conservatives emphatically professed their shock at the students' violation of sacred norms, and excoriated liberal educators such as Jing Ziyuan for their complicity in this outrageous offense to public standards. The radicalization of Zhejiang's May Fourth Movement, in that sense, served to induce a more heated polarization of opinion across a broad range of cultural and political issues that had already divided provincial political opinion for some time.

In the aftermath of the May Fourth Movement, the Zhejiang conservatives successfully forced the removal of Jing Ziyuan from his presidency of both the First Normal School and the Zhejiang Provincial Educational Association. The conservatives thus won a major political victory over a liberal enemy. The students, however, already aroused by their May Fourth taste of mobilization and grateful for the patronage of the liberals, were not about to submit to the conservatives' tattered claims to deference and discipline. Even as the province was closed off to liberal thinking in the 1920s, the conservatives found themselves confronting an increasingly unruly student body that waited impatiently for the next opportunity for action to appear.

ELITE SCHOOL

The First Normal School in Hangzhou was a public institution founded in 1904 under the administration of Zhang Zengyang, governor of Zhejiang, who launched an educational reform project in the province that year.[6] Zhang's action was part of a comprehensive plan of political reform, known as the New Policies (*Xinzheng*), that was adopted by the Qing court in 1901. The most portentous aspect of the New Policies was educational reform, which, decreed in 1904, called for the conversion of the old system of Confucian academies into a hierarchy of modern schools in counties, prefectures, and provinces to teach a Japanese-style curriculum that combined Chinese and Western subjects.[7] The First Normal School, financed by the governor's office, was to function as the key institution of this new system in Zhejiang's provincial education. Located in the former examination hall (*gongyuan*) of the province, its mission was to train county elementary school teachers in mathematics, arts, crafts, music, and physical education—"Western" subjects never taught in Confucian academies— plus old-fashioned literary skills.[8] These teachers were also to function as leaders to promote a new civic spirit in the local community.[9]

In April 1912, after a brief interruption with the change of political authority during the Xinhai Revolution, First Normal resumed instruction under the headmastership of the classically educated Jing Ziyuan.[10] The following year, the new Republican Zhejiang Provincial Assembly voted to have the school officially named the Zhejiang Provincial First Normal, and renewed its charter.[11] Although funding for the school came from the provincial budget that was under the management of the governor's office, the Provincial Assembly became the authority to which Principal Jing submitted requests such as salary increases for the teachers and staff. It was also to the assembly that the principal answered concerning the conduct and speech of the teachers and students in the Normal School.

As the foremost public educational institution in Zhejiang, First Normal was the most generously funded of all provincial schools in the early Republican years. It also had the largest faculty and student body in the province.[12] With an annual budget of forty-two thousand yuan, First Normal alone took up nearly 20 percent of Zhejiang's public education budget. With a total enrollment that averaged about four hundred, it accounted for approximately 40 percent of Zhejiang's advanced normal school students. The school graduated at least one thousand students during the first decade of its existence.[13] The Provincial First Middle School in Hangzhou, by comparison, enrolled less than three hundred students, and was allocated sixteen thousand yuan by the government.[14] These two institutions, which together accounted for 55 percent of the education budget, attracted the best students in the province.

Teaching in those days was viewed by the public as a highly respectable profession with an important social mission, even though the likeliest future awaiting most First Normal graduates was a career teaching elementary students in some county school in Zhedong. Of the eighty students admitted in the fall of 1917 out of a pool of nearly five hundred applicants, it was rare, indeed, for someone to fail to profess, in his Chinese examination papers, his dedication to elementary teaching as a vocation. Many had studied for years to prepare themselves for the exam. In the case of those who had successfully applied to other Hangzhou schools—and there were quite a few who had done so—First Normal invariably turned out to be their ultimate choice.[15]

During the first decade of the Republic, therefore, First Normal was among the most distinguished academic institutions in the province, admitting students only of top quality. Once admitted, they were guided through a demanding curriculum in the classics. They were also drilled by Principal Jing about an educated man's moral character and political responsibility. Jing Ziyuan was the most articulate among his contemporaries who believed that the purpose of education was to contribute to the construction of a new Chinese republic via the vocation of teaching. During his headmastership he turned First Normal into a center of the Republican ideal and of old-style moral and literary teaching.

GENTRY CONNECTIONS

When Jing Ziyuan (courtesy name: Hengyi, 1877–1939) assumed the headmastership of the Zhejiang Provincial First Normal School in 1912, he was a mature man of thirty-five who had already seen quite a bit of the world outside of Zhejiang. A native of Shangyu (Shaoxing) south of the Qiantang River, Jing Ziyuan came from a prominent merchant family that had experienced fluctuation in its fortunes in the course of the nineteenth century. It was also a family that had built up an extensive network of connections with both the merchant elites and the officialdom of the Jiangnan area.

Jing's grandfather, Wei (courtesy name: Qinggui, 1803–65), launched the family on its course of ascent. Unable to support himself in the hometown in his youth, he went to Shanghai at the age of fifteen to make a living, and rose to become the proprietor of dozens of native banks, tea dealerships, and shipping operations in the city. He shared his wealth by serving as the director of several orphanages and charitable organizations in Shanghai. These activities put him in contact with a sizable circle of gentry elites and government officials in the Jiangnan area, including Zuo Zongtang, governor of Zhejiang, who placed him in charge of the construction of water dikes along the coast of Haining. Jing died in 1865 before the completion of the project. In recognition of his dedicated service, he was awarded the honorary title of "prefect" by the government.[16]

Jing Wei's oldest son, Jing Yuanshan (courtesy name: Lianshan, 1841–1903), inherited his father's many operations and brought them to new heights.[17] Jing Yuanshan became the full proprietor of the Renyuan native bank and the principal director of the Tongren Fuyuan Tang, a charitable organization. Unlike his father, Jing Yuanshan happened to be active in an era when newspapers were in circulation. He was sensitive to the use of the press as an instrument for communication and succeeded in achieving a scale of business operation that was nearly national in scope.

The importance of *Shenbao* (Shanghai times), China's first commercial newspaper of significance, was apparent in Jing Yuanshan's charitable activities in the 1870s. Jing Yuanshan became aware of the disastrous drought and the subsequent famine in Henan in the winter of 1877 as a result of reading *Shenbao* reports. Moved by the reporters' vivid descriptions of family tragedies and influenced deeply by Buddhist notions of benevolence, Jing Yuanshan called together a group of friends and joined together the resources of several charitable organizations to launch relief efforts. He used his native bank to collect donations from Shanghai gentry-merchant elites on behalf of the refugees. He then transferred these funds over to the charitable hall for delivery and distribution in the disaster area. Time and again he printed open letters addressed to fellow Jiangnan merchants in the pages of *Shenbao* to elucidate the principle of cycles of fortune, the balance sheets of bliss and disaster kept by Heaven, and the importance of doing good. He also publicized lists of donors and balances in the charitable hall's accounts to keep his contributors informed of the activities on the relief front.[18]

Jing Yuanshan's messages were apparently aimed at his fellow merchants and ordinary people rather than the notably wealthy, who had been promised official ranks by the government in return for large contributions.[19] Instead of a top-down fund drive, Jing's was a mobilizational campaign that galvanized an informed segment of Jiangnan society that had become aware of the severity of the famine as a result of reading Shanghai newspapers. Because of his efficient and scrupulous handling of the relief funds, Jing's charitable hall came to be seen as a much more effective provider of relief than the government, which, with its staff of corrupt officials, was viewed with suspicion. Jing Yuanshan's growing reputation with the gentry-merchant elites in Shanghai, which rose in tandem with the circulation of *Shenbao*, soon made it possible for him to extend the scope of his relief operation to include three additional disaster areas— Zhili, Shaanxi, and Shanxi. He was subsequently elected president of a federation of charitable halls that collected funds in over two dozen central and southern Chinese cities, including Suzhou, Ningbo, Fuzhou, Jiujiang, Anqing, Hankou, and even Yantai (Shandong). These organizations were also in contact with overseas Chinese communities in San Francisco, Yokohama, and Nagasaki. By November 1879, Jing's charitable hall had succeeded in collecting and delivering more than 470,000 taels in silver from Shanghai to famine victims in China's north and northwest.[20]

Jing Yuanshan's active involvement in the relief campaign of the late 1870s earned him the attention of Li Hongzhang, governor general of Zhili. It also initiated his friendship with Sheng Xuanhuai, one of the main architects of state-sponsored modern business enterprises in the late Qing.[21] In the summer of 1880, Jing was named by Li Hongzhang to become a codirector of the newly created Shanghai Machine Weaving Bureau, which was among the earliest attempts to mechanize weaving in China. Jing had difficulty getting along with the officials appointed to the bureau by the provincial government. He opted to resign in a matter of months, but was soon appointed, also on the nomination of Li Hongzhang, to the directorship of the Shanghai Telegraph Bureau, another state-sponsored Western-inspired enterprise. The Telegraph Bureau, like many other state-initiated modernizing enterprises of the 1880s, was organized along the lines of "official supervision, merchant management." Jing Yuanshan proved to be a capable manager. He put in considerable effort educating the official and the business communities about the use of the telegraph, and under his directorship the Telegraph Bureau, which was a virtual monopoly, extended its service into dozens of cities and began generating a profit. Jing Yuanshan was not nearly as successful managing his personal fortune, however; he lost a significant amount of investment during the financial crisis that hit Shanghai's native banks in the mid-1880s and was forced to reevaluate the strategies of Westernization sponsored by reform-minded bureaucrats such as Li Hongzhang.[22]

Jing Yuanshan next turned his attention to the creation of new-style educational institutions. He launched the Jingzheng Academy in late 1893 in Shanghai, and invited Liang Qichao, among others, to lecture on current events and "new learning."[23] The goal of the academy, like the Zhejiang Provincial First Normal School decades later, was to educate students "in Chinese as well as Western subjects." Jing launched the project well before China's gentry elites recognized the importance of such a curriculum, which did not occur until after the First Sino-Japanese War (1894–95). In this regard Jing Yuanshan, along with some of his merchant friends who had been exposed to Western enterprises in Hong Kong, Macao, and Singapore, could be regarded as a pioneer in new educational thinking.[24]

In late 1897, Jing launched a second institution, the Chinese Women's School (Zhongguo nüxuetang), to teach mathematics, medicine, and law to the daughters of the Jiangnan elite. The project was sponsored by scores of individuals bearing titles such as alternate district magistrate, prefectural candidate, deputy minister, scholar in waiting, candidate for educational commissioner—wealthy members of gentry-merchant society who, like Jing himself, had purchased rather than earned their civil service ranks. It was also endorsed by young progressive thinkers such as Liang Qichao and Tan Sitong, British and American missionary educators such as Timothy Richard and Young J. Allen, and Shanghai newspaper publishers such as Di Baoxian and Wang Kangnian.[25]

The goal of the school was to nurture a new style of educated women who might combine time-honored female virtue with literary refinement and modern knowledge. Students were given classes on sewing, poetry, foreign languages, and other practical subjects.[26] Among the teachers were Timothy Richard and Young J. Allen, and among the students was Sheng Xuanhuai's daughter Sheng Jingying, who later became Jing Yuanshan's daughter-in-law by marrying his third son. When the school gave a fundraising party on December 6, 1897, it was attended by nearly three hundred elite women from prominent gentry-merchant families together with their foreign guests, who included scores of wives of consular officials and missionary doctors.[27] Jingzheng Academy and the Women's School both depended on voluntary contributions for their existence and operation. The academy, for lack of sufficient funding, was eventually folded into the Nanyang College when Sheng Xuanhuai launched the latter project with state resources in 1897. The Women's School also became a part of Nanyang.[28]

Jing Yuanshan's educational initiatives and social contacts placed him in the midst of the gentry reform politics of the 1890s. He became a strong supporter of the aborted Hundred Days Reform of 1898. When the Empress Dowager Cixi, in the reform's aftermath, plotted in 1900 to have the Guangxu Emperor deposed, Jing Yuanshan used the Telegraph Bureau to drum up voices of opposition; he mobilized 1,231 gentry leaders to endorse, on January 26, a petition urging the emperor to resume personal rule.[29] Hundreds of gentry leaders in Shanghai followed suit and sent off telegrams to Beijing. Their collective spending at the Telegraph Bureau in the following month reached half a million taels in silver. Jing Yuanshan and his friends, meanwhile, even made plans to call for a strike of Shanghai merchants should the empress dowager persist in her plan.

The infuriated empress dowager, as expected, accused Jing Yuanshan of "assembling a crowd to engage in unauthorized deeds, using alarming language with the intent to coerce . . . harboring a design that is no different from treason," and ordered Jing's immediate arrest. With the help of Sheng Xuanhuai, Jing Yuanshan boarded a British steamship and fled to Macao. The empress dowager held Sheng Xuanhuai personally accountable and demanded that Sheng deliver Jing within thirty days. Pressured by the court, Li Hongzhang, then governor general of Guangdong and Guangxi, asked the Portuguese authorities in Macao to put Jing Yuanshan under arrest. A team of French attorneys based in Hong Kong put up a vigorous defense on Jing's behalf. These lawyers succeeded in preventing him from being extradited to China, which in turn saved him from the death penalty that the court had in store for him.[30]

In addition to being such an active public presence, Jing Yuanshan was a much respected and feared patriarchal figure within his family. He did not hesitate to give detailed advice to his younger brothers, for example, on how they should conduct themselves as well as their businesses when they were sent on relief missions to north China on his behalf. Nor did he hesitate to send a strongly worded letter chiding a nephew for neglecting to write, after the young man had spent some time in Shanghai before returning home to Zhejiang. In the summer of 1880, Jing Yuanshan led the family to build its ancestral shrine in Shangyu. He personally drafted the lineage rules that spelled out regulations concerning the clan school, the ancestral temple, burial rites, marriage practices, the compilation of the genealogy, and the maintenance of the communal lands.[31] Although he spent most of his time in Shanghai, Jing Yuanshan remained a powerful presence in his family home in Shangyu.

Jing Ziyuan came under the influence of his uncle at an early age when he was still receiving a classical education at home. He became politically awakened at the age of eighteen during China's humiliating defeat in the First Sino-Japanese War, an awakening that was closely connected with Jing Yuanshan's critical reactions to the Qing court's handling of the war and his attempt to raise a volunteer army to fight the Japanese.[32] After the death of his mother, Jing Ziyuan joined his uncle in Shanghai. There he became an active member of the latter's social circle of gentry reformers and bureaucratic Westernizers.

In January 1900, Jing Ziyuan, along with his uncle and cousins, signed his name to the telegram addressed to the empress dowager. That same month, he accompanied his uncle in his flight to Macao. While Jing Yuanshan stayed on in Macao in semiconfinement, Jing Ziyuan secretly returned to Shanghai on receiving news of the Boxer Uprising in the north.

As a member of the younger generation, Jing Ziyuan moved in more radical circles than his uncle's in the post-Boxer years and was soon drawn into a nexus of connections centered around Cai Yuanpei, Jing's fellow Zhejiang coprovincial from Shaoxing. Cai became an instructor at the reformers' elitist engineering school, the Nanyang College in Shanghai, in 1902.[33]

Nanyang College was a product of Westernization measures vigorously pursued by the bureaucratic reformers of the 1900s. After the Qing court announced its intent to adopt the New Policies, Nanyang's faculty and students followed the development of the constitutional movement with keen interest. Its bureaucratic sponsors and administrators, however, had their reservations. This tension came to a head in 1902, when the administrators attempted to hold the constitutionalist sympathies of the students in rein by invoking school discipline. Students demanded permission to read journals published by Liang Qichao, a leading advocate of constitutional monarchy, who had been in exile since the failure of the 1898 Reform. They also insisted on joining the Wei xuehui (Study society), a voluntary association organized by the anarchist Wu Jingheng.[34] When the administration of Nanyang ordered the expulsion of more than a dozen students who insisted on their political rights, Cai Yuanpei and Wu Jingheng, both on the faculty of Nanyang, openly expressed their strong support for the defiant students.[35]

The episode ended inconclusively, with students simmering in rage over what was regarded as the arbitrary and authoritarian conduct of the Nanyang administration, and with the faculty divided into opposing camps caught between the students and the school officials. In November a minor incident, involving an unpopular teacher and a defiant student over a pot of ink, quickly escalated into a full-scale student protest against the conservative administration.[36] More than two hundred students walked out over the issue. Cai Yuanpei rose to the occasion and led the protestors to form a separate institution, the Patriotic School (Aiguo xuexiao).

In 1905, as the head of the Patriotic School, Cai Yuanpei organized a group of like-minded educators and gentry reformers to form the much celebrated forum for educational change, the Chinese Educational Association. The association was so centrally involved in attempts to overthrow the Qing that it is difficult to determine whether it was primarily a revolutionary organ or a professional organization. The revolutionaries in the association sought to build a radical following among the new-style school students in Shanghai. They also encouraged association members to contribute incendiary political commentaries to revolutionary organs such as *Subao*.[37] The Chinese Educational Association was apparently one of the several Shanghai organizations that formed a group of antecedents to the Revolutionary Alliance (Tongmenghui). Cai Yuanpei himself had earlier joined Sun Yat-sen's Restoration Society, and in 1906 he ran a branch of the Revolutionary Alliance in Shanghai.[38]

Cai Yuanpei's friendship with Xu Xilin, a fellow Shaoxing native who was later executed as a revolutionary in 1910, supplied an additional personal tie that subsequently involved the Patriotic School in the armed uprisings of secret societies in the hills of Zhedong. Beginning in the spring of 1906, the Patriotic School became a safe house for the Zhejiang revolutionaries in Shanghai as they plotted to overthrow the Qing.[39]

It was in Shanghai in the 1900s, in the circles centered around Cai Yuanpei, that a republican political agenda was suffused with a sweeping vision of educational reform. The reformed schools were seen both as a microcosm of an idealized republican society and as a powerhouse for social changes that would lead to the creation of the new republic. To Cai Yuanpei and those who shared his beliefs, the inclusion of Western scientific and engineering subjects into the school curriculum, a central component of the educational reform program sponsored by the imperial court, was but a matter of secondary importance. The much more significant point to them was to nurture the sort of campus atmosphere in which teachers and students could intermingle in a spirit of egalitarianism, and to knit a community of scholars on the basis of a shared dedication to the twin tasks of educational and social reform.

At the Patriotic School, Cai was determined to foster this egalitarian spirit by way of contrast to the formalistic and authoritarian hierarchy that was imposed on Nanyang students by their school officials. Whether this egalitarian emphasis could be directly attributed to Russian anarchist influence or not, there was implicit in Cai's pedagogical formulation a political view that saw the creation of the Republic not merely as the overthrow of the monarchy, but also as a fundamental restructuring of social relationships that began with the schools.[40]

Jing Ziyuan made the acquaintance of Cai Yuanpei in 1902 and left the following year for Japan. He had earlier shown an interest in science and engineering. Despite his initial hope of mastering Rousseau's *Emile*, Jing became a student in mathematical physics at Tokyo's Higher Normal School. That same year his uncle, who had been financing his education, died in Shanghai. The senior Jing's death must have been a loss as well as a liberation for the nephew.[41] Although it was not at all clear whether Jing Yuanshan himself would have opposed a republican revolution in the climate of the 1900s, his death nonetheless relieved Jing Ziyuan from his residual obligations to the constitutionalists. Jing Ziyuan joined Sun Yat-sen's Revolutionary Alliance when the league was formed in 1905; he also became a member of Cai Yuanpei's Chinese Educational Association.[42]

When Jing Ziyuan assumed the headmastership of First Normal in 1912, the provincial school was able to claim, through him, a direct link to the intellectual agitation of the revolutionary decade in the national and international arenas of Shanghai and Tokyo. Drawing on his own experience, Jing had nothing but contempt for those who regarded normal school education as mere vocational training for elementary school teachers. The corruption of the ideal of teaching as a calling, Jing declared, began with those who treated it as just a means to make a living. He envisioned instead a moral education that emphasized the "education of human character" (*renge jiaoyu*). This moral education was necessary not only to prepare teachers for their role as moral paragons to their future pupils, but also for all members of society as a whole.

MORAL EDUCATION

In his various speeches and statements, Jing Ziyuan frequently invoked *renge jiaoyu*, but he rarely explained it. What he meant by the term can only be inferred by examining the variety of contexts in which the notion appeared, and by sketching its boundaries as they must have appeared in Jing Ziyuan's own mind. Moral education was, first, something of intrinsic value that stood on its own, autonomous, devoid of all utilitarian considerations. In that sense it was opposed to the much more concretely defined "vocational education" (*zhiye jiaoyu*) advocated by leaders of the Jiangsu Provincial Educational Association.[43] That form of education stressed the training of practical skills useful for urban employments. It enjoyed the backing of Shanghai's emerging bourgeoisie and was aimed at the economic modernization of China.[44] The Jiangsu association, furthermore, took the view that classroom layout and pedagogical techniques were of greater consequence than the moral examples set by individual teachers in the transmission of knowledge and skills. It turned the association's journal, *Jiaoyu zazhi* (Educational journal), into a forum for the discussion not only of the practical results of a variety of plans, programs, and techniques, but also of the pedagogical philosophies and school systems of Japan and Western countries.

Jing Ziyuan, however, regarded such training as diminishing the true significance of the educational enterprise. He saw no reason to deny Jiangsu its wish to pursue a course of action that might suit Jiangsu's needs, "but Zhejiang has its own circumstances, and vocational education in Zhejiang is quite inappropriate."[45]

As he denied utilitarianism and pragmatism, Jing Ziyuan at the same time embraced a secular activism that affirmed the meaning of social action. True morality, according to Jing, entailed an active life that was oriented toward this world and embedded in social interactions; it should never be confused with the seeming purity of an otherworldly orientation that permitted withdrawal from meaningful social engagement. "Humans are nothing but social beings," he told his students.[46] When Li Shutong, the art and music teacher, firmly announced his intention in the summer of

1918 to resign from the faculty of First Normal in order to retreat into the mountains and become a Buddhist monk, Jing Ziyuan had to search hard for polite words to soften his strong disapproval of Li's choice at the farewell gathering. "Personal moral attainment," Jing told an audience of First Normal students, "is the one and only measurement of a lifetime's attainment." This attainment was possible only through an active engagement with the affairs of this world, because only by experiencing the vicissitudes of secular life could one learn the full dimensions of humanity and uncover the true meaning of morality. Master Li's choice to set the world aside in his pursuit of Buddhist enlightenment was something "highly respectable, but such deeds should never serve as examples to our students." Jing Ziyuan thereupon declared a new school ban that forbade the students to read Buddhist texts on any occasion whatsoever.

Buddhist influence, however, was everywhere in evidence. West Lake, where First Normal students spent so much of their time boating through islets of lotus blossoms, was surrounded by Buddhist temples that sounded their solemn gongs and chimes from dawn to dusk. To strengthen their moral resolve, Jing Ziyuan advised his students to stay away from the natural poetry and religious aura of the lake, lest they be tempted to give up their social mission.[47]

The maturation of individual moral qualities took place not in isolation from social interaction, Jing Ziyuan cautioned, but rather in the coming together of two different social beings, and in their active nurturing of a lasting friendship. Friendship in this sense was built on a shared moral understanding. It was open to all who had resolved to live out the moral meaning of their lives. It was therefore diametrically opposed, in its social expression, to the particularistic association based on a shared native place of origin. Of the 380-plus students at First Normal, sixty-five counties were represented. "Our countrymen invest much in native-place feelings, and very little in interpersonal friendship." Yet there was nothing that harmed a principled friendship more than an unprincipled partisanship such as native-place ties. "Moral friendship leads to the promotion of public good. Native-place partisanship, on the other hand, merely fosters selfish interests." Jing himself refused to make use of the Shangyu Native-Place Association's lodging facilities while traveling to Beijing, for it had seemed "so provincial and parochial for us to search only for our fellow natives from home, when we have in fact traveled to the nation's capital and mingled with tens of thousands from all parts of the country."[48]

Jing Ziyuan's notion of moral education sought to liberate the individual from his particularistic bonds and partiality to one of the tens of thousands of villages and counties that had traditionally acted as centrifugal forces in the late imperial Chinese polity. The higher goal of all this moral nurturing, Jing freely pointed out, was the inculcation of a love for the nation and an awareness of China's integrity as a whole. "These days people speak of a multitude of educational philosophies. There is 'aesthetic education,' 'civic education,' 'moral education,' 'vocational education,' to name but a few. Educators vie to differ from each other with novel ideas. . . . In the end all this diversity points to but one unifying theme: the nurturing of an awareness of China's integrity as a nation-state."[49]

Jing Ziyuan's notion of the nation-state readily reflected the dominant influence of the Social Darwinism of his time, which had powerfully stimulated the rise of Chinese nationalism at the turn of the century.[50] In his most extreme formulation, Jing Ziyuan saw the moral education of the human character as a political act rather than an ethical endeavor. "Moral education" as such was, in fact, utterly devoid of intrinsic humanistic significance. "Can we ever speak of educating the people without reference to the nation-state?" Jing asked; "For there to be true education, there must always be the nation." True education led to a correct understanding of the meaning of the nation-state, while false education produced such confused thinking on the subject that instead of serving the nation, citizens were taught to betray the nation for personal gratification. True education, in other words, facilitated the republican ideal, while false education produced scandalous ambitions such as Yuan Shikai's attempt to restore the monarchy. At this stage of human history republicanism was the true political cause to follow, because nation-states, Jing told his students, "are units for struggle and competition among the human race." Education in that context was "the sort of enterprise that prepares members of a nation for such a struggle and competition." Moral education was therefore the inculcation of the correct political understanding that turned unattached individuals into constituent members of the nation-state. This civic education would help ensure the survival of the collectivity in fierce competitions with other members of the human race.[51]

Although it was the power and strength of the nation-state that ultimately validated his moral enterprise, Jing Ziyuan continued to accept Neo-Confucian doctrines on ethical matters and frequently cited the great masters to direct the young in making concrete moral choices. On commemorating the 2,468th birthday of Confucius in 1917, Jing Ziyuan quoted at length the sayings of Wang Yangming, the fifteenth-century Neo-Confucian master from Yuyao (Zhedong), and urged First Normal students to strive toward attaining Confucian sagehood. Quoting Yangming, Jing said that sagehood was attainable by all through the cleansing of the mind of imperfect thoughts, coupled with an incessant endeavor to foster the full manifestation of the heavenly principle that was innate in humans.[52] And what was the external manifestation of that heavenly principle, which since Zhu Xi's time had been manifested in the rituals regulating hierarchical relationships between superior and subordinate? Although Jing Ziyuan had rejected the monarchy and along with it the traditional bonds of loyalty between the ruler and his ministers, he did not isomorphically reject the bond of filial piety between father and son. In fact, Jing showed no sign at all, in his praise of innate principles, of struggling against conventional Confucian familial ethics. First Normal's code of student conduct included the rule that one must be a filial son to one's parents and a deferential junior to one's older brother, in accordance with the Confucian notions of five cardinal bonds.[53]

When Confucius was solemnly honored in Republican state ceremonies, however, Jing Ziyuan took pains to point out that this was due to the sage's attainment of high virtue in the past. Confucius was an outstanding historical figure in a progressive scheme of things, instead of a universal paragon of timeless validity. His teaching in general continued to form "the basis of our present-day moral cultivation," but the precise relevance of Confucius's specific texts to the present age depended entirely on the "benefit that Confucian teachings bring to the social well-being of the future."[54] The moral canons of the past were to be subjected to the test of their utility to the vision of a better future society, which was increasingly identified with a smoothly functioning nation-state capable of asserting its sovereign rights in a Darwinian jungle of nation-states.

Jing Ziyuan's "moral education," when examined for what it was *not* as well as for what it was intended to be, appeared to be a hodgepodge that mixed elements of nationalist ideas inspired by Social Darwinism with personal moral doctrines inherited from the Neo-Confucian tradition. Given the primacy of the nation-state over the individual in Jing's thinking, he stood ready to relegate aspects of Confucian teaching to the past, so long as such a move was deemed necessary for the future strength and benefit of China as a whole—an intellectual strategy that called to mind the political reformers of the 1890s, who opted to save the "Chinese nation" by abandoning the "Confucian culture," to seek the "preservation of the state" (*bao guo*) over the "preservation of the faith" (*bao jiao*)—when there appeared to be conflicts between the two.[55] Whereas the cultural conservatives of the 1910s continued to insist that the radiant virtue of Confucius the Sage was to shine on all corners within the four seas through eternity, Jing Ziyuan's espousal of Confucianism was a qualified one which valued the power of the nation-state over the moral meaning of individual lives.[56] Jing was a "liberal," therefore, only in his seeming readiness to modify aspects of conventional Neo-Confucian practice in order to help retain its social relevance. In his insistence on discipline and dedication, Jing Ziyuan was far from accommodating—hard driven as he was by a strong sense of social mission and a deep commitment to personal principles.

PRINCIPAL JING

As the principal of First Normal School, Jing Ziyuan lectured his students frequently. It was his sole responsibility as the principal to teach a course titled "Moral Cultivation" (*Xiushen*), which was required of all students throughout their four years. In addition, many school occasions required some form of the principal's ceremonial benediction. Such occasions ranged from the seasonal opening and closing of a semester, the ritualized welcome, farewell, and commencement of incoming and departing students, the biannual kick-off and medal-awarding of athletic meets and alumni meetings, the official birthday of Confucius, the required celebration of National Day, the solemn marking of National Humiliation Day, to the sudden turn of current events such as Yuan Shikai's promulgation of the Hongxian monarchy, China's declaration of war against Germany, or an announcement that feuding provincial warlords had reached a temporary peace accord. Jing delivered almost all the lectures in the school's auditorium. These lectures were then dutifully transcribed for publication in the student newsletter. On several occasions between 1912 and 1919, faculty and students also gathered in the Lingyin Temple on the shores of West Lake to hear the principal deliver eulogies for students who had died prematurely—mostly of illness, but also of accidents—during the previous year.[57]

To his students Principal Jing was their moral legislator, political commentator, health advisor, emotional guide, character evaluator, and the ultimate controlling hand of the school in which they worked, played, and lived. For those who paid attention, the principal must have made himself quite well understood early in their student years. It was characteristic of Jing to adopt a stern tone of voice and to be straightforward with his points. He held firm to his moral and political beliefs, and regarded it his duty as an educator to convert others to his views. For the disciples on the receiving end of his instructions, the challenge was putting his words into practice and achieving the sort of "unity of knowledge and action" as taught by Zhejiang's great Neo-Confucian master of the fifteenth century, Wang Yangming.

Soon after he became principal of First Normal, Jing Ziyuan adopted a five-point motto for the school: diligence, prudence, sincerity, forbearance, and composure. He insisted that First Normal students try their best to live up to the ideals that these words suggested.[58] On the first day of the new semester on February 8, 1917, following the Chinese New Year's holidays, the principal spoke up sharply on students' tardiness returning to school. "Shops open on the fifth day of every first month, and the clerk who misses his place in that morning's worship of the God of Wealth loses his job. Those of you who are not here today have de facto given up your standing as a student at this school. . . . In my house I ordered my children to put away all means for New Year's amusement promptly on the third day. There is a time for everything. . . . Do not argue with me that it matters little to miss just a bit at the beginning. All those utterly corrupt people out there doing great harm to our society began their moral descent with a minor breach of rules at the beginning!"[59]

Because he considered the school to be where the ideal society would find its first realization, Jing was careful in building up a community of like-minded scholars and students who shared his goal of turning the school into an exemplary place to the outside world. After three years as principal, at the opening ceremony for the fall of 1915, Jing remarked with satisfaction that every student in that audience of four different grades had been personally interviewed and selected by him. "We are therefore united in spirit, which makes us unique among all schools. The purer we are in spirit, the more closely connected a body we become."[60]

LITERATI ELEGANCE

First Normal students inhabited a world of old-style literati culture rich in poetic imagery and historical allusions, which placed high value on a free-flowing life of aesthetic pursuit and metaphysical reflection. Much of this literati culture found expression in leisurely moments, in a pattern of pastime that revolved around the West Lake.

To forge a sense of community among his faculty and students, Jing Ziyuan personally led the school in extracurricular activities such as sports and hiking. Many First Normal students spent long hours boating on the West Lake and climbing up its surrounding hills. The paved steps through the bamboo groves behind the thirteenth-century tomb of Yue Fei led eventually to the Purple Cloud Cave, where the Buddha Guanyin's image appeared mysteriously on its rocky wall with a purple glint. A walk along the lake at dusk brought one last glimpse of the sun's final splendor, set against the silhouette of the teetering Leifeng Pagoda. The structure finally collapsed in 1923, releasing the spirit of the seductive White Snake who had been imprisoned under its mortars and bricks for five hundred years, or so the folktale went. Earlier in the eighteenth century, the Qianlong Emperor himself had spent treasured moments around the lake. He found the aesthetic experience so serene that he proceeded to canonize it by erecting stone steles at ten selected sites, each of which was described as the paragon of a particular sort of beauty in an aesthetic hierarchy.

With each legend and anecdote, each painting and poem, West Lake gradually became the focus of a literary and aesthetic tradition that must have begun in earnest in the twelfth century, when Hangzhou was the site of the Southern Song imperial court. Youthful wanderers of the early twentieth century saw in the hills and lake not only the passing clouds and changing lights; they saw—via the verses and songs of an older time that still reverberated in the culture—the wide variety of scenes and sentiments that had once been enacted and invoked on the lake.[61] There were the southern courtesans and their literati patrons singing, laughing, and drinking on a moonlit spring night. There was also the solitary monk in his bare room in the hills above the snow-covered lake, and the distant sounding of the evening drums and bells. With each remembrance and recitation those moments of pathos, captured in words and images, were once again evoked. It was not an aimless literati gesture, a careless or fatuous mimicry, for young scholars to roam the West Lake. The wandering was a purposeful journey to reclaim the tangible expressions, the recollected mystiques, and the lingering traditions of the literati life of the past.

Although Principal Jing endeavored to impart a somber tone to the campus as a moral community, First Normal was nonetheless fertile ground for a strong literati culture that evolved around its Chinese curriculum, which was rooted in Zhejiang's long history as culturally the most sophisticated region in late imperial China.[62] Despite Jing Ziyuan's effort to project a new image of the educated, society as a whole continued to judge his students on the basis of their literary competence in the classical tradition. The spectacle of uniformed First Normal students marching like trained cadets on one of their formal school hikes might have truly impressed on many observers how times had changed. The credibility of the school, especially in the hill and coastal counties of Zhedong, however, continued to rest largely on the demonstrated classical literary proficiency of its graduates.[63]

The tone of the literary curriculum at First Normal was set by Shan Pei (1879–?) of Xiaoshan (Zhedong), who, in his late thirties, was the youngest of the three Chinese instructors as well as the most dynamic and popular. Shan Pei was a renowned essayist of the prestigious Tongcheng School, a masterful textual critic trained in Han Learning, an adherent of Neo-Confucian ethical teaching, and a celebrated moralist whose extraordinary behavior toward his mother placed him among the paragons of filial piety of his era.[64]

Shan Pei won student admiration in the classroom not by elucidating the highly classicist textual criticism of the Confucian canon, as was common for Han studies scholars, but by teaching the rhymed prose on emotionally charged themes written by the nobles and elites of the Southern Dynasties (420–588). He chose as teaching material such pieces as Qiu Chi's "Letter to Chen Bozhi," a masterpiece of ornate elegance that was the stately aristocratic literature in its most personal voice of emotional appeal, set in the landscape of Jiangnan in late spring. He took the students far beyond the conventions of a subjective empathizing with the essay, and instead employed philological techniques that showed the construction of the prose through intertextual references. Master Shan's classroom explication was remembered by many of his students as a tour de force that demonstrated his extraordinary command of the classical literature. The reading was done with such extensive use of annotations, quotations, and philological and phonological exegeses that even a text of only a few hundred characters took a full two months to explore in depth.[65]

Shan Pei's two senior colleagues on the Chinese faculty were Xu Daozheng (courtesy name: Bingwu, 1866–?) and Liu Yupan (courtesy name: Zigeng, 1867–?). Xu, from Zhuji (Shaoxing), earned the juren degree in 1903 and held a Bachelor of Arts degree from National Beijing University.[66] Liu, from Jiangshan, was an authority on *ci*, the rhymed verse of irregular length that was the genre of many master poets, especially in the Song. Because of both their seniority and an ingrained regard for their subject matter, these two men asserted an authority among First Normal's faculty and students next only to that of Principal Jing.

First Normal in the mid-1910s had a faculty of twenty-three members, including the principal. Among colleagues there was a deference toward seniority. The official faculty roster was arranged, for instance, by age, with Master Xu, at forty-nine, heading the list. There were over a dozen young teachers in their late twenties and early thirties, almost all from Hangzhou, who taught mathematics, physical education, English, science, and arts, the inclusion of which in the curriculum distinguished the new schools of the twentieth century from late imperial Confucian academies. It was not uncommon for the younger teachers to assume certain clerical functions. The twenty-nine-year-old math teacher Zhu Quan, for instance, was also the school's part-time accountant. The thirty-seven-year-old science teacher Li Zhen, meanwhile, served as the school custodian of teaching equipment.[67]

Despite the stated importance of the new subjects in the school's formal curriculum, none of these younger teachers was able to make his presence felt in school journals and newsletters. The situation was in some ways a matter of literary and artistic style. Except for an occasional set of rhymed couplets from the physical education teacher, few of these men who had acquired expertise on "Western" subjects proved capable of composing in an acceptable classical literary style. Outside of the classroom they had a limited role to play in an extremely active campus life that revolved around literary and artistic societies devoted to poetry, seal cutting, stone rubbing, landscape painting, and calligraphy—mutual interests that fostered friendship between many teachers and students.[68]

Jing Ziyuan, in contrast, was quite at ease in the efflorescence of this literati culture at First Normal. He was himself a famed calligrapher, and he composed enough in the classical style to have his own poetry collection circulated in manuscript.[69] The pace and lifestyle of First Normal as a literary society, however, were in direct conflict with Jing's vision of it as a community of purpose and resolve. Although the school offered an ideal situation for individuals to pursue their own interests, it was Jing's goal to forge unity out of individual differences. While the literati style permitted the ease and leisure of a quiet afternoon in the Zhejiang Provincial Library on West Lake perusing Buddhist texts,[70] the drive toward moral education was informed by the conviction that schools ought to be places where individuals were quickly shaped into political beings as members of a nation. In the literati universe a vigorous youth would fancy himself as striking a much admired pose of philosophical melancholy by repeating clichéd phrases such as "in a drunken stupor I sang a song of sorrow," or "how my hair has turned silver gray!"[71] At the athletic meet presided over by Jing Ziyuan, the same student would be asked to blend his voice with everyone else's and sing in unison:

> Valiant youth showing off their strength on the athletic field. Upon their courage depends the safety of hundreds, upon their leadership the hopes of tens of thousands! The national flag flutters in a gusty wind.

The dragon sword unsheathed, the glint as cold as killing frost. The sky is high, the land is broad. The song, loud and clear, fills heaven and earth.

The wind blows, the rolling and tumbling clouds transforming our continent. The weak falls prey to the strong. To strengthen the nation, build the body first. A robust physique rejuvenates the spirit.

The warring clouds thicken the sky. A valiant youth bolsters his spirit. His song rises and falls to the beat of the drum. The voice is courageous and strong. Hearts and thoughts reach up and surpass the stars.[72]

These two strands of life coexisted in latent incongruity at First Normal up to the very eve of the May Fourth Movement. Jing placed emphasis on the martial, the valiant, and the competitive, because he believed that new-style education should answer to China's political crises and contribute to the building of a strong nation-state. He therefore sought to create a campus community of the fittest, both as a building block for, and as a microscomic image of, an emerging Chinese nation among competing nation-states. But as a way of life and as a regional tradition, the literati cultural canon continued to hold sway. It was not until the New Culture Movement reached Zhejiang that the elite's comfortable assumptions about literati culture were subjected to serious scrutiny.

Although Jing Ziyuan never intended First Normal to be set apart from the society at large, by fashioning the students and scholars into a community of the like-minded who were to reform the country, he infused his school with a proud and distinctive sense of its lofty standing. Such a communal sense of purpose was the fruit of Jing's relentlessly nurturing efforts, when the centripetal hold of the community seemed constantly threatened by the centrifugal pull of existing societal forces. His sense of dedication to his mission and his perception of the magnitude of his task were so compelling that he found it difficult to accept the tradition of summer recess. For the majority of First Normal students, summer was the time to return to their homes in Zhedong, where, in the principal's opinion, a variety of factors existed to corrupt a student into an unreformed way of life. Thus, on the last day of the semester on July 10, 1917, Jing Ziyuan sounded his usual theme that students must not see summer as a time to relax their acquired discipline of school life. "Summer recess is in fact detrimental to the development of a scholar. Does life's striving ever come to a hiatus in the summer? To say that summer heat justifies a full summer's break is to say that there should be no schools at all in the tropics!"[73]

Jing Ziyuan's suspicion of summer recess was not entirely unjustified. Each summer, it turned out, several students would die. In the summer of 1914 three died, one of long-standing lung problems, one of undiagnosed fever, and one reportedly of heat rash. The following summer three more died of "poor health," and in 1917, the school lost five students, including one who drowned in a creek in his home town.[74] There was no particular reason to think that First Normal students ran a higher risk of mortality than anyone else, but other hazards awaited when they journeyed from the Hangzhou school back to their homes. Such hazards, indeed, were sometimes the essence of a provincial boyhood.

5   A Provincial Boyhood

As Zhejiang's highest-ranking academic institution in the early Republican years, First Normal School drew students from all parts of the province. Its enrollment base extended beyond the immediate vicinity of Hangzhou, where the school was located, to the provincial boundaries of Zhejiang to include a small but significant number of students from Anhui and Jiangsu.[1]

Despite its geographical disparateness, there was, however, a distinct profile to First Normal's student body. Compared to the Zhejiang Provincial First Middle School, the only other state-funded secondary institution in Hangzhou, First Normal was favored by Zhedong students of middle-county background, whereas First Middle School was favored by sons of the Zhexi commercial and gentry elites. The former received their education in full anticipation of becoming elementary school teachers in the province. The latter, in contrast, were preparing themselves for an advanced education in colleges and universities in Shanghai and Beijing. Geographically, First Middle School was the more restrictive of the two—drawing the bulk of its students primarily from the northern five prefectures of Hangzhou, Jiaxing, Huzhou, Ningbo, and Shaoxing, but excluding representation from the middle counties and the coastal towns of the province. Academically, First Middle School placed considerable emphasis on foreign language subjects and was more responsive to trends set in Shanghai, linked as it was to the city by the future plans of its students.[2] In contrast, First Normal, under the leadership of Jing Ziyuan, strove to articulate an educational ideal that stressed Zhejiang's coherence as well as uniqueness as a provincial entity, although such efforts by no means entailed closing itself off to modernizing influences emanating from Shanghai.[3]

SOCIAL ORIGINS

Of the three-hundred-odd students at First Normal, those of Zhedong origin increasingly outnumbered those of Zhexi. This trend, already in evidence by the mid-1910s, became ever more pronounced as the years went by.[4] In the 1910s the middle counties, especially those situated along

94

the midstream of the Qiantang and in the upper reaches of the coastal riverine systems—Zhuji, Shengxian, Dongyang, Jinhua, Yiwu, Pujiang, Longyou, Lanxi, Wuyi—supplied First Normal with an increasingly significant block of students to each year's incoming class.[5]

Whether a student hailed from counties on the peripheries of the commercialized north or the largely agrarian middle counties, there was a marked tendency for First Normal students to come from the middle level, rather than the upper crust, of the county society. Records of student addresses show that an overwhelming majority of First Normal students lived in towns and villages outside of the county seats and at a distance from prefectural centers. A student with a family residence within the commercial and administrative centers of the county would have given his address typically as the following: "Chen Weiyuan, South Street, Xiaofeng," or "Xuan Qigong, No. 11 West Taiping Lane, Hangzhou." The predominant majority, however, gave their addresses as the following: "Feng Airan, the Feng Family Residence, Town of Shangtang, Yuyao County," or, as in the case of Shi Cuntong, the nineteen-year-old freshman from Jinhua, "c/o Gongda Store at the Jade Spring Temple in Jinhua County, to be forwarded to Ye Village, in Donghua Village."[6] Mail for nearly everyone was directed first to a commercial establishment in the county seat, and then forwarded via private couriers to the home address outside the city. Zhou Bodi was a nineteen-year-old student from Yuyao, a prosperous county that fell within the inner-core zone of Shaoxing Prefecture, and he gave his address simply as: "c/o Yuanxiang Native Bank, Yuyao," a business that was owned by the family. Yu Xiaofang, a nineteen-year-old native of Zhuji who had moved to Hangzhou with his family, also directed his mail in care of the family's business: "c/o Midachang Tobacco Store, Hangzhou, to be forwarded to Cifeng (Charity Peak), via Hezhen (The River Town)."[7]

Whether the instructions were simple or complex, it is worth noting that except in a few instances for residents of Hangzhou, street names and numbers were rarely used.[8] The county stores bore no numerical designations, and oftentimes no locations were given in relationship to streets either, as if the mere mentioning of the store's name was sufficient to alert the county's mail couriers. Thus to reach Xiang Zhitao via his family's business at Lanxi, one would simply write "Xiang Zhitao, c/o Tongyi Store, Lanxi."[9]

This lack of specificity in the mailing address—or rather, this lack of specificity in reference to an overall spatial mapping that purported to be an all-inclusive representation of an area divided up into named streets and numbered buildings—applied to rural residents as well. In lieu of a sequential specificity, there was instead a visual concreteness in country addresses that vividly described the main landmarks of the terrain. Incoming mails were to reach individuals "By the Stone Creek Crossing," "Behind the Water Pump," "By the Shrine," "In the Lower Field," "By the Phoenix Tree," "In Front of the Barnyard," "On the Lake," "In the Mountain," as well as "In the Old Mountain Village," "In the Lotus Peak Village," or "In the Water Pavilion Town." There was, in short, a sense of being not a number, but rather embedded in a familiar village and geography.

Families such as those of Yu, Zhou, and Shi were not members of the top-tier provincial elite whose network of connections reached beyond provincial boundaries. Instead, these were middling county families close to the land, sufficiently well-off to have a stake in the county's commercial activities. The better-off among, for example, First Normal's entering class of 1917, came from local creditors who operated native banks, leased salt-distributing permits, dealt in jewelry, or collected rental payments for goods stored in their warehouses. The most penny-conscious were sons of the owners of market-town convenience stores that reaped a meager profit in the retail of household consumer items such as candles, thread, paper, and tobacco. Between these two extremes stretched an array of county middlemen and distributors of a variety of agricultural products and handicraft goods that ranged from rice, dye, bamboo, cloth, dried goods, soybeans, and silk fabric to herbal medicine. Trading in these goods (as discussed in Chapter 1) constituted the staple of Zhejiang's traditional inland and riverine commerce, which had been vitiated by the rise of maritime trade centered on Shanghai. Some of these operations might have been launched with a capitalization of as much as several hundred taels of silver—no small fortune by local yardsticks, but a mere pittance when compared with the size of commercial capital in Hangzhou and Ningbo, which was measured by the tens of thousands. The majority of students appeared to have come from backgrounds of single-store distributing outlets at the lower end of the inland trading network in the Qiantang Valley.[10]

Taken as a whole, the social composition of First Normal's freshman class was a microscopic mirror image of Zhejiang's middling county society. In the context of the 1910s, it also meant that, unlike the First Middle School students, their families were much more likely to see their social standing eroded, rather than enhanced, by the rise of the modernized provincial elites based in Zhexi.

It was against this social backdrop that First Normal's unique tuition and fees structure became a feature of special attraction to middle-county students. Other secondary schools of Hangzhou—one public and two private—required from their students full payment of tuition and fees in addition to the costs of living. Provincial normal school students, on the other hand, were exempted by the Provincial Assembly from all such payments, besides being given government subsidies for room and board. Generally speaking, the cost for an education at the First Normal was less than half of that at its closest rival in academic reputation, the Zhejiang Provincial First Middle School in Hangzhou.[11] For those mindful of their budgets, First Normal School represented an exceptionally attractive educational opportunity.[12]

The affluent and expensive First Middle School attracted students of quite a different sort. One such student entering the First Middle School in 1918 was Ruan Yicheng, son of Ruan Xingcun (courtesy name: Xunbo, 1874–1928), an acknowledged legal expert, member of the Zhejiang Provincial Assembly, founder of the private Institute of Legal and Political Studies in Hangzhou, owner of the new-style Zhejiang Printing Company, and heir to landed and commercial wealth in Shaoxing as well as in Xinghua (Jiangsu), where Ruan Xingcun's father once served as a private secretary to the local district magistrate.[13] Ruan Xingcun was, in fact, Jing Ziyuan's closest ally and friend in Zhejiang's provincial politics. As fellow students in Japan in the 1900s, the two men had shared a great deal in background and outlook. Like Jing, Ruan was a native of Shaoxing in Zhedong. The family remained rooted there, but had developed extensive connections outside of the province. In the first years of the Republic, Ruan Xingcun, as head of the lineage, decided to take up permanent residence in Hangzhou, where he purchased a new residence and became centrally involved in provincial politics. The ancestral hearth and the account books in Shaoxing, meanwhile, were left to the care of his still robust though aging mother.[14]

Ruan Yicheng had spent much time during his childhood with his grandmother in Xinghua and Shaoxing. Once in Hangzhou, he had little difficulty adjusting himself to life in the provincial capital—the only care he had to take was to purge his speech of the less than perfectly respectable Xinghua accent of the Subei area. With the help of a private family tutor he studied the subjects on the new curriculum. He sat for and passed the highly competitive entrance examinations in Chinese, English, and mathematics, and was admitted into the First Middle School as one of the 40-member incoming class, selected from a pool of 350 candidates.[15]

Although most of his classmates had journeyed to Hangzhou from home and lived on campus, Ruan Yicheng commuted daily by walking the one and a half miles between home and school, escorted by a servant assigned to look after him. He could have been chauffeured back and forth, had Ruan Xingcun not insisted that the young man learn the virtue of a life of simplicity and frugality.[16]

Ruan Yicheng's classmates either shared his background or had other claims to provincial distinction. His close friend Zha Mengji, a native of Haining, for instance, was the descendant of an unbroken line of Zhexi gentry-official-scholars of national eminence since the sixteenth century. His fellow Shaoxing native Wang Naikuan, with whom he shared a desk in school, also came from a wealthy family.[17] It was indeed rare for someone of Ruan Yicheng's background to shift from First Middle to First Normal even though the school's academic reputation, under the leadership of Jing Ziyuan, rose to the top in the province. But in 1920, before going off to Shanghai to attend the private China College, Ruan Yicheng withdrew from First Middle to spend his final year of secondary education in Hangzhou at First Normal in order to take advantage of its superior academic offering. He chose to attend as an auditor and not as a formal student, however, even though his own father had been briefly a lecturer at the school.[18]

PROSPECTS

One major consideration that turned the provincial elites away from the First Normal School was the prescribed career pattern for its graduates. As was already evident by 1919, elementary schoolteaching in Zhejiang was a career that opened up few possibilities either for upward mobility within the province or for outward mobility into other parts of the nation or world. The system, first designed under the last years of the Qing, had made few provisions for the continuing intellectual growth of normal school students once they had completed their schooling and begun elementary school teaching. For graduates of middle-county background without independent means, teaching meant a respectable career of stifled prospects. Zhexi elites consequently discarded elementary school teaching as a career option, since it was well within their means to choose a general secondary program other than the normal school. It was as much by default as by choice that First Normal came to enroll a high percentage of middle-county students.

The high representation of Zhedong natives at First Normal developed gradually. When the school first opened, Zhexi was much better represented than in later years, and some students might have earned the diploma not in order to get a job, but simply for the certification that it represented.[19] Almost every student returned home after graduation and took an elementary school teaching position in his home county. The only exceptions were the two students who had been asked to stay on in Hangzhou to teach in the elementary school affiliated with First Normal. This honor and opportunity were about the most that a First Normal graduate could hope for. These two—Wang Shouhou and Chen Zujing— taught specialized subjects (art, music, and physical education) to different classes of students divided according to their level of abilities. Wang and Chen were able to continue developing their own interests and expertise while at the same time experimenting with various pedagogical approaches. They worked with a group of fourteen teachers, each with his specialized interest. There were clear divisions of labor in the administration of the school, as well as plenty of collaborative projects among colleagues. The total enrollment at First Normal's affiliated elementary school, at over 350, was among the province's largest at the time. All pupils were from Hangzhou and collectively represented possibly the best behaved as well as the most highly motivated elementary students in the province.[20]

Those who taught in county schools outside of Hangzhou, by comparison, were often asked to teach any subject that had to be covered in the curriculum, to run the entire school together with a handful of others, and to handle a mixed group of pupils with a wide range of ages and capabilities, numbering from several scores to over two hundred.[21] It was rare to receive appointment as a principal, unless, as in the case of Ma Qichen of Yuyao, it was the headmastership of one's own lineage school, supported fully by the family's charitable estate,[22] or, as in the case of Xiang Zhitao, it was a middle-county village school.[23] The vast majority received teaching appointments only and saw little opportunity to move upward for many years to come.

Local conditions differed from place to place, entailing dramatic discrepancies from school to school. In the mountain county of Jiangshan, conservative lineage heads continued to wield great power, and new-style normal school graduates were greeted by this old-fashioned community with scorn and hostility rather than respect.[24] Elementary education could hardly be high on the local agenda in a declining community like Jiangshan, where the infant mortality rate was high, female infanticide was widely practiced, and poor children were often sold into servitude to other parts of the province; publicly funded elementary schools in these southern counties existed sometimes at best in name.[25] Where schools were in operation at all, pupils were rowdy and unruly, "behaving as if they had never been taught about the importance of showing respect to their teachers."[26]

Whereas there were still teaching jobs available in Zhexi counties in the early 1910s, by 1917 less than one-third of First Normal's fifty-seven graduates that year could find jobs in the Zhexi plains (including Jiangnan). The bulk of available teaching positions were in Zhedong, which meant that a First Normal graduate would have to contend with the uncertainties of teaching in a hostile environment. In the opinion of the Zhedong village elders, an old-style teacher in his middle age, who had been educated during the last years of the civil service examinations system, was far better fitted to teach their children than the young normal school graduate with his impious, newfangled ideas. This situation was particularly common in a provincial cultural backwater such as Lanxi, which also happened to have the largest number of elementary schools in the province, thanks to the Neo-Confucian emphasis on education that had been the proud tradition of the middle county.[27] Those "old hands with dated knowledge who could offer nothing but rote teaching and corporal punishment" (reported a new-style educator with indignation) had no qualms about acting simultaneously as the village community's scribe, herbalist, astrologer, geomancer, and fortune-teller. Thus tightening their hold on the minds and souls of the villagers, such "unqualified teachers" reinforced the very evils that the normal students had been taught to battle.[28]

An education at Hangzhou's elite First Middle School, where the students were primarily from the urban parts of Zhexi, facilitated one's advance into a college or university in Shanghai. A Shanghai college graduate had several options, including advanced studies abroad in Europe, America, or Japan. Ruan Yicheng, the fourteen-year-old freshman at First Middle in 1918, studied in Japan after his graduation from Shanghai's China College. He returned to Hangzhou during the Nanjing decade and served for many years as Zhejiang's minister of civil affairs.

An education at First Normal, by comparison, served primarily to direct a young man back into the hills of Zhedong from whence he had most likely come. He might have mingled in the provincial capital with his contemporaries at the elite First Middle School, but on graduation their paths would most probably never again cross. While the First Middle School graduates headed outward toward metropolitan centers beyond the provincial boundaries, the First Normal graduates headed inland and up into the woods and valleys of the central and southern parts of the province to become elementary school teachers. Once they took a post in a Zhejiang local school, they were likely to stay on for decades. From such a position they watched as conditions in the local society deteriorated through the Republican years. Their own standing as teacher and intellectual eroded as the years went by.

These journeys back into the middling counties of the Qiantang Valley, so remote and insulated from the forces of change transforming northern Zhejiang society, were more than a matter of differential social mobility. To First Normal graduates who headed back, the valley was of primordial significance as the homeland of their ancestry and childhood. But the schooling at Hangzhou had opened their minds to a modernizing world and a different way of life. This homeward journey was thus no joyous home-coming; it entailed passages across different kinds of cultural space. Their loyalty toward the *guxiang* (old hometown), as Lu Xun titled one of his most poignant short stories, was ambivalent and confused. This provincial passage eventually was to have profound political consequences for a significant number of First Normal intellectuals.

THE LANDSCAPE

Each July, scores of First Normal students set out from Hangzhou for the summer recess at home. Traveling often in small groups, they sometimes took the time to visit scenic spots and historical relics. The trip frequently required several days and a variety of transport—a coastal steamship, the train, Qiantang steamboat, walking, and so forth—to complete.[29] Once home, these students visited friends and relatives, went fishing and hiking, met local leaders to discuss public affairs, and occasionally succeeded in launching projects such as a new village school.[30] The fruition of a summer's sights and thoughts was often reported in school journals the following fall. These were hometown snapshots by native sons. Collectively, they form an oddly darkened picture of Zhedong viewed through the lens of the new-style education in Hangzhou.

The landscape of Zhedong, sometimes arid and sometimes lush, was viewed above all as old. Steles, half buried, stood on the banks of the lower Qiantang like tombstones, engraved with fragmentary recollections of events from long ago.[31] Clusters of ancient graves, unmarked and unattended, dotted the hills. Hamlets by the roadside often held no more than one or two decrepit hostels "that seem a hundred years old." "A middle-aged woman, aging before her time, showed us to our bare and dusty room which was illuminated only by the moonlight."[32] Whereas Hangzhou was colorful and bright, everywhere "thriving and flourishing," the hills of Zhedong were gray and ancient, shadowed and decaying.[33]

Even with its thousands of villages and centuries of cultivation, the land was still far from tame. The threat of death lurked near home, as Shang Kui, of the sixth class of First Normal (entering in 1918), vividly remembered from his own childhood. There were rapid undercurrents and hidden whirlpools in the seemingly soothing creek that murmured through the bamboo woods behind his village. One summer afternoon, while swimming with his cousins, he was swept away and nearly drowned. He had been visiting the Temple of the Immortal Ge, which sat on top of a cliff with a commanding view of the hills beneath it and was visited by hundreds of pilgrims each summer. The mountainside path leading up to it, however, was narrow and slippery. As Shang was coming down the hills from the temple with his father and uncles, he lost his footing on the moss and dropped toward the dry creek. He was saved only by the bushes several tens of feet below. Even the rocks and stones, around which children played, harbored fatal surprises. One day, while chasing crickets, the young Shang came upon a large stone and turned it over to find two snakes, intertwined, with chicken feathers scattered about. Both were poisonous, and he was lucky to have been bitten only on his shoe.[34]

Other images of Zhedong punctuated this tired land of uncertain chances. Bandits roamed in the woods as well as by the swamps, and they picked unfriendly terrain, such as where the waterway narrowed between sharply rising cliffs, to mount attacks on helpless travelers.[35] So many residents seemed to have died an unfulfilled life in the wilderness that their ghosts wandered on in search of vengeance. Since the distinction between the worlds of the living and the dead had never been firmly drawn, a growing number of villagers experimented with codes of communication with the other world—sleeping in the graveyard in expectation of a nocturnal visit with the spirits, for instance—in order to enlist the netherworld's critical assistance in matters such as gambling.[36] In this mood of supernatural fear, "most villagers entrust their fate to spirits and ghosts, and few have any interest in schools. . . . Those who speak of magic and supernatural deeds attract a large following. New-style educators who seek to break down such beliefs, on the other hand, encounter stiff resistance."[37]

It was in one of these middle counties of Zhedong that Shi Cuntong, a founding member of the Chinese Communist Party, spent his childhood and adolescence before entering the First Normal School in Hangzhou.[38]

THE HOUSEHOLD

Shi Cuntong was born in 1899 in Yecun, a village about eighty li to the northeast of the county seat, in the rougher part of Jinhua. There were one hundred or so households in this village of about 450 inhabitants, many of whom traced their ancestry to migrant settlers from Jinhua's eastern neighbor Yiwu in the seventeenth century. Yecun was a small community with much personal knowledge and a long memory. Centuries after the initial settlement, fellow villagers still recalled each other's nonlocal ancestry and carefully maintained the minute linguistic differences—whether by the way one referred to chicken eggs as *jidan, jizi,* or *jiluan*—or by one's articulation of *chai* (firewood) versus *she* (snake)—that distinguished one source of origin from another.

Shi Cuntong was born into a large, extended family headed by his grandfather Shi Shizhu.[39] The Shis of Yecun were in a part of Jinhua that was home to several prominent lineages—Ye, Qi, Feng, Zhu—with an exalted genealogy of office-holders that went back to the Song and the Ming. Those lineages produced steles, tombs, and compounds. They also built bridges and temples. The Shis were clearly not among them: only two ancestors had ever distinguished themselves by earning lower-level degrees in the eighteenth century. What they lacked in distinction was compensated for by numerical presence. Several villages bore the surname Shi: Shanxia Shi (The Shis at the foot of the hill), Dong Shi (The Shis on the east), Qian Shi (The Shis on the front), Hou Shi (The Shis on the back side), Shi Hu Zhai (Shi-Hu dwelling).[40] Many Shis could also be found in other villages, as in the case of Shi Cuntong's forebears, who moved into Yecun (the Ye village) after the Taiping Uprising. Like most other Shis in this area, the Shis of Yecun tilled the land for a living. By hard work and humble frugality, they became, by the time of Shizhu, the wealthiest in the village.[41]

Shi Shizhu, who owned about fifty mu of land, was the head of a household of around thirty members. He had two sons: Changchun and Changyin. He also shared the household with his younger brothers and their wives and children. The old patriarch personally worked at the head of his family members in the field. Thrift and diligence were their mottoes, and the Shis could be seen in their fields year-round, including New Year's Day.

Shi Cuntong was the first child born to Shizhu's older son, Changchun (1870–1941), and his wife Xu (1873?–1919), also of peasant background, from the neighboring village Changtang, which lay about three and a half miles away. Of Xu we know very little: Yecun villagers referred to her either as "Changchun's wife" or "Cuntong's mother"; they were unable even to recall her first name. Xu, who came from a slightly more elevated background than the Shis and had a brother who later became a military officer, was apparently the first of her family to marry into Yecun. Her relationship with her husband was described by fellow villagers as "ordinary." This meant that in her lifetime she neither suffered unusual abuse nor performed extraordinary deeds—just a plain peasant wife and mother of three.[42]

Around 1905, Shi Shizhu decided to divide up his household among his sons and brothers. Shi Cuntong's father, for some reason, was given a tiny parcel that barely yielded enough to support a wife and three young children. Shi Cuntong insisted that this happened because the old man was prejudiced against his older son. Although Yecun was too small a place for a stark contrast, the village was not without its fine gradations between the rich and the poor. The society had, roughly speaking, three tiers: a top level, consisting of but two or three large households, each owning about fifty mu of land; a middle sector of forty or so households that owned around ten mu and made up about half of the village society; and a lower level consisting of individuals who worked as farmhands, woodcutters, and firewood carriers. On the margins of this hierarchy was a mobile population that quarried limestone in the hills and transported Jinhua's rice and salt into Zhejiang's southern mountains for sale—an itinerant group that sometimes included migrants. Social distinction was by no means rigid, and there was considerable interaction across all levels. Many small owners, for example, cut their own firewood. But the villagers were mindful of their relative standing vis-à-vis each other and took careful note of matters such as whether, when entertaining an important guest, a family lay out a meal with two or three chicken eggs.[43]

As the result of his grandfather's action, Shi Cuntong's family was instantly plunged from the top into the middle-lower level of Yecun society. The old man's decision was the subject of much village gossip. Some of the elders predicted that within three years the new nuclear household would drop further down the scale into degrading poverty. Shi Cuntong's parents were proud people, however; "they refused to give in under such circumstances, and worked all sorts of miscellaneous chores day and night." The eight-year-old Shi Cuntong, together with a younger brother, were put to work as well. Shi spent most of his days collecting kindling in the woods around the village. He helped care for his junior siblings and regarded himself "a most filial son to the family in those days."[44]

Fellow villagers apparently noted nothing unusual about Shi Changchun's behavior toward his family, although he had a reputation of being somewhat "short-tempered" and "strict with his children."[45] The struggle to stay self-sufficient took its toll, however, and the child Shi Cuntong saw both parents as ill-tempered and unreasonable. Verbal rebukes and beatings were daily occurrences in Shi Cuntong's childhood, and the eight-year-old, unschooled and overworked, quickly learned to defy and to provoke. His parents responded with even more beatings. In retrospect, Shi Cuntong felt little resentment toward his mother, for her actions seemed justifiable punishments. But he felt strongly against his father, who seemed to have such a violent character and unpredictable temper. Shi Cuntong, in the end, was convinced that his father did not care for him at all,[46] nor did he believe that anyone else, except for his mother, cared much for him.

Shi's negative feelings found expression in his aggressive behavior toward others. Shi Cuntong often bullied his wealthier cousins and behaved defiantly toward his numerous uncles and aunts. These incidents led to frequent complaints against him made to his parents, who often reacted by giving him a sound thrashing in public, coupled with their own apologies to the offended relatives.[47]

In private, however, Shi Cuntong's mother showed him much sympathy. She also invested in her oldest son many hopes of her own. "My mother often told me about her own sufferings. She also encouraged me to become a worthy son to the family." This was to be done by moving into the larger world beyond the confines of the village and by bringing home power and wealth beyond the wildest dreams of the villagers. Shi Cuntong recalled, "It was her hope that I might someday avenge our family for all the injustice and humiliation that we've had to endure." He was to punish the better-off for their mistreatment of the less fortunate.[48]

CONFUCIAN SCHOOLING

One source of imagination that permitted the indulgence of fantasy, including Shi Cuntong's own vision of revenge, was the village opera. Each autumn after the harvest and every winter during the New Year's celebration, the opera was staged for four nights and three days in the village. The performances, by itinerant troupes, usually took place on makeshift stages erected in the open space where villagers dried out their grains. The repertoire, known as the *Wu xi* (Jinhua opera) for its use of the Jinhua dialect and popular throughout the Jin-Qu Basin, was typically noisy, action-packed, and often lewd, with male characters showing off their martial arts skills and females cast in seductive roles. The shows were loved for their fast-paced scenes and happy endings. Among the favorites were, for example, variations of a play called *Seng ni hui* (A Buddhist monk meets a Buddhist nun), which tickled villagers' imaginations by depicting encounters between teenage novices that led to marriage. Another series featured the Daoist Lü Dongbin, which gratified peasant viewers by dramatizing the immortal as a trickster who singled out pompous mortals as his victims. For Yecun residents, these operas were no doubt the year's most colorful moments, punctuating an otherwise dreary existence of hard work and routine.[49]

Women and children, of course, were among the audience gathered in front of the stage. Shi Cuntong and his mother went to these village operas whenever they could. One time they came upon a fantastic play called *The Primus*, about the empire's top examination candidate, and both became quite excited. "Mother described to me at great length what being a primus was all about: the primus addresses the emperor directly, he gets appointed a high official, and he gets all his wishes granted." "This is exactly what I had wished for myself all along," Shi went on, "I was so happy to learn about the civil service examinations and the primus! For when I earned my top palace degree I'd be able to exact a price on all these relatives who have slighted me and my parents!"[50]

Shi's mother further told him that becoming the primus by ranking first in the metropolitan examinations was within the reach of any young man talented enough to excel in the study of Confucian classics and dynastic history, regardless of family background. Shi was quite convinced: not only did the local opera encourage such an ambition; the archways, banners, and gentry compounds in the county seat attested to the tangibility of great power and high status. The idea of joining the officialdom provided a powerful incentive for him to work harder, when, at the age of ten, he was enrolled in an old-fashioned village school. The Qing court, however, abolished the civil service examinations system in 1905 and redirected its resources to the creation of a system of new schools. By Shi Cuntong's own later account and as a measure of his benightedness prior to the May Fourth Movement, he was unable to abandon all hope about upward mobility through the exams system until age seventeen, the year of Yuan Shikai's aborted attempt to restore the monarchy.

Shi Cuntong's literary education began at the age of ten with enrollment in Yecun's village school. Learning was achieved by rote with primers, and Shi made some progress learning to read and write. Two years later the village school was taken over by a new-style elementary school, and the traditional master was displaced by two self-styled educational reformers. Shi Cuntong and about thirty other pupils became the first class of students in this school. The expanded curriculum consisted of geography, history, physics, moral cultivation, Chinese, classics, and mathematics. Shi Cuntong was a bright child who effortlessly earned good grades, but in his own way he was restless and angry; he was a schoolyard bully as well as a petty thief. Once he took a brush. On another occasion he slipped into his pocket someone else's ink stick. "My reasoning was simple: Why should others, and not me, get to have the use of fine writing brushs and ink sticks? So I pocketed them for my use."

The Confucian moral doctrines that he was required to study, however, imparted a sense of right and wrong. He was particularly impressed by his teacher's enunciation of the differences between a Confucian "gentleman" (*junzi*) and a "mean man" (*xiaoren*). "I was genuinely moved by all the moral talk about benevolence and righteousness. So much so that I was resolved to become a gentleman." To give himself a fresh start, he gathered one day his collection of stolen goods and dropped them quietly into a pond outside the village. He took it upon himself to act out exemplary deeds after the fashion of the ancient sages. When quarrels broke out among villagers, Shi Cuntong assigned himself the new role of moral umpire, citing the sages, reasoning with the parties involved, mediating and judging. Now that he had acquired a moral vocabulary of authority, he even quoted Confucius one day when his parents were arguing.

After one year the new-style educators were forced to abandon their positions in the elementary school. A lower-degree holder (*xiucai*) of the abolished civil service examinations system was invited to teach instead. He promptly revived the traditional curriculum and banished from the classrooms the new-style textbooks printed in Shanghai. Shi Cuntong thus was taught to read the *Analects* and *Mencius* in the full editions.

The literary texts of the classics posed little difficulty for Shi Cuntong, and he thrived on the challenge. In the pages of the *Analects* and other classics he looked for heroes rather than moral paragons among Confucius's disciples, and found his favorite in the young Zilu (courtesy name: Ziyou), a resolute and courageous man who had no qualms about acting out his convictions. According to the classics, this personality trait of Zilu was the ultimate cause of his untimely death at the hands of an assassin hired by his rivals. But for Shi Cuntong, Zilu's fervor of conviction and his uncompromising attack on his enemies were qualities to be valued much higher than his ability to survive in a treacherous world. He had such admiration for Zilu's ability to act, sometimes on the spur of the moment, that he gave himself the courtesy name Zhiyou, literally, "resolved to be just like [Zi]you."

Shi reserved his highest admiration, however, for Confucius himself. Confucius, he learned from the classics, brought peace and order to the state of Lu in less than three months after assuming the reins of state affairs. With remarkable ease the Sage was able to put an end to all disputes, bickering, theft, and robbery in the rugged hill country of Lu through the sheer power of moral persuasion. "Upon learning this, I was overwhelmed with admiration for Confucius. I was determined to become a faithful follower of the Confucian Way. . . . I shouted out against heresy and denounced its evil influence whenever anyone uttered any criticism of the Confucian Way. I was so fearlessly devoted in my defense of the Sage in those days that even the most conservative would have to commend my dedication!"

Shi Cuntong's compositions at this time, written in classical Chinese, were filled with a longing for the bygone "rule of the Sage" and the reigns of the deceased "former kings of the Three Dynasties." He quickly mastered the literary conventions suitable for such a stereotyped grand nostalgia coupled with an appropriate lamentation for the moral decline of the present age. "My teacher was quite impressed, and often commented on how I was to have a bright future. I was so pleased! Indeed, wasn't it something remarkable in itself, that a thirteen-year-old boy was able to conduct such discussions on the Way of the Sagely Kings?"

Yet even as Shi Cuntong immersed himself in the study of the halcyon days of the Sage's personal rule as recorded in the classical canons of Confucianism, the Confucian world was falling apart around him. Shi felt betrayed that the teacher, even as he cited the moral doctrines of Neo-Confucian masters, was himself a hopeless opium addict. "We preach sagely teachings daily. But we are not obliged to carry them out ourselves," Shi discovered. "It was my teachers who gave me such ideas with what they professed and what they did; I supposed that I should feel no qualms about trying this out myself."

Shi Cuntong learned decisively about the flawed personal character of moral preachers one evening when he agreed, on request, to stay on in the schoolhouse and keep one of his teachers company. The village school, located in the Temple of Echo (Huiyin si), stood by a hillside about half a li away from the main clustering of village houses, in an area little traveled during the night.[51] When the twelve-year-old fell soundly asleep in this quiet temple, Teacher Jin got up and descended on him. The child woke up struggling and screaming. He was forcefully muffled and sodomized. Teacher Jin, it turned out, had repeatedly imposed himself on a number of his pupils. Like his other abused classmates, Shi Cuntong was so stricken with fear and shame that he told no one about the incident, which was the usual reaction of younger males in the sexually segregated environment of the era. The pupils' silence merely emboldened their aggressors. When a new teacher named Shi arrived, Shi Cuntong was once again molested. Filled with silent rage, Shi Cuntong vowed to himself that he would someday, somehow, take revenge on "such beasts whose flesh would be detested even by dogs and pigs!"[52]

It was about this time that the monarchy fell in the 1911 Revolution, and Shi Cuntong rushed out to be among the first in his village to embrace the Republican cause. In a real-life episode that calls to mind the famous passage in Lu Xun's fictionalized account of the revolution, "The True Story of Ah Q," Shi Cuntong became the first person in his hometown to cut his queue. "They saw my hair, and they said it was ugly, looking just like a chicken's tail. I retorted that chicken tails were better than pigtails. They then warned me solemnly that the emperor was soon to return to the throne to cut off the heads of those without the pigtail. I figured that I'd be in good company losing my head with the [other] chicken tails. So I resolutely parted way with my pigtailed fellow villagers, and declared myself a citizen of the new Republic."[53]

As the revolutionaries and the provincial militarists wrangled with each other to gain control over pieces of the crumbling empire, however, the Republic had little to offer to adolescent republicanists such as Shi Cuntong, mired in the shambles of small-town Confucian morality. Right after the revolution, all schools in Yecun were closed for lack of funding. The birth of the Republic put an end to his childhood at home and in the village school. He was sent away to his maternal grandmother's village, where the elementary school remained in operation. With his pigtail cut and respect for teachers and emperors shorn—in a universe that had been constructed on the moral authority of "heaven, earth, emperor, father, and teacher"— there was little to hold him within the bounds of Confucian morality, except for what he still felt about his mother.

If Shi Cuntong's experience in his grandmother's village was any indication, rural schools in the early Republican years appeared to have deteriorated considerably compared with their late Qing predecessors. Cheating at exams was rampant and condoned by the teachers. Cheating took away all the pride and joy that Shi Cuntong once had as the brightest pupil in his village school. He took out his anger one day by using a bamboo stick to tear off the names of the cheaters posted on the wall as achievers of high scores. This gesture was instantly emulated by other students, especially those whose names appeared as low achievers on the wall poster. The principal rightfully saw Shi Cuntong as the instigator of the incident and took disciplinary action against him. "The principal assembled the entire student body and delivered a stern lecture. He demanded that I admit my wrongdoing in the presence of everyone. I was afraid that refusal on the spot would lead to expulsion, so I did his bidding. Afterwards a few older students said to me that I was timid and should have insisted on [my innocence] all the way through to the end. Yet they themselves were not about to have any trouble with the teachers."[54]

Shi felt humiliated and increasingly reckless after that episode. He allowed himself to be driven by his impulses. He had long harbored fanciful thoughts about young male actors on the stage, "who seemed to be always enjoying themselves with three to four pretty 'wives,' male or female." As a fourteen-year-old in an all-male school, Shi Cuntong soon found himself ganging up with four or five buddies, both to prey on fair-looking younger males by compelling them to behave as their "wives" and to protect themselves from being preyed on. "Someone had stated that 'the school was a microscopic image of the nation,' and I believed in that whole-heartedly. The weak fell prey to the strong, and only the fittest survived—that was certainly the proven truth."[55] The "fraternal" as well as the "conjugal" bonds forged under such circumstances were highly volatile. The loyalty of teenage "brothers" and "wives" had to be secured constantly with gifts or by fists. Shi Cuntong's social standing in the schoolyard was measured by the number of acknowledged followers at his command. He thus spent a good part of his early adolescence fighting like an embattled wolf over leadership of the pack in a Darwinian jungle.

The same village was notorious for its addiction to huahui gambling, the popular lottery that originated in the mid-nineteenth century with the peasants of coastal Guangdong and Zhejiang, and in the Wenzhou area in particular. A complex game that essentially required the gamblers to lay their bets on one of thirty-four to thirty-six possibilities, the huahui lottery was operated by seasoned gamblers who moved from district to district. These migrant rural gangsters began by selecting a quiet clearing in the hills at roughly equal distance to several villages. There they threw together a few shacks and opened each day for several hours of business. The spot of choice was often large enough to hold hundreds of villagers drawn from a circumference of about fifty li. The hills came to life as villagers, lured by the chance to win, left their fields for the clearing. Candy hawkers, food vendors, itinerant merchants, and acrobatic entertainers converged in pursuit of customers. The gambling site took on the air of a fairground. The high point of each day was, of course, the hour when the lottery operators announced the day's winning bet. The announcement was greeted with cheers by some but with sighs by many others. After shouting and laughing there came the busy footsteps of wooden sandals grating against the dirt and gravel and the sound of copper coins clanging on the countertop. By sunset the day's business was over and the noisy villagers dispersed, restoring the hillside to the comings and goings of mountain birds and beasts.[56]

A huahui lottery in the vicinity often skewed a village's life by drawing the entire community into the rhythm and rituals of its operation. Whether it was the bets, the bargains, the candies, the entertainment, or the sheer presence of the crowd, men, women, and children each found a reason to be on the lottery square. In the end the lure of the game was so powerful that even youngsters became addicted. The gambling entailed serious economic consequences. For instance, it stimulated superstitious practices, as gamblers entrusted their fortune to ghosts and spirits and allowed themselves to be completely dominated by the instructions of omens and signs. Many spent their entire savings on offerings promised to the supernatural. Crops in the field were left unattended. Usurers thrived.

A vigilant Confucian scholar would have shielded his pupils from the influence of even village religious festivals and opera performances, not to mention the lottery.[57] With the increasingly prevalent opium addiction of the schoolmasters, however, village schools of the sort that Shi Cuntong attended were no haven from the contagious communal addiction to the huahui lottery. The contest for male friendship had necessitated expenditure beyond his means, and Shi Cuntong was eager for new sources of income. Lured into the game by the hundreds of copper pieces that he won on his initial try, before long he found himself as feverishly addicted as everyone else and allowed himself to be consumed by the lottery day and night. The thriving lottery operation near his grandmother's village did not escape the attention of bandits from outside the area. When these gangs finally appeared in the clearing to exact their share of profits, they also took the opportunity to loot the nearby villages and, in the midst of the chaos, set fire to the schoolhouse. With the school reduced to ashes, Shi Cuntong packed up and went home to his parents.[58]

The next half a year spent at home convinced him that "my family life was like hell to me. . . . I suffered enormously in a home of utter darkness, abused by an ignorant father of vile temper!"

> My father often beat me up for no good reason. . . . One day, I happened to step into the house when my mother was beating my younger brother. My father picked up the stick and began beating me. I asked

him what I had done. He answered, "You surely enjoyed watching it!" . . . Some people might think that my father punished me because I had not tried to stop my mother from beating my brother. I knew for certain that this was untrue. . . . My mother had never permitted any intervention while she was punishing someone. She would have punished me had I tried to intervene, and this was well known to the entire village. My father knew that well. He beat me not in the least because I had not stopped her from punishing my brother. He hit me so that I was victimized as much as my brother.[59]

Relations between father and son were no better when they worked side by side in the field. "After two and a half years at school I wasn't quite as good at farm work as I should have been. My father showed little consideration, and forced me into heavy chores that I couldn't do. He beat me and berated me even when I was feeling ill, saying that I had faked my illness and ordered me to go out into the baking heat. . . . When my mother interfered on my behalf, she too was much berated by my father. I had never dared to defy my father to his face, but how I had come to hate him to the deepest of my bones."[60]

Shi Cuntong finally ran away from home one day and headed for Hangzhou, where he hoped to enlist in the army. Penniless, he was unable to go very far. After a day without food and a night in a deserted temple, he went to the house of his mother's married sister in the next village for help; a few days later an uncle came by and retrieved him. The following fall Shi Cuntong's father sent him off to the Changshan Higher Elementary School in Jinhua County, where a relative (Shi Changchun's cousin) practiced medicine and had an interest in an herbal medicine store. This connection made it possible for Shi Cuntong to leave the village and thus ended the last summer that he was ever to spend with his parents at home.[61]

At the higher elementary school in Jinhua County he settled without hesitation into a pattern of cheating, gambling, and masturbation. As before, he ganged up with a group of fellow students to assure that they would all receive good grades and high honors in school without having to work very hard. This "gang of five" cheated openly during exams and beat up other students if anyone happened to earn good grades honestly.[62] Assured of good grades and having succeeded in undermining school discipline, Shi Cuntong was thereupon able to concentrate on activities to his own liking.

He frequented the local opera house and pursued his favorite pastime as a pubescent teenager, which was to spot attractive young women. "I loved to watch pretty women, but such women were hard to find. Some of my buddies took it upon themselves to spot pretty women for me. But I was always saying that what they had found were no beauties. One day they called me out to say that they spotted a truly beautiful one in the theater. I went with them to the theater to see her, and still said that she was no good. How disappointed my buddies were! I looked over women most carefully, as if they were some sort of an object. I was opposed to footbinding, but I wanted women to have dainty feet. A woman without dainty feet was no beauty at all." Shi insisted, however, that he had never visited prostitutes.[63]

Although school education did little to guide and foster his academic studies, Shi Cuntong was, after all, interested in reading, and through his own effort mastered the classical prose form of the Tang-Song style. He spent the bulk of his time at the county school reading classical romances and historical narratives. In the world of fiction he sought heroes and heroic deeds, and his favorite readings during this time included the *Romance of the Three Kingdoms* and *Journey to the West*. This total immersion in the classical romance fed an active imagination that mixed the fantastic with the heroic, which colored his attitudes and responses to public events in his late teens. On learning that the Chinese government had been pressured into accepting Japan's Twenty-One Demands in April 1915, for instance, Shi Cuntong was outraged. He set out to mobilize his classmates to join the army and fantasized about commanding an expedition against the Japanese. Like the Boxers of 1900, he firmly believed that the magical power of the Monkey King in *Journey to the West* would ensure a Chinese victory over the Japanese in naval encounters.[64] When he learned that Yuan Shikai had betrayed the Republican constitution and launched the Hong-xian monarchy, Shi Cuntong was again enraged. He made wild plans to single-handedly right the wrongs of the day by assassinating Yuan Shikai, following the plots described in Tang short stories of knights-errant.[65]

These fantasies of personal heroism and derring-do in the fashion of the popular romance found expression on the eve of graduation, when Shi Cuntong entered a sworn brotherhood with three friends. Using dead chicken and pork as sacrificial offerings, the four young men swore oaths, exchanged pledges, kowtowed to heaven and earth, smeared blood, and then proceeded to get wildly drunk. The ceremony emulated a famous episode in the *Romance of the Three Kingdoms*, in which the heroes swear brotherly loyalty to each other in a peach orchard before going out to conquer the world and found a new dynasty. It was, of course, a commonly practiced initiation rite among members of the secret society that was active in the Jinhua area.[66] In this case, the performance of the blood oath contributed little to the substance of the relationship, and the brotherhood for a "great enterprise" dissolved in no time at all when these friends went their separate ways after graduation.[67]

By the time that Shi Cuntong graduated from the Higher Elementary School of Jinhua County, he was an unruly teenager seasoned in the petty vices of middle-county life and had little respect for established local authority figures. His knowledge about the Confucian Way did little to keep him in his place in the village community. Instead, it exposed to him the glaring discrepancy between what was preached and what was practiced, and alerted him to the moral decay, the parochialism, and the loss of will permeating the society around him.

It was clear enough that his parental home and native village were no longer suitable for him, but it was not clear where he should turn next. His parents could not afford to send him to any more schools. The literacy he had attained, meanwhile, led to no jobs in the countryside. Instead of going home to the ancestral village, Shi Cuntong headed downriver to Hangzhou, where an uncle—a brother of his mother—was stationed as a military officer. After repeated trial and error he finally sat for the entrance examinations for the Provincial First Normal School. Even he was surprised to learn that he had passed the exams and was admitted. The day he saw his name on the roster of First Normal's 1917 incoming class a great sense of relief came over him. It was a momentous event in Shi Cuntong's life, for "only after that date did I begin to acquire some correct understanding on what life was all about."[68]

A FRESH START

At First Normal, Shi Cuntong began a new life. The moral insistence and Republican patriotism of Jing Ziyuan's pedagogical philosophy inspired in Shi a new sense of purpose and direction. "I wanted nothing but to be a hard-working student and a new-style educator, to be of real contribution to society. . . . I had a high sense of pride, not that sort of vain interest in grades, but a genuine concentration on the substance of my study. I wished to be an exemplary student to all, and was rather strict in self-discipline." Echoing Principal Jing, Shi Cuntong went on: "I found my correct views of life, and understood that no one could exist out of one's social context. I had benefited from societal generosity, and mustn't simply be a filial son to my parents, but should also try to be a useful member of society. I saw education as my lifetime calling. I did not wish to be a mere teacher, but wanted to be an inspiring educator. I was, indeed, on the right track."[69]

Shi Cuntong found an unusual friendship with his classmate Zhou Bodi, the sort of friendship that Shi had never enjoyed before, and one that was to last for life. "It was something that I could not describe. We were not very close in temperament, nor did we think the same thoughts. It was a nameless something that was perhaps what [the principal] had called 'the confluence of two moral characters.' We confided in each other and shared our feelings. Once I had to take leave from school to visit my sick mother, and he saw me off with tears in his eyes. We gave each other advice and were vigilant about each other's moral flaws. . . . Besides Bodi I also formed a few other close friendships, and they have all had significant influences on me. This was the year that I truly benefited from such friendships."[70]

In this setting he found a new sense of moral community and changed his personal attitudes and lifestyle altogether. With Zhou Bodi, Zhu Zantang, and Yu Shousong (all of Zhedong origin), Shi Cuntong "decided to take on as our personal responsibilities the revitalization of the moral fiber of society. We set aside all self-centered thoughts, and thoroughly renounced and repented the wrong things that we had done in the past." Together these friends embarked on a private moral campaign ultimately aimed at the reform of society, but beginning with the moral rectification of the self. They resolved to refrain from such common vices of the provincial society as cheating and gambling. In addition—and much in accord with the declared doctrines of the anarchist society Xinshe (The Heart Society) of 1912—they were to refrain from drinking, smoking, and wasting time.[71] They exercised vigilance over each other's moral lapses and spurred one another on in serious intellectual pursuits. They spent so much of their time talking earnestly about moral subjects that they were dubbed the "Neo-Confucianists" (*Daoxue xiansheng*) by their classmates. Toward the end of his First Normal days Shi Cuntong was able to declare proudly: "I was able to rein myself in and adhere strictly to important principles. In my two and a half years at First Normal I had never wasted a penny, never once rode in a ricksha, never smoked a cigarette or touched a drop of alcohol," not to mention any other more serious offences.[72]

As he found new meaning to his life at First Normal, Shi Cuntong was compelled at the same time to reexamine his relationship with his own past. Jing Ziyuan's "moral education" gave him a sense of membership in a larger sociopolitical order that transcended the confines of the familial and lineage network. From this new perspective Shi Cuntong saw himself no longer as the abused and unloved son to his father, but rather as a highly valued normal school student who was going to help revitalize the nation and reform Chinese society.

Whereas the middle county of Jinhua had once been to the young Shi Cuntong merely his native place, to Shi Cuntong the educator and reformer it became transformed into a scene of social malaise and a prime object for moral reform. In Hangzhou, his personal embedment in the middle counties of the Qiantang Valley ceased to define the full content of his social being. Instead, his childhood was safely relegated to a past that could be reconstituted into a useful piece of social information. Armed with that insight, he could then better carry out his task as a moral reformer against the evils of the very middle-county society from which he came. "Without the pain and abuse that I had personally suffered I would never have been able to gain such an understanding of its dark side, nor would I have been so fervently devoted to social reform and family revolution." In the past, without the protective mediation of the reformer's vision and zeal, Shi's reencounter with his village had goaded him at one point to run away from home. As a student of First Normal School in Hangzhou and speaking in his new voice as an educator, he was ready to return and bring about the salvation of his homeland. Even his hated father had been transformed, in this new perspective, from an all-important and brutal oppressor into an object of Shi's moral campaign and a recipient of his help: "My father was a very unfortunate person deserving of sympathy. Of course he was among the ones that the social reform would save."[73] Indeed, where else was Shi Cuntong to act out his moral triumph, if not against his immoral home county?

Whether the middle-county society of Zhedong was likely to submit to the moral instruction of Shi Cuntong and his classmates was a question involving several other factors beyond their control. Were the district governments, for instance, actually ready to fund a greater number of elementary schools? Did First Normal graduates stand a better chance than the old-fashioned educated in obtaining a teaching position in these communities?

Between 1917 and 1919, as the employment prospects for normal school graduates in Zhedong steadily worsened, the Zhejiang Provincial Educational Association, headed by Jing Ziyuan, took up the leadership of three campaigns with vigor and persistence. In response to the growing frustration and anxiety of normal school students about their job prospects, the association sought to urge on the Provincial Assembly the adoption of three proposals: the creation of a Zhejiang University in Hangzhou, the immediate adoption of a public-funded and compulsory educational plan for the entire province, and a stringent review of the teaching credentials and professional qualifications of all elementary school teachers in Zhejiang. The political dynamics unleashed by these developments, as the next chapter will show, shaped the manner in which the May Fourth Movement played itself out in the provincial capital of Hangzhou. They also fashioned the future of Shi Cuntong, who moved from adolescent rebel to adult radical.

6 The Association

The Zhejiang Provincial Educational Association was a voluntary organization of school administrators and other urban professionals who shared certain beliefs about the use of education in the creation of a better society. Founded in 1912 with the blessing of the new Republican provincial government, it was headed by Jing Ziyuan in his new position as the head of the Zhejiang Provincial First Normal School. Intended to facilitate educational reforms, the organization represented the province's most progressive voice on such matters. Members of the association did not restrict their concern to schools, however. Many of these men, formed by events in the final decade of the Qing, were also ardent supporters of a republican form of government as opposed to the imperial system. In the context of Republican politics of the 1910s, this meant firm opposition to conservative attempts to restore the emperor—efforts that culminated in the Hongxian monarchy of Yuan Shikai and the suspension of the Republican constitution in 1915.

This strong belief in republicanism, coupled with considerable influence over the province's academic circles as well as educated public opinion, often strained the association's relationship with the provincial government, which was dominated by conservative militarists. But the mixing of politics with education did not begin with the Republican era, nor was the tension between cultural conservatives and educational reformers purely a provincial matter. The divisions could be traced to circumstances in the late 1890s, when the Qing court, in response to intensified Japanese, German, Russian, French, and British territorial and economic interest in China after the Chinese defeat in the First Sino-Japanese War, began contemplating drastic measures of reform that included a total overhaul of the Chinese educational system. The educational associations, along with the new schools, were products of the New Policies pursued by the Qing court from 1898 to 1911, a period of heightened national crisis and impassioned political contention. To place in sharper focus the role of the Zhejiang Provincial Educational Association in the making of the May Fourth Movement in Hangzhou, it is useful to review briefly the evolution of the association in the first two decades of the twentieth century.

NEW POLICIES AND THE
EDUCATIONAL ASSOCIATION

The first educational associations, created in 1906, were gentry organizations called into existence by the state to help the government implement the reform of the national school system. The new school system, of which Zhejiang's First Normal School was a part, was outlined in imperial decrees in 1898 and 1901 and gradually put in place through regulations promulgated in 1902 and 1904. The system displaced the traditional network of state-sponsored academies linked to the civil service examinations, which were abolished in 1905. It also called into question the pedagogy of the tens of thousands of village and lineage schools taught by a single master—a curriculum that offered literacy and classics and functioned as a sort of feeder preparing students for lower-level civil service examinations held under the supervision of the county educational commissioner.

Under the new school plan, state authorities at various levels of the bureaucracy took responsibility for the creation of a three-tier school system. The Beijing central government announced in 1898 the creation of a reconstituted Imperial Academy (Jingshi daxue tang), which became the institutional precursor of Beijing University in the Republican period. Provincial governors took steps to transform the old state-sponsored academies into secondary schools, aiming to create at least one such school in each prefectural seat. County governments, meanwhile, were instructed to set up at least one elementary school in their districts. Regional variations inevitably occurred in the process, and local authorities devised their own means in response to central government directives. By the mid-1900s, the Qing was nonetheless able to speak of a comprehensively reformed national system of new schools.

Problems and tensions developed almost immediately with the launching of the new system. Like many other state-initiated reforms under the New Policies, the new educational plan recast the role of the state from a somewhat detached arbiter and setter of examination standards to a much more involved activator and supervisor of actual schools, without, however, making provisions in administrative infrastructure and funding support commensurate with the task. Despite its impulse for centralized control, the court in Beijing was in no position to provide funding for the creation of local schools, nor was it able effectively to supervise the operation of a multitude of such institutions. Provincial governments were no better equipped than the center for the task. Gentry participation was thus indispensable, and both the court and the governors sought to mobilize gentry support.[1]

Gentry leadership had traditionally been substantial in local educational affairs.[2] Gentry elites at the turn of the century, furthermore, had long been aware of the urgent need for reform, and agitation by gentry progressives in the 1890s had created the political climate for the imperial court's adoption of sweeping changes under the New Policies. From the viewpoint of some of these gentry progressive reformers, it was the state rather than the society that was lagging behind in keeping up with changing times.

To penetrate the vast hinterland, it was necessary to draw into the cause of educational reform an even larger number of local gentrymen, who would dismantle the old system at the subcounty level. To help these local leaders identify resources for schools, the government, on the suggestion of Governor General Zhang Zhidong, the architect of the new system, gave permission to potential school-founders to take local Buddhist temple properties for their use. In addition, the court allowed them to exact special levies (te juan), mainly on small-town shopkeepers and peasants, to pay for the schools. From Jiangsu to Sichuan, Shanxi to Guangdong, gentry educationalists explored a variety of resources to help fund their schools, and often fought local monks, shopkeepers, and peasants over additional taxes and temple property. As part of the campaign, gentry reformers sought to ban village operas and divert shopkeepers' festival contributions to the construction of local schools, denouncing the temples and religious fairs as "feudal," and calling themselves "the forces of enlightenment and progress." Angry peasants, for their part, often responded with riots, attacking reformers and setting fire to local schoolhouses.[3]

While antagonizing the villagers, gentry educational reformers also made enemies out of conservative elements in their own ranks. Gentry militia leaders, who had established previous claims on the disposition of temple properties and special levies, were particularly reluctant to relinquish these resources. To counter the new-style educators, they turned to political allies of their own, which often included the militia bureau directors and military men in the provincial capital. Together they sought to undermine the credibility of the new schools by spreading rumors designed to revive old village fears and prejudices against the teaching of Western subjects.[4]

In the course of mobilizing gentry support for the new school system, the state was instrumental in setting off two processes. By creating conditions for local leaders to rally for reform, the state empowered the educational reformers on policy and fiscal matters in their own locale. This empowerment went beyond ad hoc administrative latitude to find institutional expression, in 1906, in state authorization for the organization of provincial educational associations and county *quanxue suo* (literally "centers for the exhortation of learning"), which were vested with extensive powers. By mobilizing local elites in the first place, the imperial government pitted cultural conservatives against educational progressives from locale to locale. Educational reform consequently divided opinion not only between elite gentry progressives and conservative bureaucrats at the center but also between upper and lower gentry in the provinces—a division that factionalized local society along with court politics in the late Qing.

The Qing government publicized the first set of rules governing the organization of educational associations in 1906.[5] On the provincial level, these rules called into existence associations of eminent gentry leaders who were to advise and assist provincial governors on educational matters. To perform that function, each provincial association was given the responsibility to collect information on education within the province, supervise the operation of all levels of schools, build public libraries, finance school administrations, set goals and formulate pedagogical philosophy, review and approve textbooks, compile statistics on education, and exercise a broad influence of "moral transformation" (*jiaohua*) on provincial society. Like the old provincial educational commissioners under the unreformed system, the association was to popularize the imperial "sacred instructions" (*shengyu guangxun*) among the commoners. It was also charged with combating evil customs by organizing moral campaigns against misbegotten popular practices such as sectarian heterodoxy, cult worship, female infanticide, and footbinding. Members of the association met on a weekly basis to allocate their responsibilities. They also formulated proposals that were forwarded to the provincial governor by the new provincial commissioner of education (*tixue shi*). Members of the association drew no compensation for their service; it was often their responsibility, instead, to make financial contributions on their own.[6]

Once progressive gentry elites found an arena for action in educational associations, their disagreements with high-ranking bureaucrats became more pronounced. Much of the tension had to do with differences over basic educational philosophy. Governor General Zhang Zhidong and other conservative but reform-oriented officials—most notably Yuan Shikai and Liu Kunyi—envisioned a new school system modeled on the Japanese system, which they believed was critical to Japan's successful military modernization. Abiding by the formula "Chinese learning as essence, Western learning for application" (*Zhongxue wei ti, xixue wei yong*) made famous by Governor General Zhang in his treatise *Quanxue pian* (Exhortation of learning), these officials placed heavy emphasis on the teaching of Confucian ethics in Chinese schools, insisted on doctrines of patriotism and loyalty to the ruler, and saw the new schools as instrumental to the realization of a statist vision of nation building and modernization under a centralized bureaucracy. Impressed with Japan's vigor and ability to project national wealth and power, the conservatives were willing to work with Japanese teachers and advisors in Chinese schools, especially normal schools that trained secondary and primary schoolteachers. They upheld the value of discipline and authority and, for the post of provincial educational commissioners, favored the appointment not of practitioners of new-style education but of former Hanlin scholars—classicists and holders of the highest civil service examinations degree who could be relied on to teach Confucian values and to inspire deference.[7]

Gentry progressives, in contrast, thought of the new schools in terms of a reconstitution of knowledge and a revolution in teaching. They pressed for the introduction of Western subjects and insisted on fundamental changes in pedagogical methods. Their goal was to educate not just an elite minority but as many students as possible and to train not loyal subjects but citizens for a rejuvenated Chinese nation. The Japanese system, in their view, was both authoritarian and elitist. It stressed higher education over elementary schools and required a heavy investment on the part of the students and their families in time as well as money. Among the gentry progressives were those willing to explore alternatives in educational thinking; less than a decade later, this willingness crystallized into a rising demand to abandon the Japanese model for an American one. For the post of provincial educational commissioners the gentry preferred the appointment of elementary and secondary school teachers and administrators rather than Hanlin scholars.[8]

The rift in educational philosophy overlapped with the rift in political ideology, and gentry educationalists were quite often vigorous agitators for a constitutional form of government and for local elections and self-rule. The Qing court, under mounting pressure, finally yielded to gentry demands to speed up the schedule for constitutional reform and held the first elections for provincial assemblies in 1909.[9] Two years later the dynasty collapsed, and the Republic was announced. In the arena of educational reform, however, the 1911 Revolution did little to crack the backbone of conservative influence. Nor did the birth of the Republic resolve the differences between the conservatives and the progressives. It simply altered the context within which that struggle took place.

In 1912, the new ministry of education issued its regulations governing the organization of educational associations. Under these rules provincial educational associations were ostensibly allowed to address many of the issues identified in the Qing regulations. Instead of communicating with the provincial government, however, the association reported to the provincial assembly, and rather than supervising schools and drafting policies, the association was asked to concentrate its energy on the proper conduct, correct ceremonies, family ethics, social mores, and the "moral transformation" of the community. The new government, furthermore, made it clear that the associations had no claim on provincial funds. Membership in these organizations, which in the past involved voluntary contributions, now entailed payment of membership fees, with which all association activities were to be financed. No restriction was placed on the size of the association's membership.[10] The Republican provincial educational associations, compared with their Qing predecessors, had been transformed from an elite, semiofficial advisory body attached to the provincial government to a membership association at considerable remove from the executive branch of the state.

Gentry associations, once called into existence, acquired an ability to function on their own. Government regulations did not produce immediate changes in gentry attitude and behavior. Nor did the announcement prevent the association from petitioning for money. What the gentry progressives and educationalists lost in immediate provincial political influence with the state, they compensated for with activities such as annual conferences of educational associations of all provinces, and by the publication, in increasing numbers, of journals and newsletters to keep themselves well informed of each other's activities. The first such conference, proposed by the Zhili (Hebei) Provincial Educational Association in 1914, took place in April 1915 in Tianjin. It was attended by delegates from thirteen provincial educational associations, including that of Zhejiang. The delegates adopted thirteen resolutions and handed them over to the ministry of education, which proceeded to consider them for adoption. The meeting was extensively reported in several Shanghai-based professional journals for educators. It concluded with the delegates adopting a resolution to meet annually thereafter.[11]

In subsequent meetings the delegates voted to create a permanent staff to coordinate the annual national conferences. They also identified problems in the new school system, and showed a remarkable ability to focus attention on issues over time. In 1915, the Hunan Provincial Educational Association opened up discussions on whether the Japanese school system, favored by Qing bureaucrats, was a suitable model for the Chinese to follow. After studying the problem for years, the associations voted, in the post–May Fourth atmosphere of 1922, to abandon the Japanese model and to create a much less centralized school system, particularly in the area of secondary and vocational education, patterned after American schools. Through a skillful deployment of public opinion and professional authority, the associations were able to persuade the ministry of education to adopt their resolution. An important refashioning of Chinese schools, presented both as more in tune with the Chinese past and more pragmatically fashioned for the present, was under way.[12]

By constituting themselves into a national network of educated opinion, Republican progressive educators, although without official standing, gained extensive voice and influence in national educational affairs. This development took place against the backdrop of the rise of an increasingly proactive state in national affairs, although the early Republican government, preoccupied with military and political problems, gave low priority to its role in education. This transformation of the state stemmed also from the New Policies of the late Qing. Within the context of provincial politics such as those in Zhejiang, it meant that the Zhejiang Provincial Educational Association, despite its network of gentry allies and professional educators outside the province, confronted the power of a provincial government that (compared with its Qing predecessors) was able to muster much greater strength within the province. Republican provincial governors, like the central government in Beijing, had at their disposal not only a modernized new army, a police force, and a court system after the Japanese model, but also a much more elaborate bureaucracy reaching into many more areas of social life, buttressed by an enhanced capability to extract tax revenue. The Provincial Educational Association enjoyed no special privilege in this official structure that was dominated, for a full decade after 1917, by military men from Anhui. Whether the provincial government, with its military and administrative power, or the educational association, with its gentry pedigree and intellectual authority, ought to have the last word on Zhejiang's educational affairs was by no means self-evident in the early years of the Republic. The May Fourth Movement, in Zhejiang's provincial politics, was a moment of contest in the cultural domain between these two forces.

The Provincial Educational Association, despite its national visibility, hardly enjoyed the full endorsement of all levels of Zhejiang society. The ideological split that separated the metropolitan elites from subcounty militia leaders over Qing reform politics persisted into the Republican period. In Zhejiang, lineage heads and landowners from the largely agrarian south repeatedly opposed the progressives and professionals of northern cities over issues of reform. For much of the first decade of the Republic, southern landlords, with the help of the province's Anhui military governors, were able to dominate the Zhejiang Provincial Assembly. Southern provincial assemblymen, who long harbored misgivings about northern progressive trends, were, in fact, the first people to voice criticisms of Jing Ziyuan's liberal leanings prior to the May Fourth Movement. The Provincial Assembly thereafter formed an alliance with the provincial government in conservative attacks on Jing Ziyuan and his circle. In that sense, the May Fourth Movement in Zhejiang was a contest between different kinds of power and influence, as well as a struggle between different cultural outlooks and social orientations, in which the government and the assembly, no less than the association, were key players.

ZHEJIANG POLITICS AND THE ARRIVAL OF THE ANHUI MILITARISTS

Although the 1911 Revolution had succeeded in overthrowing the Qing dynasty, Republican ideals were far from being established in provincial politics. In March 1912, Yuan Shikai, the last of a line of late imperial viceroys with personal authority over an army as well as a critical role in the central bureaucracy, was elected to the presidency of the Republic. Sun Yat-sen, the leader of the Revolutionary Alliance, stepped aside to help preserve national unity. This development had broad local ramifications. In Hangzhou, Jiang Zungui, the gentry leader who helped to overthrow the Qing, was forced to resign from his post as the military governor of Zhejiang. Zhu Rui, a Yuan follower and a native of Haiyan, Zhejiang, was installed as military governor of the province in August 1912. Zhu's close friend Qu Yingguang, a Zhejiang native from Taizhou Prefecture, was appointed the civilian governor at the same time.

Zhu, a secondary degree-holder (juren) under the abolished civil service examinations system, had at his disposal the New Army units of Zhejiang formed during the New Policies period. From 1912 to 1916 the Zhejiang provincial government, under the control of the conservatives, gave strong support to the central government in Beijing under Yuan Shikai, who suspended the new republic's National Assembly as well as its provisional constitution in 1913. Yuan also instigated the assassination of Song Jiaoren, leader of the newly formed Nationalist Party in the National Assembly, at Shanghai's train station. In response, Sun Yat-sen and his former Revolutionary Alliance comrades launched a "Second Revolution," resorting to military means to dislodge Yuan Shikai from power. Sun and his fellow republicanists, however, were unsuccessful in their attempts. Emboldened by his opponents' defeat, Yuan Shikai attempted in 1915 to abolish the Republican constitution and make himself the Hongxian emperor. Zhejiang, under the military governorship of Zhu Rui, offered little resistance to Yuan's dynastic ambition. Zhu readily declared his support for Yuan's monarchy. In return, he was made a duke of the first degree by the new emperor.[13]

The Hongxian monarchy was short-lived. As soon as the monarchists lost out in Beijing, Zhu Rui lost his control over the province. On the night of April 11, 1916, he fled his military governor's office in disguise, just as a coup was staged by Xia Chao, the provincial police chief, together with Tong Baoxuan, commander of the Second Battalion of the Zhejiang New Army stationed in Hangzhou—two revolutionary sympathizers whom Governor Zhu was at that very moment plotting to capture and murder.[14] Zhu Rui's departure was followed shortly afterward by the death of Yuan Shikai of illness on June 6, 1916. In September the Zhejiang Provincial Assembly was restored, and, for a brief period, Shen Xuanlu (courtesy name: Dingyi), the Guomindang member who later acquired fame as an anarchocommunist, served as its president.[15]

Police Chief Xia, however, was a member of the Wubei Clique of Zhejiang military officers trained in Japan and, in the aftermath of the coup, fell instantly into a fierce power struggle with members of the Baoding Clique—fellow Zhejiang officers who were cadets at the Baoding Military Academy in Hebei. As the two factions fought for control over Zhejiang, Prime Minister Duan Qirui in Beijing seized the opportunity and appointed Yang Shande, commander of the Fourth Battalion of the Northern Army and garrison commander of Shanghai, to become the new military governor of Zhejiang.[16] Yang, a fellow native from the prime minister's home province of Anhui, marched into Hangzhou in January 1917 at the head of several Northern Army units, bringing along Qi Yaoshan as his civilian governor. Yang died of illness in August 1919, leaving the military governorship of the province to Lu Yongxiang, a fellow militarist of the Anhui Clique. Zhejiang then fell into the firm grip of the Anhui Clique for the ensuing decade.

The rule of the Anhui Clique's northern military governors (1917–27) has often been referred to as a dark period in Zhejiang's modern history. With the Provincial Assembly dominated by a conservative majority, military units and police forces were significantly expanded at the expense of public schools. Government income steadily increased both through the tightening of tax-collecting measures and through the imposition of an array of new commercial taxes. This provincial treasury was used to support the military and the police.[17]

The rule of the Anhui militarists also meant that Zhejiang was drawn into the protracted power struggle over the control of the central government that unfolded between the Anhui, the Zhili, and later the Fengtian militarist cliques in the ensuing decade. These struggles took many forms, including, in the mild form of an early stage, a vigorous quarrel over whether China should declare war against Germany.[18] The Nationalists, led by Sun Yat-sen, renewed their efforts to revive the Republican constitution from their new base in Guangzhou. One way to perceive the provincial politics of the time in Hangzhou was as a contest between the conservatives and the progressives over the articulation of Republican aspirations. Without access either to the military or to the legal and financial powers of the state, provincial progressives nonetheless did their best to develop their influence in urban society. The activities of the Zhejiang Provincial Educational Association, led by Jing Ziyuan, offered a prime example of attempts by progressives to translate their influence in education and public opinion into an effective political force.

THE ZHEJIANG EDUCATIONAL ASSOCIATION MEETING IN 1917

On May 6, 1917, a few months after the Anhui militarists took over the Zhejiang provincial government, the Zhejiang Provincial Educational Association convened its annual meeting. Held on the campus of the First Normal School, the meeting began early in the morning with a procession and a performance by the school's student band, military style, on the playing field. The assembly then moved into the auditorium, where President Jing Ziyuan formally opened the session by delivering a warm welcome, thanking all present for an exceptionally large attendance that totaled 392.[19]

A large part of the meeting, as it turned out, had less to do with local schools than national politics. The morning's speeches juxtaposed reports of war in Europe with rumors of embezzlement and bribery in Beijing's ministries of finance and communications. Much of the conversation evolved around Beijing politics and China's declaration of war against Germany.

One speaker recalled that it was exactly one year earlier, in May 1916, that the Beijing government touched off a banking crisis by ordering the two government-regulated banks, the Bank of China and the Communications Bank, to suspend cashing their own paper notes with silver—an order that threw the money market into chaos and required the presence of police on the street to enforce. A full year had passed, and there was still no sign in the north that things were going to change. Rumors were rife that the Anhui militarist faction in the government, to solve its deepening financial problems, was ready to declare war on Germany in order to secure fresh Japanese loans, while the Zhili Clique, with the support of the Nationalist Party, was determined to block such a move in the National Assembly. The Zhejiang educators engaged in lively discussions about the political intrigues and financial scandals in the capital seven hundred miles to the north. They asked aloud from time to time what educators could do to make a difference. In the end the majority decided to their own satisfaction that war was unjust, and that educators should oppose the Anhui Clique for resorting to such means to hold on to power.[20]

In the afternoon the delegates discussed the state of Chinese schools and compared it with educational systems elsewhere in the world. They also linked the state of schools to politics and types of political systems, concluding, more or less, that better governments in more mature republican systems produced better schools. A strong implication was the necessity for political reform as a condition for successful educational reform.

The meeting then moved on to the business items of the association. Elections were held. Jing Ziyuan, with 279 votes, won reelection to the presidency. Sun Zengda, with 171 votes, was elected vice president. In addition, the delegates elected a twenty-four-member advisory committee, which supposedly consisted of two members from each of Zhejiang's eleven prefectures,[21] but was overly represented by delegates from the five northern prefectures of Hang-Jia-Hu and Ning-Shao; the other committee members, purportedly representing the remaining Zhedong prefectures, were in fact sojourners who had established residence in Hangzhou.[22]

After the election He Shaohan, the executive secretary of the association, steered the discussion to the necessity of fundraising for the association. Unlike gentry organizations in an earlier time, the Provincial Educational Association did not have natural local constituencies such as lineages or village communities to which it could turn. An association built on shared concerns with educational reform, it was further denied by the state access to provincial revenue, and had little choice but to devise untraditional means for self-support. The annual meeting, however, functioned better as a meeting place and a debating society than a fundraising session. Delegates took up the financial issue, but no concrete results were produced. It was left to Jing Ziyuan and his small group of advisors to work out the association's organizational problems.

Jing Ziyuan, who served as the association's president from 1912 to 1920, turned out to be an active and resourceful institution builder. To obtain for the association a permanent office with a sizable endowment for operating costs, he dedicated himself to fundraising. To amplify the group's voice on provincial matters, Jing launched the association's own journal, *Jiaoyu chao* (Tides in education), and invited his fellow Shaoxing native Shen Zhongjiu (1887–1968), a man with strong anarchist leanings, to serve as the chief editor. To reach a clientele of secondary school students, the association formed, in March 1919, the Zhejiang Youth Corps, which aimed to organize Hangzhou's students by sponsoring a variety of cultural and recreational activities.[23] Through these efforts Jing Ziyuan hoped to project for the association both a presence and a following.

Meanwhile the Zhejiang Provincial Educational Association kept up its frequent contact with educators of other provinces. In publishing as well as in other activities, the Zhejiang educators maintained a particularly close tie with the Jiangsu Provincial Educational Association, based in Shanghai. Five months after the annual meeting of the Zhejiang members, Jing Ziyuan hosted the third annual national conference of the provincial educational associations, which now referred to itself as the National Federation of Educational Associations (Quanguo jiaoyu hui lianhe hui) and brought delegates of seventeen provincial and three other educational associations to Hangzhou.[24] Although the national group refrained from direct political involvement, in the eyes of the provincial government the association represented a source of influence with a political agenda of its own. This distrust led to the provincial government's repeated refusal to grant petitions submitted by Jing on behalf of the educators.

FINANCING THE ASSOCIATION

When the Provincial Educational Association came into existence in 1912, no provision was made for its funding. For years the organization operated without office space and a budget of its own. Its presence bordered on nonexistence. Between 1912 and 1917, Jing Ziyuan repeatedly petitioned the Provincial Assembly, to which the association was required to report, for funding support from the provincial government's educational budget. These petitions were "either set aside without discussion, or set aside after some discussion but before votes were taken."[25] The association was compelled to rely on a small sum of contributions collected from its members.

In May 1917, shortly after the conclusion of the association's annual meeting, Jing Ziyuan petitioned the Provincial Assembly for the third time. Jing reported that the advisory committee of the association, after some discussion, had "adopted a resolution to locate a site on the shore of West Lake and to engage contractors for the construction of an association building." While the construction cost for the main building was estimated at twenty-five thousand yuan in silver, another twenty-five thousand was needed for embankments, infrastructure, and the interior. The association asked that the assembly contribute ten thousand and reported that it had already received a pledge of twenty-five thousand yuan from private sources.[26]

The private sources were two large donors and a cluster of small ones. Li Yuanhong and Chen Chunlan each pledged a gift of ten thousand yuan. Chen Chunlan was a wealthy merchant with extensive business connections and a fellow townsman of Jing Ziyuan from Shangyu in Shaoxing. A friend and a supporter, Chen presented Jing Ziyuan with another large gift in the aftermath of the May Fourth Movement, in 1920, when Jing was forced to resign from the headmastership of the First Normal School. On that occasion Chen provided funding for the creation of a secondary school at Shangyu and invited Jing Ziyuan to return home to be its headmaster. Jing eventually took up the offer and arrived with several fellow progressive teachers from First Normal. He devoted the rest of his years to the Chunhui School on Shangyu's scenic White Horse Lake.

The other major donor was Li Yuanhong, a former president of the Chinese Republic. Considered a member of the Zhili Clique that had formed an alliance with the Nationalist Party in Beijing's National Assembly, President Li had hoped to project for himself the image of an enlightened supporter of the republicanists' educational agenda in Zhejiang. In 1917, he was unceremoniously forced out of the presidency by Prime Minister Duan Qirui, head of the Anhui Clique. Thus a gift to Jing Ziyuan—a Nationalist Party member in a province dominated by the Anhui Clique—was a gift to the enemy of one's enemy, which Li was more than happy to make. The remaining five thousand yuan was contributed by scores of smaller donors, including Jing Ziyuan himself.[27]

The Zhejiang Provincial Assembly, however, once again rejected the association's plea to fund the construction of its permanent building. It offered instead the use of a piece of government land at the north end of Pinghai Road, near Hangzhou's New Market. The educators were unhappy with the suggestion because that location would take them away from the scenic West Lake, but without the cost of lakeside embankments the building expenses were considerably reduced. Although Jing Ziyuan calculated that he would still be short by about ten thousand yuan, construction began in time for the building's inaugural opening in October 1917, when the third annual meeting of the National Federation of Provincial Educational Associations was held in Hangzhou.[28]

The following year Tang Erhe—a Zhejiang native, republicanist, friend of Cai Yuanpei (who was by now president of Beijing University), and one-term minister of education in Beijing—presented two hundred thousand yuan to the Zhejiang Provincial Educational Association as a gift. At the next annual meeting of the association in June 1918, Jing Ziyuan reported extensively on "this unprecedented act" that "set a first in personal giving in China." With his gift Tang Erhe had shown his "great faith" in the goals set by the association, while the Provincial Assembly had stubbornly shown little. With his characteristic forthrightness, Jing Ziyuan could not help but dwell publicly on the contrast between Tang's generosity and the Provincial Assembly's persistent refusal to offer any help.[29] More important, with such a generous private gentry contribution deposited under the association's name, Jing Ziyuan was well endowed for action.

BUILDING A STUDENT FOLLOWING

One of Jing Ziyuan's initiatives was the creation of the Zhejiang Youth Corps, which was formally launched in August 1918 at a well-publicized ceremony to which many notables, including the military governor, sent their congratulations. The corps sought to realize certain progressive educational ideals through the organization of secondary school students' extracurricular lives. It organized instruction in music and art, encouraged students to picnic, hike, and travel, presented lectures on current events, and offered civic training in Republican ideals. The stated goal of the corps was to nurture a broad range of interests among secondary school students, to bring forth in them a cosmopolitan outlook, to create a community of brotherly love in which "none of the artificial hierarchies of 'class,' 'sec-

tion,' 'year,' and 'school' that existed within the formal school structure"
would be allowed to divide up the student body.[30]

Educators including Jing Ziyuan rightly perceived that the social environment was often harsh and that it was a constant personal struggle for
provincial teenagers such as Shi Cuntong to acquire a sense of purpose and
discipline in their lives. By creating a group such as the Youth Corps, the
organizers hoped to provide a community of moral support for Zhejiang's
adolescents during the most critical years of their development. Jing emphasized that members of the Youth Corps should speak their minds to each
other as equals and friends. The corps idealized the horizontal linkages
between individuals "truthful to their moral integrity" instead of the
vertical ties of master-disciple relationships that formed the backbone of
traditional social networks.[31]

Jing and his supporters had hoped that the Zhejiang Youth Corps would
draw into its local branches students in all secondary schools throughout
the province. Membership enrollment in Hangzhou soon reached 2,100,
but elsewhere, especially in the south, it proved difficult for the organization to attract members.[32] Some of the obstacles stemmed from the
charter of the Youth Corps. To join as a core member, a boy had to be at
least fourteen, to have completed an elementary school education, and to
be able to afford about twelve yuan for the uniforms.[33] These conditions
greatly reduced the number of qualified members in places outside of the
urban centers in the north.

Some of the activities that the corps sought to promote, furthermore,
ran against conventional notions of the purpose of education. Acting, for
instance, had traditionally been regarded as a profession of ill repute.
New-style drama, however, under Western influence and performed in the
vernacular, was much valued by progressives as a vehicle to disseminate
political messages. Organizers of the Zhejiang Youth Corps disagreed on
whether dramatic activities should be included in the organization's programs, although this same group reached consensus on the educational
merit of music, arts, gymnastics, archery, and team sports without any
difficulty.[34] The conservatives of the province consequently viewed the
activities of the Youth Corps, in this connection, as either frivolous or
downright inappropriate.

The Youth Corps also organized lectures on contemporary events. It
invited speakers who voiced open criticism of the province's Anhui militarists, which displeased the authorities. In the early months of 1919 the
Youth Corps Monthly, the newsletter of the organization, began voicing
its support for the New Culture and May Fourth Movements in Beijing.

These developments pushed the Youth Corps toward an ever closer identification with the liberal progressives in the north as opposed to the cultural conservatives in the south. The Youth Corps' activities also gave grounds to the conservative suspicion that the organization functioned as a following for the political opposition.[35]

PROMOTING CHANGE THROUGH PUBLISHING

The intellectual arm of the Zhejiang Educational Association under Jing Ziyuan was the association's official journal, *Tides in Education*. Between April 1, 1919, and its suspension by the Zhejiang provincial government in January 1920, the journal produced six issues at irregular intervals.[36] The theme of the journal in its first incarnation was the importance, the necessity, the naturalness, and the inevitability of change. "Tides are natural wonders," said the inaugural editorial, "They are infinitely complex in split seconds, and they are so overwhelming. . . . They break new ground endlessly, rejuvenating life with this incessant force of change." The tides "sweep away the decayed and break up the hollow." Tides are nature's way of releasing the hold of the old and hastening the birth of the new.[37]

What was the relevance of such changing coastal tides to Zhejiang's educational scene? According to the editor, Shen Zhongjiu, they were embodiments of a universal law of nature that inspired people of intelligence to think of the inevitability of change. Contrary to what some cultural conservatives would have liked to believe, moral teachings and classical doctrines were not immutable; they themselves must change to keep up with the changing times. Shen Zhongjiu welcomed novel ideas and urged fellow educators to do the same.[38]

The global trends for the new century, Shen believed, were headed toward a greater respect for humanitarian qualities and greater freedom for the individual. "It is the kind of thinking that is centered upon man, that sees the world as a world inhabited by man, that is opposed to all the established ways that refuse to treat man as the center of things." The "established ways" of the past were those of violence, invasion, military force, capitalist exploitation, and imperialism, all of which "dehumanized" human beings by turning them into objects or subjects of oppression and exploitation. The new trends of the century, on the other hand, were those of democratic rule, national self-determination, and communal sharing of wealth. Unlike the old order that was driven by greed and violence, in the new world it would become possible for individuals to pursue self-interest without sacrificing communal good.[39]

The responsibility of the new-style educators in this changing world was to come to a full appreciation of the global force of change and, by "yielding and responding" (*shunying*) to the emerging trends in human affairs, to conduct their affairs in such a way as "to hasten the passing of the old way that goes against the currents of time," to "facilitate the birth of a new order" that was for the benefit of all. A sensitive educator should have known by 1919, for example, that the "search for national wealth and power" was over and that "survival of the fittest" was something of a past credo. The new guiding principles were that educators, instead of teaching their students to become loyal subjects to state authorities, should place emphasis on the teaching of individual moral character; that schools must foster spirits of spontaneity, freedom, self-rule, and self-discipline; and that students should receive training in scientific reasoning. The purpose of this "new order" education was not to train compliance and obedience, but to give every educated person an independence of mind that would arm him against forces of coercion, while liberating him from constraining devices such as nations and boundaries.[40]

The first issue of the journal included a contribution by Jing Ziyuan entitled "On Education and the Times," which echoed Shen Zhongjiu's educational philosophy. Shen also gave himself ample space for the presentation of his views. He was the author of two additional pieces that were headlined "Democratic Education" and "What To Do about New and Old Ways of Thinking." He also wrote a highly critical open letter to Zhejiang's Provincial Assembly; he was not shy about showing them the right way of thinking and the right actions. Among his recommendations were the implementation of plans for local self-rule in Zhejiang and the creation in Hangzhou of an institute of higher education. Both proposals were aimed at the promotion of self-rule and the intellectual autonomy of the individual.[41]

The publication of the second issue of the journal coincided with the outbreak of the May Fourth Movement in Beijing. Shen Zhongjiu devoted his journal to the New Culture and student protests. When school resumed in fall 1919, he turned *Tides in Education* into a forum for the promotion of New Culture ideas such as linguistic reform and literary revolution, which were championed locally by First Normal's new-style Chinese teachers. In an effort to show that Zhejiang educators had their own contributions to make to the May Fourth Movement, the journal also publicized in its fall issue of 1919 the regulations of the student self-governing body at Zhejiang First Normal. The student government there was hailed as firsthand evidence of how democratic goals could be realized on school campuses where the correct educational philosophy had been recognized.[42]

Prior to the May Fourth Movement, Jing Ziyuan and Shen Zhongjiu were the main contributors to the early issues of the journal. Thereafter, the list of contributors expanded to include progressive faculty members and students of the First Normal School. Among the teachers who were also frequent contributors were Xia Mianzun, Liu Dabai, and Chen Wangdao—Chinese teachers who joined the faculty in fall 1919 and who enthusiastically supported the New Culture Movement. Among the student contributors were Yang Xianjiang, Wang Yuquan, and Shi Cuntong—student activists who became radicalized by their experience during the May Fourth Movement.[43] By late October 1919, these students were also editors of the iconoclastic student journal *Zhejiang xinchao* (Zhejiang new tide weekly). The editorial boards and contributing authors of *Tides in Education* and *Zhejiang New Tide Weekly* formed an interlocking network of teachers and students who shared iconoclastic views on a broadly defined range of cultural and political questions.

MENTORS AND FOLLOWERS

In secondary school circles in Hangzhou, several channels coexisted that exposed students to progressive ideas in the late 1910s. While a new approach to teaching began to appear on the campuses of many schools, thanks to the agitation of the Provincial Educational Association, many students were at the same time led in the direction of new cultural and political activities through their participation in extramural organizations such as the Youth Corps. Journals like *Tides in Education* played an important role in voicing viewpoints otherwise censored by the conservative authorities. More important, personal contacts and social interactions at public events, such as at the speeches and classes held in the Zhejiang Provincial Educational Association, brought together likeminded students and their mentors. Fu Binran, a senior student at First Normal, paid frequent social visits to Shen Zhongjiu at the latter's editorial office in the summer of 1919. Sometimes he went alone and sometimes in the company of a few schoolmates. Shen Zhongjiu had studied in Japan in an earlier decade and was well read in anarchist writings, which had been his interest since then. He introduced Fu Binran to anarchist literature, and Fu in turn shared his new discoveries with his First Normal classmates, including Shi Cuntong. Shen also had a wide network of friends and acquaintances among intellectuals and educators, and was familiar with the new-style publishing world.[44]

During the May Fourth Movement, Shen Zhongjiu played the role of advisor and a mentor to these students. It was on his suggestion that in October 1919 Fu Binran wrote to Ruan Yicheng, a student at the First Middle School, and took the first step in a series of developments that led to the creation of the Zhejiang New Tide Society shortly thereafter. Shen's advice also guided the editorial policies of the journal from its inception.

Under the leadership of Jing Ziyuan, then, a nexus of conjoined coteries was formed. Individuals were brought together through organizations such as the Youth Corps and the Provincial Educational Association. These organizations extended their influence to a much larger literate audience through the publication of new-style journals that propagated new cultural and political ideas. As editors and contributors, the progressive members of urban schools gained visibility in a national network of similarly oriented publishing activities. Writing and publishing led to a broad network of contact with progressives and reformers in other provinces. When confronting the militarists in their own province, the Zhejiang progressives, in that sense, were not acting in isolation. They were acting out their beliefs in full knowledge of fellow progressives based in Beijing, Shanghai, and other provincial capitals such as Changsha and Wuhan.

Jing Ziyuan held no formal post either in the provincial government or in the Provincial Assembly. So long as he continued to serve as the president of the First Normal School, ministry of education regulations prevented him from running for a seat in the assembly and from serving as the head of any professional association other than that of education.[45] Although Jing believed that the Provincial Educational Association should concern itself primarily with matters of education, he also believed that the nation's political future was rightfully the concern of educators. He regarded education as a critical instrument for the creation of a new social order and pursued organizational means that bordered on campaigns for social mobilization. In the eyes of some members of the Provincial Assembly, Jing was using the association and the First Normal School as institutional foci to build a personal following for his political agenda. From a loosely defined ideological or organizational perspective, the province's conservative authorities thought that they had good reasons to suspect in Jing's activism a threat to their interest. They therefore pinned high hopes on the provincial bureau of education and county educational offices to counter the association's influence.

GOVERNMENT INFRASTRUCTURE
IN PROVINCIAL EDUCATION

Although there was a ministry of education (*jiaoyu bu*) in the Republican government, reconstituted on the basis of the board of learning (*xuebu*) of the Qing, there were no provincial bureaus of education (*jiaoyu ting*) until September 1917, when the Beijing government promulgated a nine-article "temporary provision" defining their organization and jurisdiction. This delay reflected the early Republican state's hands-off attitude toward the actual funding and operation of local schools in the country, despite the government's desire to assert centralized control. The ministry of education, in its conception of that control, placed emphasis on regulatory stipulations and on official supervision. To avoid any possible collusion between officials and local elites, the government followed the rule of avoidance (that is, no official could serve in his home province), as had the imperial government previously. Among the dozen or so men appointed to become provincial educational ministers in 1917 was Wu Chongxue, chief of the general education section of the ministry of education and a native of Jiangsu, who was appointed to Zhejiang.

The National Federation of Educational Associations, arguing that local contribution was critical to the new school system, had previously petitioned the central government to exempt provincial educational appointments from the rule of avoidance. The state rejected the plea.[46] Members of the National Federation of Educational Associations, including Jing Ziyuan's Zhejiang association, nonetheless welcomed the creation of the provincial educational office, because they regarded it as a step toward the eventual professionalization of educational administration and had hoped to find in the official the understanding of a fellow educationalist. In Zhejiang, prior to the arrival of Minister Wu, the educators had to present their petitions for funding to the Provincial Assembly, which was by and large unsympathetic to their requests. In Jiangsu, the Provincial Educational Association often complained about dealing with "nonexperts" who understood little about "principles of education." The creation of a provincial bureau of education meant that educators would thereafter deal directly with the new minister, who might share the outlook of a new-style "education expert." The National Federation of Educational Associations, in fact, had repeatedly called for the appointment of such a provincial official in its annual meetings.[47]

In connection with the creation of the provincial educational office, the state revived, at the county level, the sub-bureaucratic *Quanxue suo*, or

"Centers for the Exhortation of Learning." This Qing-era creation under the New Policies took its name after Governor General Zhang Zhidong's treatise, *Quanxue pian* (Exhortation of learning), which had been named after a chapter in the classic *Xunzi*. The Quanxue suo, which drew on existing local leadership and resources to offer assistance to the county government, was defined by the ministry of education as an organ authorized "to take general charge of all educational matters" in the county. In the chain of administrative control the Quanxue suo was to provide the linkage between the county magistrate's office and lower-level districts. All communications on educational matters between the county and its lower-level districts were to be routed first to the Quanxue suo, then to the administrative unit on either end of the hierarchy.[48] The county Quanxue suo, according to Zhejiang's governor Qi Yaoshan, was the "central command in county educational affairs. It makes recommendations to the county magistrate, exercises direct supervision over subcounty offices, and reviews all educational activities in the county."[49] Unlike the Provincial Educational Association, the Quanxue suo was made into a link in the formal bureaucracy.

Within two months after Minister Wu's assumption of office in Hangzhou, all seventy-five counties in Zhejiang were equipped with an educational office. Shortly after that, Minister Wu called a general meeting in Hangzhou attended by the directors of all counties. The gathering, which lasted for a full ten days, began on November 24, 1917, in the auditorium of the First Normal School in Hangzhou and was attended by Wu together with his section chiefs and clerks from the bureau of education.

Wu opened the meeting by telling the county directors that they should "appreciate the officialdom's wish to bring order to local education," while at the same time "undertake measures that are in harmony with local opinion."[50] He then turned the podium over to the chair of the conference, elected on the spot. The sessions followed procedures adopted by the Zhejiang Provincial Educational Association in its annual meeting. County directors, representing their districts, presented proposals, discussed petitions, and put issues to vote. The Shaoxing director raised a concern with county educational funding and suggested that the state close down the studies run by old-style private tutors and divert their resources to new-style schools. The Jiangshan director opposed the suggestion and spoke at great length on how in his part of the province—the upper Qiantang hills, where old-style schoolmasters were greatly respected—reform and innovation must proceed with caution so as to "secure the good will of the people." But when the delegates voted to create a permanent staff for the conference of county directors of education, Minister Wu intervened and filled the positions with officials from his office.[51]

In the following months Minister Wu's position as the province's highest ranking education official came down to two basic points. On funding, he had little to offer, except to encourage the counties to be self-reliant and resourceful in coming up with their own solutions. "Educational development depends upon local development," he told another gathering of county representatives. "Counties must do what they can and explore means to do so to their own best ability. Only by enduring hardship will there be real gains."[52]

On schools, Wu's main interest was in tightening up student discipline. Time and again he sent orders to school principals instructing them to "put the campus community into proper order" by paying greater attention to student behavior. Principals, in particular, were enjoined to "supervise and control rigorously" their students so that all would learn to "love the country" and "set themselves up as examples to the rest of the society." Even the teachers, according to Wu, would benefit from some firm reminder of their duties of loyalty to the state. An ideal campus was a "serious and disciplined" place where everyone knew where he stood in the hierarchy and all behaved with deference and propriety. Wu regarded it as a particularly serious mistake to allow students to indulge in "merely intellectual pursuits" that placed them under undue "outside influence," such as that of Russian political thinking.[53] Altogether, the minister's comments resonated with those made by late Qing bureaucrats, who placed a similar emphasis on discipline and loyalty.

THE PROVINCIAL EDUCATIONAL ASSOCIATION'S AGENDA

While Minister Wu sought to rein in the county students, Jing Ziyuan concentrated instead on the creation of administrative and personnel regulations to professionalize the system. Jing was the author of an eighteen-article document entitled "Regulations on the Hiring of Full-Time Instructors," which spelled out in detail the terms governing matters such as employment contracts, teaching responsibilities, security of employment, salaries, promotions, ranking, retirement plans, life insurance, and so forth for the teachers. To put the draft into practice, he called a meeting that brought together the principals of Hangzhou's major secondary schools. After some discussion, the principals voted to adopt his draft. Since they were acting well within the range of their authority, they put Jing's

recommendations into effect immediately. The minister was simply notified of the matter in a polite letter that asked for his blessing.[54]

Jing Ziyuan then invited Minister Wu to attend the next meeting of
the Zhejiang Provincial Educational Association in the summer of 1918
and to share the podium with himself. The two men gave their respective
speeches to the assembled delegates and put emphasis on their different
concerns. Jing, already in tune with the spirit of change of the New
Culture Movement, spoke of eternal rejuvenation. Wu, still employing
the bureaucratic reformers' language of the late Qing, discussed the importance of a "citizen's education" (*guomin jiaoyu*) of loyalty to the state
and of proper observance of rites and rituals.[55] The latter, as he had
previously stated, referred to the "ritually proper behavior as prescribed
by the ancients." To train students in this behavior, "the teachers must
unite in one heart" and students must make the rituals "a part of their
everyday life."[56]

Where Wu stressed the moral and the hierarchical and invoked Beijing
as well as the ancients, Jing Ziyuan continued to busy himself with fraternal alliances with gentry progressives elsewhere. He attended, on behalf of the Zhejiang Provincial Educational Association, both the fourth
and fifth annual meetings of the National Federation of Educational Associations, which were hosted respectively by Jiangsu and Shanxi. There
he talked about the necessity to push for government funding of education, to create endowment funds for public schools, to implement plans for
compulsory elementary education. He also discussed the employment
prospects of secondary and normal school students on graduation, and, in
response to the call for vernacular literature by intellectual leaders of the
New Culture Movement, he evaluated the merits of vernacular Chinese in
teaching.[57]

From the mid-1910s onward, it had become increasingly difficult for
Zhejiang's normal school graduates to find suitable teaching positions.[58]
In response to the situation, the Zhejiang Provincial Educational Association devoted its energy, between 1917 and 1919, to the promotion of
several measures in the hope of restructuring the profession of teaching.
The group argued, first of all, for the implementation of a public-funded
compulsory educational plan for the entire province. Within that context,
the association insisted on a stringent review procedure of the teaching
credentials and professional qualifications of all elementary school teachers in the province. To complete the system within the province and to
provide opportunity for further education for graduates of Zhejiang's
secondary schools, the association proposed that the provincial govern-

ment consider creating a Zhejiang University. Altogether, the goal was to strengthen the system through its popularization, professionalization, and intellectualization.

Jing Ziyuan was clearly not the first person to demand that the state pay for compulsory elementary education. The National Federation of the Educational Associations had been agitating for it since 1917, and many gentry educators had voiced their support. Neither the state nor the gentry elites, however, possessed enough resources to make this possible. Even though the association was able to create a favorable climate of opinion for the plan, little was accomplished in this regard during the Republican period.

The call for standards in teaching qualifications was implicit in the progressive educators' overall drive toward the professionalization of new-style teaching. Drawing on theories of learning psychology and pedagogical methods made available in Chinese through translations, these educators discussed modern teaching in professional journals such as the Shanghai-based *Jiaoyu zazhi* (Chinese educational review) and insisted that the essence of new-style education was none other than pedagogical reform. This view placed the new educators in direct conflict with old-style schoolmasters, who continued to dominate village schools in many parts of the province. The goal of the new educators was no less than the total elimination of the old schools, and the teaching qualifications clause was but a first step in that direction. Minister Wu, caught between the Provincial Educational Association and many county educational associations in the south, was unable to commit himself to either position. As a gesture of response, he created the Review Committee on Zhejiang's Elementary School Teachers, and appointed the county educational directors to the task.[59]

The third proposal, which called for the creation of a Zhejiang University, ran into opposition with both the provincial government and the Provincial Assembly. Part of the problem had to do with a basic understanding about the new school system. To conservative minds that thought of the new system by analogy to the late dynasty's civil service examination system, universities were structural equivalents to the former imperial academies. The funding of a university, therefore, was the privilege—and responsibility—of the central government. Was it not a ritual usurpation, conservative politicians asked, for a province to sponsor a university at all? This scenario, however, does not fully explain the intensity with which the two sides clashed in October 1919. One cause, as we shall see, was simply the May Fourth Movement itself. Another was the political constitution of the assembly's membership and the alliance it formed with the Anhui Clique, which stood behind governors Yang Shande and Lu Yongxiang.

THE COMPOSITION
OF THE PROVINCIAL ASSEMBLY

On the eve of the May Fourth Movement the Provincial Assembly was dominated by an overrepresentation of delegates from the southern coastal prefecture of Taizhou, a rather isolated part of the province that served as a midway station for coastal trade between Ningbo and Wenzhou. The rise of the Taizhou faction in provincial administration began in 1912, when Qu Yingguang, a native of Taizhou's Linhai County, became the civilian governor of Zhejiang. As governor, Qu Yingguang appointed to the provincial bureaucracy in Hangzhou a large number of his fellow townsmen. To assure that Taizhou received a special share of representation in the Provincial Assembly, Qu Yingguang rigged the electoral process and manipulated the allocation of local representatives. In the Republic's first Provincial Assembly, which was elected to office in 1913, Taizhou supplied 23 percent of the assembly members, sending more representatives than all three prefectures of the western Zhejiang plains—Hangzhou, Jiaxing, Huzhou—combined, and more than twice as many as the affluent Ningbo Prefecture of coastal Zhejiang. In the second Republican Provincial Assembly, elected to office in 1918, Taizhou and its southern neighbor Wenzhou jointly held 114 of the 152 seats of the assembly. The election rules of the province at this time ostensibly called for individual prefects to contribute representatives in proportion to qualified electors. The results of the election census released in early 1918 showed, however, that of the three million Zhejiang residents with electoral rights (almost 15 percent of the population), almost 75 percent were in the hilly prefectures of Taizhou and Wenzhou on the southern and eastern coast. This could not possibly be in line with the reality of population distribution in Zhejiang, since a later population census, taken in 1933, showed that the Zhexi plains had one and a half million more inhabitants than Taizhou.[60]

To secure a dominant position in the Provincial Assembly, the Taizhou faction formed various political alliances with representatives from other prefectures and managed to bring under its leadership a bloc of southern assemblymen from the coastal hills and upper and middle Qiantang valleys of Wenzhou, Chuzhou, Jinhua, Quzhou, and Yanzhou. In 1918, Duan Qirui, the prime minister of the Beijing government and himself a native of Zhejiang's western neighbor, Anhui, sent delegates of his political faction, the Anfu Clique, to Hangzhou. The Anfu deputies made contact with the southern delegates in Zhejiang's Provincial Assembly and secured the latter's support for the Anhui Clique's position in the government in Beijing. In return, the Anhui Clique backed the southern assemblymen's choice of Zhou Jirong, a Taizhou representative, to become president of the Zhejiang Provincial Assembly. Zhou was elected over the opposition of the northern elites of the Zhexi plains and lower Qiantang: Hangzhou, Jiaxing, Huzhou, Ningbo, and Shaoxing. Riding on their recent victory, the southern assemblymen subsequently formed a political club—the Chenglu Club—which managed to elect two of its candidates to the vice presidency of the Provincial Assembly. At its organizational meeting, Jiang Bangyan, the leader of the Chenglu Club, addressed the faction's fifty-some members and declared that the conservative southern prefectures could now assert their interest against the liberal gentry reformers of the north.[61]

Assemblymen of Zhexi and the northern prefectures of Zhedong, in response, organized a Society of the Virtuous (Liangshe) in April 1919, which drew its membership largely from the constitutional law experts (or the republicanists) of the Provincial Assembly. Many members of the Society of the Virtuous were not only legal scholars and gentry reformers, but also former followers of Sun Yat-sen's Revolutionary Alliance in Tokyo and current supporters of Sun's ideas for a republican government with a constitutional parliament.[62] The organizer of the Society of the Virtuous was none other than Ruan Xingcun, the legal expert and Yuyao representative of Shaoxing Prefecture, who was Jing Ziyuan's close ally and strong supporter in the Zhejiang Provincial Educational Association.[63] Although Jing Ziyuan's membership in Sun Yat-sen's revolutionary party was inferred rather than confirmed at this time in the public's eye,[64] the conservative majority of the Provincial Assembly nonetheless attributed the organizational build-up of the Zhejiang Provincial Educational Association to the growing influence of the Guomindang within the province. Since it was Sun Yat-sen's declared goal to launch a military northern expedition and bring down the unconstitutional government dominated by the militarists in Beijing, national struggles over the political future of China were thus joined with regional contests within Zhejiang's provincial context, as the Chenglu Club and the Society of the Virtuous fought over issues that brought home to Zhejiang the daily significance of larger national political and cultural divisions.

A CLASH

The Provincial Assembly conservative majority's distrust of Jing Ziyuan and his educational association came to a head in April 1919, when Shen Zhongjiu, the editor of *Tides in Education*, published "An Open Letter to Members of the Zhejiang Provincial Assembly" in his journal, urging the legislators to accept Jing Ziyuan's proposals to create a Zhejiang University, to begin funding compulsory elementary education for all county schools, and to establish a public institute for the translation and compilation of new textbooks. Representatives of the largely agrarian south viewed these measures as attempts not only to enhance the influence of the professional elites of the culturally liberalizing north, but also to facilitate the dissemination of dangerous new ideas that threatened to undercut their conservative base in the provincial hinterland. They were particularly suspicious of the motion to create a Zhejiang University, which had long received the vocal support of such prominent national figures as Cai Yuanpei, president of Beijing University.

The petition to create a Zhejiang University was first presented to the Provincial Assembly in May 1918. In a written statement to the assembly, Jing Ziyuan pointed out that no institutes of higher education had ever been created in Zhejiang, except in specialized areas of law and medicine. Zhejiang secondary school graduates in pursuit of higher education consequently had to leave the province, a condition that "resulted in a major loss of our best talents to other places." In addition, the province as a whole had lost touch with its own cultural tradition—so much so that "young scholars of the present day no longer recognize the names of Wuyuan (Zhu Xi) and Yaojiang (Wang Yangming)," the two leading masters of Song and Ming Neo-Confucianism who had made Zhejiang their home. Without a modern-style institute of higher education, the province risked becoming a cultural backwater, in which "the talents of many young students are wasted, because they find it difficult to sustain distant travel. Some have consequently been forced to give up their desire to pursue advanced study."[65]

Although the proposal was enthusiastically embraced by the progressive elite, it was flatly rejected by the Provincial Assembly. Jing petitioned his case a second time in April 1919, timing his presentation with the publication of Shen Zhongjiu's article in *Tides in Education*. The Provincial Assembly refused to reconsider. The petition was once again turned down.[66]

In October 1919 the Provincial Educational Association presented the petition a third time. By then the political atmosphere in Hangzhou had become charged by the student demonstrations and intellectual iconoclasm of the May Fourth Movement during the previous summer. Jing Ziyuan presented a thoroughly revised petition, in which he made explicit the New Culture outlook that informed the association's support for such a motion. He told the Provincial Assembly that "global trends of thought are in a state of change and rejuvenation." The sagely norms of Confucian masters were subject to the law of evolutionary progress as much as everything else. For Zhejiang to keep alive its cultural life at all, there had to be a university that would serve "to entertain the great diversity of new thoughts in their entirety, to adjust the province to the rapid changes of the present time, and to guide young students toward an understanding of the evolutionary process." Echoing an iconoclastic view first enunciated by political revolutionaries, Jing Ziyuan went on to state that the future of the province as well as the nation rested with the daring youth of the present day, instead of their conservative seniors as in the past. Young students "are pillars and saviors of the nation." A university in Zhejiang was necessary not only for the educational benefit of individual students—it was for the benefit of the nation as a whole that Zhejiang's talented youth receive advanced instruction in the latest knowledge.[67]

The Provincial Assembly met shortly after the publicization of Jing Ziyuan's proposals. After heated debates with members of the Society of the Virtuous, the conservative majority, led by the Chenglu Club, rejected Jing Ziyuan's initiative and then proceeded to vote for an increase in salaries for its own members. The discussions and voting took place in the presence of a group of First Normal students who had come to the assembly in the hope of witnessing the creation of a Zhejiang University. Disappointed and irritated by what they saw, some students shouted insults at the assemblymen. Guards were called and fights broke out. As emotions ran high, First Normal students burst forth on the floor of the assembly and began smashing up the hall. In the ensuing brawl "the air of dignity" of several conservative members "suffered a serious blow."[68] Jing Ziyuan's allies in the Society of the Virtuous—those who "recognize the importance of educational funding, uphold justice, and oppose the salary increase for assembly members"—on the other hand, were treated with respect and ushered out of the chaos with much dignity.[69] It was understandable that Jing Ziyuan was firmly held by the conservative majority of the Provincial Assembly to have been the instigator of this unruly student mob.

Many strands of development, as the next chapter will show, had joined together in the months between April and October 1919, to stretch the long-existing tension between the conservatives and the progressives to the bursting point of open hostility. In late spring, the May Fourth Movement erupted in Hangzhou. Thousands of students swarmed Hangzhou's streets shouting slogans against the conservative provincial authorities. By early fall, Hangzhou students were publishing radical journals, openly forming intellectual alliances with radical iconoclasts in Shanghai and Beijing, espousing their goals, and shunning the state celebration of Confucius. Jing Ziyuan and his First Normal students were serving notice that they had rejected the political language of the Confucian state. Conservatives in the assembly decried Jing Ziyuan's abuse of provincial resources as the head of their best-funded public educational enterprise. Funds entrusted to Jing's headmastership, indeed, had been used to help promote "Russian radicalism," to denounce Confucius, and to destroy ethical norms. With much anger and outrage, the conservatives charged that the progressives were attempting "to bring down the sacred order of our ancestors."[70]

7 The May Fourth Movement in Hangzhou

When news about the Beijing student demonstrations of May 4, 1919, reached Zhejiang, Hangzhou's secondary school students mobilized to respond. Delegates of fourteen schools met on May 9 to discuss plans for action. Three days later, at eight o'clock in the morning, more than three thousand students of all grades gathered in the Number Two and Number Three Parks by West Lake. Shouting slogans such as "Assert our nation's rights internationally!" and "Punish the traitors among us!" they proclaimed the creation of the Hangzhou Student League of National Salvation, as rally organizers raised a huge banner featuring the league's name, which billowed over them as they paraded back into the city, waved small national flags, and distributed handbills as they marched along.[1]

The procession marched first to the office of the military governor of Zhejiang, the ailing Yang Shande, and shouted "Return our Qingdao"—the Shandong city in dispute—three times. It then marched to the office of the governor of Zhejiang, Qi Yaoshan, where the same slogan was repeated six times. The procession finally reached the Zhejiang Provincial Assembly and presented a petition demanding that the assembly, in turn, petition the Beijing government to reject the Versailles Peace Treaty and punish the three Chinese negotiators—Cao Rulin, Zhang Zongxiang, and Lu Zongyu—as traitors. The assembly accepted the written petition.[2] After a full day of marching and demonstrating, students dispersed peacefully before dusk.[3]

The primary weapon of the students in Hangzhou, as in other places during the May Fourth Movement, was the boycott of Japanese goods. Organizing the boycott required the support of influential local merchants. The Hangzhou Merchants' Association (Shanghui) was a federation of self-regulating merchants that acted on the one hand as tax broker and on the other as regulator of trade practices. It also served as a chamber of commerce to represent merchant interests. Like similar chambers in other Chinese cities that summer, it responded sympathetically to the students' patriotic appeals to support a boycott against Japanese goods. The Merchants' Association consequently authorized the Hangzhou students to organize teams of inspectors who went about the streets conducting inventory checks of local stores. Armed with that authorization, the student inspectors confiscated contraband goods and forced store managers to cancel their outstanding orders of Japanese imports. Recalcitrant shopkeepers were threatened with retaliation and sometimes coerced with the unpleasant prospect of a parade down the streets for public denunciation.

With the support of their teachers, Hangzhou students also mobilized for a campaign to arouse the patriotism of the public. Classrooms were abandoned, with students taking to the streets to distribute handbills and give lectures. Some went as far as they were able to into the outskirts of Hangzhou to lecture peasant women and children in the villages. To keep attention focused on the issue, from time to time a group of students would file past the tightly shut gates of the Japanese consulate, waving little paper flags and shouting "Return our Shandong!" Some spent their day at the train station to intercept citybound cargoes of Japanese imports. Participants in these historic events remembered that the students at the railway station more often than not amused themselves with improvised games of pebbles to pass the time as they waited for the next train to arrive.[4]

As the momentum started to flag in late May, Fang Hao, a student representative from Beijing University and a native of Zhejiang, arrived home from Beijing. The sagging student movement in the province was temporarily revived. Fang Hao gave numerous public lectures and worked to forge a link between the demonstrators in Beijing and Hangzhou in preparation for a national student strike. On May 29, three days after nearly ten thousand Shanghai students met to declare their strike, the student union of Hangzhou announced its own strike[5] and called on all secondary and normal schools in the rest of the province to do the same.[6]

As police chiefs from Jilin to Fuzhou, from Shanghai to Wuhan, cabled reports of strikes and incidents involving impassioned students and local resident Japanese, the Beijing government became increasingly nervous about the ramifications of the spreading unrest.[7] The ministry of education's initial attempt to restore order by putting pressure on school administrators had yielded negative results, especially after Cai Yuanpei, the president of Beijing University, resigned in protest. The police thus became the only means for the central government to bring students back to the classrooms in the capital.

On June 4, when thousands of Beijing students defied government orders and once again staged street demonstrations, over three hundred were arrested by the military and the police. Minister of Education Yuan Xitao resigned immediately. When news of the police repression spread, it touched off in Shanghai and Guangzhou not only major student demonstrations in support of the arrested patriots but also mobilization among industrial workers for the first time. In Shanghai, nearly seventy thousand workers walked off their jobs, spearheading a general strike that shut down schools and factories as well as shops and services. The general strike, organized with the support of Shanghai's General Chamber of Commerce, instantly plunged the financial market into chaos. Cabled messages were sent to Beijing "like snowflakes" with urgent reports of the runs that had been started on several branches of the state-owned Communications Bank.[8]

In Zhejiang, railway workers in Hangzhou and Ningbo were the first ones to strike in response to the action taken by their fellow mechanics, conductors, operators, and porters on the Shanghai end of the line. Dockworkers in Ningbo refused to handle Japanese goods and demanded an increase in their wages. By mid-June, not only had the shutdown of factories, shipping, and transportation facilities spread to include among the affected areas Hangzhou, Ningbo, Shaoxing, Wenzhou, and Ruian, but it had also drawn into the movement the shopkeepers and their clerks in these cities.[9]

Hangzhou student movement diverged significantly from student responses in Beijing and Shanghai—to the alarm of activists within the Hangzhou student association. The flagging of energy in late May had been only temporarily forestalled by the efforts of Fang Hao. On May 30, just one day after the student association's call to strike classes, the Zhejiang provincial government announced that summer recess for Hangzhou students was to begin immediately. On that same day the majority of Hangzhou students set out on their way home, dispersed into the scores of counties in all parts of the province.[10] Student protestors in Hangzhou thus never acted in conjunction with the province's striking workers, and, later, the striking shop clerks. Also unlike their counterparts in Beijing and Shanghai, they acted with considerable restraint, observing government orders such as the ban on student gatherings. The Hangzhou students' alliance was able to bring out only a few dozen delegates to its meetings, and most of its efforts consisted primarily of the issuance of prepared statements.[11]

In Hangzhou, order was restored by the provincial government with surprising ease, and the authorities had no need to call on the armed police and the soldiers. These developments left the radicals among the students, including Shi Cuntong and Fu Binran of the senior class of First Normal School, angry and disappointed. Their restlessness was further enhanced by a sense of shame when they read sharp criticisms of Zhejiang students in the Shanghai-based publication *Xingqi pinglun* (Weekend review).

The journal, a weekly attached to the daily *Minguo ribao* (Republican daily), was coedited by Dai Jitao and Shen Xuanlu, senior members of Sun Yat-sen's Guomindang and prominent statesmen in early Republican politics. Beginning publication in the aftermath of the May Fourth incident, the journal's declared goal was to engage in "uninhibited criticism" (*ziyou pipan*) of contemporary Chinese philosophy, literature, society, and political life. The editors sought "friends who share our views" as well as "friends who spur us on to sharpen our moral sensitivity."[12] Regular contributors included not only Sun Yat-sen's other close associates such as Liao Zhongkai and Zhu Zhixin, but also Shen Zhongjiu and Liu Dabai, of Hangzhou's progressive intellectual circle. The journal featured, among other subjects, discussions on women's liberation and Confucian familial ethics. It was a radical voice that was highly influential, especially among intellectuals in the coastal southeast of China.

The very week that Hangzhou students went home for the summer, *Weekend Review* printed a scathing commentary on the May Fourth Movement in Hangzhou. The sentiment was most likely supplied by the frustrated Shen Xuanlu, who had been the president of Zhejiang's Provincial Assembly for a brief while in 1916, before the Anfu Clique seized control of the province. The article expressed deep disappointment with the docility of Hangzhou students. It observed that the level of political consciousness of Hangzhou students was far below that of their counterparts in Beijing and Shanghai. "The tidal bore at the mouth of the Qiantang River had always impressed viewers with its majestic power," wrote the commentator; yet the tide of student demonstrations, which engulfed the country from north to south, was effortlessly stemmed with mere verbal commands by the authorities. On receiving those official instructions, "the seemingly fearless students [of Zhejiang] . . . beat a hasty retreat and dispersed instantly like birds and beasts into the woods without a trace. . . . Shouldn't these deserters feel ashamed of themselves, seeing how others elsewhere have courageously charged into enemy ranks and taken outposts and fortresses?" In a backhanded fashion, the report went on to absolve the students of personal responsibility for their behavior. It fixed the blame on the educational system and attacked the "servile," "rigid," "mechanical," and "commercialized" nature of school education in Zhejiang. These imperfect schools produced deficient students incapable of independent action and thought. Consequently, at moments of revolutionary significance such as the May Fourth Movement, Zhejiang students were able to show only "the qualities of tamed slaves" in their inability to act.[13] Comments in this vein, coming from a group of respected intellectual leaders, embarrassed students like Shi Cuntong deeply, and Shi was accordingly impelled to act on his beliefs regardless of the outcome.[14]

THE ACADEMIC REORIENTATION
OF THE FIRST NORMAL SCHOOL

Although the May Fourth Movement in Zhejiang failed to reach a level of societal mobilization comparable to that in Beijing and Shanghai, it nonetheless opened the floodgate for a wider dissemination in Hangzhou of iconoclastic journals and vernacular literature associated with the New Culture Movement. Through printed words and shared ideas, campus life in Hangzhou underwent a subtle reorientation toward an emerging national culture of iconoclasm. For guidance and inspiration, radical students in particular began to look to Westernized intellectual and political leaders in Beijing and Shanghai, and away from venerable masters of Confucian learning in their own province. The students did not entirely turn their backs on Zhejiang's scholastic traditions in their effort to embrace the New Culture Movement, however; they brought some of those very special ethical concerns of Zhejiang's Neo-Confucian learning to the new tide, resulting in a May Fourth iconoclasm of unique intensity and fervor.

The new orientation coincided, during the summer of 1919, with a significant shift in the academic atmosphere at the First Normal School, attendant on a crucial change in personnel in the Chinese faculty. After the first wave of May Fourth agitation swept over First Normal's students, Shan Pei and his senior colleagues—all leading members of what might be called the "old school"—resigned. The three replacement teachers were Xia Mianzun, Liu Dabai, and Chen Wangdao, younger and all with foreign educational experiences.[15] All three favored the teaching of vernacular over classical literature, and all were outspoken in their criticism of traditional moral norms. They were not erudites and classicists, but poets, essayists, editors, translators, and political activists. Unlike their predecessors, they did not trace their intellectual genealogy up the Qiantang into the middle counties of Zhejiang's glorious Neo-Confucian past. Though natives of Zhedong, they had acquired their training in places like Shanghai and Tokyo, and were connected with a network of fellow intellectuals who were busy writing, publishing, teaching, and translating in metropolitan centers. All three later achieved considerable eminence in Republican history as cultural and political figures in their own right. Although information is sketchy on what these men taught at the First Normal School in the fall of 1919, there is a wealth of material about their thoughts and deeds in the 1920s. On the basis of these later developments, it is possible to surmise what must have been already in the air in the fall of 1919, when the new teachers began to reorient the school's curriculum.

The most senior of the three teachers was Xia Mianzun, who had been educated in Japan and earned national fame in 1926 as the translator from Japanese of the best-selling Italian novel *Cuore* (Heart), by Edmondo de Amicis (1846–1908).[16] In 1933 Xia published, along with Ye Shengtao, an essay collection entitled *Wenxin* (The heart of literature), in which he detailed his views on reading and writing for an audience of secondary school teachers and students.

Cuore, translated into Chinese as *Ai de jiaoyu* (Education of love), was a story about an elementary school pupil's moral education, told principally in the form of the child's diary kept over a period of ten months. Besides the daily entries, there were longer chapters that purported to be the child's notes on the teacher's instructions. These chapters appeared at monthly intervals and consisted of didactic tales on national honor, moral self-assertion, independence, and the virtues and rewards of hard work.[17]

Cuore, as Xia Mianzun noted in the translator's preface to the Chinese edition, "idealized the affective bond between father and son, teacher and student, the bond that brings friends together and unites the community and the nation." Itself a product of the nationalistic fervor of the Italian risorgimento, *Cuore* lavished praise on civic virtues and glorified military feats.[18] Although the ethos of the novel marched in perfect step with Nationalist China's quest in the 1930s for a civil society based on communal spirit, military discipline, and the virtues of endurance and diligence, for Xia Mianzun and his secondary school readers the special appeal of *Cuore* lay in its emphasis on the power of moral persuasion by example, plus its sentimental treatment of family relationships. In translation the novel was melodramatic and didactic, with rivers of repentent tears and heartfelt embraces of reconciliation. For its Chinese readers, the book affirmed the value of emotional expressiveness as opposed to ritual appropriateness. Xia's translation was highly popular among China's youth in the Republican period. Excerpts from it were also used in secondary school textbooks.[19]

Xia Mianzun's essay collection *Wenxin* presents his literary and pedagogical views on reading and writing in the voice of a secondary school student in the "First Middle School" in a certain "H. City" that was about half a day by train from Shanghai.[20] Because *Wenxin* was intended to be studied in the classroom, it contained discussions of literary genres and the grammar of the Chinese language. The more significant part was Xia's discussion of composition.

There are basically two kinds of composition, Xia Mianzun writes: those that perform a certain function and those that permit a particular expression. The former type of composition is used for reports, legal contracts, and diplomatic treaties; it argues, persuades, and concludes. Composition of the latter type is aesthetic and can be further divided into two categories: an aestheticism that permits the expression of genuine feelings and thoughts, and an aestheticism that derives its sense of delight from the form, rhythm, imagery, and allusions of the language. Xia Mianzun endorses unequivocally the aestheticism of self-expression and equates the aestheticism of formalism with literary classicism. Because language, like any other social and cultural institution, develops over time, Xia Mianzun argues that classical Chinese, along with the literary genres of the past, is an anachronistic artifact that cannot adequately serve the needs of the modern Chinese for communication and self-expression. It becomes the responsibility of modern students, therefore, to develop and enrich the vernacular language.

As for reading, Xia Mianzun reminds his readers to keep in mind the historical changes that have taken place in society and to disengage themselves from the charm of the past by restoring classical literature to its proper historical context. Take, for example, the reading of the six idyllic poems entitled "On Returning to My Home in the Countryside" (*Gui tianyuan ju*) by the Jin poet Tao Yuanming (365–427). Tao's vocabulary, Xia Mianzun points out, has lost its original meaning as a result of changes in socioeconomic circumstances.

> The majority of us do not have acres of land that we may retire to in the countryside. We are caught in the web of mundane relationships in the cities. We live in rooms for which we pay a monthly rent to the landlord. We consume rice for which we pay ten-some yuan per *dan* to the rice merchant. We wear fabrics woven on a machine. We walk on streets crowded with vehicles and pedestrians. . . . Tao's vocabulary bears no relevance to our urban existence in the modern age. We must, therefore, enjoy idyllic poems only as the urban rich would enjoy a vacation in the countryside, as a change of pace and a form of diversion. These poems are but a form of pastime for us.

The modern countryside would never again produce a poet like Tao Yuanming and poems like "On Returning to My Home in the Countryside."

Xia continues: "Every period in history is characterized by its special circumstances. Those of us reading literary works of the past in the present day must keep in mind those historical considerations. The ancients might not have intended to mislead us. We must always be alert to such historical differences in order to avoid a confusion in time." A poet of our own time, Xia Mianzun suggests, should be like the Russian poets who praise the intense rhythm of work in modern factories, using vocabulary such as *workshop, iron, furnace, hammer,* and *uniform* to eulogize the power and efficiency of the machine.[21] These factory poems are genuine products of our time, according to Xia, because they convey thoughts and experiences present not in the literary tradition but in the everyday reality of the present.

Xia Mianzun did not wish to go so far as to suggest that the classical literary tradition should be completely banished from modern classrooms. He was careful to relegate classicism to the past, however, and to admit only its historical and scholarly relevance. Like Hu Shi and Chen Duxiu during the New Culture Movement of 1917–19, Xia Mianzun strongly favored the use of vernacular over classical Chinese. He encouraged secondary school students to discover fresh imagery and to enrich the living language by using the vernacular as a vehicle for self-reflection as well as to describe real social phenomena. The purpose of writing was neither to celebrate the classical tradition nor to strike a literati posture, but to engage oneself with contemporary socioeconomic issues and give words to one's true feelings.

Xia Mianzun's colleague at First Normal, the poet Liu Dabai, shared these basic tenets about the historical evolution of language and literature.[22] Classical Chinese, Liu believed, was an arcane language that had been drained of living substance by his time. Its domination of high culture in imperial times was never challenged, however, because it served as such a convenient linguistic instrument for the gentry and the bureaucracy to exercise their political domination over the people. As a result of this domination, moreover, ordinary people were deprived of a medium of expression in the political realm; they had no voice of their own.[23] Liu vehemently attacked the leading modern classicist Zhang Taiyan for obfuscating the written language, the better to perpetuate this intellectual hegemony over a politically voiceless population.[24]

Because in the Confucian moral order, according to Liu, the power of the ruler was based on the power of the patriarch, the ethical foundation of the imperial political order was the family. Liu Dabai spent much of the summer of 1919 writing vernacular poems and essays for the *Weekend Review,* in which he attacked that ethical foundation outright. In a short piece entitled "The Prisonhouse of Thought" (*Sixiang de jianyu*), Liu assailed the most fundamental moral teachings of Confucianism. He charged that the sacred norms of ritual appropriateness, the "three bonds" and "five constants" that structured every aspect of relationships in the Chinese family, were in fact cruel and draconian prison rules that had deprived the Chinese for thousands of years of intellectual freedom, emotional sensitivity, and personal happiness. Confucius, in Liu's depiction, was the supreme prison god; and all the Confucian masters of the past two thousand years had functioned as jail wardens guarding the high walls and defending the eternal darkness that ruled beyond death.[25]

Liu Dabai's influence on the students of First Normal in the fall and winter of 1919–20 appeared to stem from sources other than just the purely intellectual. Liu was a prolific poet in the vernacular, and in the late 1910s he wrote primarily to chronicle the vicissitudes of his unconventional love affair with his future wife, He Fuxia.[26] He was conscious of the provocative nature of his courtship and romance in the eyes of cultural conservatives, and he defended himself by attacking their traditional norms:

> The norms of proper behavior created an oppressive atmosphere. As a result, Chinese men and women of the past several thousand years had never been allowed to express their romantic feelings. . . . The system of oppression has now collapsed, swept away by the strong current of the new tide. Romantic love can now be expressed. Modern poets turn to love poems, and as they are liberated from the restrictions of traditional literary forms, are able to express themselves fully and without inhibition, through the new linguistic medium. Their poetic creations are far superior to the traditional poems in expressiveness and affectiveness. Is this not the most encouraging sign in the development of poetry of the present day?

Liu Dabai went further than Xia Mianzun in linking his championship of vernacular literature to a new course of action—whether political in his overall endorsement of the Nationalist enterprise in Guangzhou, or personal in his pursuit of romantic love and rejection of the conventional norms of appropriate behavior. His saga seemed so intriguing to his students that years later some still entertained ideas of turning their teacher's love story into a novel.[27]

Before his appointment to the Chinese faculty of the First Normal School, Liu Dabai had served as a personal secretary to Shen Xuanlu, the president of Zhejiang's Provincial Assembly in 1916. In 1919, he was a frequent contributor to Shen's Shanghai-based journal, the *Weekend Review*, where he published vernacular poems and essays on women.[28] He was thus able to provide the critical introduction of the young radicals at First Normal, such as Shi Cuntong, to Shen Xuanlu and his coeditor, Dai Jitao.[29] This association was significant in two respects. First, it helped to bring the events in Hangzhou to the attention of the intellectual and political progressives in Beijing, Shanghai, and Guangzhou.[30] Second, Shen Xuanlu and Dai Jitao were both noted in the late 1910s for their progressive thinking and their radical concern with social and economic issues. Shen Xuanlu's interests in this regard became a major source of influence on Hangzhou student activists during 1919–20. His own political connections paved the way for the Hangzhou students' involvement with the Marxism Study Society in Shanghai the following year.

It was not until 1923 that Shen Xuanlu's socialist leanings found full expression in his sponsorship of a land reform experiment in his home county of Xiaoshan, where he liberated his own tenants.[31] This action prompted tenants elsewhere to revolt. The experiment culminated in a sizable tenant uprising in Yaqian, which was put down mercilessly by the landlords. Although Liu Dabai was the author of a long poem in 1923 that was dedicated to the memory of Li Chenghu, the leader of the Yaqian uprising, there is no evidence in Liu Dabai's collected works that his sympathy for the poor led him to believe in the necessity of a socialist revolution in China.[32] In fact, after the establishment of the Nationalist government in 1927, Liu Dabai took up high-ranking positions first in Zhejiang's bureau of education and later in Nanjing's ministry of education until his resignation in 1930. He was later denounced by the Communists and accused of refusing to exercise his political influence to save the life of a former First Normal student, Ye Tiandi, who was executed in 1927 by the Nationalists as a member of the Communist Party.[33]

While Xia Mianzun and Liu Dabai concentrated their energies on the literary and linguistic aspects of the New Culture Movement, Chen Wangdao, the third new member of the Chinese faculty, was a major influence in the politicization of First Normal students in 1919. Whereas Liu was a new-style poet who had rebelled against his old-fashioned literary training, and Xia was a sentimental pedagogue with an eloquent prose style, Chen Wangdao was an unabashed ideologue who arrived at the First Normal School with a bachelor's degree in law from Chuo University in Japan.[34] At First Normal he taught the use of phonetic alphabets and punctuation and presented the rules of grammatical and rhetorical analysis, placing emphasis on the "scientific" precision of his teaching.[35] More important, Chen Wangdao formed and directed student interest in contemporary social and political issues, such as the living conditions of common laborers and the role of women in traditional Chinese families. He also led the students to examine the ethical meaning of traditional practices such as prearranged marriages and concubinage.[36]

Chen Wangdao's emphasis on these issues found full expression in the articles that he contributed to the journal *Laodong jie* (Labor circle),[37] which appeared in the fall and winter of 1920–21, and a series of articles on marital arrangements, divorce, inheritance law, and women's right to education that were published in the "Funü pinglun" (Commentaries on women's issues) section of the *Republican Daily* between 1920 and 1923, which he also edited. Meanwhile, Chen Wangdao devoted himself to the study of theories of socialism. In the winter of 1920 he completed the first unabridged Chinese translation of the *Communist Manifesto*, which appeared in print the following spring in Shanghai as one of the earliest publications on socialism issued by the Marxism Study Society.[38]

Chen Wangdao's importance to the First Normal radicals became evident in 1920, when developments in Hangzhou compelled reformers and activists, including Chen, to leave the city. Chen Wangdao moved to Shanghai, where he joined the Chinese faculty of Fudan University in September 1920. He became actively involved in the organization of the Marxism Study Society and the Communist Youth Corps (Gongchanzhuyi qingnian tuan), and served twice as the editor of *New Youth* in the winter and spring of 1920–21 when Chen Duxiu, the founder of the Chinese Communist Party, left for Guangzhou to become the dean of the Nationalist Party's Sun Yat-sen University.[39]

As will be discussed later, when First Normal radical students such as Shi Cuntong and Yu Xiusong arrived in Shanghai in April 1921, it was their former teacher Chen Wangdao who introduced them to the radical intellectuals who had been part of the *New Youth* circle based in Beijing.[40] Chen Wangdao's presence in Shanghai helped channel the socialist leanings of the Hangzhou iconoclasts into actual membership in an organized Communist movement, although Chen himself preferred not to join.[41]

Although these three teachers later turned out to take considerably different political positions, in the fall of 1919 their ideas and activities presented, each in its own way, powerful challenges to the authority of the provincial conservatives. With the support of Principal Jing Ziyuan, the iconoclastic young teachers proceeded to reform the Chinese curriculum of First Normal. Open-ended seminar discussions took the place of old-fashioned lectures, and active explorations of social issues displaced the philological and textual scholarship of the past year. Along with the use of the vernacular language a new kind of teacher-student relationship developed that was far more egalitarian than the deferential hierarchy of masters and disciples copied by Shan Pei from the age of the classics and celebrated in the schools of Neo-Confucian learning.[42] Education, in the final analysis, was to help advance social changes and to be at the service of a political program. Regardless of whether they turned out to become supporters of the Nationalist or the Communist Party, the three teachers were as one in their efforts to bury the bookish classicism that had been Zhejiang's pride for centuries. Together they encouraged their students to open up the province to the new tides that were rising and swelling in centers such as Shanghai and Beijing.

CHANGES IN STUDENT LIFE
AT THE FIRST NORMAL

In the fall of 1919, Shi Cuntong and Fu Binran, a fellow senior at First Normal, opened on their own initiative a student bookstore called the New Life Book Society, which was dedicated to the dissemination of New Culture publications in the province. The best-sellers on their stands were *New Youth* magazine and *Weekend Review*. The new tide of iconoclasm was certainly sweeping over Hangzhou's students. More than four hundred copies of these two journals were sold weekly on the First Normal campus alone, which was roughly the school's total enrollment.[43] Shi Cuntong also went out twice a week with a few friends to the public athletic field at West Lake, where they set up a mobile distribution center to display over a dozen new-style journals in the hope of reaching a larger general audience.[44]

Jing Ziyuan openly declared in the fall of 1919 that the May Fourth Movement had convinced him of the province's urgent need for a new kind of education and that he intended to carry out the necessary changes at the First Normal School. To train and nurture the pupils' civic virtues as citizens of a democratic republic, Jing permitted First Normal students to elect their own representatives and to create a self-governing body that replaced faculty supervisors of student affairs. On the critical question of "deportment" in particular, faculty members were relegated to the position of mere advisors, while students were expected to carry out fully their "self-rule" (*zizhi*). When Shi Cuntong wrote to Shen Xuanlu to discuss the matter, the Shanghai editor responded enthusiastically with an article in the *Weekend Review*. Student self-rule encouraged not only a new way to exercise moral authority in schools, but a voluntary code of conduct against "the evil habits of the old society," such as drinking, smoking, gambling, and visiting prostitutes. The ascetic ethics of the students were built on a modern conception of socially moral behavior: in the equal sharing of manual labor, in wholesome recreation, in communal cooperation, and in mutual caring and respect for all members of the society. Self-rule in school was thus an all-important first step toward the ultimate realization of an egalitarian society built on mutual love and self-regard.[45]

To develop the students' ability for critical thinking and self-expression, Jing Ziyuan authorized a complete curriculum reform in the Chinese program. Under the new program modern vernacular Chinese, instead of classical literary Chinese, was formally adopted as the language of study. For classroom instruction, extensive usage was made of vernacular essays published in contemporary journals, in place of literary collections and classical canons compiled in the past. Pedagogical approaches were revised accordingly. Students were urged to read critically and to embark on research of their own, to familiarize themselves with contemporary intellectual debates and social issues, to present materials and develop viewpoints on topics of their own choice instead of at the teacher's behest, and to give lectures and engage in open-ended discussions on their findings.[46] The emphasis of training was shifted from high literacy and erudition to the development of a student's ability to express himself in the vernacular on issues of contemporary social and cultural significance, such as familial relationships, female chastity, literary genres, and so forth. Leading iconoclasts of the New Culture Movement—Chen Duxiu, Qian Xuantong, Liu Bannong, and Hu Shi, who mounted extensive attacks on nearly all aspects of Chinese cultural tradition and social institutions—became the new icons in the eyes of the students and displaced the Confucian sages.[47]

THE RITES CONTROVERSY

With Confucianism under heavy attack as the outdated ethical norm of an inferior past and as the source of contemporary conservative political power, it was only natural that Confucian rituals on the campus of First Normal, so reverently preserved and performed in an earlier time, should also come under attack. In the autumn of 1919, when Governor Qi Yaoshan, the former personal staff aide to the conservative Governor General Zhang Zhidong, was preparing to lead the annual ceremony in the Confucian temple to commemorate the Sage's birthday, the students of First Normal refused to take their usual part as ritual dancers in the temple courtyard. The governor, whom the students contemptuously nicknamed *liuli dan* (slippery egg), took this as both a personal affront and a scandalous breach of sacred protocol.[48] He also recognized in it the defeat of cultural conservatives by educational progressives in the field of teaching, which led the students to violate sacred norms in their pursuit of new ideas.

To make matters worse, Principal Jing, who also had an important ritual role to play in the worship and was duty-bound to rein in the students, announced his own plan to be away in Shanxi to attend the fifth annual meeting of the National Federation of Educational Associations. On September 28, the officially designated birthday of Confucius, while Governor Qi and his subordinates knelt and bowed in solemn ritual worship before the statue of Confucius in the temple, a group of First Normal students deliberately went out to West Lake to spend the day visiting the tomb of the anarchist Liu Shifu.[49]

The symbolic meaning of the First Normal School's conspicuous absence from the Confucian birthday rituals was lost on no one. By refusing to perform their parts in the ceremony, the First Normal students, in collusion with their principal, had openly avowed their determination to reject the ethicopolitical order sanctified by the collective worship of the founder of the Confucian school. This ritual breach, which marked the beginning of deliberate efforts to marginalize Confucian teachings in daily life, was magnified by the performance of a ritual act of the iconoclastic students' own invention—a pilgrimage paid to the tomb of Liu Shifu, the most prominent anarchist at the time. With this insult the students sought to oppose Confucianism with anarchism. In the semiotics of worship, it also called to mind the pilgrimages made by late imperial sectarian followers to the tombs of cult founders, which the Confucian state had persecuted so relentlessly as heterodoxy in the past.

The ritual affront did not stop there. Back on their own campus, First Normal radicals dislodged the statue of Confucius from the pedestal that was standing in front of the main administration building and dumped it ignominiously into a cottage at the back of the campus, together with an icon of the disreputable fox maiden (*huxian*), the animal spirit of enchantment and seduction.[50] The worship of Confucius, which had been officially inaugurated by Han Gaodi, the founding emperor of Han, in 195 B.C. as a major state ceremony, had by the late Qing developed into an elaborate system of public rituals and ceremonies governing the lives of the educated both in and out of the bureaucracy, thanks largely to the perfection of the civil service examinations system and the network of academies. In rejecting that ritual, First Normal students not only rejected a political culture nurtured by the examination system, but also severed a vital link between the educated and officialdom.

The toppling of Confucius's statue, like the dismantling of Mao's giant stone statue on the campus of Beijing University (Beida) nearly seventy years later, was a vivid symbol of the momentous changes of the time. Whereas Mao's statue came down at Beida with the blessing of the authorities, Confucius's image was removed by a group of students while the governor persisted in his worship. Also, the spirit of revolt found expression in Hangzhou not in large-scale, politically mobilized street demonstrations as in Beijing, but rather in the daring intellectual iconoclasm of a handful of serious radicals whose local political influence was severely limited. Paradoxically, these same radicals, suppressed at home, were able at the national level to push the May Fourth Movement to new ideological heights through their skill and energy as writers and publishers.

THE PUBLICATION OF STUDENT JOURNALS

The first student journal published in Hangzhou in the wake of the May Fourth Movement was *Mingxing yuekan* (Star monthly), which appeared on September 25, just three days before the official birthday of Confucius.[51] The one-thousand-character inaugural editorial, written in the vernacular, was composed by Ruan Yicheng, the fifteen-year-old student at the elite Zhejiang Provincial First Middle School in Hangzhou. The journal appeared primarily as an attempt to emulate student publications elsewhere. "Zhejiang has always taken pride in its cultural leadership in the country. But in the New Culture Movement the leadership has bypassed the province," observed Ruan. "We, the editors of *Star Monthly*, would like to do our very best to rectify this situation." In a private letter to a friend earlier on September 11, Ruan Yicheng was even more explicit: "Nowadays every school in Jiangsu and in many other provinces has its own publications that spread new ideas. We therefore must also make plans to launch our own journal."[52]

Ruan Yicheng's coeditor was a classmate at First Middle School, Zha Mengji. Zha, also fifteen, was a descendent of the Zha lineage in Haining, Jiaxing, which had maintained its eminence in Confucian scholarship and gentry-bureaucratic standing since the Ming dynasty.[53] When Zha sat for the examinations that admitted him into the socially prestigious First Middle School in the fall of 1919, he wrote his examination essay in vernacular instead of classical Chinese. Those who learned about what he had done half expected his essay to be disqualified. It certainly sent a message to the educated circles at large when the faculty committee placed

Zha first on the admissions ranking list on the basis of his brilliant but demotic vernacular composition.[54]

Star Monthly printed essays written in the vernacular, used the new punctuation system adopted for vernacular composition (as opposed to the practice of no punctuation or periods only as used in classical Chinese), and argued enthusiastically in favor of the novel ideas about language and literature advocated by the New Culture intellectuals in Beijing. Ruan Yicheng and Zha Mengji did all the writing. The cost of printing for the first issue was borne by ten students of the First Middle School. Ruan had no difficulty engaging the service of a printing house, since his father, Ruan Xunbo, owned the Zhejiang Printing Company, the firm that pioneered modern-style printing in Hangzhou.[55]

To the disappointment of the editors and their friends, the first issue, printed on eight-by-twelve-inch newsprint, found no paying readership. The copies had to be distributed free of charge, and the *Star Monthly* was compelled to fold. On September 29, four days after the first appearance of the journal, Ruan Yicheng wrote to friends to announce the publication's demise. He was not about to give up, however, and instantly agitated for the creation of a new magazine. The business aspects of the publishing activity received considerable emphasis this time. Ruan stressed the importance of involving individuals who knew how to promote sales. A capable essayist and editor would be all the more attractive if this person could also bring funds with him for contribution. After some exploration among friends and acquaintances, seven students of the Zhejiang Provincial Institute of Industry, introduced by a close family friend of the Ruans, agreed to join the original group of First Middle School students for a new publication. Among the Institute of Industry students was the nineteen-year-old Shen Naixi (Duanxian), a native of Hangzhou and a younger member of a gentry family in decline, who published at this time under the name of Shen Zaibai. In the 1930s he became the leading playwright and principal Communist Party figure in Republican drama and film circles under the pen name Xia Yan.[56]

The first issue of the new publication, a biweekly named *Shuangshi* (Double ten), appeared on October 10, 1919. Compared with *Star Monthly*, the new journal drew from a much wider circle of editorial talent and ceased to be Ruan's one-man enterprise. An editorial board was formed with a rotating chairmanship. Contributors were invited to express viewpoints on any subject of their choice, without guidance or restrictions from preestablished editorial guidelines. Ruan's major responsibility was to coordinate the overall operation. He handled the correspondence and acted as a sort of business manager. Whether the journal was to have a future, the members soon realized, depended on its ability to attract a readership. Half a yuan was allocated for promotion, while another six yuan covered the expenses of printing and mailing. Members of the publishing group were also urged to promote circulation with their own resources.[57]

The inaugural editorial of *Double Ten* was composed by Zha Mengji, who set a strident tone for the journal by declaring, "We publish this biweekly to spread new ideas. We are here to offer advice and guidance to the conservatives." The journal's teenage authors stirred up controversy immediately with their denunciation of the social pages of Hangzhou's major newspapers as stale, vulgar, and reactionary. They charged that the editors and reporters were perpetrators of vice. The literary supplements of Hangzhou's newspapers also came under sharp criticism. These pages contained nothing but old-fashioned, middle-brow "Mandarin Ducks and Butterflies" fiction—a genre of urban entertainment that had been associated with escapist fantasy and literati decadence and was regarded by progressives as a vehicle for outdated and pernicious values.[58]

For the most part, the journal addressed its critical voice to issues relevant to the students' own concerns. The student editors of and contributors to *Double Ten* discussed the physical and moral aspects of formal education in their schools. They commented on the conservative nature of Zhejiang's new-style elementary schools, and stated boldly that there were serious problems with the province's educational system as directed by the provincial bureau of education. The journal praised the New Culture Movement in Beijing, issued a warning to "conservative-minded youth," printed one student's irreverent thoughts during a Confucian ceremony, and declared that Confucian rites bore little relevance to a true appreciation of the teaching of Confucius. It offered its own guidance on "the road to a new society" and challenged its readers to indicate their preference for "political activism by students or soldiers." It echoed the protests of Beijing college students on May 4 in its review of China's role in World War I and its critical assessment of the nation's "reward" in the peace conference at Versailles. As there was no sign that Japan's ambition toward China had been thwarted, *Double Ten* asked rhetorically, "Is This What We Had Hoped to Achieve by Boycotting Japanese Goods?" and it offered by way of an answer, "A Few Words of Remonstrance to Xu Shichang," the president of the Republic. The students were fearless in their attacks on the conservative and recalcitrant. They were just as swift in showing support for their fellow students and friends. "Welcome to Our Friend, *First Normal Alumni Association Biweekly*," declared *Double Ten*, when students and alumni of the First Normal School launched a journal of their own.[59] *Double Ten* turned out to be a success: the first issue went into four printings, and the second issue into six.

Up to this point new-style publishing by Hangzhou's secondary school students was undertaken principally by those who were drawn to the literary and linguistic agenda of the New Culture Movement. These youths were sons of northern Zhejiang's progressive gentry elites who were well able to afford the expenditure of publishing. They shared with their progressive parents a general concern with cultural and educational matters. Just as their forebears financed the publication of poetry collections, the generation of May Fourth turned to the publishing of vernacular essays. The overtly political and iconoclastic writings that we commonly associate with May Fourth youths did not take place until this group was joined by middle-county radicals.

CONFLUENCE

The content of *Double Ten* attracted the attention of the radical group of students in the senior class of First Normal whom we have already met in preceding pages: Fu Binran, Shi Cuntong, and their ardent friends of the middle counties. Trained to become teachers in county elementary schools, they had taken Neo-Confucian moral teachings seriously. As we have seen, they had also been exposed to anarchist ideas through readings and personal contacts, such as with Shen Zhongjiu, the editor of the Zhejiang Provincial Educational Association's organ, *Tides in Education*. Attracted by the iconoclastic tone of the new journal, Fu Binran and Shen Zhongjiu each sent a letter to Ruan Yicheng, the business correspondent of *Double Ten*.

Shen wrote primarily to offer his help and suggestion on the publication's editorial direction. He applauded the boldness of *Double Ten*'s editors, compared the journal's appearance in Hangzhou to "the rise of a brilliant star" against the dark sky, and hailed these secondary school students as pioneers and pathbreakers. Shen went on: "You should have no fear of darkness. You should be concerned only when you fail to expose the darkness. You should have no fear of the government's censorship and imprisonment. You should indeed be concerned if you fail to provoke the censors and prosecutors." Shen Zhongjiu also drew attention to the importance of the labor problem and emphasized that ideas became worthwhile only when used as guidance for social action. "The social reform of China can be achieved only through an alliance of the students and laborers," Shen wrote. Because students and laborers represented the hopes for China's future, Hangzhou student journals ought to address themselves especially to these two groups in the area. The journal should report truthfully on the conditions in local schools, news media, and the work place, and should offer criticisms as well as suggestions for action.[60]

Shen Zhongjiu stressed, furthermore, that *Double Ten* ought to differentiate itself from major national journals and publications by concentrating its resources on issues of local relevance, in order to engage the interest of a local audience and make its influence felt. Shen belabored the point that publishing was merely a first step in the making of a new society. This was to be understood both in the sense that the advocacy of iconoclastic ideas represented a first step toward revolutionary social action, and in the sense that the thrust of publishing and cultural activities was to lead to the mobilization for and organization of a larger political movement. Publishing was the vehicle that allowed the iconoclasts and revolutionaries to identify their fellow comrades. The goal of publishing activities was to create a basis of support for the revolutionary movement.

While Shen Zhongjiu wrote as a seasoned editor, an established intellectual figure, and a self-styled mentor, Fu, an active contributor to the *First Normal Alumni Association Biweekly*, wrote to suggest that the *Double Ten* group and his friends at First Normal combine efforts in writing and publishing. Fu Binran wrote in the passionate voice of a fellow student, an ally, and a comrade: "I read the first issue of *Double Ten* with great excitement. Earlier, during the May Fourth Movement, I felt deeply ashamed about the response of us Hangzhou students. How I had hoped that Hangzhou students could have behaved differently! I fear that some of us had been so thoroughly crushed by the old slavish system that we would never be capable of action. Now *Double Ten* has appeared as a happy surprise just as my despair about us was increasing!"

Fu applauded the journal's audacious attack on Hangzhou's conservative cultural establishment and announced his intention to call a meeting of "the worthy and progressive young students in Hangzhou to discuss the future of Chinese culture." He invited *Double Ten*'s editors and contributors to take part, so that "we shall be able to spread our influence to more people, and we can offer each other moral support in the impending cultural struggle." Fu called for the end of *Double Ten* and the birth of a new journal, *Zhejiang xinchao* (Zhejiang new tide), jointly published by the students of the three major schools in Hangzhou: the First Middle School, the Institute of Industry, and the First Normal School.

Ruan Yicheng and his friends were delighted by these developments. A first meeting took place in Ruan's parental house, followed by more meetings held in the Zhejiang Provincial Educational Association.[61] A group of twenty-eight students, including Shi Cuntong, Fu Binran, Zhou Bodi, Yu Songshou (Xiusong), and Zhang Weizhan of the First Normal School, subsequently formed a new society, the Zhejiang Xinchao She (Zhejiang new tide society), and began the publication of the *Zhejiang New Tide Weekly*. With the help of Shen Zhongjiu, the new society was given the use of an office in the Zhejiang Provincial Educational Association. To launch the journal, each member was asked to contribute one yuan. Several faculty members of First Normal, especially the new Chinese teachers who had arrived just that fall, also made contributions to support the students' activity.[62] Thus *Double Ten* concluded after two issues, and the enterprise was folded into the *Zhejiang New Tide Weekly*.

The smoothness with which the transformation took place from one student journal to another masked a major departure in the Zhejiang New Tide Society's organizational principles. The two earlier publications, *Star Monthly* and *Double Ten*, had been launched by a small group of personal acquaintances acting together in friendship. *Zhejiang New Tide*, on the other hand, was the result of an alliance of two disparate groups joined together by a sense of shared mission. The earlier journals were centrally focused on literary and linguistic issues. Ruan Yicheng and Zha Mengji were drawn primarily to the literary aspects of the New Culture Movement and sought to build up a publishing enterprise to facilitate Zhejiang's participation in the national movement. The radical First Normal members of the Zhejiang New Tide Society, however, had gained some exposure to writings on anarchism, were keenly attentive to the social meaning of political action, and were eager to bring about fundamental changes in ethicopolitical norms. The latter group sought to destroy evil social practices, while the former placed emphasis on gradual changes and literary innovation. The latter were newly liberated from the Confucian values of their home and past. The former, as sons and scions of northern Zhejiang's progressive gentry, had long been exposed to the progressive politics—if not New Culture—of their fathers, to whom they turned for support. The creation of the Zhejiang New Tide Society marked the confluence of youths from two distinct backgrounds in the publication of Zhejiang's student journals. From the viewpoint of someone like Ruan Yicheng, the membership composition of the Zhejiang New Tide Society seemed far more complicated than that of *Star Monthly* or *Double Ten*. "The New Tide Society," he ruefully recalled, "brought in quite a few radicals!"[63]

THE NEW TIDE

The First Normal students, older and more seasoned, soon assumed editorial control over *Zhejiang New Tide*. They quickly pushed their junior partners into minor chores. Institute of Industry student Shen Duanxian was put in charge of the mailing list. His assignment in the society was to put the printed journal into envelopes, jot down the names and addresses of subscribers, and carry the packages down to the post office. Ruan Yicheng, the founder and editor of the first two journals, was replaced by First Normal student Huang Zongzheng as the business correspondent of the new publication. Although it was initially agreed that members of the three schools would take turns overseeing the editorial work of *Zhejiang New Tide Weekly*, First Normal students quickly let it be known that they lacked confidence in the ability of their junior partners. When Shi Cuntong and Zhou Bodi, seniors at First Normal, proofread sample copies of the second issue of the journal that was edited by First Middle students, they complained about "numerous absurd errors" and proceeded to exercise editorial discretion when the articles were on the printing press.[64] Shi Cuntong subsequently suggested that he alone take full charge of the journal's editorial work. Because the weekly was receiving more articles from its members than it could print, the job of editorship entailed considerable power of discretion over what to print. Ruan Yicheng remembered, half a century later, that his one essay on Hangzhou education was never published by the new journal.[65]

With the First Normal students at the editorial helm, the new journal took a radical turn. It adopted an ever intensifying tone of urgent pleading coupled with self-righteous defiance. An editorial in the second issue of the *New Tide Weekly* spoke of a morally regenerated and enlightened "we" arrayed against a besotted and inert "they." "We," the twenty-eight comrades and members of the New Tide Society, "have been awakened to the light of the truth," whereas "they," the majority of Hangzhou students, remained "poisoned by a mindless system of education." The Hangzhou Student Association showed so little understanding of the tasks confronting it, indeed, as to permit its members to go home at the order of the Zhejiang bureau of education at the height of the May Fourth protests! Members of the Zhejiang New Tide Society, in contrast, had demonstrated their awareness through their gestures of protests and defiance, such as refusal to take part in the Confucian rites, and had drawn a clear dividing line between themselves and the rest of the society.[66]

Compared with the opening remarks of the two earlier journals, the inaugural editorial of *Zhejiang New Tide Weekly* dwelled on the theme of individual awakening and sketched the outline of an ideal future society, clearly reflecting the influence of contemporary anarchist thinking.[67] It delineated an ideal society in which all people were blessed with personal dignity and happiness, and then contrasted this image sharply with a reality depicted in terms of institutionalized oppression, widespread misery, and social stagnation. Life, happiness, and progress, the journal passionately declared, were the universal goals of human existence in this world. Yet everywhere men were deprived of their entitlements by the oppressive structure of society. There were four classes of people: politicians, capitalists, intellectuals, and laborers: "Politicians and capitalists are oppressors, aggressors, and exploiters, and the enemies of individual freedom, mutual aid, and productive labor." These classes had the help of intellectuals, who, in return for petty privileges and minor pay-offs, spun specious theories and guarded authoritarian norms that "justify and maintain this system of injustice." The laborers, or the bulk of humanity, on the other hand, performed all the productive work in return for nothing but hardship. Because this inequity had been institutionalized in kinship relations, religious beliefs, legal practices, political institutions, economic relationships, clan organizations, and so forth, a fundamental social reconstruction was necessary to correct the situation. The laborers would become the natural leaders in this revolutionary change, because they alone represented the social class with unimpeachable integrity.[68]

With a characteristic "cosmic optimism" that has been linked to the Mencian philosophy of human nature,[69] the editors evinced great confidence in the innate goodness of ordinary men and women while blaming the social system for human misery. "Not only do most of us lack adequate food, clothing, or shelter; we are inhibited from showing our feelings, deprived of educational opportunities, and unemployed. Not only do we receive no help; we are prevented from offering help to others." Society, as it was, alienated brothers from brothers. The first step toward a regenerated future, therefore, was a sweeping destruction of those norms and institutions that erected artificial social barriers. In the new society there should be no authority but that of individual conscience; no intrigue and competition, only brotherly love, harmony, and mutual assistance; neither burdensome toil nor wasteful idleness, but honest productive labor, from each according to his ability.[70] A cherished moment would be the time of harvest, when hope, faith, harmony, peace, gratitude, and contentment would all find their expression, as was captured in Jean-François Millet's

The Gleaners (*Les glaneuses*, 1857) and sentimentally eulogized in an essay by Xia Mianzun, the teacher and mentor at the First Normal School.[71]

The iconoclastic editorials in *Zhejiang New Tide Weekly* were considered as the first steps to prepare the vanguard groups, especially the laborers, for their role in the coming revolutionary struggle. Because the majority of Chinese laborers were illiterate and hence beyond the reach of printed words, however, Chinese students must shoulder the responsibility of serving as the workers' teachers and organizers.[72] This task could only be assumed by "awakened" intellectuals: educated men who had renounced their own class and past, dedicating themselves to the cause of the common laborer. It was the inevitable conclusion of *Zhejiang New Tide*'s editors, then, that they must concentrate their efforts on "awakening" and organizing their student audience to train them to arouse the workers into drastic action.

The journal encouraged its readers to spread the messages of awakening to an ever widening circle of audiences in the schools, at street corners, through printed words, and via mass education. "If we unite and work for our common goal, we shall be able to sustain each other with moral force and we can resist external pressure. We may begin by forming small groups that will develop into larger ones. We may begin with the awakening of but one person; this beginning will lead us to groups of individuals. Eventually we will then be in a position to destroy the existing social order!"[73]

The editors invoked images of darkness versus light, hypocrisy versus truth, animal behavior versus human dignity, and vowed to wage war on "all dark, false and beastly behavior." "We stand for humanity and truth, and we will confront the forces of darkness. . . . There will be difficulties and setbacks . . . censors and police, prison cells and even the execution ground . . . uphill struggles against government suppression and mass ignorance. . . . [But] we shall have no fear, only pride. . . . As long as darkness, falsehood and jungle-style behavior continue, our fighting spirit will never die."[74]

Although the editors mentioned no intellectual authority in this article, the influence of Pyotr Kropotkin (1842–1921) was evident. Kropotkin's writings and the idea of mutual aid had been introduced to First Normal students through the pamphlets and journals issued by a Guangzhou-based group of anarchists led by Liu Shifu, the man now lying in peace by West Lake. The Guangzhou group had drawn on the anarchist theories developed during 1903–5 by sojourning Chinese intellectuals in Paris, principally Wu Zhihui and Li Shizeng. They were the publishers of the journal *Xin shiji*

(New century) and had been exposed to the ideas of Jean Grave, editor of *Les temps nouveaux*.[75] Like the Paris group of early Chinese anarchists, the Hangzhou students accepted the evolutionary scheme of human history and placed their faith in a better future of universal culture and freedom. Whereas the Paris group embraced modern science and technology and believed in the power of education and propaganda to transform society through nonviolent means, however, the Hangzhou radicals showed little interest in machines and the wonders of science. They attacked "capitalists" alongside "politicians" and deplored economic as much as political inequality.

The Hangzhou youth echoed other anarchist voices best articulated by Liu Shipei, whose ideas had been published in the journal *Natural Justice* when he was studying in Tokyo between 1902 and 1904. Liu believed that the necessary condition for the future age of freedom from want was a simple, arcadian life of equally shared agrarian labor. The principal source of inspiration for his anarchism was not the modern West, but a faith in an idealized Chinese antiquity of harmonious self-sufficiency, such as described in the pages of *Li ji* (Book of rites). This ideal state, which was blissfully ignorant of political and ethical divisions, Liu believed, was destroyed by the great imperial centralizers, Qin Shihuang and Han Wudi. Although Liu Shipei reached this belief through philological training in the school of Han Learning, in Tokyo he was much inspired by Leo Tolstoy's equation of capitalism with "false civilization" and deeply influenced by the militancy of the Japanese anarchist Kotoku Shusui. Liu was prepared to adopt violent revolutionary means to achieve a simpler society of shared labor and equality.[76]

The Hangzhou student radicals plainly preferred Liu Shipei's vision of a simple, halcyon society over Wu Zhihui's Parisian-influenced view of a future society built on modern science and technology. Although they responded to Wu's idea about using education and propaganda as means to reform society, they were also ready, like Liu, to conduct revolutionary struggles. Thus even though the Zhejiang New Tide group was eclectic in its acceptance of elements of both major strands of anarchist thinking available in Chinese at the time, it showed a clear penchant for a simple communitarian life unencumbered by the complex products of modernization.

Above all, the Hangzhou student radicals believed that they were ready to take immediate action to attain a simple society of equality and security for everyone. An immediate target for destructive action was the social reality at hand. Hangzhou students did not simply denounce the vices of traditional society in general or the regime of warlords in distant Beijing in particular; they attacked the ethicopolitical order that prevailed in everyday life at home and that consequently legitimized the practices of the provincial government. While their metropolitan counterparts rallied in street demonstrations to express anti-imperialist patriotism, Hangzhou's youth organized small publishing societies to challenge the values on which a whole way of life had been built.

CONNECTIONS

The first issue of the *Zhejiang New Tide Weekly*, dated November 1, 1919, attracted the attention not only of Hangzhou's students and educators but also of the educated public. The first thousand copies were sold out in less than three days. A second printing of another thousand copies lasted a few days more. By the time the next issue of the weekly appeared, subscription orders had arrived by mail from Beijing, Changsha, Guiyang, Chongqing, and Guangzhou.[77]

The *Zhejiang New Tide Weekly* gained national prominence even before the first issue actually appeared, when it was prominently featured in an article entitled "The Cultural Movement in Zhejiang" that appeared on October 27 in *Shishi xinbao* (Current affairs), a major Shanghai newspaper favored by the intellectuals and second in its volume of circulation only to *Shenbao*.[78] Shortly after that, the editors of the *Zhejiang New Tide Weekly* began corresponding with Zhang Dongsun, the editor of *Current Affairs*, which later featured their exchanges.[79] Fu Binran, Shi Cuntong, and other First Normal members of *Zhejiang New Tide Weekly* also began corresponding with Jiang Menglin and Luo Jialun, student leaders of the May Fourth Movement in Beijing and principal contributors to *Xinchao* (Renaissance), the new-style literary journal of a group of Beijing University students.[80] In mid-November, Dai Jitao of Shanghai's *Weekend Review* wrote to offer his comments. Even more impressive, a letter arrived from no less a figure than Chen Duxiu, editor of *New Youth* magazine and intellectual leader of the New Culture Movement in Beijing. This initial contact led eventually to the organization of the Marxism Study Society (Makesi zhuyi yanjiu hui) in Shanghai the following year, which lay the foundation for the organization of the Chinese Communist Party.[81]

This network of intellectual contacts, like Jing Ziyuan's circle of progressive educators, reached beyond provincial boundaries and grew through the printed media. Compared with Jing's colleagues, this emerging radical alliance was heard both in a handful of urban professional journals subscribed to by teachers and school administrators, and in leading Shanghai and Beijing journals and newspapers with an educated audience. It was joined, in one variation or another, by the voices of hundreds of campus publications mushrooming among the students, who mobilized to form reading and publishing societies of their own. Organizationally, no effective national confederation grew out of this disparate collection of student bodies, despite Beijing student leaders' efforts along those lines in the summer of 1919. But the potential for organization certainly seemed real enough—a possibility that was readily recognized by the Guomindang opposition as well as by the military authorities.

Just as the *Zhejiang New Tide Weekly* appeared to be linking up with a broad network of intellectuals with New Culture reputations and Nationalist Party connections, Zhejiang's authorities struck out against the young radicals and ordered the Zhejiang Printing Company to stop all printing activities with the journal. While the authorities had long regarded Jing Ziyuan and his circles with distrust, the crackdown was precipitated by the publication in the journal's second number of an article by Shi Cuntong that bore the title "Fei Xiao" (Decry filial piety!). The article, which drew on personal experience, attacked filial practices in provincial society and portrayed the author's father as a callous patriarch. Although the term *fei xiao* had its classical origin in the pages of the *Book of Filial Piety* (*Xiaojing*), generations of commentators had made it clear that those who "have the audacity to disparage it [*fei xiao*] lack a feeling and loving heart [*wu qin*],"[82] and such heartlessness sowed the seeds of great disorder (*da luan*). Shi's essay thus attacked one of the most inviolable norms in Confucian teaching and pushed Hangzhou iconoclasm to a new height in confrontation with the conservative authorities.

In contemporary rhetoric this fresh attack on filial piety (*fei xiao*) by Hangzhou's radicals was instantly paired with their earlier attempt to dispense with the Confucian temple rites (*fei Kong*) during the May Fourth Movement. These two transgressions were invoked by the conservatives in conjunction with their own summary of what the anarchocommunist youth wanted: "communal wives" (*gong qi*) and "communal property" (*gong chan*). Together these four threads of dissent touched on the subjects of women, private property, social ethics, and political rituals, and represented the most comprehensive and dangerous assault on the existing social order at the time. Although the province had failed to come into full swing with Beijing and Shanghai in the student demonstrations and civilian mobilization of the previous summer, by late 1919 Hangzhou had earned for itself, along with Changsha, the capital of Hunan, the reputation of being one of the two most intensely radical centers in thinking and publishing throughout the country.[83]

Although he wrote with passionate conviction, Shi Cuntong himself was not without despair and hesitations. "Decry Filial Piety!" for him was more than an abstract intellectual position. The choice to publish the article was painfully made, and whether he succeeded in transcending his dilemma by doing so, it represented an honest effort to resolve some of life's difficulties by bringing to bear a set of principles that he had come to believe as superior and true. As the next chapter will show, conversion to those principles entailed considerable personal anguish, caused by the necessity of tearing himself loose from his own origins.

8 "Decry Filial Piety!"

In October 1919, shortly before the first issue of *Zhejiang New Tide Weekly* was published, Shi Cuntong received a letter from home informing him that his mother was dying. He hastened back to his home village in Jinhua County, where he found, to his grief, that his mother was indeed very ill. She was able to sit up in bed and still had an appetite; she laughed and talked. Yet "she was uttering nonsense, and her limbs were as cold to the touch as ice." To his indignation, he found she was "clothed in rags, brought only leftover, unheated food, and left alone most of the time." Shi learned that the village herbalist, a second cousin and one of the few who had been to the county seat, had earlier declared her case to be incurable. The family then had offered earnest prayers and offerings to gods and ghosts on her behalf, but when those efforts produced no visible results, she was given up for lost. No more medical help was sent for, nor was the patient given special nourishment or attention—the reasoning was that the family's resources should not be spent on a hopeless case.

Shi Cuntong had brought home with him a small sum of money that he had earned as a freelance contributor to Hangzhou newspapers. When he offered it for his mother's care, his father refused. The money, Shi's father argued, would make it possible to arrange for a respectable funeral and burial in accordance with ritual propriety. These rites had been passed on from generation to generation. They prescribed the socially accepted expression of appropriate grief and filiality. Proper observance of these rites reflected favorably on the survivors for families that aspired to local standing.

Shi Cuntong disputed his father's notion of filiality, which placed emphasis on formal rituals and public ceremony. It was much more important, he thought, to perform caring deeds and follow filial sentiments. Formal filial duty required that Shi obey his father. Yet it also dictated that he take care of his dying mother. Filiality was clearly an all-encompassing demand with multiple manifestations. Confucian teachings, however, did not discriminate between the absoluteness in filial duties required of a child toward his father versus those toward his mother. Since in real lives men and women rarely stood on an equal footing in the hierarchy of the patriarchal household, Shi Cuntong found himself confronting the power and opposition of his father as the son attempted to act out his filial sentiments toward his dying mother.

As Shen Xuanlu had observed of his contemporaries, under patriarchy sons were taught "only to look toward their fathers but not their mothers" (*dan zhi you fu, bu zhi you mu*).[1] The episode thus brought into sharp relief a point of ambiguity in a value system that in its past practices and normative injunctions seldom addressed the issue of real power and of that power's capacity to bias the teaching of morality. Shi Cuntong confronted a situation in which Confucian patriarchal authority, backed by formalized conduct and reified expectations, clashed with Confucian moral imperatives. Neither the sacred edicts of emperors nor the canonized teachings of the sages had much to offer on an appropriate course of action, since it had always been assumed that the exercise of patriarchal power would be humane and benevolent. When the patriarch flouted the pious expectation of benevolence, the precarious union of the ethical and the political orders in familial relationships was inevitably compromised to the detriment of the ethical.

This gap between the two orders of arrangement presented, on one level, a serious moral deadlock for Shi Cuntong. He spent three days at home agonizing over his options, and in the end decided to return to school, partly in flight from his excruciating dilemma. Because he was bound by his filial duties not to take a stand against his father, he felt powerless in not being able to live up to his cardinal ethical duties toward his mother. Instead of watching her die, "I felt that I must return to school before I myself died of anger and frustration."[2]

The uncoupling of the political and the ethical led Shi to the conclusion that, in a majority of Confucian practices, the ethical had merely been used to mask the political. This realization evoked an intensely charged reaction against what Shi Cuntong regarded as the coercive being masked as the normative—precisely because he had been so deeply committed to the integrity of the ethical. Although he had given up on the home front and had refrained from personally challenging the authority of his father, on his way back to Hangzhou he turned the matter over and over in his mind. By the time he reached the First Normal School he had resolved to launch an open attack on the use and abuse of filial piety as practiced in the middle counties.

Even though his mother was still alive and lingered on, he too had tacitly accepted the hopelessness of her condition and the inevitability of her death. Instead of striving, perhaps in vain, to bring her comfort and relief, he turned her into a case and a cause, and committed himself to a fierce struggle to redefine the normative operation of filial piety and to reform the familial structure. "It was too late to try saving my mother," Shi later reflected. "I thereupon resolved to save all other women who in the future might find themselves in similar circumstances."[3]

What had happened to Shi Cuntong's mother consequently struck a nerve for many others witnessing the decline of the middle counties and discovering the same disjuncture between power and value, with the latter reduced to mere legitimizing symbols. As a normal college student in 1919, poised between the two cultural spaces of school and home, Shi stood at a particularly critical intersection where personal experiences and larger intellectual trends conjoined. He had been steadily exposed to the progressive thinking of liberals at the provincial capital, as well as to the New Culture publications emanating from Shanghai and Beijing. Inspired by provincial progressives and cosmopolitan intellectuals alike, Shi Cuntong came to believe that beyond Confucianism there was an even higher plane of evolutionary ethics. The rage and grief over the lack of caring shown toward his mother allowed him to grasp and shape Hangzhou progressive ideals by infusing them with the radicalizing anguish of a middle-county youth. Conversely, when progressive messages were brought to bear on his personal circumstances, Shi also reached a transformative juncture in his life. Thereafter his biography took on a different meaning, both in terms of his self-understanding and of his stance in relation to home and community. This repositioning paved the ground for his subsequent transformation into a man of pronounced ideological conviction.

SHI'S INTELLECTUAL TRANSFORMATION

When Shi Cuntong arrived at First Normal School, he was absorbed in Neo-Confucian teachings.[4] In his early days at First Normal, he followed the moral teachings offered by Principal Jing Ziyuan, which were far from unconventional. Faith in a constitutional republicanism inspired Jing Ziyuan to give his loyalty to an impersonal nation-state. Jing had never raised doubts about a son's filial duty to his parents, however, nor did he ever step beyond traditional bounds on the issue of male and female relationships within the Confucian family. Jing's concerns were mainly with the restructuring of political institutions. He did not raise questions about the nature of moral authority.

Shi Cuntong's questioning of Confucian practices, based on his own experience growing up in the middle county, developed over a period of time. An avid reader who kept up with journals and newspaper publications, Shi was among the first of his friends to discover the Beijing-based monthly *New Youth*, in the fall of 1918. In the pre–May Fourth days when First Normal continued to emphasize old-style literati culture, *New Youth* was not among the materials promoted in the classroom. Shi kept copies of the journal under his pillow while traveling by boat from home to school, reaching for the magazine whenever he had a moment to himself.[5]

Shi Cuntong was not instantly converted to the iconoclastic cultural messages championed by *New Youth*. His immediate response to several of Chen Duxiu's pieces on Confucianism, in fact, was outrage.[6] These essays were pointed attacks on reactionary attempts to restore the Qing Emperor in 1917.[7] Chen Duxiu did not just take aim at the political program of the monarchists, who were flaunting their Confucianism during the attempt to restore Puyi, the last Qing emperor. Rather, Chen went beyond the immediately political to attack their underlying cultural assumptions. By attributing the conservative political agenda to a misplaced loyalty to the teachings of Confucius, Chen was also calling for a thorough denunciation of Confucianism in order to stem its pernicious political influence.

Shi Cuntong was both perplexed and shocked by Chen's irreverent accusation. He had been sufficiently exposed to the revolutionary rhetoric and the evolutionary view of history among the political progressives of Hangzhou to be firm in his belief that republicanism was superior to monarchy. Yet he was not shaken enough from his deep commitment to Confucian moral teachings to see the pernicious implications of Confucianism as a state ideology. Chen Duxiu, after all, wrote with the authority of being dean of the College of Letters of National Beijing University, China's leading academic institution.[8] Not knowing where to turn, Shi Cuntong preferred to set Chen's daring arguments aside for the time being.[9]

With that first taste of iconoclasm, Shi Cuntong found himself drawn to issue after issue of *New Youth*, driven by a growing desire to pursue the matter to its logical end. He followed the debates carefully, his attention riveted on the issue of Confucianism and politics. He watched the printed exchanges between major intellectual figures as well as their public performances on the nation's political stage. When Kang Youwei, the renowned Confucian scholar of the New Text School and the living "Sage of the South Sea (Nanhai)," openly called for the demise of the Republic and the restoration of the monarchy, Shi Cuntong thought that he had learned enough to draw his own conclusions. Kang had spoken, it seemed to Shi, against the evolutionary principle of history by insisting on a political form that belonged to a superseded past. Shi reasoned that Kang's inability to place Confucian teachings in their historical context, in a way that Principal Jing Ziyuan had been able to do, prevented Kang from embracing the higher form of political republicanism. Shi Cuntong began to see Chen Duxiu's points as he, too, linked reactionary politics to an unqualified adherence to Confucianism as a timeless norm. With this newly gained insight, Shi Cuntong approached the cultural iconoclasts and Westernizers of the New Culture Movement with fresh appreciation. As Shi wrote, "Initially I was only half persuaded by the arguments laid forth in *New Youth*—I had doubts about the journal's attack on Confucianism. But by the second half of 1919, I was fully won over—whatever was stated in the pages of the journal, it could not possibly be misguided." He sought in the journal's writings guidance and inspiration for personal action and began treating the views of Chen Duxiu, Hu Shi, Qian Xuantong, Liu Bannong, and other leading iconoclasts with the fervor and conviction of a self-styled disciple.[10]

Shi Cuntong became so earnestly engaged in the pursuit of new ideas that, in April 1919, he organized his First Normal friends into a New Life Society (Xinsheng she) to study the issues of *New Youth*. These friends also gave themselves a reading list of Western political thought in Chinese translation. They began with essays on Social Darwinism by Yan Fu and his translation of John Stuart Mill's *On Liberty*—writings in wide circulation that had asserted a tremendous impact on an earlier generation of intellectuals at the turn of the century.[11] As the reading program progressed, Shi and his friends also discovered recent translations of Kropotkin—especially his *Appeal to Youth* (*Gao qingnian shu*) by Ba Jin (Li Feigan) and *Modern Science and Anarchism* (*Jindai kexue yu wuzhengfu zhuyi*) by Huang Lingshuang.[12] They studied closely the articles published in Chinese anarchist journals such as *Minsheng* (Voice of the people), *Ziyou lu* (Chronicle of freedom), and *Jinhua* (Evolution), and began to regard mutual aid as superior to the survival of the fittest.[13]

Voice of the People, which began publication in Guangzhou in 1913, was the organ of the Cock-Crow Society (Huiming she), the first significant anarchist organization inside China.[14] Led by Liu Shifu (Sifu), the society and its journal became a major source of inspiration that spawned similar anarchist societies, especially in central and south China.[15] *Chronicle of Freedom*, which first appeared in July 1917 in Beijing, was published by the

Truth Society (Shi she) founded by a group of university students and journalists dedicated "to the search for anarchist organization in politics and advocacy of the true principles of communism in economics."[16] *Evolution*, first issued in January 1919 in Nanjing, was the journal of the Evolution Society (Jinhua she), which combined the publishing activities of several anarchist societies in Guangzhou, Beijing, Shandong, and Nanjing; under the editorship of Chen Yannian, son of Chen Duxiu, it came close to resembling the organ of a "national" anarchist organization.[17] All three journals favored, by and large, an anarchist alliance with the common laborers for the purpose of achieving social goals through immediate action. This social radicalism contrasted with a different strand in Chinese anarchism that placed emphasis on anarchism as a social philosophy, which pinned hopes on the long-term transformative effect of education.[18]

Shi Cuntong's intellectual transformation began with changes in political belief, followed by a fundamental reconsideration of familial ethics.[19] This sea change began with Jing Ziyuan, whose single-minded attention to the nation nonetheless paved the way for the demolition of the Confucian ethicopolitical order in Shi's reasoning.[20] The transformation gained momentum as Shi was exposed to Jing's circle of progressive friends among Hangzhou's educators, who in turn drew his attention to recent journals circulating in Shanghai and Beijing.

Jing Ziyuan instilled in Shi Cuntong, first of all, a sense of loyalty to the republic. He showed Shi Cuntong an active commitment to the ideal of creating a republican nation-state, which was to take primacy over individual interest. Like Sun Yat-sen, Jing posited a dichotomy between national citizenship and particularistic loyalties to lineage and village communities. He argued that emotional obligation to such "natural" communities was inimical to the creation of a superior political entity, the "Chinese nation," which embodied a higher stage in the evolutionary scheme of history. Since nation-states were incessantly struggling for survival in the universe that Jing Ziyuan had framed through Yan Fu's Social Darwinian perspective of the 1890s, the wealth and power of China should be the ultimate goal of all its citizens' endeavors, including the task of educating the country's elementary and secondary school students.

While Shi Cuntong readily accepted Jing Ziyuan's critique of village particularism, he and his friends regarded themselves as being able to move to an even higher stage on the evolutionary ladder, embracing the superior ethics of mutual aid as opposed to the survival of the fittest, and transcending undue fixations on the nation-state in order to address all of humanity. Shi Cuntong's understanding of anarchism owed much to the

encouragement of Shen Zhongjiu, Jing's secretary at the Zhejiang Provincial Educational Association, who believed in the importance of anarchist social action through an alliance of students and laborers. Shen opened
up to the students the library of the Provincial Educational Association,
which featured an up-to-date collection of Shanghai publications, edited in
many instances by Shen's fellow provincials of Zhejiang and former classmates in Japan. In March 1919, for instance, the literary supplement of the
Shanghai-based daily *Current Affairs* serialized Li Shizeng's translation of
Mutual Aid. Later that year *Weekend Review* serialized *The State.*[21]
Writing by and about Kropotkin became an intellectual staple. By the
summer of 1919, Shi and his circle, after reading Huang Lingshuang's
rendition of *Modern Science and Anarchism*, were ready to embrace mutual aid as the norm dictated by the modern natural sciences as well as social
sciences. In September, one month before he set out for home to visit his
ailing mother, Shi Cuntong announced that he had liberated himself from
all reverence for the family as a social institution and that he embraced
instead the ideal of "an anarchist communism of true freedom and equality." He now saw the teachings of "the three bonds and five constants" as
a repressive atavism.[22]

While an evolutionary view of history had led senior progressives
such as Jing Ziyuan to denounce provincial attachments as parochial and
to relegate Confucian monarchy to the past, the same notion of human
progress persuaded younger radicals such as Shi Cuntong that the cardinal Neo-Confucian construction of familial relationships had to be displaced by anarchistic communism. In the utopia to come, the family would
perish as the basic social unit, and human beings everywhere would inter-
act as brothers and sisters.[23]

THE ATTACK ON FILIAL PIETY

Against this backdrop of intellectual transformation Shi Cuntong confronted his father about caring for his mother and the issue of filial
obligations. The encounter served as a catalyst that brought about Shi
Cuntong's emotional break with his past. His subsequent heartfelt essay,
"Decry Filial Piety," appeared in November 1919 in the second issue of
Zhejiang New Tide Weekly. Although other writers before him had eulogized the utopia of selfless love and virtue, Shi was the first to attack the
coerciveness of filial piety. Not only did he declare that Confucian ethics
was doomed to pass, he attacked the entire sociopolitical order that was built
on these rites, icons, and norms.

Echoing the anarchism of Liu Shifu, Shi argued that the private ownership of property was the source of all social evils. Would not his mother have fared better if a public health care system had existed to look after her medical needs, regardless of her financial capability? Did not private property relations erect social barriers that prevented even neighbors and friends from assisting her in distress? Private property was collectively held in families and lineages under the control of household heads. This economic control, coupled with the patriarch's normative claim to filial obedience, effectively deprived sons of all independence that was contrary to their father's fiats. Since the normative claims also validated, and were in turn validated by, political power, Confucian patriarchy amounted to a total system of control that denied women and youth their possessions and autonomy.

Filial piety in this hierarchically structured order based on personal property, Shi concluded, was no different from "the virtue required of a slave" (*nuli de daode*).[24] "An ethical norm that stresses reciprocal obligations at its origin," wrote Shi, "has been used in reality as an instrument that justifies the exercise of absolute power by one party to this bond over the other. To invoke the imperatives of filial piety these days is for the elders to demand absolute obedience from the younger generation."[25]

Shi perceived his mother not merely as one unfortunate woman, but as the victim of the flawed socioethical practices of Confucian China. Shi Cuntong himself sounded far from being a confident rebel preaching from an intellectually superior position. He projected himself as an aggrieved son who had sought in vain to redress the power balance between the father and the mother in his family. In the still Confucian language of everyday practice, Shi depicted himself as having elected to be an "unfilial son" to his father because he was outraged by the callous treatment of his mother. He laid the blame firmly on the Confucian patriarchy itself for permitting him no other choice but unfiliality in order to be human.[26]

Although he was slashing at the most vital cord in the net of Confucian ethical relationships, Shi managed to maintain the conviction that his moral intention, even by Confucian standards, was beyond reproach. It was not he but his own father who had betrayed the true intent of the Confucian ethical tenet. Still, Shi Cuntong was detached enough to recognize that his father was conforming to expectations deeply seated in the collective practices of the village community. Even though short-tempered, his father held no particular malice toward his wife and son. He was just "another unfortunate person" imprisoned in middle-county society. Whether individuals were acting as victims or victimizers, however, they were all caught in an iron cage of ritual texts and iconic practices that condoned the suffering of women as the weaker members in the uneven power distribution of hierarchical society.[27]

The ritual subjugation of women and children, Shi believed, was in basic conflict with the nature of human beings, who, in their uncorrupted state, desire freedom, equality, and fraternal love. Although Shi Cuntong mentioned the writings of neither Mencius nor Rousseau, he was clearly invoking natural law to oppose the ethical imperatives of Confucian patriarchy and using his rights of "being human" to contest his obligations as a filial son. Here Shi articulated a wish to escape altogether from the ethical universe of Confucian patriarchy. To the extent that this meant rejecting particularistic local ties, his reasoning was analogous to Jing Ziyuan's attack on narrow personal loyalties. Whereas Jing the nationalist wanted to see the rise of a modern Chinese nation-state, however, Shi Cuntong the anarchist preferred a simple community open and caring to all.[28]

IMAGES OF THE CONCRETE

Theoretical constructs such as anarchism, according to philosopher Ludwig Wittgenstein, are often at their most concretely persuasive when a factor—whether symbol or model—is present that allows the theory to "be taken in at a glance and easily held in the mind."[29] Marx contributed to the method of making concepts "concrete" by turning them into images. He noted that "mental fact" or "conceptual totality" is "by no means a product of the idea which evolved spontaneously and whose thinking proceeds outside and above perception and imagination, but is the result of the assimilation and transformation of perceptions and images into concepts." Concepts as such derive from images, containing the tension between the concrete and the abstract in the unity of diverse aspects. "The correct scientific method" (to use a favored phrase in socialist China) in grasping an abstract theoretical construct is "the recovery of its own origins" in "a reproduction of the concrete situation" it was designed to explain.[30]

For Shi Cuntong, the last visit to his dying mother produced the concrete situation that his anarchism was designed to explain. He chose at his mother's bedside to break ties with his father and the middle-county society of his boyhood. In December, his mother died. He was not summoned home, nor was he even notified until a full month afterward. His subsequent fury and grief are thus understandable.[31]

The articulation of "Decry Filial Piety" marked for Shi Cuntong a critical threshold in a student life of reading and reflection that moved interactively between ideology and biography. In the autobiographical account written in the summer of 1920, Shi Cuntong showed how the readings that he did with the New Life Society spoke directly to his experience. Unlike many others who simply idealized freedom and brotherhood, Shi Cuntong did not approach issues of social and economic hierarchy in abstraction. As a result of specific encounters concerning his mother's death, he located society's malaise in an established way of life rooted in Jinhua, and he denounced his own father in the process of his intellectual transformation.

Like many other youths of his time, Shi Cuntong was exposed to the journals and pamphlets published in Beijing and Shanghai. He was, in that sense, influenced by the writings of Chen Duxiu and Chen's fellow Beijing intellectuals. To suggest, however, that Shi's radicalism was the result of an ideological conversion through printed words emanating from metropolitan centers and projected unilaterally into the provinces—a mere product of outside influence—is to deny the significance of his biography. It is also to deprive his reading and thought of the elements of agency and autonomy. During the May Fourth Movement in Hangzhou, many other youths had gained exposure to New Culture ideas, but not all of them turned into anarchocommunists. Among those who did, a disproportionately large number of the province's radicals hailed from its middle-county society. This radicalization was driven by an experience with middle-county life that, in its sheer concreteness, could not be reduced to a mere reflection of metropolitan ideology.

The strong presence of Confucian patriarchy in middle-county society, furthermore, generated a particular form of anti-Confucianism that focused its destructive energy on familial norms. This tendency contrasted with May Fourth iconoclasm in Beijing, where intellectual leaders reacted to Confucianism largely in terms of state ideology and attacked it as an instrument in the hands of monarchists and reactionaries. Although the metropolitan articulation paved the way and revealed the patterns of connection between ideology and various aspects of social reality, Hangzhou iconoclasm, charged by a rage and a fervor emanating from middle-county society, selectively displayed intensity in certain areas over others and was no pale reflection of metropolitan input. In reading the metropolis, Hangzhou radicals brought to bear on this dialectical process social conditions and cultural traditions that were inseparable from their locale and their biographies. Without the appearance of these provincial radicals, the New Culture in Beijing would have been a movement of leaders without followers. To the extent that the center depended on the activation of the provinces in order to be the center, middle-county radicalism represented more than local dialogue; it supplied the energy to fan the fire of iconoclasm across the prairie, a process that was bound to change the tenor of iconoclasm in the metropolis.

Hangzhou's conservative authorities, like its youthful radicals, duly recognized the concreteness of the iconoclastic threat. The moment for action had arrived.

THE COUNTERATTACK

The provincial government's first angry reaction was to curb the circulation of the *Zhejiang New Tide Weekly*. The journal by then was circulating well beyond Zhejiang's provincial boundary, and copies of earlier issues were being reprinted and resold in Shanghai's foreign concessions. Lu Yongxiang, Zhejiang's military governor, sent the police to order the Zhejiang Printing Company to stop all printing jobs for the New Tide Society. Together with Qi Yaoshan, Zhejiang's civilian governor, Lu cabled Beijing on November 25 in confidence. They described the journal as a product of "volatile youths" falling under the influence of "instigators" and "conspirators" who exposed them to drastic ideas of "social reform and family revolution." This unfortunate development, Lu suggested, was by no means unique to Zhejiang, but part of a national problem. These youths, Lu went on, "treated labor as sacred . . . viewed loyalty and filial piety as vice . . . disrupted order . . . [and] corrupted fine custom." Because irreverence was in vogue, many young people rushed to embrace radical ideas out of a fear that they "otherwise might appear to be behind their time [*hou shi*]." Young students "clustered and hovered about like ants and bees" to follow the instigators down the wrong path, behaving, in the eyes of the governor, "as if they had lost their human nature."[32] Invoking the country's publication code, Governor Lu reported that he had ordered the police to stop all future publications as well as mail distribution of the journal. He had also ordered the provincial bureau of education to conduct an investigation into the publishing activities of *Zhejiang New Tide Weekly* so as to determine individual responsibility. He urged the Beijing government to help curb the circulation of the journal into other provinces. A week later, the State Council (Guowu yuan) in Beijing, in response to Lu's request, banned the printing and distribution of the journal throughout the country.[33]

The mood in the New Tide Society's next meeting was tense and despondent. The governor's cable to Beijing reflected a particularly hostile strand of conservative opinion in the provincial capital, which attributed Hangzhou iconoclasm to youthful frenzy and volatility. It also purported to see behind the iconoclasm a broader political conspiracy masterminded by a distinct collection of enemies. In a language that called to mind the late imperial government's campaigns against heterodox religious sects, young radicals were portrayed as having been beguiled and became dangerously out of touch with their true nature. The situation required firm measures of intervention by the authorities for the well-being of the students as well as for the good of society as a whole. By presenting the case in this light, Lu showed that the government had armed its will to act.

Confronted with the wrath and the power of the state, the society's members were divided in their responses. Younger members from the First Middle School, who had been uncertain about the journal's radical turn in the first place, were ready to give in as well as to give up. Shi Cuntong, however, insisted that the journal should carry on its struggle against the provincial authorities in Hangzhou and that the group should print the third issue of *Zhejiang New Tide*. This was to be done in an even larger number of copies and distributed free of charge. Shi vehemently declared that he himself would welcome the prospect of a direct confrontation with the Hangzhou police, and, if necessary, "die a martyr's death." During the intense discussion that ensued, Shi Cuntong "went into a fit, uttered strings of vicious curses as if seized by sudden madness."[34] Shi's fierce determination carried the day. Members of the society voted to accept the offer of Dai Jitao and Shen Xuanlu, coeditors of the Nationalist Party–sponsored *Weekend Review*, to print the third issue of *Zhejiang New Tide* in Shanghai's French Concession, which, along with Shanghai's International Settlement, lay safely outside the jurisdiction of the Chinese state. When the printed copies of the third issue were brought by train from Shanghai to Hangzhou, Zhejiang authorities acted again, threatening to throw into jail anyone who attempted to distribute the journal and ordering the confiscation of all copies sent through the postal service. Only a handful of copies of the journal, therefore, gained circulation among the immediate circle of friends of the editors. For all practical purposes the *Zhejiang New Tide Weekly* had been forcibly put out of existence in Hangzhou.[35]

The conservative faction within the provincial capital, meanwhile, launched its attack on Jing Ziyuan and his liberal allies. On November 25, a bureau of education official arrived at First Normal to interview the principal and to indicate the government's intention to put the school "back in order." Jing Ziyuan was held responsible for the publication of *Zhejiang New*

Tide—fourteen of the society's twenty-eight members were First Normal students—and was asked to punish Shi Cuntong with expulsion.[36] On November 28, fifty-one assemblymen petitioned the governor to demand the immediate dismissal of Jing Ziyuan as principal of the First Normal School. The assemblymen also asked for a thorough investigation into the activities of the Zhejiang New Tide Society.[37] On December 7, the assembly adopted a resolution based on a draft prepared by the Taizhou assemblyman Ruan Shangfu, which called not only for a public denunciation of Jing Ziyuan's "pernicious influence" on young students, but also for criminal proceedings against him as the "instigator" inciting Zhejiang's youth to radical activities. The assembly then cabled its resolution to Beijing to the offices of the president, the prime minister, and the minister of education. To press forward with the charges against Jing, on December 29 another fourteen assemblymen wrote to Zhejiang's governor Lu Yongxiang and urged him to commence the legal process immediately.[38]

The actual task of purging the First Normal School of Jing Ziyuan and his radical students fell on Xia Jingguan, the new minister of Zhejiang's provincial bureau of education.[39] A supporter of Liang Qichao and his party of constitutionalists, Xia Jingguan was a respected classical essayist and a former director of Shanghai's private Fudan College in the 1900s. On receiving the order, he realized that he was about to be caught between a conservative faction entrenched in the provincial political system and a liberal-progressive network with ready access to a national audience of the educated via Shanghai- and Beijing-based journals and professional associations. Xia Jingguan tried to avoid turning Jing Ziyuan into a moral hero and political martyr. Instead of openly forcing Jing out, Xia suggested that Jing resign from the headmastership of First Normal School. Jing, however, flatly refused.

To appease the conservatives, Xia Jingguan then tried to get Jing Ziyuan to purge May Fourth radicals and supporters from the First Normal School. Jing Ziyuan refused to be instrumental to this process. Xia was forced to take the action himself. He ordered the immediate expulsion of Shi Cuntong and other radical students from their school. He also dismissed the four Chinese teachers who had been supportive of the radicals: Xia Mianzun, Liu Dabai, Chen Wangdao, and Li Cijiu. Jing Ziyuan, still the principal, offered a vigorous defense on behalf of the assailed teachers and students. He argued, as did his long-time friend President Cai Yuanpei at Beijing University, that no immoral deeds had been committed, just the articulation of iconoclastic ideas. He stressed, furthermore, that student behavior on campus was strictly a matter for the educators and not for the police.

It was none of the business of the state, in short, to intrude on the school campus. Jing Ziyuan's stance vis-à-vis the provincial educational minister greatly enhanced his stature in the eyes of his students. It also incensed the conservatives.

Further exchanges took place between the bureau and the school, until Xia Jingguan finally succeeded in forcing Jing Ziyuan's resignation from the First Normal School by simultaneously announcing Jing's promotion to advisor to the provincial bureau of education, and the appointment of Wang Gengsan as the new principal of the school. When he learned of Xia's announcement, Jing Ziyuan promptly resigned. He left for his hometown in Shangyu (Shaoxing), resigning from the presidency of the Zhejiang Provincial Educational Association as well.[40]

Wang Gengsan, the new appointee, was formerly dean of academic affairs at First Normal. To show his solidarity with the faculty and students in opposition to the provincial government, Wang refused to assume his new office. Xia Jingguan then offered the post to Jin Bu, an official in the provincial bureau of education. By this time Jing Ziyuan had already departed. Confronted with the prospect of a bureaucratic appointee as their new principal and deprived of the guidance of the senior liberals of the educational association, members of the Student Self-Rule Association (Xuesheng zizhi hui) of the First Normal School mobilized to take matters into their own hands.

The creation of the student association on the campus of First Normal dated back to the fall of 1919, when, in keeping with the spirit of "liberation" (*jiefang*) associated with the New Culture Movement, Jing Ziyuan introduced several measures onto the campus of First Normal and brought important changes into his students' lives. He recognized, first of all, that too often in contemporary schools power was concentrated overwhelmingly at the top in the hands of the principal—so much so that the majority of faculty members and students felt denied their autonomy and participation. They consequently lost their commitment and motivation. In addition, Jing believed that the essence of educational reform lay not in coming up with new "isms" and goals with which to harangue the students—a mere preoccupation with "what" to teach the students—but in coming up with new attitudes about teaching—the "how" in motivating and interacting.[41] He decided, therefore, to embark on a thorough administrative restructuring of the school based on the principle of student self-rule, and to turn the student body into an active entity in the administration of student affairs.

To delegate responsibilities and decentralize the administration, Jing Ziyuan created a sixteen-member faculty committee and vested it with full administrative authority. This committee set itself to the task of reorganizing First Normal's academic curriculum in the fall of 1919. The most radical measure, from the viewpoint of the conservatives, was the decision to stop teaching Confucian classics and classical literature in all Chinese classes, and to offer, instead, modern vernacular essays written by contemporaries—a measure that reflected the educational philosophy held by First Normal Chinese teachers Xia Mianzun, Liu Dabai, Chen Wangdao, and Li Cijiu. Instead of being taught to recite poetry and rhymed couplets, students were trained to analyze and to synthesize. Unprecedented in many ways, and to the great disapproval of the conservatives, much emphasis was also placed on speech, debates, and verbal presentation.[42]

Jing then organized the students into a self-governing body and empowered it not only with the formulation and enforcement of all rules pertaining to student conduct, but also with the management of all student affairs, including the dining commons. Students were allowed to assess and collect their own fees, supervise the dining hall staff directly, and maintain their own accounting records without the school administration's involvement. They also made their own rules on such matters as overnight leave of absence on weekdays and the ban on smoking. On October 16, 1919, Jing announced a "Draft Regulations for Student Self-Rule" and formally divided administrative responsibility at First Normal between the faculty committee and the student self-rule body. The faculty committee became the highest authority that made all decisions on academic matters. The student self-rule body took charge of all matters concerning student life on campus, including extracurricular "research and scholarship," "thoughts and speech," "moral conduct," "discipline and punishment," and "social service."[43]

When Shi Cuntong's article "Decry Filial Piety" appeared in *Zhejiang New Tide Weekly* later that November and stirred up a major controversy, therefore, it fell not on First Normal's faculty and administration, but on its Student Self-Rule Association to offer a response. Jing Ziyuan had earlier expressed his reservation about Shi's piece, criticizing it for failing to offer "a new definition of filial piety" and for focusing too much on the negative aspects of filial piety without providing something positive in its stead. One First Normal student, Ling Dujian, actually wrote a rebuttal of "Decry Filial Piety," using his own money to print it for circulation. Consequently, when the province's conservative authorities ordered Shi Cuntong punished, the Student Self-Rule Association not only found him blameless, but summoned Ling Dujian instead to appear before its tribunal and questioned him closely on whether he had been acting at the behest of the authorities.[44]

With its handling of campus issues of all sorts, the Student Self-Rule Association, by the end of the fall term, developed a strong sense of identification with the liberal progressives in provincial politics and a close involvement in the daily operations of the school. Because this was a direct result of Jing Ziyuan's campus reform in the aftermath of the May Fourth Movement, support for student self-rule was translated into support for New Culture values, which were equated with the measures and doctrines espoused by Jing Ziyuan.

On February 9, 1920, Jing Ziyuan resigned from the headmastership at First Normal and left Hangzhou. The Student Self-Rule Association strongly demanded that he be reappointed. It also refused to allow Jin Bu, the new appointee, to take up his duties on campus. In the next few weeks First Normal students held numerous meetings, raised an emergency action fund, drafted several proclamations, and sent delegates to petition the provincial government. Even though February was traditionally the month for New Year holidays on the lunar calendar, many First Normal students, especially a core from the Jin-Qu Basin, chose to stay in residence to offer a timely response to the provincial government. To prepare themselves for action, they sent delegates out into several counties in the Shaoxing and Huzhou areas to alert students who had gone home to the imminent confrontation and to ask for their immediate return to school.[45]

In mid-March, rumors reached the students that the bureau of education planned to have the school disbanded. First Normal students, in anger and agitation, held a campus rally and adopted a resolution that required everyone "to insist to the end on the cultural movement . . . to take no action without the consent of the student body as a whole . . . to stay on campus until the administrative crisis reached a satisfactory resolution . . . not to leave Hangzhou unless forced to do so by the military and the police . . . [and] to prepare for ultimate sacrifice until the authorities reappoint Jing Ziyuan." Fourteen students were elected to draft proclamations and petitions. Another four—including Xuan Zhonghua, who was later executed in 1927 by the Guomindang as the head of the Zhejiang provincial committee of the Chinese Communist Party—were elected to present the documents to the governor and to the provincial minister of education. The students' meeting with Xia Jingguan, publicized in several Shanghai and Beijing newspapers but especially in the pages of the Shanghai Guomindang newspaper *Republican Daily* on March 18, produced little results. First Normal students, meanwhile, organized themselves into guard units, both to maintain order on campus and to control all traffic in and out of the school.[46]

During the following week student delegates tried in vain to present their views to the provincial authorities. Cai Yuankang (courtesy name: Guqing), head of the Zhejiang branch of the Bank of China, member of the Zhejiang Provincial Educational Association, and Cai Yuanpei's younger brother, volunteered to carry messages back and forth between Governor Qi Yaoshan, Jing Ziyuan, and the students. Cai was unable, however, to persuade the governor to soften his stance, nor was he able to persuade the students to give up. When the new principal Jin Bu arrived at First Normal campus on March 22, Jin and the faculty and staff that he had assembled were forcefully turned away by the student guards. The Student Association, meanwhile, issued an invitation to Shen Zhongjiu, the anarchist editor of *Tides in Education*, to come and lecture. Two days later Shen arrived to speak. On the same day the bureau of education posted a notice on the front gate of First Normal, announcing that the school was to be closed down immediately. The following morning the students woke up to find forty-some armed policemen standing on guard to the entrance of their school. The policemen had forced the student guards to retreat from their position, and their mission was both "to protect school property" and "to disperse the students immediately from the campus."[47]

First Normal students refused to give in. They sent telegrams to Shanghai newspapers to plead their case, and continued on with their petitions and meetings. On March 27, they marched to the bureau of education en masse and demanded that the government withdraw the police and reinstall the former faculty and administration of the school. Minister Xia responded by asking the students to transfer to other schools. When the students tried to march over to the office of the military governor Lu Yongxiang, Lu's guards burst on the student crowd and dispersed it with drawn bayonets.[48]

The following day the Hangzhou Student Association sent a five-member delegation to meet with Governor Qi Yaoshan to plead for the preservation of First Normal. This delegation included Chen Dezheng, a First Middle student who later became a member of the Guomindang leadership in Shanghai. The governor rejected the plea, lectured the delegates on the importance of Confucian ethical teaching, chided them for their absurd audacity in criticizing filial piety and in preaching mutual aid, gender equality, and social equality, and then concluded by telling the Hangzhou Student Association delegates that he had intended to outlaw their organization in the first place.[49]

The Hangzhou students' general support for First Normal students clearly had served only to antagonize the governor even further. Shortly before dawn on March 29, hundreds of armed policemen and soldiers surrounded the campus of First Normal with orders to disperse the students by force. They burst into dormitory rooms wielding clubs, dragging the students out of their beds. Only a few managed to escape in their pajamas. The majority was rounded up and herded onto the athletic field, where the students were ordered to sit down on the cold and damp ground. Gripped by agitation and consternation, many students, especially those still in their late teens, began wailing and screaming. The soldiers shouted out their orders and demanded that the students disperse. First Normal students shouted back saying that they would "rather die than leave." One person snatched a drawn bayonet from a soldier and attempted to use it against himself. Although he was restrained in time, the commotion drove many others to hysteria.[50]

Those students who had escaped went about spreading the news, and by dawn students from other Hangzhou secondary schools, including First Middle, the private Zongwen Middle School, Women's Normal School, Women's Vocational School, and Women's School of Sericulture, marched to the assistance of their besieged comrades, shouting and wailing as they pushed their way through the lines formed by the soldiers and police. Teachers and school administrators also rushed to the scene, bringing food for the surrounded students. Some students began lecturing the policemen on the value of the New Culture Movement. Several policemen, unlike their professional successors under the Nationalists as well as the Communists, were said to be moved to tears by the students' ardent desire to bring about social equality. Negotiations with the governor immediately commenced. As a result of the mediation of Cai Yuankang and the province's other gentry notables, Governor Qi agreed to call off his armed units. He also agreed to allow the school to remain open if the students were to accept the appointment of Jiang Qi, a prominent educator, as their new principal. By noon the siege was over, and the chastened students were able to save their school from immediate closure. They were also forced to accept the departure of Jing Ziyuan and the liberal members on the Chinese faculty.[51]

In April 1920, instruction resumed and order was restored on the campus of First Normal. Jiang Qi kept his promise not to reverse the restructuring adopted by Jing Ziyuan. With the Zhejiang Provincial Educational Association also thoroughly reconstituted, however, the First Normal School lost much of its influence and importance. The government never fully set aside its mistrust of the institution. In 1923, after a bizarre incident involving the poisoning of hundreds of First Normal students for which the chef and two students, including a former activist of the Student Self-Rule Association, were sent to the gallows, the school was reorganized and folded into the First Middle School, thereby ceasing to be a distinct institution.[52]

DEPARTURE

Sometime before the confrontation over Jing Ziyuan's dismissal reached a point of crisis in February 1920, the authorities, as they closed down *Zhejiang New Tide Weekly*, also pronounced their judgments against the twenty-eight members of the Zhejiang New Tide Society, both of the First Middle and of the First Normal schools, and demanded their immediate expulsion from their schools. At First Normal, Jing Ziyuan refused to carry out the order. Shi Cuntong and his friends, however, came under such heavy political pressure that they had to leave Hangzhou.

At the First Middle School, where Principal Wu Wenkai, like Jing Ziyuan, was eventually forced to resign, the authorities ordered the expulsion of ten students on charges of involvement with the New Tide Society and for organizing a First Middle School student self-rule association. Among the affected were Zha Mengji and Wang Naikuan. Zha returned to his ancestral home in Haining (Zhexi) and gave himself a classical education utilizing the library collection and resources at home. In the late 1920s he was invited back to teach at the First Middle School, and he eventually became a professor of Chinese at Yingshi University in Shanghai in the late 1930s and 1940s. Wang Naikuan left for Shanghai, enrolled in Pudong Middle School, received his bachelor's degree from another prestigious private institution, the Nankai University in Tianjin, and went on to study aviation in the United States.[53] The wrath of the provincial government forced these students to depart from Hangzhou but did not deprive them of either support or opportunities elsewhere.

When handing out punishment, Zhejiang authorities and the school administration were especially lenient to Ruan Yicheng, the founder of the journal that led to the New Tide Society. They gave special consideration to the fact that Ruan was the only son of a provincial assemblyman, who was also president of Hangzhou's Bar Association and of the city's private Zhejiang Institute of Law and Political Studies. Instead of demanding Ruan's dismissal, they recommended only the delivery of a "remonstrance" (*xungao*). Ruan's father, a close friend of Jing Ziyuan, rejected this gesture of leniency. To expel others and to hand down but a remonstrance to Ruan

Yicheng, he stated in a letter to the authorities, would mean that students in the Zhejiang New Tide Society case "had been punished unevenly on the same charges." If Ruan Yicheng were to accept this differential treatment, Ruan's father went on, he would be guilty of "betraying his friends" in a time of difficulty.[54] The senior Ruan therefore withdrew his son from the First Middle School. Like his best friend Wang Naikuan, Ruan Yicheng went on to attend private schools in Shanghai. He later graduated from the private China College during Hu Shi's tenure as college president.

Middle-county radicals who involved themselves in Hangzhou's May Fourth Movement, by contrast, experienced none of the official leniency or family support known to the First Middle students. Their critique of Confucian ethnical norms had cost them not only the opportunities for formal schooling, but also kinship ties with the Confucian patriarchal order back home. Unlike Jing Ziyuan or Zha Mengji, these radicals were no longer able to return to the family homestead. Neither were they given a second chance for formal schooling, for it was well beyond their means.

More than their First Middle comrades, however, First Normal radicals had acquired national fame on the basis of their words and deeds, and a firm connection with metropolitan intellectuals in Shanghai and Beijing through a network of reading and publishing. It was these connections, ideological and political, rather than personal and familial, that enabled Shi Cuntong and his friends, as uprooted provincials, to leave for big cities such as Beijing and Shanghai.

A NEW BEGINNING

Radical iconoclasm during the May Fourth Movement in Hangzhou, as the history of Shi Cuntong and his First Normal classmates shows, was not a sudden outburst in a dramatic moment of change, discrete and disassociated from events before or after. Many factors, structural as well as circumstantial, entered into the process of its making. It owed a great deal to the pioneering efforts made by Jing Ziyuan and gentry progressives of his generation, who had taken iconoclastic positions in significant ways and showed the young radicals how to organize their attacks on a well-established order of conservatism. The sons of these northern progressive gentry liberals often matured into liberal progressives themselves. Those who became radicals were instead sons of conservative fathers and students of progressive teachers.

Hangzhou radicalism, therefore, was not produced by the forces either of modernization or of tradition in mutual isolation. Rather it occurred when cultural spaces were crossed, causing perspectives to change, expectations to alter, and the dissonance between the two worlds to be sharply felt. In Hangzhou, new ways of thinking that trickled down from metropolitan centers via pamphlets and journals, handbills and newspapers, translations and memoirs did not in themselves produce iconoclasm; it required the human agency of middle-county youth to realize their potential for radicalism. Cultural iconoclasm during Hangzhou's May Fourth Movement was a consequence of the dialectical interaction between the quickening pace of change in urban centers and the petrifying weight of traditionalism in the agrarian heartland. At the provincial capital, earnest upriver youth suddenly found themselves straddling a larger and larger gap between home and school, personal past and present. The result was a profound erosion of faith in the integrity of an established way of life at home, and a quest for a new future by the generation standing at a transformative juncture in the province's life.

In early 1920, the contest between the progressives and the conservatives, which had begun with the New Policies of the Qing government twenty years earlier, came, at least for the moment, to a point of total defeat for Jing Ziyuan and his fellow gentrymen of the Zhejiang Provincial Educational Association. As the conservatives tightened their grip over the province's cultural and educational matters, leading figures of Zhejiang's May Fourth Movement departed for other parts of the country.

Of the mentors, Xia Mianzun and Shen Zhongjiu taught briefly at the Chinese faculty of another provincial normal school, the Hunan First Provincial Normal School in Changsha, where, with Mao Zedong as the director of its affiliated elementary school, another major center of radical thinking developed during the May Fourth period.[55] The authorities there, however, were no less hostile than their Zhejiang counterparts to progressive gentrymen and liberal intellectuals. Xia was pressured to leave for Shanghai by the end of 1920. With resources pooled from his family and friends, including a widowed sister and Jing Ziyuan, he started a bookstore in the Shanghai International Settlement called the Kaiming Publishing House. Xia devoted the rest of life to the chief editorship at the bookstore, turning it into a major publishing house on cultural subjects and secondary school reading materials.[56]

Shen Zhongjiu, following a different schedule, arrived in Shanghai in the early 1920s. In 1924 he became the editor of an anarchist journal called *Ziyou ren* (Free man). He served, in 1927, as the chief editor of another anarchist weekly, *Geming* (Revolution). In 1934 he joined the secretariat of the Fujian provincial government and eventually became a personal secretary to General Chen Yi, a senior figure in the Guomindang military and a native from Zhejiang. In May 1944, the Nationalist government set up in Chongqing a Taiwan Investigation Committee (Taiwan diaocha weiyuanhui) in anticipation of Japan's eventual defeat. Chen Yi, who chaired the committee, brought Shen Zhongjiu onto it. In October 1945, Shen arrived in Taiwan with Chen Yi, then governor of Taiwan. Shen served Chen in the provincial government and directed the flow of paper in and out of Chen's office during the February 28 Incident of 1947. The incident, reported back to Nanjing by the Taiwan provincial government as mob riots instigated by the Communists, led to a bloody military suppression by government troops that continues, to this day, to breed Taiwanese resentment against the ruling Nationalist Party. Chen Yi was later nominated by Chiang Kai-shek to become governor of Zhejiang.[57] Shen Zhongjiu returned to the mainland with him. In the 1950s Shen became an editor with the Zhonghua Bookstore and the Pinmin Bookstore in Shanghai. He also served as a member of the city's Office of Literature and History (Wenshi guan) until his death at the outbreak of the Cultural Revolution in April 1968.[58]

Liu Dabai and Chen Wangdao, unlike Xia and Shen, moved directly from Hangzhou to Shanghai, where from their rented quarters in the French Concession they made a living writing and editing. Liu spent the 1920s producing several literary volumes, including a collection of love poems in the vernacular. He remained a man of letters throughout his life, despite his iconoclastic approach to language.[59] Chen filled in as the editor of *New Youth* magazine in 1920, when Chen Duxiu, the chief editor, was invited by the Nationalists to teach in Guangzhou. A former student in Japan, Chen became a pioneering translator of Marxism from Japanese into Chinese.[60] He also began teaching at Shanghai's Fudan University and eventually reached the height of his career as the first president of Fudan University appointed by the Communist authorities after 1949.

Unlike their mentors, Shi Cuntong and his friends set out in early 1920 not for Shanghai but for Beijing. There, besides auditing university lectures on ethics and sociology, they joined the Work-Study Mutual Aid Corps (Gongdu huzhu tuan) to lead an anarchocommunist life of self-government and self-support.

Members of the corps lived and worked together, addressed each other without using family names, accepted women into full membership, and supervised each other's moral conduct according to the covenants of the corps. Quite apart from the financial difficulties that the corps had to face, the presence of women proved to be considerably more problematic than anyone had suspected. For his "indescribable sense of delight" whenever Qunxian—the daughter of a National Assemblyman who had fled her home—was present, Shi Cuntong was ready to defend her reputation "to the point of death" and nearly broke his friendship with Fu Binran and Yu Xiusong, his two best friends from Hangzhou. Shi Cuntong insisted that his feelings toward Qunxian amounted to "a pure love that was not romance"; he simply "felt happy—the whole universe brightened up— whenever I saw her; and felt amiss whenever she was away." Qunxian, on her part, confessed that life was agonizingly difficult because dozens fell in love with her wherever she went. The corps fell apart after less than two months. Qunxian disappeared. Shi Cuntong and his friends headed south for Shanghai, where, rejoined with several of their former mentors, they moved into Shen Xuanlu's office at the *Weekend Review*.[61]

Within the next eighteen months, these May Fourth provincial radicals would transform from anarchocommunists into founding members of the Chinese Communist Party, and from social idealists into revolutionary practitioners with distinct ideas about labor, propaganda, and organization. In Shanghai, Shi Cuntong and his friends commingled with provincial radicals from Jiangsu, Anhui, Hunan, Hubei, Sichuan, Guangdong, and elsewhere. Crammed in small rooms in the back alleys of Shanghai's French Concession and moving in and out under the watchful eyes of the Concession police force, Shi Cuntong and his friends nonetheless traveled far and wide, gained exposure to Marxist ideas through Japanese translation, and became activists during the First United Front both at Shanghai University and in the May Thirtieth Movement.

The diaspora in early 1920 of this nucleus of Zhejiang intellectuals thus had considerable political consequences. Expelled from the provincial capital, Hangzhou radicals, reconvening in Shanghai's foreign concessions, worked out their distinct versions of urban communism. Some concentrated their efforts on learning and publishing, others on the development of a revolutionary political party. In either case they created new institutional forms and continued the quest for a new social order in a fresh metropolitan setting. The expulsion from Hangzhou was not an ending but rather the beginning of a new, broader phase of cultural iconoclasm.

3

9 Uprooted Provincials

May Fourth rebelliousness in provincial society had focused attention on two issues: normative bonds that structured relationships within extended families and lineage ownership of property. When Shi Cuntong and his friends arrived in Beijing in January 1920 to join the Work-Study Mutual Aid Corps (Beijing gongdu huzhu tuan), they had high hopes for the instant realization of an ideal way of life free from the constraints of Zhejiang society. With Jinhua more than a thousand miles away, the provincial worries that drove them away from home seemed far behind. Hangzhou radicals soon discovered, however, that their quest for a new order was not about to be answered by the simple move from the provinces into the cities, from ancestral homes into a larger society. As Wang Guangqi, the founder of the Beijing Work-Study Mutual Aid Corps, put it, "Chinese society was a thousand times more treacherous and corrupted than the traditional family."[1] Barely four months after his departure from Hangzhou, Shi Cuntong deplored: "There is not a single spot of peace and moral purity that is to be found anywhere under heaven in today's society."[2] Whether from Hangzhou or via Beijing, the journey toward a better future turned out to be much more arduous than anyone had ever suspected.

The Work-Study Corps that Shi Cuntong joined unraveled in less than three months. A number of factors contributed to that result. The most important was the state of emotional exhaustion into which the young rebels worked themselves as the full impact of their social alienation and financial difficulty sank in. To compensate for the loss of home and connection, they turned avidly to each other for sustenance and support. The corps was like a hothouse in which emotions ran high, with idealistic young men and women unselfconsciously caught in romantic entanglements, placing impossibly high demands on each other for purity and honesty.

One day in the winter of 1920, one of the young women in the group, Qunxian, announced that she and her boyfriend Mengxiong were practicing free love (ziyou lian'ai). Qunxian fully expected to receive the brotherly approval of the other men in their circle, but Shi Cuntong reacted ambivalently. A couple of days later, after a particularly intense afternoon wandering around the snow-covered grounds of Beijing's Central Park with a group of friends chiding him for his impure and distinctly un-brotherly feeling about Qunxian, Shi Cuntong contemplated suicide. That evening, as he made his way slowly back to his sleeping quarters in the corps, Shi reviewed in his own mind the occurrences of the past six months, and asked himself, "Why live? There is nothing left in life. But how does one kill oneself?" He spent the next hour devising means. When Yu Xiusong, Zhou Bodi, and his other Hangzhou friends came looking for him sometime later, they found him utterly dazed and semiconscious, having spent too much time in the cold winter night. The friends helped him back to his bedroom. On regaining consciousness, Shi Cuntong burst into tears. He was joined by the others who sat at the foot of his bed weeping and wailing. After they had all exhausted themselves crying and talking, Shi Cuntong assured Yu Xiusong that he would not take his own life. The weary friends finally dispersed to their own sleeping quarters. Word about the episode got around; further discussions were generated and emotions again ran high. A few days later Qunxian left the corps without notifying anyone. A group of corps members summoned Shi Cuntong to their meeting and furiously denounced him for behaving like a "beast" (*qin-shou*) and a "subhuman" (*fei ren*). Within days the Work-Study Corps fell apart.[3]

With the collapse of the Work-Study Corps in Beijing, Shi Cuntong and his fellow radicals hit the nadir of their radical career. Shi, who had been confident about his ability to cope with nearly all problems, "no longer dared to boast that I'd never end my own life."[4] Shaken by the demise of the corps, Shi Cuntong and Yu Xiusong left Beijing for Shanghai, where they took refuge with Shen Xuanlu, the one-time president of the Zhejiang Provincial Assembly, attaching themselves to Shen's editorial office at the *Weekend Review*.

THE *WEEKEND REVIEW* CONNECTION

When Shi Cuntong and Yu Xiusong left for Shanghai, they had no clear plans about their future course of action. The *Weekend Review* Society, presided over by Shen Xuanlu and his Guomindang comrade Dai Jitao, was their last recourse. The two friends moved into the office of the society and began sharing living quarters with the two senior figures plus half a dozen other radical students.

Shi Cuntong's acquaintance with Shen Xuanlu and Dai Jitao, as noted before, dated back to fall 1919, when he had organized a New Life Society on Hangzhou's First Normal School campus and began distributing journals published in Beijing and Shanghai. The publication and consumption of new-style journals during the May Fourth Movement created a national network that linked radical youths in a handful of provincial capitals to progressive intellectuals in the two major metropolises. The emergence of this network facilitated the departure of radical youths from their home provinces, and functioned to sustain the uprooted provincials in the big city.

Of Shi's teachers at the First Normal, Chen Wangdao, Liu Dabai, and Shen Zhongjiu had all been contributing authors to the *Weekend Review*. In addition, Liu Dabai was not only a fellow Shaoxing native with Shen Xuanlu, but also Shen's erstwhile personal secretary during his brief tenure as the president of Zhejiang's Provincial Assembly in 1916. From their days at First Normal through the early years of *Weekend Review*, Zhejiang progressives in Shanghai were linked by co-provincial ties as well as by collegial connections developed in Hangzhou's new-style educational and civil organizations. When Shi Cuntong and Yu Xiusong arrived in Shanghai, they found at *Weekend Review* a cluster of their former teachers, mentors, and provincial elders—paternalistic figures and also fellow progressives who regarded it as their responsibility to provide the young radicals with shelter and support.[5]

The *Weekend Review* was a Guomindang (officially the Zhonghua gemingdang until the name change that took place on October 10, 1919) publication launched in June 1919 on Sun Yat-sen's instruction. Its appearance represented an early effort on the part of Sun to reform his party and capture the dynamics of May Fourth student protests in order to aid his political struggles against the military government in Beijing. It was distributed as a weekend supplement with the Guomindang's party organ in Shanghai, the *Republican Daily*, which featured the literary supplement section "Awakening," edited by Shao Lizi, another senior Guomindang member. Shao had dedicated his literary pages to the propagation of vernacular literature and new cultural values in the summer of 1919. With a distribution list of nearly thirty thousand copies, the weekly and the newspaper represented the Guomindang's two serious attempts to ally itself with emerging social forces and the new cultural politics.[6] Affiliation with the *Weekend Review* thus exposed the Zhejiang radicals to the larger Guomindang publishing network in Shanghai, and Shi Cuntong eventually became a contributor to the *Republican Daily* himself.

The *Weekend Review*'s leading contributors, Dai Jitao and Shen Xuanlu, had both been law students in Tokyo in the 1900s. Although Chen Wangdao was not a member of Sun Yat-sen's political party, he, too, shared this educational experience, and had gained exposure to socialist concerns and theories of historical materialism while in Japan.[7] With the editorial staff at the *Weekend Review* serving as a nucleus, Zhejiang radicals were placed in touch, on the one hand, with members of the Guomindang such as Shao Lizi and, on the other hand, with fellow intellectuals with Japanese training and socialist leanings.[8] This connection opened up for Shi Cuntong a world of books on Japanese socialism. It also launched him on his quest for a better understanding of scientific socialism—a quest that sent him to Tokyo the following summer.

Recent studies in the social history of Republican Shanghai have drawn considerable attention to the importance of co-provincial (*tong xiang*) ties and native-place associations in the social formation of the city. These studies have shown that because of the powerful presence of particularistic ties (kinship, lineage, and village) among Shanghai's immigrant workers and sojourning merchants, it was difficult to speak either of the rise of a "working-class consciousness" or of a "middle-class civil society" that laid the foundation of an urban community.[9]

While the network of relationships that evolved around the publication of *Weekend Review* drew on co-provincial ties with origins in Zhejiang, it was not limited to that circle of associations. Unlike migrant laborers and guild merchants from the hinterland of Shanghai, provincial radicals uprooted from their hometowns were not intent on the reconstitution of their native communities in the city. They were, on the contrary, interested in the creation of a new social order that did away with lineages and private property. This higher aspiration did not prevent them, in practice, from activating co-provincial ties, especially in moments of need. Because they envisioned a different society, however, neither were they constrained in their associations by considerations of provincial origins.

The *Weekend Review* network was the sort of organization that permitted its own growth and development along organizational and ideological lines through its members' nonparticularistic associations. The teacher-student relationship, developed back in Zhejiang, gave Hangzhou radicals an initial foothold in Shanghai. Thereafter the network fostered a variety of wider allegiances that, in the end, made claims on a person's primary loyalty. This openness diluted the exclusivity of particularistic connections, enabling provincial radicals to discover new comrades in Shanghai's cosmopolitan setting.

For Shi Cuntong and Yu Xiusong, the *Weekend Review* network made a crucial difference in their lives. The senior figures at the society did not hesitate to offer advice to the despondent young radicals. Shen Xuanlu, above all, convinced the newcomers that the failure of the Work-Study Corps had little to do with their personal problems and had everything to do with structural injustices in Chinese society. Under the tutelage of the senior editors of the *Weekend Review*, Shi Cuntong learned to focus his attention on economic issues, which he came to regard as of greater consequence than individual moral integrity in the creation of an ideal society.

Reading Li Dazhao's discussions of historical materialism (derived indirectly from Friedrich Engels via Kawakami Hajime's essays in Japanese), Shi Cuntong quickly converted to the notion that in a system in which economic capital was privately owned, no hard-working young man could hope to earn his living through honest labor, because "the value of his work had been systematically plundered by those who owned capital." Until laborers gained the ability to "recover from the capitalists the value of their work,"[10] Shi wrote, radical communal ideals of life that did away with kinship and private property could never hope to be realized, because an economic foundation for their creation did not exist.[11]

Shen Xuanlu, furthermore, urged Zhejiang radicals to find work in Shanghai's factories and to plunge themselves "into the midst of workers." Yu Xiusong, who followed this advice and took a job in the Housheng Steel Works in Hongkou, assembled around himself a group of fourteen provincial exiles and was delighted by the challenge and opportunity that Shanghai represented. A fast-paced metropolis thriving on the industry and finance that linked the Chinese economy to a global system, Shanghai was where young men and women found their freedom from the constraints of provincial society. Yu Xiusong, in a letter to a former teacher and family friend, described his delight in the "air of cordiality, affection, cheer, and innocence that fills the surroundings, which gives me the true pleasure of living." The robust mood and carefree atmosphere in his new circle gave him a new sense of beginning. To members of his "former family" in Zhejiang, Yu requested: "Put me out of your thoughts and let me have my freedom."[12]

In a different guise, the big city was also an inhospitable place that greeted radical youths with indifference and drove home to them their financial difficulties. Shi Cuntong, who began to develop lung problems that were to weaken his physique for life, chose, in contrast with Yu Xiusong, to see the dark side of city life. He cited theoretical writings on capitalism and disputed Yu Xiusong's delight and optimism. Personal freedom and individual self-sufficiency, Shi Cuntong told a friend, could never be realized in a society like Shanghai, because it was above all a place where capitalists exploited workers. This did not mean that Shi and his friends should give in. On the contrary, to build their ideal society, radical youths must adopt radical means of change. The factories and workplaces of modern capitalism must be infiltrated, Shi declared, because these were "the battlegrounds of societal revolution."[13] Shi called on fellow radicals to "burrow our way into the inner workings of this society . . . to conspire and achieve a radical, comprehensive reform from within."[14] The mood was grim, but Shi Cuntong was determined to act.

Between Yu Xiusong's delight and Shi Cuntong's combativeness existed a whole spectrum of moods that informed provincial youths' initial reaction to their Shanghai condition. Unlike members of the city's middle classes, these radicals occupied a dubious position in the urban setting. Although in the city, they were never of it. Free to pursue what was denied them elsewhere, they operated, nonetheless, on the fringes of urban society. The city was central in many regards to their strategies as well as to their formation. Yet the work that they did often began with their own marginalization. In a letter to a former Hangzhou teacher, Yu Xiusong wrote: "I will soon be leaving here to enter the factory, to assume a different name, to abandon my former style of clothing, and to stop writing all of you altogether."[15] In disguise and in flux, Yu was certainly able to celebrate his personal freedom and liberation. This freedom was also spurious, however, since it was predicated on a denial of his social existence and primary identity.

Whether in a mood of celebration or of despair, the *Weekend Review* Society, with the participation of provincial radicals, soon developed into a dynamic nucleus in the exploration of socialist ideas. Under the influence of senior intellectual figures like Chen Wangdao and Li Hanjun, Shi Cuntong and his friends quickly moved beyond May Fourth attacks on provincial society and acquired a new vocabulary that reflected the influence of Japanese socialism. With increasing exposure to Shanghai's labor scene, the young radicals redirected their attention away from the evils of "feudal" society to the sins of "capitalist" society. The Shanghai exposure opened up a whole world of Marxist writings, and Shi Cuntong became keenly aware of the necessity that he become better educated. He took up the study of Marxism with serious dedication. Out of the crisscrossing of members of the editorial boards of *Weekend Review, New Youth,* and the "Awakening" section of *Republican Daily* eventually emerged a Marxism Study Society of Shanghai in the summer of 1920. This society came indirectly under the advice of Comintern representatives. It laid the foundation, at a certain remove, of a "cell" organization of the Chinese Communist Party, which in turn gave impetus to the transformation of May Fourth–style study societies in various provincial capitals—Wuhan, Changsha, and Chengdu in particular—into organizations along analogous lines.

FELLOWSHIP IN THE STUDY OF MARXISM

Chinese interest in socialism, as we know from scholarly research, did not begin with the May Fourth Movement.[16] It was in the months after the Versailles Peace Treaty, however, that there was an extraordinary outburst of interest in socialism, and discussions of it nearly acquired the status of an intellectual fashion. A wide variety of European socialist theories, ranging from trade unionism, liberal socialism, and Marxism to anarchism, Communism, and histories of socialist revolutions, were presented in the pages of Shanghai's new-style publications.[17] By 1921, even the conservative monthly *Eastern Miscellany* featured selections from Marx's *Contribution to the Critique of Political Economy*.[18]

Among the New Culture publications, *New Youth* was the first that devoted considerable space, in May 1919, to the subject of Marx.[19] This coverage, however, did not attain the sort of profundity that passed muster with later theoreticians, nor did the journal have much to say about the October Revolution. Thus when Dai Jitao's attention was caught in September 1919 by Leo Karakhan's July 25 announcement on behalf of the Bolshevik government renouncing all previous czarist claims of treaty privileges gained in China, Dai became the first among his contemporaries to draw attention to the new government. In his essay Dai spoke of the sharp contrasts between the czarists and the "labor-peasant government" (*laonong zhengfu*) in their attitudes toward China.[20] He also turned his attention to the writings of Japanese Marxists. In November 1919, Dai Jitao printed his own Chinese version of Karl Kautsky's *Commentary on Das Kapital*, which was based on Takabatake Motoyuki's Japanese translation. When Shi Cuntong and his friends moved into the office of *Weekend Review* in April 1920, they found themselves exposed not only to daily conversations about conditions in Russia, but also to journals and publications by Taisho socialists.[21]

By the time Chen Duxiu arrived in Shanghai in 1920, it was surely not as if he had to spark interest in Marxism through the organization of a Marxism Study Society. On the contrary, it was precisely because so much interest had already been generated in a wide range of ideas loosely associated with socialism that the moment had arrived to turn attention to socialist action.[22]

According to the recollection of Chen Wangdao, who was present at the creation of the Shanghai Marxism Study Society in May 1920, the circumstances that surrounded the birth of the society seemed natural enough.[23] Because the two-storied house that had been rented for Chen Duxiu's use in the French Concession "happened to be not very far away" from the rooms shared by Shao Lizi, Chen Wangdao, and their Zhejiang followers at the *Weekend Review*, Chen Duxiu's living room, which also served as the editorial office (and warehouse) of *New Youth*, soon became a gathering place for friends to converge in the evenings. As the young bachelors from the provinces whiled away long hours in Chen's home, talk inevitably turned to problems of social reform. As the discussions went on, Chen recalled, "eventually some of us began to realize that some form of organization leading on to the creation of a Chinese Communist party would be desirable and necessary," for it seemed to be the only effective way for provincial radicals to fight their own sense of powerlessness in the large city.[24] There was, according to Shi Cuntong, also a thirst for broader socialist knowledge. The Marxism Study Society of Shanghai was thus born.

Rosters of the early membership of this all-male Marxism Study Society vary from one account to another. Most accounts name Shi Cuntong, Yu Xiusong, Chen Wangdao, Shen Xuanlu, Li Hanjun, Shao Lizi, and Shen Yanbing. Also present for many of the discussions were Dai Jitao, Shen Zhongjiu, Liu Dabai, and Zhang Dongsun. Even at this early stage disagreements over organizational forms undercut general compatibility in theoretical interest, and memberships in the two progressive journals—*New Youth* and *Weekend Review*—did not entirely overlap with the roster of the first Marxism Study Society. Dai Jitao, for one, refused to join, saying that he owed his primary organizational allegiance to Sun Yat-sen and the Guomindang. Shen Zhongjiu and Liu Dabai declined, because they were anarchists rather than Marxists. The anarchists were joined shortly afterward by their former colleague Chen Wangdao, who simply did not wish to become organizationally involved with any political party.[25] For all practical purposes, however, a Communist organization was inaugurated by provincial radicals who had converged in Shanghai.

Recent scholarship has dismissed either as ideologically stillborn or organizationally irrelevant this transformation of May Fourth intellectuals into early Communists. The significance of the Shanghai Communist movement in 1920 must not be exaggerated. If we ground the phenomenon in its social context and approach the revolution in practice, however, we see that the creation of the Communist cell organization in Shanghai catalyzed the entire urban Chinese Communist movement.

Urban Communism in Shanghai in the early 1920s operated in a social space that was neither bourgeois nor proletarian, but an urban enclave in a modernizing city under the rule of multiple sets of colonial and indigenous authorities. For most people living in the city, their most immediate experience with Shanghai's social landscape involved its fragmentation and inequality. The city, experienced from within, was where the rich exploited the poor and the modern was juxtaposed with the traditional. Radical youths in Shanghai experienced this inequality all the more keenly, since they were uprooted provincials hardly capable of finding a foothold in the city.

With its growing number of modern industries, printing facilities, and an expanding infrastructure in communication, in contrast, Shanghai, which was modern China's leading center of trade, finance, manufacturing, publishing, and higher education, was also a source of standardization and integration in relation to China's interior. One of the most significant outcomes of the rise of the city, as has been discussed, was Shanghai's ability to project its cultural and economic influence outward, drawing an ever widening arc of provincial society into its orbit. People who chose Shanghai as the primary stage of their action were able to make their presence felt to a much wider circle of audiences throughout the lower Yangzi region.

For Zhejiang radicals in the city, their space for action thus contracted and expanded at the same time. Marginal to the city, they found themselves confined, through a combination of tangible and intangible factors, to cramped rooms in back alleys behind Shanghai's busy commercial thoroughfares. But the metropolis was also where ideas were exchanged and people converged. Despite their small numbers, constrained field of action, and social marginality, Zhejiang radicals in Shanghai, compared with their comrades in the provinces, occupied a position of strategic centrality.

Shortly after its creation, Shanghai's Marxism Study Society became a center of communication and inspiration for study societies in provincial capitals such as Wuhan, Changsha, and Guangzhou. These organizations, much like the Zhejiang New Tide Society of the previous year in Hangzhou, were intellectual networks built on connections developed in local schools, book societies, and student journals. As the Hangzhou radicals in Shanghai transformed into members of a Communist cell organization, they set themselves up for emulation by their provincial comrades. Although the socially progressive in Wuhan and Changsha had been reading Beijing and Shanghai publications on socialism, the idea for the creation of a Communist organization originated with members in Shanghai. In the case of Wuhan, Li Hanjun's prompting was instrumental in the creation of a seven-member Communist organization in fall 1920 in the living room of Dong Biwu.[26] In the case of Changsha, similarly, a letter from Shanghai led to the formation of a "nucleus Communist organization of the Soviet Russian style" within the New People Study Society (Xinmin xuehui), a change that strained existing relationships and caused the society to split.[27] Elsewhere, Shanghai influences were exercised to an even greater extent in the creation of the first Communist organizations in Jinan and Guangzhou.[28]

The creation of the Marxism Study Society in Shanghai does not mean that this early Communist organization functioned in the manner of the Party's later central committee, to which all provincial branch organizations supposedly made their reports. Shanghai was central to the rise of an urban network of Communist organizations in the early 1920s not in the sense of an all-powerful command post that monopolized initiatives, but rather as a critical hub in the flow of ideas and information among traveling intellectuals. As the cases of the Communist Party's two early enterprises, the Foreign Language School and the Women Commoners' School, were to show, Shanghai drew many disaffected provincial youths into its orbit. Once there, the city functioned for them not only as a powerful shaping influence in itself, but also as a way station on their journey toward a larger world that sometimes reached beyond the borders of China to such faraway places as Tokyo, Irkutsk, Moscow, and Paris. It was in this sense that the Foreign Language School, with Yang Mingzhai as its principal and Yu Xiusong as its executive administrator, functioned as "the first school for the training of Communist Party cadres" that brought radical youths out of their provincial hometowns and set them off in their quest for socialism.[29]

FOREIGN LANGUAGE SCHOOL

The Foreign Language School was among the first collective enterprises undertaken by members of the Marxism Study Society in the summer of 1920.[30] Its principal mission was the instruction of foreign languages, including Russian, French, and Japanese. The school had a makeshift program of irregular curricula, and enrollment fluctuated between twenty and sixty cadres. The Russian class, with thirty to forty students, was often the largest as well as the best organized. Most students were given elementary training for three months, then sent to Moscow via Manchuria. Many Communists embarked on their revolutionary careers in this way. Among the first group of twenty-odd students who departed for Moscow's Communist University of the Toilers of the East in early 1921 were Liu Shaoqi, the future head of the People's Republic of China, as well as Peng Shuzhi, Ren Bishi, Ke Qingshi, and Wang Shouhua.[31]

The Foreign Language School, with Li Da, Li Hanjun, Wang Yuanling, and Yuan Zhenying as language instructors, was deeply enmeshed in the publishing and organizing activities of the Shanghai Communists. Much of Li Da's energy at this time was focused on the publication of the Party's first theoretical journal, *Gongchandang* (English title in original translation: *The Communist*). Much of Li Hanjun's attention, similarly, was devoted to the publication of *Laodong jie* (Labor circle), a journal on the conditions of the working class. Principal Yang Mingzhai and Voitinsky, for their part, had organized the semijournalistic Chinese-Russian Correspondence Society (Hua-E tongxun she) to render news stories about Soviet Russia into Chinese. Provincial youth who attended the Foreign Language School found themselves drawn into a wide range of mobilizational activities launched by their teachers.

The majority of the school's students came from the provinces of Zhejiang, Anhui, and Hunan. They arrived often via personal introductions. The geographical distribution reflected the places of origin of members of Shanghai's existing Communist organization. Students who arrived from Chen Duxiu's native Anhui included two literary figures who later rose to fame as writers associated with Lu Xun's circle: Wei Suyuan and Jiang Guangchi. Zhejiang natives included Wang Yifei, who was arrested and executed in Changsha in 1927, and Wang Shouhua, whose murder by the Green Gang, Shanghai's organized underworld, in April 1927 signaled the beginning of the right wing's attack on the Communist-led labor movement in Shanghai. The Provincial First Normal School of Hangzhou continued to provide a critical linkage between Zhejiang youths and Shanghai Marxists. Hua Lin, who in August 1925 became a Zhejiang delegate to the Second Party Congress of the reorganized Guomindang in Guangzhou, arrived at the Foreign Language School almost purely as a result of his school connection with Yu Xiusong. The Hunan group was perhaps the most numerous as well as the more enduring. Many of its members were drawn from the Russian Study Society (Eluosi yanjiu hui) in Changsha, which was run by Jiang Yonghan and Mao

Zedong. Its members included Liu Shaoqi, Peng Shuzhi, Ren Bishi, Luo Yinong, and Xiao Jingguang.[32]

Whether they had come to Shanghai merely for an entrée in the big city or in pursuit of a more distant dream, these provincial youths from Zhejiang, Anhui, and Hunan found themselves drawn into a particular style of life that constituted an urban enclave quite apart from the dominant order of the metropolis. Although they had come for schooling, their lives were far removed from students' ordinary existence in Shanghai's modern-style educational institutions. They inhabited rooms in the city's quiet alleys among millions of petty urbanites (*xiao shimin*). Yet their residential arrangements were diametrically opposed to average middle-class aspirations. Coming as far as they had, knowing of more distant journeys ahead, their lives in the city were nonetheless compressed into strictly limited confines—the result, on the one hand, of "capitalism's commodification of space" and their inability to pay for more, and, on the other, of the power of the state in the form of the police.

THE URBAN ENCLAVE

The Foreign Language School, at Number 6 Yuyangli, was located in a two-storied building on an alley behind the main commercial thoroughfare Route Joffre in the French Concession.[33] One of a row of identical houses built at the turn of the century, the building started out in 1919 as a rental under Dai Jitao's name, when he was working as the editor of *Weekend Review*. Dai decorated the glass windows with poems and calligraphy in his own handwriting. In the spring of 1920, Yang Mingzhai took over the lease and posted a sign that announced the presence of the Chinese-Russian Correspondence Society. That summer, after the creation of the Foreign Language School, another sign, a wooden plaque in black and white with characters done in the style of stele inscriptions of the Wei period, was added to the front wall. Because the front entrance, which faced a corner convenience store that sold cigarettes, was constantly under the surveillance of police detectives, residents of the building used the back door in the kitchen to get out to a lane which led, after two turns, to Route Joffre. For many students who had come to Shanghai for the Foreign Language School, this place was not only where they held their classes, but also where they ate, slept, and worked.[34]

The first floor was designated for classes and meals. Minimally equipped, communally shared, and loosely organized into institutions of teaching and training, Number 6 Yuyangli was intensively utilized by the early Shanghai Party for a variety of functions. The Chinese-Russian Correspondence Society, the Socialist Youth Corps, the journal *Labor Circle*, the Shanghai Mechanics' Union, and later the secretariat of the Chinese Labor Union (Zhongguo laodong zuhe shuji bu) all conducted their activities at this one site. The Correspondence Society office, furnished with but one desk, also doubled as Principal Yang Mingzhai's bedroom. The Socialist Youth Corps, equipped with a mimeograph machine, operated out of the room that the corps's secretary general Yu Xiusong shared with his comrade, the labor activist Li Qihan.[35]

The second floor was used as the students' sleeping quarters. Its rooms mainly containing beds, it was run more like a shelter than a dorm. The best beds were made of wooden frames crisscrossed by coir ropes; the next grade consisted of wooden boards placed on the floor. Then came just the space on the floor to put down one's bedding.[36] There was a tendency for the Zhejiangese, the Hunanese, and the Anhuiese to cluster into their respective quarters, but the comings and goings of the majority were apparently far too fluid for the clustering to turn territorial.[37]

These provincial youths in Shanghai were not merely language students. Following the lead of their instructors, they were also labor organizers, student organizers, propagandists, and publishers of a variety of journals. The Foreign Language School students worked as copiers, proofreaders, couriers, and distributors for the Correspondence Society as well as for *Labor Circle*. They also attended the weekly meetings of the Socialist Youth Corps, which featured evening lectures and political analyses delivered by Yu Xiusong, Chen Duxiu, Li Da, Chen Wangdao, and Shen Xuanlu.[38] Some were present to witness the founding of the Shanghai Mechanics' Union, which took place in the first-floor classrooms. Others were at hand to help with the preparation for the celebration of May Day in 1921. The intensive use of a limited space translated into a multiplication of functions performed by those who shared that space, which knitted the group all the more tightly into a community operating in its own enclave.

The living quarters of Shanghai's Communist activists were apparently as crowded as those of Shanghai's urbanites. Like all of their neighbors, occupants of Number 6 Yuyangli had to endure the intrusion of street noises that pervaded the entire neighborhood from dawn to dusk. What differentiated the Communist safe house from the middle-class home was in the former the absence of children, the elderly, and women, and in the latter the preoccupation with a mundane domesticity. The provincial radicals, in their quest for liberation from the traditional familial order, created not a new kind of urban family but a bachelors' collective. The frequent coming and going of numerous young males, each speaking with a distinct provincial accent, readily attracted the attention of the police, whose surveillance further restricted their field of action in the city.

UNDER THE SURVEILLANCE
OF THE FRENCH CONCESSION POLICE

Many houses used by the early Communists in Shanghai were located in the French Concession. Until the creation of Shanghai University toward the end of 1922, which spurred a move of its faculty and students toward Zhabei, the majority of early Party activities took place in these rented houses in the French Concession. Radical intellectuals who occupied rented rooms in Shanghai's back alleys worked on the translation of Marxist tracts, disseminated information about the new Russia, published journals, organized evening schools for women and workers, taught literacy classes, drafted party doctrines, contacted international as well as provincial Communists, and convened several Party congresses. They also organized workers and rallies to celebrate significant dates such as May Day. Often they distributed flyers and attempted public speeches on street corners.

Within this context the French Concession police force featured prominently in the story of the early Chinese Communist Party in Shanghai: as watchful detectives lurking in the shadows; as police officers who broke up rallies and public assemblies; as legal authorities who brought charges, assessed fines, issued bans, threatened arrests; and as consular officials who lectured the radicals for being wrong-headed. Chen Duxiu was charged, for example, on April 10, 1921, by the French police for "possession of inflammatory literature" and fined one hundred yuan.[39] The Mixed Court banned the sale of *New Youth* in the French Concession. Chen was consequently forced to move the magazine to Guangzhou. On April 27, 1921, the police searched Number 6 Yuyangli and hauled away hundreds of copies of the *Communist Manifesto* along with stacks of printed portraits of Marx. Xu Zhizhen, the Hunanese student at the Foreign Language School who happened to be returning on assignment to pick up an order of fifty thousand copies of May Day flyers, spotted the presence of the police detectives at the entrance to his alley just in time to turn the ricksha around and escape with his cargo. Two days later, after the flyers had been distributed at public places such as the Temple of the Heavenly Empress in the Chinese City, the Wing-On (Yong'an) Department Store on Nanjing Road, and the Zhabei factories, French police arrived and surrounded the house.[40] On July 25, in one of the often-cited episodes in Party history, the French police broke up the First Congress of the Party.[41] It was because of the French Concession police that virtually none of the original documents from the First Party Congress, including the Party "Platforms" and "Resolutions," have survived.

On October 4, 1921, shortly after Chen Duxiu's return to Shanghai from Guangzhou to assume his responsibility in the newly created position of secretary general of the Chinese Communist Party, Chen's residence at Number 2 Yuyangli, which had been used by Li Da to edit the *Communist*, was again searched.[42] In the subsequent court hearing the judge asked if it was true that Chen, as reported by several newspapers, had been advocating radical ideas such as "hatred of one's father and communal sharing of one's wife [*chou fu gong qi*]" in several of his speeches in Guangdong. Defended by his attorney P. D'Estrées, known to his Chinese clients as Ba De, Chen vigorously denied the suggestion. The next day's *Republican Daily* carried an angry public notice in which Chen denounced "those shameless cowards who dared not confront me directly in Guangzhou, and turned instead to the circulation of such slanderous rumors which . . . aroused the suspicion of the French Concession Mixed Court against me."[43] Chen's ally Shao Lizi, the editor of the paper's "Awakening" section, stepped in with an article entitled "Socialism and Communal Sharing of Women," in which he emphasized the socialist belief in true love and respect for women as the foundation of all marriages. Shao referred to Yun Daiying's translation of Engels the year before to make the point that the commodification of women in prostitution was the product of capitalist rather than socialist systems.[44] A week later, the Mixed Court judged that the materials seized at Chen Duxiu's residence, which included numerous copies of *New Youth*, the *Communist*, and *Labor Circle*, and books on socialism in several languages, "did not contain radical speech." Chen was charged with violating an earlier court order that banned the sale of *New Youth* and was released on October 26 after paying a fine of one hundred yuan.[45]

French action against Shanghai Communists in the 1920s appeared to consist mainly of surveillance, searches, fines, and dispersal of public meetings. Contrary to generalized descriptions of harsh imperialist oppression of nationalist movements as presented in official Chinese textbook accounts of a later time, French attitudes toward radical intellectuals emphasized close monitoring and intelligence gathering as opposed to harsh legal action. During the court proceedings against Chen Duxiu, the French consul went so far as to declare his own sympathy for Chen's quest, referring to his Gallic love of political freedom and the republican form of government. He then went on to caution Chen about the discrepancy that existed between the lovely theory and harsh reality of Bolshevism, drawing attention to Russia's inability to achieve self-sufficiency without Western relief.[46] The goal was to dissuade radical Chinese intellectuals from taking the Bolsheviks as their model and to turn their admiring gaze toward the nonsocialist West.

Although the police presence in the French Concession forced Chen Duxiu into public announcements and circumscribed the activities of Shanghai's early Marxists, it appeared to be far less rigid and arbitrary compared with military authorities elsewhere in China. Nor did it reach the level of methodical harshness of the 1930s, when captured Communists faced deportation, imprisonment, and execution. In their report to the First Party Congress in July 1921, Beijing Communist delegates cited the heavy presence of the military government and its police force as among the obstacles that they had to confront while engaging in Party work.[47] Among Chen Duxiu's worst fears about possible court actions against him in the 1920s was expulsion from the French Concession. The differential police pressure that radical intellectuals faced under Chinese versus French authorities channeled provincial radicals to Shanghai instead of Beijing. Shanghai's French Concession, more than any other part of the city, constituted a political asylum in the larger environment of China that permitted the growth of radical enclaves in the 1920s.

SHANGHAI, BEIJING,
GUANGZHOU: COMPARISONS

It is useful in this connection to make a few comparisons between the Communist movements in Shanghai, Beijing, and Guangzhou to gain a better appreciation of the contextual factors that contributed to local differences.[48]

The Beijing Marxism Study Society dated its formation to March 1920, almost two months earlier than the one in Shanghai. Like the group in Shanghai, the nineteen members of the Beijing society came from several core provinces: Hebei and Shanxi in the north, Hunan and Hubei in central China. It developed out of the frequent contact among a group of concerned intellectuals and laid the foundation for the creation of a Communist cell in the fall of that year.[49]

The Beijing organization was closely associated with Beijing University. Not only was the majority of its members Beida students, but many of its activities took place on the campus of Beida with the endorsement of both Professor Li Dazhao and President Cai Yuanpei. President Cai gave permission for the society's announcement to appear in the pages of the campus student journal, *Beijing daxue rikan* (Beijing University daily), and even made a personal appearance at the society's first formal meeting that marked its creation.[50] He assigned the society the use of parts of a university building that were made into an office and a library. That office was subsequently named Kangmuni Zhai, or Communist Studio. By the entrance of the studio hung a sign bearing a pair of couplets in calligraphy that read: "Out of laboratories into prisons; combining the strength and talents of North as well South"—the latter phrase referring to the convergence at the society of students from several provinces. Books collected at the library bore the stamp "Communist Studio Collection."[51] Li Dazhao pledged a monthly contribution of eighty yuan to help pay the society's expenses incurred in connection with its various activities.[52]

As a result of this association with Beida, the Beijing society developed into a semipublic organization of hundreds of members, including anarchists as well as trade unionists, guild socialists as well as social democrats.[53] There were those who devoted themselves to the study and translation of Marxism; others organized and educated railway workers at the Changxindian Station. The society "elected no leaders, designated no secretaries, adopted no organizational charts or platforms." The majority submitted themselves to no particular disciplinary rules and "came and went as they pleased."[54]

In July 1921, when the Beijing Communists made their report to the First Party Congress, they cited Beijing's lack of a modern industrial base as an explanation for the looseness of their local organization. The city was a former imperial capital, the site of China's national government, a cultural and educational center, and the home of major universities. Its largest employer was the government, which was also the source of funding for Beijing's major publishing houses, editorial offices, schools, equipment manufacturers, and the railroad system.[55] There were no modern workers to speak of, except for the two to three thousand railroad workers at Changxindian outside the city. Nor were there major capitalists, even though the city had its share of wealthy bureaucrats and bank depositors. The ricksha-pullers, fifty to sixty thousand in total, represented the largest category of laborers in the city. These men, according to the young Communists, were imbued with a deep belief in the notion that "politics is none of the business of low-class people" (*gao zhengzhi bu shi xiadengren de shi*), and they willingly endured as their fate the hierarchy and inequality of social conditions.[56] The same attitude also informed the behavior of the city's shopkeepers and petty merchants who met in teahouses and restaurants under signs that cautioned against discussions of state affairs (*mo tan guo shi*).[57] Beijing Communists thus found it a challenge to develop converts beyond the circle of their fellow students and intellectuals.

Even with the creation of the Communist cell organization, anarchist influences continued to dominate the young radicals. Beijing Communists reported, not without scorn, the anarchist tactic of "distributing pamphlets one day and going to jail the next" as their only strategy in "making appeals to the masses" (*xiang qunzhong huyu*). Yet the anarchists were able to dominate the early Communist cell organization—so much so that Li Dazhao and Zhang Guotao, the leading Communists on the Beida campus, were virtually used by them as "clerk" and "messenger," respectively (Shouchang *zuo shuwu*, Guotao *qu paolu*).[58]

Guangzhou, like Beijing, was a stronghold of anarchism. Seven of the nine members of the city's first Communist executive committee, created in 1920, were anarchists, not Communists. The principal body of workers in the city were the mechanics and transportation workers employed along the railroad and shipping lines between Guangzhou and Kowloon.[59] Although the anarchists and the Communists were active, the Mechanics' Union of Guangzhou, with more than five thousand members, was a Guomindang rather than a Communist or an anarchist organization in 1921.[60] The more than twelve thousand sailors who joined the strike that shut down the ports of Guangzhou and Hong Kong in January 1922 had also worked in collaboration with the Guomindang.[61] Thus the Communists of Guangzhou had to contend with the Guomindang as well as the anarchists for influence among the laborers.

The difficulty faced by the Guangzhou Communists, compared with their Beijing comrades, was less a product of socioeconomic conditions than of history. Both the anarchists and the Guomindang had been active in the city since the 1900s: Guangzhou was the hometown of both Liu Shifu, the leading Chinese anarchist of the turn of the century, and Sun Yat-sen, whose party controlled the Guangdong provincial government from time to time. The Communists, being latecomers as well as outsiders (Chen Duxiu with his Anhui accent, Bao Huiseng with his Hubei origin, and so forth), found themselves hard-pressed between the anarchists and the Guomindang. But the Guangzhou workers clearly represented a viable source for mobilization. A rally and street parade in January 1922, held to commemorate Karl Liebknecht (1871–1919) and Rosa Luxemburg (1870/1–1919), brought out over two thousand workers, the largest crowd in the country.[62] In addition, Guangzhou's students had a lively interest in socialist issues. These conditions did not escape the attention of Maring, the Comintern representative, as he toured southern China in December 1921 through January 1922. He reported to the Executive of the Comintern that "especially in the South, Youth Organizations are well developed." The Guomindang, furthermore, exercised considerable influence over the workers and the soldiers. The impressions that Maring formed during this visit helped to provide the impetus for his push to create an alliance between the Guomindang and the Communists.[63]

When the First Party Congress met in July 1921, Shanghai was clearly the one city where, as a result of the rapid economic growth during World War I, there existed the material foundation for the creation of a working-class movement that had not been cluttered by either an anarchist or a Guomindang past. The modern work force remained relatively small, and traditional forms of labor contract, enforced by the Green Gang, continued to dominate the lives of the laborers. More important, the city's Communists possessed neither resources nor a local foothold. Unlike the Beijing Communists, they occupied no university positions and had to make their living by writing and publishing. Unlike the Guangzhou Guomindang, they enjoyed neither local connections nor party support. Although Shanghai was China's largest industrial city, a disappointed Maring reported that "there exists no labour movement as we know it."[64]

Shanghai, nonetheless, was the one place where one could speak of workers as opposed to peasants, industrial workers as opposed to unskilled laborers. This city was also where foreign investments were concentrated, creating conditions for the rise not only of an international capitalism but also of a national bourgeoisie. With varying degrees of success, the city's small number of organized Communists, acting on their faith in scientific socialism, attempted a variety of activities that ranged from the organization of labor unions for printers, tramway workers, construction workers, sailors, railroad workers, electricians, and mechanics, to the education of women, the translation of socialist texts, the creation of correspondence societies, the organization of workers' clubs, and the publication of labor textbooks, newsletters, and socialist journals.[65]

Compared with their Beijing comrades, Shanghai Communists were able to move in and out of the city with relative ease, owing to the divided nature of the municipality, which had been carved up among the mutually distrustful authorities of the British, French, and Chinese. Unlike the Guomindang in Guangzhou, however, Shanghai Communists could not rely on the tolerance of local authorities, nor did they have access to funding. Maring was rightly disappointed by Shanghai Communists' lack of success in the early 1920s in mobilizing a large working-class following.

Through activities such as the publication of the *Communist, New Youth,* and *Labor Circle* and the creation of institutions such as the Foreign Language School, however, Shanghai Communists, together with the provincial radicals drawn into their orbit, had turned themselves into China's most advanced students of Marxism. They took full advantage of their proximity to Japan, and dedicated themselves to the search for the most effective revolutionary strategy. They engaged in intense debates among themselves and projected their findings into the provinces through their publications. Their theoretical deliberations, coupled with growing organizational experience, helped to sharpen the focus of an urban Communist ideology that, when opportunities presented themselves during the First United Front, contributed significantly to the mobilizational success of the May Thirtieth Movement of 1925.

Until 1925, however, Shanghai Communists struggled along on the edges of the metropolis. Caught in paradoxes—marginality and centrality, contraction and expansion, theirs was an unstable existence of high tension. Although the power of their movement was later released, for the time being it was a life of much stress and constraint. As the following brief sketch will show, Shi Cuntong's life in these early years involved frequent movement, acute financial difficulty, restless quests for an ideological position, fervent propagandistic endeavor, and exhausting attempts at organizational work. These activities kept him occupied and gave him a much needed sense of being. They also landed him first in a Japanese prison, and then in a state of nervous breakdown.

ON THE MARGINS

The first serious blow to the Hangzhou radicals in Shanghai came in early June 1920 when the *Weekend Review,* under heavy police pressure, was forced to close down. The weekly had been operating since its inauguration in June 1919 in the relatively safe haven of the French Concession in Shanghai. The Beijing authorities, meanwhile, had been maintaining a net of surveillance over the country's young radicals since the outbreak of the May Fourth Movement. The movement of Shi Cuntong and his friends from Beijing to Shanghai in April 1920, closely watched by the Beijing government, directed Chinese police attention to *Weekend Review* in the foreign concession, creating a condition that was not altogether unfamiliar to the former members of the Zhejiang New Tide Society.

Shortly after the arrival of the young anarchists, *Weekend Review* published issue number 47 (April 25, 1920), which contained a brief description of the history of May Day along with a lengthy article by Dai Jitao in which he declared "the bankruptcy of nation-states" (*guojia zhuyi*) and called for an international alliance to carry out a socialist revolution. Drawing attention to China's relationship with the Russians vis-à-vis the Japanese, Dai Jitao offered a harsh criticism of the policies pursued by the Beijing government, which he described as one of unwise appeasement of Japanese capitalists at the expense of China's true ally, the people of the Soviet Union.[66] Chinese authorities took action and forbade the sale of *Weekend Review* in Jiangnan cities. Instead of giving in to such signs of official displeasure, *Weekend Review*'s editors used their next issue to celebrate May Day with full-page drawings and oversized characters. They also printed vernacular verses that eulogized labor, demanded the adoption of an eight-hour day for the workers, and called on Chinese students to join the workers in direct political action.[67]

These declarations spurred the Chinese authorities' swift response. Unable to act in the concessions, Chinese authorities exerted pressure by targeting the journal for mail censorship. They choked off the distribution channels of the journal by confiscating all issues sent through the postal system, especially to central Yangzi provincial capitals. Shi Cuntong and his comrades soon found themselves in the midst of "mountains of back issues" and effectively disconnected from the bulk of their readership. Letters from provincial readers, once a steady flow, stopped coming in altogether because of interception by the provincial postal services. After nearly two months of futile resistance, the journal folded with issue number 53 on June 6, 1920.[68] The creation of the Marxism Study Society notwithstanding, Shi Cuntong and his circle of radicals were once again forced to confront the question of their future course of action.

Some comrades, like Yu Xiusong, plunged into Communist organizational work in Shanghai. Shi Cuntong, who was not a person of much physical strength, was prevented from going into the factories by his unpredictable health. Because of the considerable intellectual promise that he had shown, Shi won the special favor of Dai Jitao, who committed himself to the sponsoring of Shi's pursuits. Armed with letters of introduction provided by his senior colleague at *Weekend Review*, Shi Cuntong set sail for Japan on June 20. His intention was to study socialism, and he spent the bulk of his time in that pursuit for the next eighteen months in Tokyo.[69]

Shi arrived in Tokyo on June 26 and made his way to the Miyazaki household, where he was received by Miyazaki Torazō and his son Miyazaki Ryūsuke. The senior Miyazaki was a staunch supporter of Sun Yat-sen's

Revolutionary Alliance and a close friend of Dai Jitao. His son was a leading student activist at Tokyo Imperial University. The Miyazakis welcomed their Chinese visitor warmly. Almost immediately, Miyazaki Ryūsuke accompanied Shi Cuntong to have his lungs checked. He also arranged for Shi to move into a nearby house, at Mitsu Zakikan, which the Miyazakis were managing on behalf of its proprietor, Sun Yat-sen's revolutionary ally Huang Xing. Shi Cuntong then enrolled himself in Tokyo's Dōbun Academy to study Japanese and began to settle into a routine of reading and learning.[70] In addition to his connection with the Miyazakis, Shi Cuntong socialized with a circle of socialist intellectuals centered on Yamakawa Hitoshi, Sakai Toshihiko, and, at a slight remove, Takabatake Motoyuki. He also came under the influence of Kawakami Hajime, the Marxist economist.[71] Shi Cuntong avidly read the texts and translations produced by these Japanese Marxists and followed their activities closely.

Among the first socialist essays Shi translated into Chinese was Yamakawa Hitoshi's piece on Marx's "Critique of Gotha Program," in which Marx sought (in Karl Korsch's words) "to demolish Lassalle's conception of society, which was based on a philosophy of Right and of the State, and therefore on 'idealism,' [and] . . . to replace it, theoretically and practically, with the 'materialist' conception of history founded on the economy."[72] Marx's attack on the social democratic legacy of Ferdinand Lassalle at the time of the dissolution of the First International was taken by Yamakawa as an affirmation of the necessity for the creation of a Communist society not entirely on its own volition, but as it emerged from capitalist society. In translating Yamakawa Hitoshi, Shi Cuntong underscored the importance of the creation of a labor-peasant dictatorship (*laonong zhuanzheng*) that recognized the economic laws of a capitalist stage while preparing to seize state power for a future Communist era under the aegis of a broadly based class alliance led by a Leninist party against the higher bourgeoisie.[73] In the footsteps of Takabatake Motoyuki, whose writings he translated into Chinese as well, Shi also became an avid student of Marx as a political economist, and sent to Shanghai a steady stream of essays that were the by-products of his own study in Marxian economics.[74]

Shi Cuntong's Chinese comrade in Japan was Zhou Fohai, a Communist from Hunan who had earlier formed a close relationship with Li Da, the editor of *Communist*. Using the pen names Wuxie and C.T. respectively, Zhou and Shi became active contributors to Li Da's Shanghai journal, which was circulated among Chinese Communist cell organizations throughout the country. From Japan they supplied reports on the Japanese Communist Party and the Japanese socialist movement, and became key conduits of information between the Japanese and the Chinese Communist movements.

Although most of Shi Cuntong's published pieces in 1920 contained reflections and autobiographical sketches, by 1921 this personal voice was effectively suppressed by that of a budding ideologue who moved arguments surefootedly to incontrovertible conclusions, marshaling a formidable array of Marxist categories and vocabularies along the way. Among Shanghai's socialist readers and publishers Shi Cuntong's name became firmly associated with celebrated pieces such as "The Communism of Marx" and "To Apply Historical Materialism to China," which were received as minor landmarks in their own contexts.[75] In Japan he learned not only to believe, but also to differentiate. He had become disillusioned with his May Fourth anarchocommunism as a result of his experience with the Work-Study Corps. Under the influence of Yamakawa Hitoshi, whom he revered as an exemplary figure and saw as a kindred spirit, Shi Cuntong discovered the greatness of Lenin and the promise of Bolshevism in the Soviet Union.[76] By late 1921 he was ready to espouse Marxism and to wage war on paper against trade unionists and social democrats. These writings earned him the special attention of Chen Duxiu, the elected secretary general of the Chinese Communist Party. In *Shehui zhuyi taolun ji* (Discussions on socialism: An anthology), a special anthology on socialism published in 1922 under the direction of Chen Duxiu and announced as a required reading for all Communist Party members, Shi Cuntong's essays featured prominently along with pieces by some of his senior colleagues. Together with Zhou Fohai, he took his place next to Chen Duxiu, Li Da, and Li Hanjun as one of the early Chinese Communist Party's most important ideologues.[77]

In April 1921, in preparation for the opening of the First Party Congress, Chen Duxiu wrote from Guangzhou to appoint Zhou Fohai and Shi Cuntong co-organizers of the Tokyo cell of the Chinese Communist Party, and instructed them to develop the Party's membership among Chinese students there. Zhou Fohai, who was studying in Kagoshima at the time and had set his sights on Kyoto University, wrote to Shi to excuse himself from playing an active role, and urged his friend to assume the main share of the organizing responsibility.[78]

In addition to his own reading and writing, Shi Cuntong thus organized the Tokyo cell of the Chinese Communist Party, which, by the time the Party Congress convened in July, included more than a dozen people. Most of these members were Chinese students taking Japanese language lessons in preparation for a formal education in a Japanese school. Shi Cuntong gathered these men from time to time for meetings. Among those he brought into the Party was Peng Pai, who later acquired fame in connection with the Hailufeng Commune in Guangdong.[79]

When the First Party Congress convened later that July in Shanghai, Shi Cuntong, who was the actual leader of the Chinese Communists in Tokyo, yielded to Zhou Fohai's wish and permitted Zhou to travel to Shanghai as Tokyo cell representative. Zhou had just commenced his courtship with his wife-to-be and was anxious for a reunion with her back in China.[80]

Shi Cuntong's activities in Japan did not escape the attention of the Japanese police. Under the influence of a distinct group of Japanese socialists, Shi Cuntong gave up his anarchocommunist beliefs of the May Fourth period and transformed himself into a Marxist, a Communist, and a Bolshevik by his own recognition. It is somewhat ironic, therefore, that the Japanese police initially directed its attention toward Shi as a result of his contacts in anarchist circles, over which the police had long maintained a tight surveillance. Japanese police records at the foreign ministry archives suggest that the police had little knowledge of Shi's activities as the Chinese Communist organizer of the Tokyo cell during 1921. The police, however, had been following the activities of Japanese socialist intellectuals closely, and had kept a close watch over their interactions with foreign visitors, especially Russians, Chinese, Koreans, and Germans. A Japanese police sweep of Comintern agents in late 1921 led to Shi Cuntong's arrest and deportation, though triggered by involvements that were not nearly as central to himself as to others.[81]

Shi Cuntong caught the attention of Japanese police in December 1920, when *Ziyou* (Freedom), an anarchist journal published in Shanghai, printed a letter from Shi that included his mailing address in Tokyo. The foreign affairs bureau of the Japanese police, which had been wondering about "this person who visits the Miyazaki household and reports on Chinese events," launched an investigation into his background and discovered that Shi was none other than the famed author of "Decry Filial Piety" during the May Fourth Movement. In January 1921, Shi corresponded with a group of anarchist students in a secondary school in Wuhu, Anhui, and mailed them a reading list. The police opened the letters and decided to impose a tight surveillance on him.

By April 1921, Shi had emerged in Japanese police reports as "a Chinese in frequent contact with Chen Duxiu and Li Da and requiring watch," "a popularizer of Japanese socialist writings in China's hinterland," "an operator of clandestine publishing enterprises," and "an organizer of secret Communist meetings in Shanghai," all in collaboration with Japanese socialists such as Sakai Toshihiko. Almost immediately after Shi Cuntong launched his organizational efforts on behalf of the Tokyo cell of the Chinese Communist Party during that month, the police detectives closed in on him.

In May, Shi wrote to Shao Lizi in Shanghai to complain that he had been subjected to "constant harassment by the Japanese police as if in a bad dream." In June, he was visited by agents of the foreign affairs department and questioned extensively about his activities and intent. Shi tried to present himself as a student of economics living on a monthly stipend of one hundred yuan sent by his father from their Jinhua village. He curtailed his social contacts with the Japanese socialists and loudly professed his admiration for Hu Shi, the American-educated liberal, as the leading May Fourth thinker. The police, which had been reading his mail as well as his other writings, said nothing about their intimate knowledge of his past and chose to have him shadowed almost around the clock. Shi Cuntong tried to protest to the police for this virtual loss of freedom. The police reacted by moving an agent into a room next to his living quarters.

Japanese police intelligence reports suggest that the Tokyo bureau obtained fairly accurate information in advance of the date and location selected by the Chinese Communists for their First Party Congress in Shanghai. One possible source for such intelligence was the correspondence between Shi Cuntong and Zhou Fohai, which the police monitored, about the Tokyo group's representation. The intelligence apparently was not of sufficient interest to the Japanese police authorities to excite them to action. Zhou Fohai made his passage to China safely, and Shi Cuntong's cell members were left undisturbed.

Shi's stay in Japan corresponded with a period of time when the Comintern, beginning in the summer of 1920, established direct contact with Japanese leftists via representatives sent to Shanghai. In May 1921, Kondo Eizo, the Japanese socialist activist, met Korean and Chinese revolutionaries and Comintern representatives at Shanghai. Thereafter Kondo, armed with cash supplied by the Comintern, called together a group of militant graduates of Waseda University and in August 1921 launched the organization of the Enlightened People's Communist Party (Gyomin Kyosanto). This development, which marked the end of the "winter period" (*fuyu no jidai*) for the Japanese left-wing movement and ushered in the transformation of the Japanese socialist movement from study groups on theory to political parties for action, promptly caught the attention of the Japanese police.[82]

On October 5, 1921, Zhang Tailei, who had been traveling with Maring as the latter's interpreter in China, arrived in Tokyo. Zhang, who had never met Shi before, presented a personal letter of introduction to him written by Zhou Fohai. Zhang turned out to be on Comintern assignments to facilitate Japanese participation in the Comintern Far Eastern Bureau's forthcoming congress in Shanghai, and he asked Shi Cuntong for help.[83] Shi put Zhang Tailei up in his own apartment and took him to see Sakai Toshihiko the following morning. Sakai, in turn, arranged for Zhang to meet with Kondo Eizo. Zhang and Kondo, conversing in English, agreed on the number of Japanese delegates to attend the congress. Zhang then handed over to Kondo a stack of hundred-yen bills issued by the Bank of Korea for travel expenses. With his mission accomplished, Zhang returned to Shanghai the following week.[84]

Shortly after that Kondo Eizo was accused by the Japanese government of disseminating seditious propaganda and was arrested by the police on November 25. Kondo's arrest took place in conjunction with that of several foreigners, including a Comintern agent by the name of B. Grey, who had just arrived from Shanghai with more funds for the Japanese socialists.[85] The complete collapse of Kondo's party came one week later, when the police rounded up some forty of its members and supporters and charged them with violating the Publications Law and the Public Peace Police Law.[86] The police subsequently mounted a campaign to sweep up all foreign nationals who had acted as liaisons for the Japanese socialists. Because of the role that he played during Zhang Tailei's visit, Shi Cuntong was arrested on December 20. He readily admitted that he had been an anarchist since age nineteen and had converted to Communism and Marxism since. The court judged that his activities and his contacts with Japanese socialists posed a grave threat toward Japanese social order, and ordered his deportation on December 27.[87]

Once again, Shi Cuntong found himself thrown off his course of action as a result of police intervention. Just as the closure of *Weekend Review* ushered in a new stage, the expulsion from Japan, which cut short his study of socialist theories, forced on him the inauguration of another mode of existence. He boarded the U.S.S. *Arizona* at Yokohama under police escort on December 29 and landed in Shanghai on January 7, 1922. Several Japanese newspapers printed his photograph and carried detailed reports of his departure. Chinese newspapers such as *Shenbao* in Shanghai and *Chenbao* in Beijing, by contrast, noted his return only briefly.[88] His comrades in the Chinese Communist Party welcomed him by naming him the secretary general of the Chinese Socialist Youth Corps. Drawing on his experience in Tokyo, Shi devoted himself to organizational and ideological work in Shanghai. He emerged in the mid-1920s as one of the best-known Communist activists and ideologues of the First United Front.

FINANCING URBAN REVOLUTION

When Shi Cuntong and his friends had first reached Shanghai two years earlier, they had arrived as provincial radicals without a niche in the city. Although they found shelter and support at the *Weekend Review,* the magazine did not provide them with a source of income. Nor was it readily apparent where they would locate the resources needed to finance their various Party activities. A constant undercurrent in the lives of Shanghai's Communists at that time was an acute sense of financial strain.

To earn a living, Shanghai radicals were forced to make the best of what their highly commercialized environment had to offer. Li Dazhao and some of his followers in Beijing were able to draw on the resources available to China's leading government university, but the majority of his Shanghai comrades had at their immediate disposal only a handful of "editorial boards" of left-wing journals that produced very little income. Shanghai radicals, unique among intellectuals in early-twentieth-century China, however, did have access to the city's fast-growing private cultural enterprises—bookstores, publishing houses, and popular journals, which were rapidly turning Shanghai into the nation's capital of commercial publishing and journalism. Shanghai's commercial publishers were willing to pay in particular for popularized writings on socialism, because there was an audience anxious to read about its own social stress and personal frustration. The city thus offered unique opportunities for radical intellectuals to earn a living as writers and translators, even though these activities also placed them at the mercy of editors and publishers of commercial establishments.[89]

With the creation of a Chinese Communist Party organization, radicals in Shanghai launched a variety of activities. Each of these—the publication of journals, the organization of labor and student unions, the orchestration of rallies, the distribution of proclamations, the creation of evening schools, literacy classes, and recreational centers for the workers, and so forth—entailed costs. The printers had to be paid before rallies could be summoned with flyers, posters, and pamphlets. The postal service would not deliver without postage, and few essay contributors ever received royalties from the issues that were mailed. While students at the Foreign Language School were subsisting on a budget of a mere five yuan per person per month, the

Guangzhou Communist Party, which had to pay all its own bills, spent nearly seven hundred yuan monthly during 1921 for the publication and distribution of its organ, *Shehui zhuyi zhe* (The socialist). Shortage of funding eventually forced the Guangzhou Communists to close down not just their main labor journal, *Labor Circle*, but also two chapters of their newly formed labor union.[90] To assume responsibility for Party organizations in the early 1920s meant taking responsibility for their financing, which, as Shi Cuntong found out, was a trying task indeed, especially if one worked with colleagues in a haphazard manner without a clear organizational division of labor and responsibility.

When Shi took over as the secretary general of the Socialist Youth Corps, there were more than three thousand members nationally, including over two thousand workers in Foshan. Branch organizations existed in Shanghai, Beijing, Wuhan, Changsha, Guangzhou, Nanjing, Taiyuan, and Foshan.[91] Shi's main duty was to run the corps with the assistance of Shen Zemin, Yu Xiusong, and Zhang Tailei. In addition, Shi Cuntong oversaw the publication and distribution of the Corps' organ, the weekly *Xianqu* (Vanguard).

Yu Xiusong, Shen Zemin, and Zhang Tailei, like other Communists of their time, had assumed multiple responsibilities in the Party. Yu and Zhang, who were Shi's predecessors in the leadership role of the corps, had become preoccupied with other matters. Zhang, in particular, had been spending the bulk of his time traveling with and translating for Comintern representatives in China. Shi Cuntong ended up taking sole responsibility for the publication of *Vanguard*. He was not only the editor and the principal contributor, but also the proofreader, courier, and clerk. Party publications paid no royalties, and Shi Cuntong, who drew no salary for his work, had to compose additional articles for more commercial publications to earn a living. Yet he had to operate under such a hectic political schedule that he was hard-pressed for time to engage in those necessary additional writings.[92]

The annual budget of the corps was a mere three hundred yuan. Branch organizations—Guangzhou, for one—clearly expected the center to assume certain financial responsibilities for local activities. They did not, however, always consult the center before initiating activities. Zhang Tailei, for instance, went ahead and spent nearly four hundred yuan in March 1922 for a tea party that marked the founding of the Guangzhou Socialist Youth Corps, an occasion that was attended by nearly four hundred members. Zhang had gone into personal debt by borrowing from family and friends to finance this event; he wrote to the Shanghai headquarters, nonetheless, to request relief.[93] In a 1923 episode, Zhang Tailei, who was then the secretary general of the Guangzhou branch, wrote to the headquarters in Shanghai to report Guangzhou's failure to distribute flyers and statements after an incident in which two Chinese workers were killed by Portuguese soldiers in Macao. Zhang reported that he had his proclamations composed in time. There was simply no money to pay for the printing of the proclamations, however, and Zhang lamented that he had had to allow his essay to be appropriated by the editor of a government newspaper. It was truly unfortunate, Zhang concluded, that the Socialist Youth Corps had been unable to take a public stance on this important issue.[94] In instances like these, it was up to Shi Cuntong, as the central secretary general, to cope with and respond to Zhang Tailei's work style and budgetary demands.

Shi Cuntong did his best to build the Socialist Youth Corps into an active organization. He convened the first national congress of delegates of the corps, threw himself into strikes and rallies, orchestrated the creation of the Federation of Non-Christian Students to launch verbal campaigns against the Federation of Christian Students, and held public memorial services for the socialists Huang Ai and Pang Renquan, who were executed by the Hunan military governor Zhao Hengti. Under Shi Cuntong's leadership, the Socialist Youth Corps became prominently involved in political struggles within the Chinese Communist Party (Zhang Guotao versus Chen Duxiu) as well as in the Guangzhou government (Sun Yat-sen versus Chen Jiongming). During the presidential election campaign in 1923, Shi Cuntong lashed out vigorously against the massive corruption in the highest level of the Beijing government's electoral process, and he was thrown into jail as a result.[95]

Engaged as he was in these activities, Shi Cuntong's tenure as the secretary general of the Socialist Youth Corps took its toll. By the time the corps convened its second national congress in Nanjing in August 1923, Shi Cuntong had concluded that he was "unsuitable for organizational work." Although he was reelected to the central leadership, he firmly declined to continue in his present position. He claimed to be suffering from an acute nervous breakdown and was ready to turn the corps over to Zhang Tailei. After much discussion Shi was finally granted permission by the corps to relinquish his responsibility.[96]

Although Shi Cuntong's departure from the Socialist Youth Corps did not put an end to all organizational responsibilities for him in the future, it was significant as a landmark in his personal trajectory. Barely four years since the publication of his essay that decried filial piety, Shi Cuntong had seen the insides of prison walls in Japan as well as in China. He had, of course, anticipated the hostility of the authorities. It was clearly much more exhausting that he should become disillusioned, more than once, with his close comrades. His youth and determination, however, prevented him from giving up. Shi had survived the winter years of his radical career and emerged as an earnest Marxist, a respected theoretician, and an important figure in the early Chinese Communist Party. These qualities led him to a teaching position in the Sociology Department of Shanghai University. From there he participated in the rapid development of the revolutionary movement during the First United Front between the Communists and the Nationalists. He also contributed to the ground-level mobilization of the May Thirtieth Movement and rode its momentum with high hopes.

10   Shanghai Spring

While the early 1920s were years of wandering and searching for many of Shanghai's young Communists, the mid-1920s, by comparison, were years of much hope and action. With the formation of the First United Front in 1923, Shanghai Communists developed a close working relationship with Sun Yat-sen's Guomindang in Guangzhou. Young Communists such as Shi Cuntong and Mao Zedong worked side by side with senior Guomindang members in the Guomindang's Shanghai Executive Committee in the first months of 1924. Party workers received steady financial support for their revolutionary activities and saw the Party's membership enjoying a period of significant growth. Cell organizations multipled in neighborhoods and at workplaces. By late 1924 more than 120 such units dotted the greater Shanghai area, each with memberships ranging from a dozen to scores of people. Hundreds of volumes and thousands of articles appeared in print on the subject of socialism. Radical intellectuals found their own center of learning at Shanghai University, where they taught students drawn from dozens of provinces, who in turn spread the teaching to the city's laborers by organizing and instructing in evening classes and commoners' schools. The injection of resources during the United Front unleashed the revolutionary energy that a seasoned strategist such as Maring had long hoped to see in a city such as Shanghai. For Shi Cuntong and his fellow Shanghai Communists who felt that they had finally discovered an effective revolutionary strategy, the mid-1920s ushered in the springtime of their lives.

THE PATH

The creation of the Marxism Study Society, the Communist cell organization, and the opening of the First Party Congress signified important steps in the development of the Chinese Communist Party. In each one of these cases, Shanghai Marxists took a further step in sharpening the organizational definition of their collective entity. As these developments unfolded, however, Shanghai Communists were also forced to confront the ideological differences that divided members of their small Marxist community. Along with the quest for an effective organization came the inevitable pressure, with or without the presence of Comintern representatives, for greater ideological consensus. Yet in the still open and fluid environment of the 1920s such pressure, instead of producing conformity, led to open declarations of differences and to ideological contestations within the nascent Party. Several strands of opinion developed within the early Communist Party between the years of the first and third Party congresses (1921–23). Shi Cuntong emerged, in this spectrum of ideological debates, not only as a firm supporter of Party Secretary General Chen Duxiu but also as a committed follower of the strategies of the United Front.

It is well known that although Dai Jitao was an important intellectual contributor to Marxist writings in the early 1920s, he soon parted political ways with his Communist friends. Dai's reservation with Marxism focused on two points: class struggle and the dictatorship of the proletariat. He was unable to accept the necessity of either one of these positions. Dai soon abandoned the Communists and did not even join the Marxism Study Society.

Li Hanjun, Dai's close associate at the *Weekend Review,* enjoyed an even greater reputation as a theorist for his work on *Das Kapital* and for his grasp of historical materialism. Between 1919 and 1921, he was the author and translator of over ninety essays, published in Shanghai progressive journals such as *New Youth,* the *Communist,* and *Weekend Review,* which contained explications of Marxist principles and also analyzed their applications to Chinese conditions.[1] A learned Marxist, Li was elected by his Shanghai comrades to be one of their two delegates to the First Party Congress. He also hosted the congress, which met in his second-floor apartment in the French Concession. On that occasion Li Hanjun and Zhang Guotao, the Beijing delegate who was elected to chair the congress, were barely able to conceal their antipathy toward each other. Zhang Guotao's "reprehensible behavior" during the French police raid of Li's apartment, according to Chen Gongbo, planted the seeds of Chen's disillusionment with the Communist Party in the years to come.[2]

Zhang, a former Beijing University student and, along with Deng Zhongxia, an active labor educator and organizer among the railroad workers at Changxindian, believed firmly in action and in the importance of educating the laborers to stand up for themselves.[3] The report that he made to the First Party Congress on behalf of the Beijing Communist organization highlighted the Beijing Party's achievement in organizing the railroad workers and in stirring them up to confront the authorities.[4] In May 1921, Zhang held several meetings with Maring to discuss the development of the labor movement in north China. He was consequently designated as the Chinese Communist Party's liaison with the Comintern.[5] In the new Central Bureau (Zhongyang ju) created by the First Party Congress, Zhang Guotao was elected director of the Organization Department (Zuzhi zhuren). He stayed on in Shanghai and created, in August 1921, the Party's Secretariat of Labor Unions (Laodong zuhe shuji chu), which published the journal *Laodong zhoukan* (Labor weekly). The secretariat also served as the Party's central organ in the direction of the labor movement.[6]

In contrast Li Hanjun, a graduate of Tokyo Imperial University (Todai), a student of the Japanese Marxist economist Kawakami Hajime, and an intellectual, firmly believed in the importance of a better theoretical grasp of Marxism.[7] Li placed emphasis on the dissemination of Marxist ideas among students and intellectuals. Instead of organizing laborers, he wished to organize converted Marxists into an intellectual vanguard. Once this elite Marxist force came into being, Li believed, it would be possible for the Marxists to gain political power through legal means. From a position of power this elite would adopt social legislation on behalf of the working class. The revolution could then be won, not with violence and agitation in the streets, but through a thorough transformation of consciousness and a restructuring of social relationships.[8]

Li Hanjun's position, dubbed "legalistic" (*hefa pai*) by some of his irate comrades because of his insistence on lawful means, followed more closely the lines of the Second rather than the Third International. He viewed with considerable distrust the street tactics—fliers, speeches, songs, slogans, rallies, parades, and so forth—adopted by the Party's labor organizers, and opposed the labor organizers' call for the creation of a disciplined Party with a centralized structure of authority.[9]

This does not mean that Li Hanjun paid no attention to labor movements, especially in the early years. As the editor of *Labor Circle* in 1920–21, Li was a principal moving force behind the creation of the Machinists' Union at Yangshupu and the Textile Workers' Union at Xiaoshadu in Shanghai.[10] He strongly disagreed with Zhang Guotao and Chen Duxiu, however, over the issue of centralization of power within the Party, and Zhang Guotao was quick to call him a Kautskyite as opposed to a Leninist, a "yellow" instead of a "red" Marxist.[11] The opposition between Li on the one side and Zhang and Chen on the other came to a head in the Second Party Congress in July 1922, when Li submitted a written statement of his opposition to the Comintern proposal that the Communists ally with the

Guomindang. The alliance, Li believed, would take the Party down the road of mass mobilization without a true revolution in consciousness. Li spelled out, in addition, what he believed the Party organization ought to be: a decentralized system of a federation of provincial soviets run on local initiatives. Believing that he had thereby burned his bridges, Li refused to respond to Chen Duxiu's summons to appear before the congress. The congress, nonetheless, elected him to an alternate position in the Central Committee. He left Shanghai and headed home for Wuhan and served, for the rest of his years, as the head of the History Department of Wuchang's Higher Normal College. As Li discontinued his involvement with his former comrades in Shanghai, he was also officially expelled by the Party, which by then insisted on imposing its centralized discipline on all loyal members.[12]

The end of his Communist Party membership, however, did not put an end to Li Hanjun's interest in Marx, nor did it prevent him from being a Communist in his own regard. In Li's words, "I cannot be a member of the Communist Party anymore. But I am happy to be a Communist."[13] Li went on to create the Research Association of History and Sociology (Lishi shehui xue yanjiu hui) in Wuhan. He edited journals, published essays, taught courses on historical materialism, and converted many of his students to Marxism.[14] In the mid-1920s, Wuchang, under the influence of Li Hanjun, became a magnet for Marxists and Communists who were disaffected with Chen Duxiu's Communist Party. These Marxists turned toward leading Japanese theorists rather than able Russian organizers for access to the true Marxian vision.[15]

Li Hanjun's social democratic ideal deeply appealed to May Fourth radicals such as Shi Cuntong, who had displayed his own anarchocommunist leanings in his earlier writings. During his first months with *Weekend Review*, Shi Cuntong readily looked toward Li, ten years his senior, for guidance and direction.[16]

"HOW DO WE MAKE A SOCIAL REVOLUTION?"

Between 1920 and 1923 Shi Cuntong was an active translator and editor of numerous articles, essay collections, and treatises on Marxism and labor issues that appeared in Chinese. His extensive commentaries and translations made Shi Cuntong, along with Li Da, Li Hanjun, and Chen Wangdao, one of the leading theoreticians of the Chinese Communist Party in those years. During his stay in Japan, Shi Cuntong wrote a substantial essay entitled "How Do We Make a Social Revolution?" ("Women yao zenmeyang gan shehui geming"), which reflected the mainstream of Party ideology during this formative period.[17]

Although Shi Cuntong described his piece as tentative and preliminary, "How Do We Make a Social Revolution?" articulated a revolutionary strategy that was self-consciously positioned as a refutation of both the anarchists and the social democrats. In this essay Shi touched on a broad range of issues that were points of debate within the early Communist movement: lawful versus unlawful means, seizure of power via parliamentary versus revolutionary processes, determinism versus voluntarism, social democracy versus dictatorship by the proletariat, political versus social revolutions, leadership by a majority versus by a minority, and propaganda and education versus organization for strikes and uprisings. Discussing the material foundation of the Chinese revolution, the social composition of the revolutionary masses, and the nature or stage of development of the Chinese economy, Shi Cuntong took as his starting point the "backward," "agrarian" state of Chinese society and went on to espouse violence as the only effective means for revolutionary changes under the present circumstances (10).

Shi opened his essay with a refutation of the anarchist position. Communists and anarchists, according to Shi, ultimately shared similar goals. The tenets cherished by the anarchists—voluntary association (*ziyou zuzhi*), from each according to his means, to each according to his needs (*gejin suoneng, gequ suoxu*), and so forth—were also Communist ideals. While the Communists built their strategies on the basis of a realistic assessment of the material conditions of social revolution, however, the anarchists showed little awareness of such things. The result, according to Shi, was a strong disagreement between the two over the issue of the role of the state and the use of power in a society that was far from classless. Because the anarchists had failed to grasp historical materialism, they had been preoccupied, in their efforts to make a revolution, with the issue of liberating individuals from the constraints of the state. This orientation was utterly misdirected: the real test in the choice of any correct revolutionary strategy, Shi announced, was the question of whether it had been built on a scientific understanding of existing socioeconomic conditions (11, 17). Because the anarchists had overlooked this whole material dimension, they were unable to comprehend the class antagonisms that would continue to exist, with or without the state, until the entire system of private ownership of property had been abolished. Neither were they able to appreciate the importance of a dictatorship by the proletariat for the realization of socialist goals until all class antagonisms had been eliminated (11–12).

China's only hope, in Shi's view, lay with Communism, not anarchism. There were two ways to achieve Communist goals: a gradualist approach involving mass participation and parliamentary elections, or a radical approach under the leadership of an organized and disciplined party of vanguards dedicated to their collective goals. Using England and Russia as his two illustrations, Shi Cuntong spoke of the difference in labor movements between an advanced and a less advanced capitalist society. Because the English economy was highly modernized and industrialized, Shi argued, England had many skilled laborers with knowledge and experience, capable of looking after their own interests in a parliamentary process. They were also better able to organize themselves into labor unions for the advancement of their material well-being through the use of legal means. Russia, on the other hand, being far less advanced than England in its stage of economic development, could count on far fewer workers capable of constituting themselves into an effective labor movement. The Russians, nonetheless, had won a major success in 1917. This successful revolution, according to Shi, was attributable to the activism of an elite vanguard party that had been able to mobilize the masses for action (15–16).

In the case of China, which Shi described as an agrarian society with few industrial workers yet a multitude of illiterate and unskilled laborers who had left their homes in the countryside, revolutionaries had been debating between the choice of two revolutionary strategies: a gradualist "social democracy" or a radical "dictatorship of the proletariat." The social democratic approach, Shi wrote, would require Chinese Communists to "set aside our political agenda for the time being . . . and work on the conversion of a majority of people to our beliefs. Revolutionary action would be taken only when such a condition has been obtained. Once the revolution has successfully taken place, the state itself would be permanently dissolved" (16). Those who favored this gradualist approach emphasized the importance of education and propaganda in transforming the minds of the people. Shi Cuntong believed that this gradualism was the wrong strategy, because its advocates failed to recognize how the existing state, in its present form, was the most powerful factor in controlling the educational process. It was futile for the gradualists to battle the influence of the state in attempts to dominate the schools (ibid.).

The "dictatorship of the proletariat" approach, on the other hand, meant immediate and direct political activism by a small number of organized believers. These committed Communists would "seize the first opportunities for action for the purpose of taking political power." Having gained control of the state, the activists would turn the state into an instrument of socialist revolution and use it to suppress all class enemies. The party of the proletariat would also aggressively pursue a policy aimed at achieving the full socialization of property. Once all productive forces had been liberated from the constraints imposed by class antagonism, Shi believed, rapid economic development would take place. A true Communist society would then become possible on this thoroughly revolutionized economic foundation (16–19).

Shi declared that neither one of these strategies had any intrinsic value as such. Making revolution with speeches and essays did not make a Communist morally superior to the comrade who spent his time plotting riots and organizing strikes. The sole valid criterion for choosing between the two revolutionary strategies had to be their respective efficacy in producing the desired goals of social revolution. The only way to make this determination was by reference to the material foundation of the Chinese revolution at the present historical moment (16–19). At a later point in his life, Shi Cuntong dedicated himself to the study of the Chinese economy in the hope of establishing such knowledge on the basis of a "scientific" foundation. In this 1921 essay, Shi concluded that given China's "backward" stage of economic development, there could be no doubt about the choice of the radical over the gradualist course of action, and consequently the creation of a proletariat's state rather than the total dissolution of the state (15–16). This was the only effective revolutionary strategy for young Chinese Communists to follow, and the only issue that remained was the question of implementation.

Shi Cuntong was aware of the argument that because industrial capitalism had not yet developed in China, there existed neither modern workers nor genuine capitalists, hence no material foundation for socialism. Like Mao later, Shi separated the creation of a unified labor force from the issue of its material foundation, and regarded the use of political means as a feasible alternative to economic forces in the creation of such a labor presence (15). A revolution was made, according to Shi, as a result of both "economic necessity" and "human endeavor" (10). China's lack of economic development was consequently no hindrance to its quest for a social revolution. To launch the revolution, Chinese Communists should simply constitute themselves into a vanguard Party, with which they could develop, via organizational and propaganda means, a mass following among students, soldiers, and the "propertyless" in general. The Party would then be ready to lead its followers to power through direct action on the streets (24–26).[18]

Compared with his writings of the May Fourth period, the most striking aspect of Shi Cuntong's thinking in the 1920s was not merely his acceptance of the necessity of coercive means, but also his ready espousal of brute force in the form of collective violence. In commenting on the weakness of the Chinese industrial labor force in general, Shi Cuntong expressed his skepticism about the decisive importance of a general strike on the existing power structure in the process of a social revolution, and stated his belief in the necessity of bolstering the labor's presence with that of an army. "We must know," Shi wrote, "that might can only be opposed by might.... It is laughable for those who desire social revolution in China to oppose the use of the military for the achievement of socialist goals in this process" (26). He urged his fellow socialists to arouse the consciousness not only of the workers but also of the soldiers (24).

A mere two years earlier, Shi Cuntong had regarded Kropotkin as the embodiment of a preeminent form of ethical teaching superior to Social Darwinism and had rebelled passionately against all forms of coercion. By the time of Shi's return to China in 1922, however, he not only had become a firm proponent of the universality of historical materialism, but also had accepted a Darwinian view about the instrumental nature of ethical conduct.[19] The transformation, as noted before, began with his disillusionment with the Work-Study Corps in Beijing and was completed during his months of study in Japan. It is important to recognize that although he endorsed the use of coercive means, he accepted violence not for its own sake but as a means for the realization of a higher moral order. This paradoxical relationship between violence and morality was closely connected with his belief that moral imperfections were products less of individual flaws than of structural injustices embedded in socioeconomic circumstances. To change the world for the better, it was necessary to change the system rather than the individual.

In this process of reasoning Shi Cuntong exonerated individuals of their share of moral responsibility and came to regard most men and women, including his own father, as victims under given social circumstances rather than victimizers. His own task as a vanguard intellectual, then, was to come to grips with the material foundation of social revolution and to locate systematically the source of collective action. The validity of this scientifically generated vision lay more in its effectiveness in producing change than in its descriptive power, although this combination of the descriptive and the prescriptive remained the basic characteristic of Shi's writings throughout his career as a Marxist thinker.

In the early 1920s Shi Cuntong's description of China's socioeconomic state and his articulation of a revolutionary strategy placed him more or less in the mainstream of urban Chinese Communism, especially as it developed in Shanghai. As one of the movement's emerging ideologues, Shi had little difficulty with Chen Duxiu's insistence on the centralization of power within the Party. Nor did he oppose Zhang Guotao's call for "direct action" among the workers. He accepted Lenin's theories of imperialism and was prepared to embrace the Comintern's judgment on the nature of the Chinese revolution. Armed with these beliefs, he accepted, after 1923, the necessity of a revolutionary alliance between members of the petite bourgeoisie and the proletariat, and readily plunged into propaganda and organizational work on behalf of the Communists' First United Front with the Guomindang.

THE GUOMINDANG CONNECTION

For nearly two years, until the death of Sun Yat-sen in March 1925, the Guomindang used the provincial revenue generated by Guangdong, which it controlled, to pursue a policy of alliance with the Communists.[20] The impact of the United Front on the Communist movement was the most discernible in Guangzhou and Shanghai. In Guangzhou, Communist activities moved into the open. Communist Party members, in conjunction with their comrades in the Guomindang, developed mass organizations among women, students, shop clerks, and peasants. Increasingly after the First Party Congress of the Guomindang in January 1924, Communist activists from central Chinese provinces took up strategic positions in the central party organs of the Guomindang. The conjoined nature of the Guomindang–Communist Party operation, however, bred tension between the right and left wings of Guomindang followers, which escalated into full-scale confrontations after Sun's death in 1925.[21]

In Shanghai, where the Guomindang commanded neither the city nor an established party apparatus, the impact of the United Front on the Communist movement was no less significant, albeit in a different way. With the funding support of the Guomindang, two developments helped to unleash the mobilizational potential of the city's Communist movement amid Shanghai's large population of students and workers. First was the creation in 1923 of Shanghai University, which gave the city's Communist intellectuals an institutional niche as well as an operational base for propaganda and organization. Second was the reorganization of the Guomindang party structure in the lower Yangzi region, especially in Shanghai,

Zhejiang, and Jiangsu, under a team of veteran Nationalists and young Communists, which put in place a usable infrastructure for political mobilization.

SHANGHAI UNIVERSITY

The successful reorganization in 1923 of the Southeast Higher Normal School (Dongnan gaodeng shifan xuexiao) into Shanghai University, into which the Guomindang in Guangzhou reportedly poured "tens of thousands" of yuan in support, was a landmark event in the development of urban Communism. After nearly a full year of exploratory discussion, the Shanghai Guomindang Central Executive Committee finally placed funding for the university on a regular schedule at an impromptu meeting called by Hu Hanmin on December 28, 1923. The committee members present referred to the school as a "Party school" and considered, in addition to the problem of its operating budget, capital expenditures for the construction of a permanent campus.[22] Although funding for the school was far from adequate thereafter, the faculty and students of Shanghai University had available the use of a cluster of buildings, a collection of books and materials, a source of income from tuition and fees, a budget from Guangzhou, and a Guomindang network to turn to in times of need.

As the Guomindang looked after the funding of the university, young Communists worked toward the creation of a faculty and a curriculum that would embody their socialist ideal. After Yu Youren, a veteran Guomindang member, announced his willingness to take on the presidency of Shanghai University, many Communists assumed faculty and administrative positions under his administration. Li Dazhao, the initiator of the Marxism Study Society in Beijing, was instrumental in the appointment of several leading Communists to key posts in Shanghai University. Deng Zhongxia (1897–1933), a former Beida student and Zhang Guotao's comrade in Beijing's labor organization, was appointed to the deanship of the new school on Li Dazhao's recommendation. Qu Qiubai (1899–1935), the future secretary general of the Chinese Communist Party in 1927–28, became the head of the Sociology Department. Cai Hesen (1890–1931), Yun Daiying (1895–1931), Zhang Tailei (1898–1927), Peng Shuzhi (1896–1983), Li Da (1890–1966), and Li Ji (1894–?)—the Party's ideologues and student organizers—all joined to teach. In 1923 Shi Cuntong joined his comrades and became a professor in the Sociology Department.[23]

In the next two years Shanghai University, aided by the presence of this active community of radical intellectuals, emerged as a center of socialist thinking and organizational activity that projected its influence far and wide into many lower Yangzi cities. While the professors popularized the study of historical materialism, published their lecture notes, and initiated the teaching of Marx on Shanghai college campuses, the students were busy setting up evening schools, literacy classes, reading clubs, and after-work centers for the workers. The university, in addition, hosted a series of highly visible public lectures that featured senior Guomindang figures such as Hu Hanmin and Dai Jitao, on the one hand, and New Culture leaders from Beijing such as Hu Shi and Li Dazhao, on the other. In 1924, Shanghai University opened up two affiliated operations, a commoners' school and an "English evening school," which attracted skilled factory workers, shop clerks, trade apprentices, bookstore and printing-house employees, newspaper proofreaders, elementary school teachers, and lower-level Party workers, who were taught "revolutionary thought and class consciousness" by student volunteers from the university. The pupils were quite often former secondary school students, mainly from Sichuan, Guangdong, Anhui, Hunan, and Zhejiang.[24] More than any other endeavor previously attempted in the city, Shanghai University became a powerful source of influence that ideologized and organized these uprooted provincial youths in Shanghai, who shared the early Communists' frustrations with their home communities.

ROMANCE AND REVOLUTION

Shi Cuntong was affiliated with Shanghai University until September 1926, and he forged lifelong friendships among a group of leading socialist theoreticians. The urban enclave by then consisted of the narrow alleys and crowded back streets in the factory zone surrounding Shanghai University, where Shi and several of his comrades lived, ate, worked, and loved in semicollective arrangements under the same roof. Frequent debates on current events and political theories punctuated daily life. Relationships between friends and comrades, both intellectual and personal, were intense. It was a life dedicated to public issues and to ideas and actions with national import. It was also a life of enclosure and chronic financial distress, among a group of comrades acutely aware of their minority standing in the larger society. Romance as well as revolution was in the air, and the pursuit of personal liberation became entangled with the quest for social justice.[25] During these years at Shanghai University Shi Cuntong shared his life with Wang Yizhi, a young woman from Hunan. In the charged atmosphere at the university, the lovers occupied a first-floor room under the same roof with another couple, Qu Qiubai and Wang Jianhong, who also happened to be Wang Yizhi's best friend from her native town.

Wang Yizhi came from a gentry household in western Hunan. Although the family was financially well off, she had an unhappy childhood, which had much to do, as in the case of Shi Cuntong, with the relationship between her parents. Because Wang was her mother's only child and a daughter, her father insisted on taking a second wife. Shortly after the concubine gave birth to a son, Wang's father broke up with her mother and moved away into separate living quarters. Wang's mother, angry, depressed, and humiliated, focused her attention on her child, investing in her all the hope that other parents would reserve for a son. She encouraged Wang to do her very best in her study with the family tutor, and pressed on the child the importance of literacy and education and how these advantages might lead to a better personal future. No sooner had Wang turned fourteen, however, than her mother died of illness. Wang Yizhi blamed her mother's death on her father's callousness. She ran away from home, even before she had completed the hundred days of ritually prescribed mourning, and applied to the Provincial Second Women's Normal School in Taoyuan, which was "several hundreds of li away from home." There she spent the next five years as a student living on campus, relying fully on provincial government support for tuition, fees, books, and room and board. She also received two uniforms each year. These provisions enabled her to declare her independence from her father.[26]

In the months after the May Fourth Movement, Wang Yizhi threw herself into the reading of new publications arriving from Shanghai and Beijing—Chinese translations of Rousseau, Plato, Huxley, and Kropotkin. An avid reader of the Beijing University student publication *Xinchao* (Renaissance), she was particularly affected by articles that "opposed feudal ethical norms, exposed the ugly side of feudal families, voiced sympathy for women in their powerlessness, advocated individual liberation and equality between men and women." These essays, according to Wang, "gave voice to the thoughts that I have long held and yet never articulated" and helped to "shatter the chains that feudal norms had placed on my mind." They gave Wang "the courage to break away from feudal ethics." Echoing Shi Cuntong several provinces away, she voiced her own thoughts decrying filial piety and female chastity, and put these thoughts down in writing in classroom compositions. Together with a dozen other classmates, Wang Yizhi cut short her hair and wore it "the way men do." Such "rebellious behavior" brought these young women much criticism from families, school authorities, and local gentry society. "We were seen as strange creatures and monstrous incarnations, and exposed to much ire and ridicule." Wang and her friends, however, persisted. They demanded that the school add an English language course to the curriculum, and, when opposed by the school authorities, they even staged a strike.

In the summer of 1921, Wang Yizhi graduated from the Second Women's Normal School. Unable to pursue further education, she took a teaching job with an elementary school at the river port of Xupu in central Hunan. Filled with rage over the inequality between men and women, she gained further exposure to new publications emanating from Shanghai, including *New Youth*, now under the editorship of Chen Wangdao, and *Communist*, edited by Li Da. She felt like "an unbridled horse, poised to set forth." She also saw herself as someone "standing at a crossroads, not sure in which direction to turn." Wang Yizhi became all the more eager to leave Hunan for a place where she might "gain further knowledge, broaden intellectual horizons, and discover the right path to follow."

When she received a letter from her former classmate Wang Jianhong informing her about the new Commoners' School for Women (Pingmin nüxiao) that had just been started in Shanghai, Wang Yizhi was overjoyed. The school required no tuition, offered opportunities for work-study, and featured a faculty roster studded with names made famous by the new publications of the May Fourth Movement. Wang Yizhi thought that this was the perfect school for her to attend. It was operated, unbeknownst to either woman, by the Shanghai Communist Party, and was located, for a while, in Li Da's French Concession apartment on a block named Fude Li. Together with Wang Jianhong and four other former classmates from the Hunan Women's Normal School, Wang Yizhi boarded a steamship heading down the Yangzi for Shanghai in February 1922.

The Commoners' School, which was run much like the Foreign Language School, combined Party work, work-study, and the instruction of socialist theories under one roof. Compared with the Hunan Women's Normal School, it was a spartan place operating on an ad hoc basis. Thirty-some students were divided into two classes: beginners and advanced. The women pupils spent much of their time sewing and making socks for their "work-study." As for schooling, Gao Yuhan, the Chinese instructor, appeared to be the only person who taught his classes on a regular schedule. All the other instructors, including Chen Wangdao and Shen Yanbing (Mao Dun), were busy Party organizers, ideologues, translators, and publishers who taught as they found time. They gave lectures rather than classes and referred the Hunanese women to readings such as

the "A. B. C. of Communism" and "Anti-Duhring." It was in this haphazard setting that Wang Jianhong met Qu Qiubai and Wang Yizhi met
Shi Cuntong, the new secretary general of the Socialist Youth Corps who
had just returned from his stint in Japan.

At the Commoners' School for Women, Wang Yizhi gained exposure
not only to Marxism, but also to the mobilization of Shanghai's labor
movement. Because of her Hunanese accent, she was rarely asked to address
Shanghai's women textile workers in open rallies; instead she conducted
interviews with them in individual meetings. During the labor strikes of
1922, Wang and her friends were organized into "support teams" to ask
the public for contributions to the striking workers. These support teams
of three to five members, primarily women, often stationed themselves by
the entrances of Shanghai's popular amusement centers or by the teaming
department stores on busy Nanjing Road. They would display banners
carrying the message *"Zhiyuan bagong"* (Support the strikers) and use a
large bamboo jar with a small opening for coins and notes to collect
donations. The amount of donation ranged "from one to two mao to several
yuan," contributed mostly by men who were moved to action by the
presence of young women activists. Other passersby, who chose to ignore
the student teams, were not allowed to enter the amusement hall with a
clear conscience: "Whenever this happened," Wang Yizhi recalled, "we
would angrily point a finger at their back and berate them for their
selfishness and indifference to the workers who were our compatriots."
Wang Yizhi and her friends had to flee as soon as members of the Shanghai
Municipal Police appeared. Besides collecting contributions, she also went
out on the street distributing handbills and posting flyers.

These activities to support the strikers, although born by students of the
Commoners' School for Women, were coordinated by the Socialist Youth
Corps. To show the Youth Corps's commitment to the labor movement,
Shi Cuntong often went out into the street with the support teams himself.
Energized by Shi's dedication, Wang Yizhi joined the corps in mid-1922.
She also became a member of the Chinese Communist Party later that year.
The next summer, Shi and Wang rented a room together near the uni-
versity and were recognized by their comrades as a couple.

The union between Shi and Wang lasted for only two years. In a volume
published twenty years later and offered as a piece of advice to young
couples, Shi urged them "not to share living quarters with an unmarried
young friend on a regular basis." He also warned them to "avoid sharing
living quarters with another couple with whom one has developed a deep

friendship." This was because "these arrangements are likely going to lead to unexpected difficulties, even major tragedies."[27] Shi Cuntong was obviously speaking from firsthand experience.

In a spirit of communal partaking similar to the ambience that prevailed at the Work-Study Corps, the Foreign Language School, and the Commoners' School for Women, Shi and Wang shared their space liberally with fellow revolutionaries and offered their hospitality to comrades such as Zhang Tailei, who fequently traveled to Shanghai from Guangzhou on Party business related to the Socialist Youth Corps. Wang Yizhi, who traced her rebelliousness to her father's humiliation of her mother, had continued to feel restless after her marriage to Shi. In the charged atmosphere surrounding Shanghai University in the early 1920s, when romance commingled with revolution, she fell in love with Zhang Tailei. In February 1925, just as Shi was busily engaged in organizing the city's ill-fated strikes of that month, Wang Yizhi defiantly left Shi for Zhang, and the new couple moved away quite abruptly without announcing their destination.

This incident, widely known in United Front circles at the time, exposed Shi Cuntong to much ridicule. He reportedly "went in pursuit of them from Shanghai to Changsha, from Changsha to Qingdao." He failed to locate Wang Yizhi's whereabouts and returned to Shanghai feeling distraught. Shi then found himself embroiled in a series of quarrels with some of his Shanghai University comrades, especially the German-trained Marxist Li Ji. As in his last days of the Work-Study Corps, he was once again disillusioned about his life.[28]

During the May Thirtieth Movement in 1925, with Wang Yizhi out of his life, Shi Cuntong formed a new union with another student at Shanghai University, the Sichuanese Communist Zhong Fuguang. Zhong was a labor activist and member of the Women's Department of the Communist Party that was led by Xiang Jingyu. To mark their union, Shi changed his given name from Cuntong to Fuliang. The word *Fu* was chosen for the purpose of symmetry; the word *Liang* was chosen to form the compound *Guang-liang*—light and brilliance—with the last character in Zhong's given name. To mark the occasion, Shi Cuntong composed a poem in which he wrote of the brightness of their future together and of their fearless march forward, arm in arm. By changing his own name instead of that of his wife, he hoped to redress an imbalance in established Confucian practices that had always favored the male, but above all Shi Fuliang hoped to acquire a fresh identity and begin a new life.[29]

REORGANIZATION OF THE PARTY IN SHANGHAI

While the United Front was an arrangement that allowed Communist Party members to join the Guomindang as individuals, it at the same time launched a thorough reorganization of the Nationalist Party. The goal was to streamline the Guomindang into a centralized and disciplined organization, to initiate training, and to improve internal coordination. As Liao Zhongkai put it during an in-house work session with local Party members in Shanghai, the emphasis of this new round of reorganization (*dang wu gaizu*) was not simply to refashion the Party at its highest level, as the Guomindang had already done on at least four other occasions, but also to build Party organizations from the bottom up—to create "basic Party units" (*jiben dangbu*) such as the "district branch Party" (*qu fen bu*) at the local level in order to turn the Party into an instrument of power capable of collective action.[30]

In Shanghai, Guomindang reorganization, which took place under the supervision of the Shanghai Central Executive Committee, began with a comprehensive reregistration of all Party members in the city. The objective of this effort was both to verify Party membership and to organize Party members into cohesive units. Shanghai local Party units had developed along occupational (*zhiye*) lines in the past.[31] To facilitate interactions within the Party, Liao Zhongkai and Wang Jingwei instructed that these units were also to be clustered into subunits by residential location. Once a unit had been formed, Party members would hold general meetings to elect branch Party secretaries, who would serve as liaisons between the subdistricts, the districts, and the Shanghai Central Committee. Thereafter local branches would conduct themselves in accordance with the new Party organizational guidelines. Members would meet on a weekly basis, get to know each other, and study Sun Yat-sen's writings. Local units were required to produce rosters, addresses, and reports of activities for regular submission to the Shanghai Executive Committee. The committee, for its part, distributed numerous copies of Sun Yat-sen's writings, which, after spring 1924, included Sun's lectures on Three Principles of the People (*sanmin zhuyi*), and dispatched its top members to attend the local branch's weekly meetings.

The Shanghai Central Executive Committee, which took responsibility for all Guomindang organizations along the Yangzi, underwent significant changes as well.[32] It was reconstituted into a standing committee that met three times a week, supported by a secretariat (*mishu chu*) and a staff that held regular office hours at the Party's headquarters at Number 44 Huanlong Road. The committee divided its tasks into three "departments" (*bu*): Propaganda, Organization, and Worker and Peasant; a fourth, Youth and Women, was added a few months later. Each of these departments was staffed with secretaries to handle liaison (*jiaoji*) and administration (*zhixing*).[33] The Shanghai Committee issued all central Party orders, except for those intended for Guangdong, Guangxi, and Yunnan, and it made reports to Guangzhou on a monthly basis.[34]

This reconstitution, implemented in December 1923, regularized the Party organization in Shanghai and gave it a certain degree of stability. The principles of "bottom-up" representation and regional division of responsibility, furthermore, gave the branch considerable autonomy vis-à-vis the headquarters in Guangzhou. As the highest-level Party organization in the Yangzi, it dispatched Party members from Shanghai to carry out the reorganization of Party organs in Jiangsu, Zhejiang, Hunan, and Anhui.[35] The heart of the Executive Committee's operation remained in Shanghai, where the Party experienced growth as a result of the active participation of the Shanghai Communists.

During the early phase of the United Front, about seven hundred Guomindang members lived in Shanghai. Although this concentration was small compared to the three thousand in Guangzhou, it nonetheless made the Shanghai Party the second largest in the country. Starting late in 1923, Shanghai's Communists worked side by side with Hu Hanmin, Wang Jingwei, and Ye Chucang—senior Guomindang members who chaired the Shanghai Executive Committee. In a matter of months these men succeeded in nearly doubling the Nationalist Party's membership to fourteen hundred. Mao Zedong, as the executive secretary and assistant to Hu Hanmin at the Organization Department, undertook a tireless endeavor to keep the Party's membership registration up to date.[36] Shi Cuntong, in addition to serving as a project director under Wang Jingwei in the Propaganda Department, led the Party's Zhabei branch as its executive secretary, and completed the registration and organization of more than one hundred workers and intellectuals in this area in the brief span of only one week. Following a resolution adopted by the Shanghai Executive Committee, the Shanghai Party was divided up by locale into seven main branches, each encompassing smaller subdistrict units whenever the size of the Party membership would permit. These districts, created in December 1923, overlapped roughly with the boundaries of Zhabei, Nanshi (the old Chinese City of Shanghai), the French Concession, the International Settlement, Hongkou, Wusong, and Pudong.[37] Some of these district branches contained many more Party members than others, depending on the social profile of the locale and the respective preexisting strength of the former Nationalists and Communists.

Zhabei, where Shanghai University and the printing facilities of the Commercial Press were located, was clearly the most important district in the Guomindang's Shanghai organization. On the first all-Shanghai Party meeting held on December 23, 1923, over 300 members showed up from Zhabei to represent the printers, the workers, and the students of literacy classes and evening schools. Another 120 presented themselves from Shanghai University. In contrast, other district branches in the city—the China Steel Works of Wusong, the Southern University, and the Number One Trade School in the International Settlement, for example—were able to present no more than a few score of members at this time.[38]

Zhabei was also the first district in the city to complete its organizational work.[39] The district Party meeting was held on December 30, 1923, while other districts—Nanshi and the International Settlement in particular—did not even launch their organizational endeavor until sometime in 1924. There were six subdistricts (*qu fen bu*) formed under Shi Cuntong's direction, each a clustering with its own rationale of cohesion. The largest, with 122 members, was Shanghai University, also the largest Guomindang subdistrict in Shanghai. Its elected Party leaders included Shi Cuntong, Cai Hesen, Yang Xianjiang, and Qu Qiubai, all of whom were renowned Communists in the 1920s. Not too far away from Shanghai University were the editorial departments and the printing workshops of the Commercial Press, which contained a much smaller Party subdistrict (twelve members), yet the members were no less radical than their Shanghai University comrades. Membership in this branch included Mao Dun, the editor, and Dong Yixiang and Xu Meikun, the first workers to become Communists. Active members of the two institutions had been linked by professional contact as well as native-place origins for quite some time. Mao Dun, who later earned a national reputation as the author of the fictional trilogy *Eclipse* (*Shi*), was a member of the Communist Party and the publisher of several Marxist and Communist writers, including Li Da and Li Hanjun. Shanghai University and the Commercial Press together represented the most dynamic cultural complex in Shanghai in the production and dissemination of radical ideas.

Radical intellectuals, students, and workers affiliated with these two institutions developed close contacts with each other outside of their work environments. Like Shi Cuntong and Wang Yizhi, numerous other couples formed conjugal units and shared living quarters with their comrades. They took up residences in nearby areas and clustered into radical neighborhoods and communities. The third and fourth subdistricts of the Zhabei Guomindang, referred to as Baotong Road and Qiujiang Road in Party documents, reflected the functioning of such clusterings.

Those elected to run the Baotong Road subdistrict branch included Xiang Jingyu, Ye Chucang's assistant in the Department of Youth and Women in the Shanghai Executive Committee and wife of Mao Zedong's close friend from Hunan, Cai Hesen. Those elected to run the Qiujiang Road branch included Shen Zemin, Mao Dun's younger brother and the husband of Zhang Qinqiu, another Zhejiang radical and a close colleague of Yang Zhihua, who had by then married Qu Qiubai and was busy organizing women textile mill workers in Zhabei. Two other subdistricts, the Xiangya Company and the After-Work Association (Gongyu she), were formed by auditors and students in the evening schools run by Shanghai University students. These members had received secondary school educations in their native provinces before coming to Shanghai to find work.[40]

All six subdistrict branches of the Zhabei Guomindang, in other words, were dominated by Shanghai Communists and their less well-known followers. Because of the crisscrossing and overlapping connections of employment, residence, and after-work associations, these men and their families formed a close-knit community that did not require the creation of the Guomindang units to impart cohesiveness and identity. The existence of these ties prior to the reorganization of the Party made it possible for Shi Cuntong to initiate and complete his organizational tasks with ease and alacrity, despite the size of the Zhabei branch. The first planning session for the Zhabei branch, which took place on December 23 in the home of Yang Xianjiang, Shi Cuntong's former classmate from Zhejiang Provincial First Normal School and an editor with the Commercial Press, was a meeting of only three members.[41] The subdistrict branches created subsequently were formed simply by Shi Cuntong and his two comrades activating their network of acquaintances.

In his December 30 report to the Shanghai Executive Committee on the successful organization of Zhabei Party members into six subdistrict branches, Shi Cuntong noted that "there are others in Zhabei with whom we are not familiar," who should be added to the Party roster at a later date. Zhabei had a significant concentration of the city's underclass, the Subei migrants from the Huai River region of northern Jiangsu, who spoke a dialect and shared certain cultural traits distinctively different from those of the natives of Shanghai. There were Party members in their midst who had little interaction with Communist intellectuals on the campus of

Shanghai University and who had been overlooked by Shi Cuntong in his handling of the registration. A group of them who lived in the neighborhood of Number 55 Huazhenfang came forward in January 1924 with a roster of about thirty Party members and declared themselves a "Special District" of the Zhabei Guomindang. Unlike the majority of Subei migrants in Shanghai, these Party members, hailing from Yancheng, Funing, Huai'an, and Baoying, were all men in their late twenties and thirties who were graduates of vocational schools and normal schools. Some were army officers, several were small merchants. Gu Yuebo, who was elected to head the propaganda department for this special district, was the head of an evening school that taught English. Compared with the Shanghai University intellectuals, these men wrote deferential reports to the Shanghai Executive Committee, in a style of calligraphy that showed, especially when compared with Mao Zedong's handwriting, a painstaking attention to details and correctness. Few of the names on the Special District roster went on to achieve much fame in either party's history; in all likelihood these members chose the Nationalists over the Communists when the United Front collapsed.[42]

While the Communists showed their greatest strength in the factories and schools in Zhabei, the old Guomindang had its network in the residential compounds of the French Concession. The office of the Shanghai Central Executive Committee, adjacent to Sun Yat-sen's Shanghai residence, was itself located in the French Concession. Next only to Zhabei, the French Concession was a major locus of activity during the reorganization of the Guomindang. The scope and speed of many of its efforts toward reorganization, however, paled beside that of the Zhabei Communists. Nor was there much evidence of an increase in activities or of further growth of the Party's organizations in this area during the United Front.

The Number 18 subdistrict in the French Concession, for instance, contained fourteen Party members, who were all military officers from Anhui. Most of these were men in their thirties and forties who had been active during the 1911 Revolution and the first decade of the Republic. The Number 9 subdistrict in the French Concession, which contained nineteen members, included several former Guomindang members in the Beijing parliament and a handful of officers and newspaper reporters. Many of these men were no longer active in public life in the 1920s. A decade older than their Communist comrades, several had come to Shanghai in semiretirement, taking up residences in the quiet sections of the French Concession and enjoying politics in the way to which they had been long accustomed. Their Party subdistricts, named in Party documents after residential compounds such as "Number 10 and Number 20 at Pubo Road," "Jiyi Li," "Juxing Li," and "Meiren Li," each contained about two dozen men. Four of these subdistricts—Xinshan Li, Lao Xinshan Li, Songhe Li, Tongkang Li—were within walking distance of the Guomindang headquarters at Number 44 Huanlong Road, which the Party members sometimes used as a neighborhood gathering place.[43] The reports prepared by these former parliamentarians and military officers to the Executive Committee, compared with those submitted by the Communists, were typically brief and hasty. Irate Communists sometimes complained about how weekly Party meetings in Number 9 subdistrict were merely occasions for chit-chat.

Given the social composition of the Party in Shanghai, it was only to be expected that there was a high degree of fluidity in the constitution of Guomindang membership, a result of the ceaseless coming and going of Party members to and from the city. At the Number 3 subdistrict in the French Concession (Julaida Road, Xinshan Li, Lao Shanle Li, Songhe Li, and Tongkang Li), the Guomindang registered a total of forty-one Party members, new and old, in mid-January 1924. By March, only twenty-odd were left, the rest having either moved away or gone to Guangdong.[44] Similar situations existed elsewhere in the city with the Party's other branches. Part of Mao Zedong's job as the executive secretary of the Organization Department was to keep track of these fluctuations in membership—an endless round of registration and reregistration in the hope of keeping up with the continually changing figures. Twenty subdistricts, of various sizes and memberships, were eventually formed in the French Concession by the end of 1924, with approximately three hundred members on paper.

Outside Zhabei and the French Concession, the Guomindang faced considerable difficulty trying to create local-level Party organizations. At Nanshi, the old commercial part of the Chinese city, not much happened until mid-March 1924, when a man named Chen Bai, from the Wanzhu Elementary School, wrote to Mao Zedong and requested his attendance at an organizational meeting for the Party. The Party branch came into existence about a week later, and members met twice every month thereafter. They also used the Shanghai Bookstore, which specialized in social science texts prepared by the young Communists, as their information center. Several other units, each with fewer than a dozen individuals, were eventually formed in Nanshi. In most cases these subdistricts—at the private Qingxin Middle School, the Japanese language Toa Dobun Kan, the Educational Center of the Chinese Vocational School, the Shanghai

Bookstore, the state-funded Nanyang College, and the public Number Two Normal School—mainly involved students and intellectuals.[45]

The first wave of growth of Nationalist Party membership in Shanghai during the United Front, as the Nanshi pattern suggested, took place mainly among the city's students and "cultural workers"—those employed by bookstores, printing houses, and vocational educational centers. In Wusong and Jiangwan, as in Nanshi, the Party developed subdistricts on the campuses of Fudan University, Tongji College, and the private Wenzhi College.[46] Elsewhere in Hongkou and Pudong, where the economy was largely agrarian and where there were no major educational institutions, the Party's presence was negligible during the early phase of the United Front.

This is not to say that there was no working-class involvement in the United Front Party whatsoever. In addition to the steel workers at Wusong, the employees of the Nanyang Tobacco Company and of the Wing-On (Yong'an) Department Store, many of whom were natives of Guangdong, successfully organized subdistrict branches of the Party, by residence as well as by employment, by the end of 1923.[47] The numerical growth of workers in the Party, however, often lagged behind that of students. More often than not, the propagating endeavor of student converts was required to draw laborers into the Party.

The differential rate of the Party's growth among the city's students and workers, not at all unexpected by the Party's organizers, convinced Shi Cuntong and his fellow Communists of the correctness of their strategic thinking, first articulated in 1921 and reaffirmed repeatedly in the following years. When making a social revolution, the Party's first task was to build a vanguard elite led by the students, who would then organize the workers, the soldiers, and the propertyless into a revolutionary following for the purpose of taking power through direct action. The United Front, with its broad appeal not only to the workers, the soldiers, and the propertyless but also to members of the petite bourgeoisie, was an experience that demonstrated to young Communists such as Shi Cuntong the importance of factors such as "the concentration of power" (*liliang de jizhong*) and "the standardization of thinking" (*sixiang de tongyi*).

TRANSFORMATION

As a result of the United Front, Shanghai Communists, as members of the Guomindang, put in place an urban infrastructure serviceable as an instrument of mobilization. With the support of the Guomindang, they were able to give their full attention to Party work without financial worries. Shi

Cuntong, Yun Daiying, and Shen Zemin, for example, each drew a stipend of about eighty yuan a month for their work as secretaries and officers in the Propaganda Department. Others who took up comparable positions under the Executive Committee, including Deng Zhongxia, Shao Lizi, Mao Zedong, and Xiang Jingyu, were equally compensated.[48] Compared with the conditions that they faced in an earlier time, this source of income removed a major factor of distraction in the lives of Shanghai Communists.

The Guomindang, meanwhile, assumed the cost for a variety of Party activities in the Shanghai area. It paid, for example, for the Commoners' School in the textile factory zone of Yangshupu, initiated by a group of Shanghai University radicals in April 1924. Separately, Xiang Jingyu, who organized Party affairs for women workers in the Zhabei textile factory area, received 680 yuan for the creation of four commoners' schools for women.[49] Dozens of such schools were created in 1924 in various parts of the city, each a branch of the United Front affiliated with Shanghai's educational institutions. Shanghai University alone operated seven such schools by the summer of 1924, all with the financial support of the Party. One of these schools, for example, enrolled 364 students (301 men and 63 women). For purposes of teaching, students were divided into four categories: literate, illiterate, grown-ups, and minors. Among the illiterates were carpenters, rug weavers, construction workers, tailors, chair makers, silk factory workers, grass mowers, servants, janitors (including those employed at Shanghai University), and their apprentices. Among the functionally literate were copper workers, chauffeurs, gardeners, shoemakers, binders from the Zhonghua Bookstore, cotton mill workers, and shop apprentices. These students were taught how to read and given lectures on their social plight. The schools built institutional connections between radical youths and workers in a variety of modern and traditional trades and industries, drawing a growing number of the laborers into the Party's organizational orbit along the way.[50]

The Shanghai Executive Committee, furthermore, paid for the publication of Party journals and subsidized the associational activities of organizations such as the city's various student unions. While the well-established *Republican Daily* was in a position to hand over to the Shanghai Executive Committee a sum of seven hundred yuan in August 1924, the newly launched *Xin jianshe zazhi* (New construction), edited by Yun Daiying, had to turn to the Party for a monthly subsidy of one hundred yuan. The Party paid for the travel of members between cities such as Shanghai, Wuhan, and Guangzhou. It also sent personnel and funds into the provinces to influence the composition of Party organizations in cities such as Jiaxing and Hangzhou. Although it is difficult to determine the exact amount of the Party's regular expenditure through the Shanghai Central Executive Committee, it is safe to place it in the neighborhood of close to thirty thousand yuan per year in Shanghai itself. The source of funding for the Party's activities in the Yangzi region was the Guomindang in Guangdong. In late July 1924, just when the Shanghai Executive Committee's account balance was dropping below one thousand yuan, Liao Zhongkai arrived from Guangzhou and replenished the coffer with a fresh deposit of two thousand yuan.[51]

The infusion of Guomindang resources enabled the Shanghai Communists to expand their activities well beyond the level of the self-reliant Foreign Language School, the makeshift evening schools, and the small number of journals that they had produced previously. With the assets and infrastructure of Shanghai University, and with dozens of commoners' schools, women's schools, journals, and associations at their disposal, the organizational strength of the Party in Shanghai recorded a significant growth during 1923 and 1924. By May 1925, the Party commanded a citywide network of about 120 branches, with thousands of individuals taking part in its many activities. With the help of printed media, the Party also was able to project its ideological influence into large and small provincial cities. Within the metropolis itself, Shanghai University provided an entirely new form of support and occupation. Although it was often derided as a flight-by-night operation and an ad hoc "back alley university" by members of the middle class who sent their children to reputable educational institutions such as the well-endowed Episcopalian St. John's University and the state-sponsored Communications University, Shanghai University gave uprooted provincials a foothold in an important aspect of Shanghai life that permitted them to emerge from under the surveillance of French Concession police. To the extent that Shi Cuntong and his friends were able to attenuate their sense of marginality in Shanghai's urban society through these newly constructed points of engagement, they found themselves correspondingly better positioned to realize the strategic potential of Shanghai as the hub of modernity.

The impressive organizational presence of the United Front lay the foundation for the massive urban mobilization of the May Thirtieth Movement in 1925. As workers went on strike and syndicalists seized control, few failed to recognize that much of the energy behind this "heyday of radicalism" in Shanghai emanated from the campus of Shanghai University.[52] The university during the United Front period represented one of those rare moments in Chinese Communist history when ideology and organization were dialectically fused. For radical intellectuals intent on forming a new order designed with socialist blueprints, it must have seemed as if they were only a brief span away from the creation of a truly progressive and tolerant community in which the ethical, however tentatively, was joined to the political.

Shanghai University was also where the course of this revolution, urban and modern in nature, turned tragic, and radicals who survived the tragedy were forced to reconsider drastically the meaning of Communist revolution. As the events of the next three years were to show, although the city was where revolutionary strategies were fashioned, it could not be the sole focus of a social revolution on a national scale. The very conditions that made it possible for Shanghai to emerge as a center of revolutionary thinking also prevented it from being a powerhouse of revolutionary changes. Conditions were so different between China's urban centers and the provinces, that while Shanghai nurtured the socialist vision of radicals such as Shi Cuntong, it also undercut their effectiveness in the middle counties back home. May Fourth radicals who had turned their backs on the provinces in the 1920s thus learned a painful lesson. Their revolutionary road maps, so carefully worked out in the metropolis and so sharply focused on an antagonism against the capitalists and the imperialists, could not travel into the provinces without undergoing basic transformations. The conservative forces that controlled the radicals' provincial hometowns, and the "feudal landlords and evil gentry" that increasingly exercised a significant influence over the right wing of the Guomindang, could not be ignored without a heavy price.

Shi Cuntong left Shanghai for Guangzhou in the summer of 1926. The Northern Expedition—the Guomindang's military campaign to unify China—embarked shortly thereafter. Shi Cuntong marched along with the armies all the way to Wuhan, where he emerged, in the spring of 1927, as the director of the Political Training Department at the Wuhan campus of the Central Military Academy. There he was safely ensconced under the protection of the left-wing regime headed by Wang Jingwei when the radicals' revolution suddenly crumpled. Among the leadership in Wuhan and serving as a standing member of the Central Executive Committee of the Guomindang was none other than his former principal, Jing Ziyuan.

The Communists' success with the urban labor movement, which initially led to an explosive revolutionary expansion beyond Shanghai to the peasant associations of Hunan and the labor unions of Hubei, paradoxically fell back on itself. On April 12–13, 1927, Chiang Kai-shek launched his purge of the Communists and other left-wing progressives in

Shanghai, practically unopposed. Shi Cuntong's fellow provincials there—the entire group of Jiang-Zhe radicals who were without the left-wing Party support that Shi enjoyed in Wuhan and were thus instantly vulnerable to Chiang's attack—were rounded up and shot, nearly to the last man and woman.

Among the victims were dozens of key Communist figures in the Party organizations of Zhejiang, Jiangsu, and Shanghai, including Shi Cuntong's former classmates at the Zhejiang Provincial First Normal School (Wang Shouhua, Xuan Zhonghua, Ye Tiandi) and colleagues at the Shanghai University (Hou Shaoqiu, Zhu Jixun). In the streets of Zhabei, young workers, headquartered at the printing workshop of the Commercial Press, succumbed to the backlash that crushed urban socialist revolution in 1927. In this single act of White Terror and in waves of subsequent persecutions, Chiang Kai-shek and the right wing of the Guomindang were able to extirpate the core elements of urban Chinese Communist propagandists and labor organizers based in the lower Yangzi region, who had developed, in the dynamic environment of metropolitan Shanghai, a Communist ideology of considerable vitality and sophistication. Although the idea of urban communism, propped up by the Comintern, lingered on, the White Terror utterly changed the nature of the Chinese Communist Party, as it ceased to be a viable indigenous movement rooted in Shanghai. The Party leadership was left eventually in the hands of the more remote Hunanese provincial network that ended up rusticating the Chinese Communist Party in the rural soviets and mountain base areas. The reactionary backlash also introduced deep divisions into the ranks of the surviving Shanghai Communists, many of them middle-county radicals, who were left to ponder, once again, the drastic disjuncture between the villages they had left and the cities they had lost.

THE QUEST

Although Shi Cuntong was devastated by the events of 1927, he stood firm by the strategies of the United Front. Between the Nationalist-bourgeois Right (the "Dai Jitaoism" of Nationalist Revolution) and the Communist-internationalist Left of Chen Duxiu and the "returned Bolsheviks," he sought to follow a third, centrist position (*zhongjian daolu*) that would place socialist revolution in the larger context of national liberation, which he believed was also the true legacy of Sun Yat-sen. On August 30, 1927, he published "Beitong zhong de zibai" (Confessional statement in grief and pain) in the *Central Daily News* (*Zhongyang ribao*) in Hankou, an essay that both mourned the dead and severed his link with the Communist Party. He continued to regard himself as a member of the Guomindang and fought to revive the Party's revolutionary spirit of 1924.

Shi Cuntong moved back to Shanghai. Still entertaining hopes that the United Front might be revivable, he joined efforts, for a brief period, with the left wing of the Guomindang under Wang Jingwei and Chen Gongbo, and became a contributing author to their short-lived but influential journal *Geming pinglun* (Revolutionary commentary) (May–September 1928).

Chen Gongbo, one of the thirteen original delegates at the First Party Congress of the Chinese Communist Party, had by now come to regard the Comintern as "red imperialists" (*chise diguo zhuyi zhe*). He roundly denounced Chen Duxiu's willingness to ally the Chinese Communist Party with the Soviet Union and called for the creation of a Fourth International of the Communist Parties of "the Eastern nations"—China, Japan, Korea, and Vietnam—so as to achieve the goals of a socialist revolution within the contexts of nationalist liberation.[53]

Shi Cuntong never went as far as Chen Gongbo did in his attack on the Comintern and the Chinese Communist Party. He aimed his critical fire instead at Chiang Kai-shek, and berated the latter for betraying the socialist revolution as the head of a so-called revolutionary party that appeared to have been stricken with a pronounced phobia for the might of the masses. Shi insisted on the basic strategies of the United Front and advocated the mass mobilization of students and workers in alliance with members of the petite bourgeoisie.[54]

Shi Cuntong's "centrist" position of the late 1920s put him in the midst of heated debates over the nature of the Chinese revolution as it related to the murky terrain occupied by the "third force" between the Nationalists and the Communists. Although he was insistent on the primacy of a nationalist revolution against the forces of imperialism, he also placed emphasis on a mass-based socialist revolution as the only effective means to achieve the nationalist goal. This view proved to be far too much to the left for Wang Jingwei's Reorganization Faction (Gaizu pai) of the Guomindang, which, as self-proclaimed "centrists," preferred to achieve socialist goals through nationalist means. Shi Cuntong's relationship with the left wing of the Guomindang was thus not without tension. The Wang faction, which had no military power of its own except for the support of a loose coalition of northern warlords, was significantly weakened when the allied warlords suffered sound defeats at the hands of Chiang Kai-shek's army. Shi at that point severed his connections with the left wing of the Guomindang.[55]

Between 1929 and 1936 Shi Cuntong resumed his life as a radical man of letters, devoting himself to writing, thinking, and translating. He made his living off income from royalties, producing on contract with publishers, and catering sometimes to the reading interests of a growing audience for popularized socialism. During that period he published more than twenty volumes on a broad range of topics, including *Das Kapital*. No longer a Communist organizer but continuing to be a Marxist intellectual, Shi Cuntong was a political activist who held no Party membership. He operated in an urban setting rather than in the countryside, and his goal was to change the consciousness rather than the fortunes of those who were drawn into his orbit.

Remote from the peasants in their base areas, Shi followed the activities of bankers and manufacturers of Shanghai. His economic writings of this period focused attention on the rise of the modern sector in the Chinese urban economy. His socialist vision was built on his tireless research into the problems and principles of capitalism as well as imperialism. He commanded a sizable following in Shanghai's book market with his socialist messages, and he accused compradore capitalism along with provincial feudalism for the crumbling of the old world.

In his analysis of the Chinese economy and in his search for a materially grounded revolutionary strategy of scientific validity, Shi Cuntong reached the conclusion, as early as 1931, that the Chinese economy was a capitalist economy under a colonial system, in which imperialism and bureaucratic capitalism had important roles to play. Chinese capitalists were not ordinary members of the bourgeoisie, but compradores and brokers of imperialist interests. Chinese cities, especially Shanghai, were not ordinary urban centers that articulated the wealth of the rest of the country, but conduits through which the wealth of the colonized hinterland was drained into a global system dominated by the imperialist order. In Shi's analysis, the compradore nature of the Chinese bourgeoisie helped to account for its members' inability to rise to the occasion and carry out the mission of national revolution in conjunction with the rioting students and workers in 1927, which accounted for the disastrous failure of the First United Front that spring. To achieve the goals of national liberation (*minzu jiefang*) and socialist revolution (*shehui geming*), Shi argued, the Chinese must begin by defeating imperialism—a task that could be successfully borne only by the country's aroused masses.

Shi's descriptive analysis of the problems afflicting China's modern society had an enormous influence on Shanghai's publishing circles in the 1930s. His critique of the structural injustices of compradore capitalism was echoed, in one variation or another, in a wide range of writings—from Gu Mei's diatribe on the colonial nature of the modern Chinese educational system to Li Gongpu's diagnosis of the plight in which "vocational youth" found themselves—that appealed to a wide reading audience of urbanites and educated provincials.[56] In the wake of the Great Depression Shi Cuntong called for (and predicted) the uprising of Chinese peasants along with the urban proletariat. He envisioned a broadly based alliance among the lower middle class, the workers, and the peasants in a common struggle against the colonialists and the compradores. These ideas were later adopted by Mao Zedong during the Second United Front and New Democracy periods, but at the time they sharply divorced Shi Cuntong from the Communist Party's "internationalism."[57]

In Shanghai, where he and Zhong Fuguang looked after her aging mother, Shi Cuntong plunged with passion into the resistance movement after the January 1932 Japanese assault on the city. He published scores of essays in newspapers within a matter of months to advocate popular resistance, and became a target of the Nationalist police and secret service when they began arresting, kidnapping, and assassinating progressive elements involved in the National Salvation Movement against Japan. With the help of a few friends Shi Cuntong and his wife left Shanghai in the spring of 1933, just in time to escape an arrest order issued by the Shanghai municipal branch of the Guomindang. With no other place to turn to, Shi decided to go home to Jinhua, where his father and two brothers still lived in Yecun.[58]

The trip back, over paths trod by twelve hired hands carrying Shi's library of Japanese books and Chinese socialist treatises in baskets suspended from shoulder poles, could have been awkward for Shi Cuntong after his forced departure from the province thirteen years earlier. He was, after all, returning to the hometown that he had abandoned, uncertain of his ability to find a place among the relatives and townspeople he had long ago left behind. Like previous gentry-scholars who had sojourned in the larger world, however, he was at the same time confident that he had acquired a vision that could be shared, the realization of which would be for the benefit of everyone.

His fellow villagers greeted him respectfully. Shi Cuntong to them was a man who had seen the big world and perhaps served as an official, a source of silver and gold who nonetheless did his best not to put on city airs. But they were also reportedly disappointed when they discovered that Shi's baskets were filled with mere books. Shi's manner and behavior defied village expectations about how an accomplished man returning from the big city should conduct himself. Conscientiously visiting and talking to peasants while he, his wife, and his father built, brick by brick, a large house in the middle of the small village, Shi was unable to find the vocabulary with which to make himself intelligible to them. He tried to speak of the value of labor, but few were able to get the point. On the completion of the house he graced the entrance with the time-honored Confucian motto "Tilling and Studying"—finally finding a gesture acceptable both to himself and to the locals who had such high expectations about him as an educated gentryman.[59]

THE HOMEWARD JOURNEY

Shi's active support for the anti-Japanese resistance movement in the 1930s led to his increasing identification with the democratic center—what was to become eventually the "third force." The two phrases that he had helped to coin, *minzu jiefang* (national liberation) and *minzhu gaizao* (democratic reconstruction), ultimately became the platform of the third force. After the outbreak of the war of resistance, the Nationalists and the Communists announced their Second United Front. In November 1937, on the eve of the fall of Shanghai, Shi prefaced one of his volumes with an essay entitled "Yige chengshi de shengming" (An honest statement), in which he reflected on his own career since 1927 and expressed a survivor's profound guilt and grief over the death of former comrades killed by the Nationalists a decade earlier. This statement, offered as a piece of self-criticism, did not escape the attention of the Communist Party and paved the way for his reconciliation with Yan'an. Shi and his family journeyed to China's southwest later that year, first to Kunming, then in 1940 to Chongqing. There he resumed contact with members of the Party, especially Zhou Enlai. In Chongqing he worked for a journal affiliated with a bank and published extensively on the subject of the Chinese economy. He made the acquaintance, meanwhile, of many bankers and industrialists. Together with Huang Yanpei, Zhang Naiqi, and a few other leading members of the former National Salvation Movement and the Democratic League (Min meng), he launched the Society for the Democratic Construction of the Nation (Minzhu jianguo hui), which was devoted to the mobilization of members of the "national bourgeoisie" for a "centrist position" that would lean toward neither the Left nor the Right.[60]

The third force, including the Society for the Democratic Construction of the Nation, sought to mediate between the Communists and Nationalists after the outbreak of civil war in 1946. The political outcome of that conflict, however, was decided on the battlefield instead of in the pages of the journals and periodicals to which Shi Cuntong continued to contribute. Shi's Communist sympathies became increasingly pronounced by the conclusion of the civil war. Although few could challenge his credentials as a Marxist economist, he was nonetheless presented to Chairman Mao at a dinner party in Beijing in April 1949 as the head of the Society for the Democratic Construction of the Nation. As an external ally rather than a Chinese Communist Party member, he once again pledged his allegiance to the Party that he had helped to create nearly thirty years earlier. Later that year he was named a deputy minister of labor under Li Lisan.[61]

The position was a sinecure as well as a United Front gesture, and Shi devoted his attention to the "democratic reform" of members of the "national bourgeoisie." In 1954 he suffered a partially paralyzing stroke and gradually dropped from public sight. From the early 1950s onward, Shi had been put increasingly on the defensive over his record of taking a "centrist" position. He came repeatedly under pressure to recant, but he refused to renounce that earlier faith. Consequently, during the Cultural Revolution he was made an object of attack, and he died of illness in November 1970. His death, like a good part of his existence in the late 1950s and 1960s, took place in seclusion without attracting much public attention. It also took place after his witnessing the heyday of the Mao cult, when throngs of Red Guards assembled at Tiananmen Square to shout their salute to socialist China's Great Helmsman.

Twenty-two years later, in February 1992, Zhong Fuguang passed away as well. Life had changed considerably since the days of the Cultural Revolution, and the Party, under the Four Modernizations policies of Deng Xiaoping, was ready to retreat from a single-minded focus on Mao and his legacy. Zhong Fuguang—who had served as a delegate to the Party's Women's Association and enjoyed long friendships with women leaders such as Deng Yingchao (Zhou Enlai's spouse) and Zhao Junman (Premier Li Peng's natural mother)—was able to win from the Party an honored place of burial not just for herself but also for her long-forgotten spouse, who was interred in the government cemetery at Babaoshan, in the hills west of Beijing.

In May 1992, the first paved road ever was opened into Yecun, and workmen began to build a mounded mausoleum for Shi Cuntong's ashes, alongside a piney set of hills a thousand yards northeast of the village and the Shi family house. The villagers welcomed the commemoration, both because it brought Shi's and Zhong's remains back to the community along with a certain kind of fame, and because the road connected them with the outside, making it possible to think of transporting their orange harvests by motorized vehicle to markets far beyond. Except for the county Party secretary, who was given the task of composing the inscriptions on the tombstone, few villagers were able to recount Shi's accomplishments during his lifetime, although all took pride in him as a native son.

Like the central administrative center of Jinhua, where the most important shrine now is the tomb of the historiographically correct Taiping prince Li Shixian, Yecun remains very much a middle-county backwater. While Shanghai plans to displace Hong Kong and Tokyo as the financial center of Asia during the twenty-first century, Jinhua's Yecun can only dream of buying a refrigerator truck to ship the village's fresh chicken eggs over the Jiangshan pass down to the Shenzhen Economic Zone in Guangdong. And while Shanghai lionizes Milton Friedman and the Cato Institute, Yecun's white-washed schoolhouse, built in the 1950s as a gift to the village by Shi Cuntong, still has portraits of Marx, Engels, Lenin, and Mao looking down on pupils proud of their red kerchiefs and Young Pioneer salutes.

Meanwhile, above the village, home again forever, rest the ashes of Shi Cuntong. Encased in the mausoleum, now resurrected as a Communist revolutionary icon, Shi's remains have become part of that earlier landscape of Confucian graves and shrines that immured Jinhua from challenge and change. "He had traveled a tortuous journey. . . . He had deviated from the path . . . but he found his way again," intoned the *People's Daily*. He was "a man of clear-cut love and hatred . . . a man who dissected himself with much moral courage," said his Zhejiang biographers.[62]

The tomb, the inscriptions, and the printed remarks would not have appeared had there not been a major change in socialist China's domestic agenda in the 1980s. The construction of the tomb broke the silence that had long been imposed on Shi's memory. Shi Cuntong's childhood world, with its Confucian patriarchs and ritualized norms, has disappeared. Those who ponder the meaning of his life find in it, meanwhile, a quest for a socialist ideal that stood quite apart from the power structure of the Chinese Communist Party, and tells a different story of China's transformation from Confucianism to Socialism. The ethical and the political, in the present as in the past, are grievously divided. Yet from the peaceful vantage of the shrine, where the wind soughs through the pines while the village rests below, Shi's passionate hopes, which launched him on his provincial passages decades before, seem far from gone.

Notes

INTRODUCTION

1. Chow Tse-tsung, *The May Fourth Movement: Intellectual Revolution in Modern China* (Cambridge, Mass.: Harvard University Press, 1960). See also Benjamin I. Schwartz, ed., *Reflections on the May Fourth Movement: A Symposium* (Cambridge, Mass.: Council on East Asian Studies Publications, Harvard University Press, 1972).

2. See, for example, Li Zehou's attempt to reconceptualize modern Chinese intellectual history in *Zhongguo jindai sixiang shilun* [Essays on modern Chinese intellectual history] (Beijing: Renmin chuban she, 1979), which considers the significance of new developments from Hong Xiuquan (1840s) to Lu Xun (1930s). For Li's reevaluation of the legacy of the May Fourth Movement and the place of intellectuals in modern Chinese society, see especially pp. 450–71. On the seventieth anniversary of the May Fourth Movement in 1989, Li Zehou offered reflections in "Wusi huimou qishi nian" [Seventy years since the May Fourth Movement: A backward glance], "Wusi de shishi feifei" [Rights and wrongs of the May Fourth Movement], and "Qimeng de zouxiang—Wusi qishi zhounian jinian hui shang fayan tigang" [Path toward enlightenment: An outline of remarks delivered on the occasion of the seventieth anniversary of the May Fourth Movement], all in Li Zehou, *Zou wo ziji de lu* [Following a path of my own] (Taipei: Fengyun shidai chuban gongsi, 1990), 525–40, 541–65, 566–81. Li Zehou, born in 1930, is widely regarded as contemporary China's most prominent thinker and philosopher. For reflections on the May Fourth Movement offered by a younger generation of Chinese thinkers, see Gan Yang, "Bashi niandai wenhua taolun de jige wenti" [A few problems in the cultural discussions of the 1980s], in Gan Yang, ed., *Zhongguo dangdai wenhua yishi* [Contemporary Chinese cultural consciousness] (Taipei: Fengyun shidai chuban gongsi, 1990), 9–50. Gan Yang was born in 1952. A native of Hangzhou, he spent eight years in the remote province of Heilongjiang in northeastern China during the Cultural Revolution. On the "unfinished" quality of May Fourth as a cultural campaign, see Yu Ying-shih, "Wusi—yige wei wancheng de wenhua yundong" [May Fourth—an unfinished cultural movement], in *Wenhua pinglun yu Zhongguo qinghuai* [Cultural commentary and Chinese attachments]

(Taipei: Yunchen, 1988), 65–72. Many of the problems exposed by the May Fourth Movement, as Vera Schwarcz notes, remained unresolved in "People's China." For much of the seven decades between 1919 and 1989, Chinese intellectuals "held on to the allegory of May Fourth as a means of keeping alive the spirit of criticism and of chastising those who would consign it to the past." See Schwarcz, *The Chinese Enlightenment: Intellectuals and the Legacy of the May Fourth Movement of 1919* (Berkeley: University of California Press, 1986), 240–302. The quotation is from p. 241. For examples of recent Western scholarly attempts to reconceptualize modern Chinese cultural history in light of a reevaluation of the May Fourth Movement, see Ellen Widmer and David Der-wei Wang, eds., *From May Fourth to June Fourth: Fiction and Film in Twentieth Century China* (Cambridge, Mass.: Harvard University Press, 1993).

3. For students of Chinese history, mere mention of core and periphery calls to mind the influential work of G. William Skinner, whose descriptive analysis of Chinese urban hierarchies and macroregions has powerfully shaped the spatial conceptions of China that have for decades informed scholarly work. Almost as a tribute to the overarching scope of the Skinnerian conception, meanwhile, a significant amount of scholarly energy has also been poured into the examination of individual macroregional boundaries in the hope of redrawing the maps first suggested by Skinner himself. The core and peripheries identified in the theory of macroregions have been based, by and large, on a hierarchical conception keyed to the distribution of human and economic resources. Skinner's model aptly captures the tension between a bureaucratically imposed administrative structure of the late imperial Chinese state on the one hand and, on the other, the "natural" networks of gradations of markets and central places that were articulations of the socioeconomic forces of late imperial Chinese society. There were, in other words, major economic centers in the urban hierarchy that had not been assigned comparable weight on the administrative hierarchy of the state, and vice versa. When it comes to cultural and educational factors, however, the Skinnerian model neither argues for nor denies a perfect congruence between economic and cultural centers on the Chinese map. As a spatial model that commands considerable historical depth, it has for the most part left the question of cultural-political dynamics out of the picture.

But because of what Skinner has characterized as the bureaucratic-agrarian emphasis of the Chinese political system and the geographically uneven distribution of urban and commercial development across the Chinese landscape, culture was precisely the arena in which tensions between the bureaucratic and the commercial found expression. Given the antimercantile bias of Confucian moral philosophy, commercial centers in late imperial Chinese society were not necessarily sites imbued with a sense of their own cultural centrality. Too much commerce and wealth in fact served to undercut the authenticity of such a claim. What this book will try to show—where it differs from the spatial conception of the Skinnerian model—is that in the cultural arena, competing sets of values, exclusively linked to neither socioeconomic factors nor political-bureaucratic ones, coexisted in constant tension. Thus the core and the periphery on the cultural map did not necessarily correspond to those same spheres on the socioeconomic map. They were more a matter for subjective negotiation than for objective quantification. The contentious nature of these values and the dynamics for change that stemmed from such multiplicity ultimately forced the dissolution of a spatial conception with a unitary core and a hierarchical periphery. For Skinner's classic presentations of his spatial conceptions of China, see especially the five essays in G. William Skinner, ed., *The City in Late Imperial China* (Stanford: Stanford University Press, 1977). For a most instructive application of the Skinnerian conception to an explanation of the political history of Zhejiang, see R. Keith Schoppa, *Chinese Elites and Political Change: Zhejiang Province in the Early Twentieth Century* (Cambridge, Mass.: Council on East Asian Studies Publications, Harvard University Press, 1982), especially the discussion of "the four Zhejiangs," pp. 13–26. On county-level studies of revolution and change in the Republican period, see R. Keith Schoppa, "Contours of Revolutionary Change in a Chinese County, 1900–1950," *Journal of Asian Studies* 51, 4 (November 1992): 770–96; Stephen C. Averill, "Local Elites and Communist Revolution in the Jiangxi Hill County," in Joseph W. Esherick and Mary Backus Rankin, eds., *Chinese Local Elites and Patterns of Dominance* (Berkeley: University of California Press, 1990), 282–304, and, in the same volume, Lenore Barkan, "Patterns of Power: Forty Years of Elite Politics in a Chinese County," 191–215.

4. In the 1980s, new published sources appeared that made it possible for Western scholars to approach the early history of the Chinese Communist Party (CCP) from new perspectives. A most promising start has been made recently by Arif Dirlik in his book *The Origins of Chinese Communism* (New York: Oxford University Press, 1989). Dirlik stresses the strong anarchist presence in early-twentieth-century Chinese radical culture and shows that most Chinese radicals were anarchists and Marxists of various persuasions until they were shaped decisively into Leninists on the creation by the Comintern of the Communist Party. Dirlik's argument, framed around the question of whether Chinese Marxism was more "Chinese" or "Marxian," begins with a somewhat mechanistic observation about the global nature of capitalism. Because China had entered into a capitalist mode of production during the period of World War I (1914–18), according to Dirlik, the material foundation was in place for Chinese intellectual life to acquire the characteristics of socialism. Few of these

intellectuals, however, supposedly had any inklings of Lenin and his doctrines about the vanguard party and the dictatorship of the proletariat.
Although the tenets of Leninism were fully spelled out by Shi Cuntong and
other Marxist ideologues in the pages of *Gongchandang* (The Communist)
well before the founding of the Party, Dirlik argues that the rise of a
Leninist ideology in China was a consequence rather than a condition for
the creation of the Communist Party organization in July 1921. The rise
of the organization, conversely, put an end to the dissemination of Marxism
and the development of radical culture as an indigenous and spontaneous
expression.

To account for the decline of anarchism and Marxism relative to Leninism, Dirlik places emphasis on the organizational intervention of the
Comintern that led to the creation of a Communist Party along Leninist
lines. To the extent that Dirlik may have placed too much emphasis on the
organizational presence of the Comintern and its effectiveness in struc-
turing a coherent Leninist Party, his work provides a convenient foil for
Hans Van de Ven, who criticizes Dirlik for being insufficiently alert to the
internal divisions that continued to exist in the CCP after the founding of
the Party in 1921. (See Van de Ven, *From Friend to Comrade: The Founding
of the Chinese Communist Party, 1920–1927* [Berkeley: University of
California Press, 1991], 55–59.) Van de Ven focuses his attention on the
many years that it took for a Leninist-style operation to establish itself.
There were no instant Bolsheviks, he points out. Like Dirlik, Van de Ven
pays attention to the provincial study societies that lay the foundation of
Communist cell organizations. Citing Maring's report to the Comintern in
1922 (which was presented on July 11, 1922, in Moscow and is available
in published form in Chinese; see Zhishi chuban she, ed., *Yida huiyi lu*
[First Party Congress memoirs] [Shanghai: Zhishi chuban she, 1980],
91–103). Van de Ven argues that the central Party in Shanghai was ineffectual as a central organ for provincial party organizations, which were
embedded in local settings and functioned with self-sufficiency. To the
extent that Van de Ven takes as his central theme the rise of a Leninist-style
Party organization within the early CCP, he regards 1927 as a much more
significant year than 1921, since it was not until the late 1920s that
members of the young Party learned to shed their scholar-intellectual
frame of mind and became members of a Bolshevik Party. Van de Ven's
stress on provincial study societies, however, seriously underestimates the
cultural radicalization of Shanghai Party members during the United Front
period.

Moreover, when Van de Ven does pay attention to the style of behavior
of early Chinese Communist Party members as heirs to their own cultural
tradition and as products of their own social backgrounds, he tends to blur
crucial individual differences. Whereas Dirlik introduces fine ideological

differentiations among anarchists, Marxists, Leninists, and Communists, Van de Ven speaks of "Communists" mainly in organizational terms. Party members were "Chinese" before they were Communists, and even with the help of the Moscow-led Third International, Van de Ven suggests, it took a long while to turn elite intellectuals steeped in their own national culture into acceptable cadres by the yardsticks of an international Bolshevist. And whereas Dirlik has made a conscious effort to distance himself from a Mao-centered perspective, Van de Ven's presentation only gains persuasive coherence by retaining a single-minded focus on a form of the Party recognizable from a later perspective.

By focusing his attention on the historical emergence of a Leninist Party, Van de Ven, in his historical search for "the CCP," appears to have overlooked the reconstitution of the Party as opposed to its evolution. As the final chapters of this book will show, the sort of CCP that Van de Ven describes had emerged at the expense of the majority of the Party's early membership. The Party of 1927 was different from the Party of 1921 not just because the latter managed to introduce discipline and centralized directives, but because it was built on a different composition of membership. Those who disagreed with the Leninist doctrines and organizations did not transform themselves into Leninists; they had either withdrawn from the Party or had paid for their involvement with their lives.

CHAPTER 1: ZHEJIANG

1. The compound *Zhe* and *Jiang* conjured up images of a crooked waterway. The character *Zhe* was made up of the verb *zhe*, meaning "to break, to bend, to set back, to frustrate," with the water radical attached to it. See the definition in the dictionary *Cihai* (Taipei, 1981 edition).

2. Qiantang jiang jixing bianxie zu [Editorial team, "Journal along the Qiangtang River"], *Qiantang jiang jixing* [Journal along the Qiantang River] (Shanghai: Shanghai jiaoyu chuban she, 1981), 1.

3. Lyman P. Van Slyke, *Yangtze: Nature, History, and the River* (Menlo Park, Calif.: Addison-Wesley, 1988), 8–10; Terry Cannon and Alan Jenkins, eds., *The Geography of Contemporary China: The Impact of Deng Xiaoping's Decade* (London: Routledge, 1990), 87.

4. Zhang Qiyun, *Zhejiang sheng shidi jiyao* [Historical geography of the province of Zhejiang] (Shanghai: Commercial Press, 1925), 8–9.

5. The Fujian county Pucheng shares borders with Zhejiang's Jiangshan. Jiangxi's Yushan and Leqing share borders with Zhejiang's Changshan. Anhui's Xiuning and Wuyuan share borders with Zhejiang's Kaihua. Jiangshan, Changshan, and Kaihua on the Zhejiang side of the border are contiguous. Xianxia Pass on the southern border of Jiangshan, Caohui Pass, Caoping Pass, Huilong Bridge (Coiled Dragon Bridge), and Fangcun Pass

in Changshan County are all treacherous mountain passes famed historically for strategic military and commercial importance. Wei Songtang, ed., *Zhejiang jingji jilue* [Outline of Zhejiang economic geography] (Shanghai: n.p., 1929), 371–72, 380.

6. Maritime activities centering on the Zhedong coast in the earlier centuries have received much scholarly attention. See, for example, Wang Gungwu, "The Nanhai Trade," *Journal of the Malayan Branch of the Royal Asiatic Society* 31 (1958), pt. 2: 1–135; Lo Jung-pang, "The Emergence of China as a Sea Power during the Late Sung and Early Yuan Periods," *Far Eastern Quarterly* 14, 4 (1955): 489–504; Lo Jung-pang, "Maritime Commerce and Its Relation to the Sung Navy," *Journal of the Economic and Social History of the Orient*, 12, 1 (1969): 57–101; Lo Jung-pang, "The Decline of the Early Ming Navy," *Oriens extremus* 5, 2 (December 1958): 149–68. On the depression of this trade and on coastal trade linking Ningbo to Shanghai, Fuzhou, Shandong, and so forth in the Ming and Qing, see discussion in a later section of this chapter.

7. Zhejiang in Ming times was the province that produced the largest number of *jinshi*, or first-class metropolitan examination degree-holders, for the country as a whole. Of the eleven prefectures of Zhejiang, only the two poorest, Quzhou and Chuzhou, in the southern mountain areas, failed to produce at least two jinshi. This record is surpassed only by that of Jiangsu in Qing. In the Ming period Hangzhou, Jiaxing, and Huzhou prefectures produced a total of 1,351 jinshi which represented 41.2 percent of such degree-holders produced in the province as a whole. After the dynastic change in 1644 this figure rose to 70 percent. Hangzhou alone produced 1,004 jinshi under the Qing. The city, energized by the wealth of Huizhou salt merchants, boasted the largest number of major national library collections among late imperial Chinese cities. Huzhou, with 421 jinshi during the Qing, was the prefecture with the highest density of such examination success in the nation. Ping-ti Ho, *The Ladder of Success in Imperial China: Aspects of Social Mobility, 1368–1911* (New York: Columbia University Press, 1962), 246, 252–53.

8. The phrase in Chinese is *Shang you tiantang, xia you Su-Hang*. For a historical description of Suzhou, see Michael Marme, "Heaven on Earth: The Rise of Suzhou, 1127–1550," in Linda Cooke Johnson, ed., *Cities of Jiangnan in Late Imperial China* (Albany: State University of New York Press, 1993), 17–45. On Hangzhou during its heyday, see Jacques Gernet, *Daily Life in China on the Eve of the Mongol Invasion, 1250–1276*, trans. H. M. Wright (New York: Macmillan, 1962), and Pang Dexin (Pong Tak-san), *Songdai liangjing shimin shenghuo* [Original title in English: Daily Life in the Sung Capitals as Reflected in the *Huaben* of the Sung, Yuan and Ming Periods] (Hong Kong: Longmen shudian, 1974). In the eighteenth century Suzhou, along with Hangzhou and Nanjing, dominated

the market hierarchy in the lower Yangzi. Suzhou was "the center for the national rice trade and for the cotton and silk industries," and had supplanted Nanjing, Ming imperial capital under Zhu Yuanzhang, "as the region's central metropolis." Hangzhou and Nanjing "continued to function as regional metropolises," although their days of glory were in the past. Suzhou's population eventually grew to seven hundred thousand in the mid-nineteenth century. Susan Naquin and Evelyn S. Rawski, *Chinese Society in the Eighteenth Century* (New Haven: Yale University Press, 1987), 152.

9. Jiangnan and Zhexi were leading rice-producing regions in the Song-Yuan period. From the sixteenth century onward, however, peasants there turned to a highly intensive form of farming, but they rejected attempts for a secondary crop, despite the rising cash price for rice and the ready accessibility of the market. This was because silk weaving often brought in profits four times the amount obtainable from rice growing. In Suzhou, peasants rejected increasing yields in favor of sericulture, which would augment their income. Evelyn S. Rawski, *Agricultural Change and the Peasant Economy of South China* (Cambridge, Mass.: Harvard University Press, 1972), 52–55, 151–59.

10. There is a rich historical scholarship on this subject. See, for example, Fu Yiling, *Mingdai Jiangnan shimin jingji shitan* [Preliminary research on urban economy in Jiangnan under the Ming] (Shanghai: Renmin chuban she, 1957), 24–51, 79–87; Liu Yongcheng, "Shilun Qingdai Suzhou shougongye hanghui" [Handicraft guilds in Suzhou during the Qing dynasty], *Lishi yanjiu* 11 (1959): 21–46; E-tu Zen Sun, "Sericulture and Silk Textile Production in Ch'ing China," in W. E. Willmott, ed., *Economic Organization in Chinese Society* (Stanford: Stanford University Press, 1972), 79–108.

11. Jonathan D. Spence, *Ts'ao Yin and the K'ang-hsi Emperor: Bondservant and Master* (New Haven: Yale University Press, 1966), 82–103; Lillian M. Li, *China's Silk Trade: Traditional Industry in the Modern World, 1842–1937* (Cambridge, Mass.: Harvard University Press, 1981), 39–61.

12. Wei Songtang, *Zhejiang jingji*, 8–9. There is an extensive body of secondary literature on urban guilds and merchant associations in late imperial Chinese cities. See the seminal works of He Bingdi (Ping-ti Ho), *Zhongguo huiguan shilun* [Historical essay on Chinese *Landsmannschaften*] (Taipei: Xuesheng shuju, 1966), and G. William Skinner, "Introduction: Urban Social Structure in Ch'ing China," in Skinner, *The City in Late Imperial China*, 521–53; see also, in the same volume, Peter J. Golas, "Early Ch'ing Guilds," 555–80, and the various chapters in Mark Elvin and G. William Skinner, eds., *The Chinese City between Two Worlds* (Stanford: Stanford University Press, 1974), especially Susan Mann Jones, "The

Ningpo Pang and Financial Power at Shanghai," 73–96. For recent studies, see William Rowe's *Hankow: Commerce and Society in a Chinese City, 1796–1889* (Stanford: Stanford University Press, 1984) and *Hankow: Conflict and Community in a Chinese City, 1796–1895* (Stanford: Stanford University Press, 1989). See also Ye Xian'en, *Ming Qing Huizhou nongcun shehui yu dianpuzhi* [Rural society and the system of tenant servants in Huizhou under the Ming and the Qing] (Anhui: Renmin chuban she, 1983), especially 122–44. A well-known Huizhou local saying urged these youths on: *Bu yao huang, shi ri dao Yu-Hang* (Do not panic; just ten days and you reach Yuyao and Hangzhou). To equip themselves for such a trip, all it took was a letter of introduction into a fellow provincial's shop in Hangzhou, and a string of especially hard-baked wheat cakes worn around the waist, guaranteed to be both edible and indestructible even beyond the duration of the entire journey.

13. Wei Songtang, *Zhejiang jingji*, 8.

14. On the activities of the Luo Sect in the Gongchenqiao area in the eighteenth century and official response, see Yeh Wen-hsin, "Renshen zhijian: Qianlun shiba shiji de Luojiao" [Mortals and immortals: On the Luo Sect in the eighteenth century], *Shixue pinglun* [Historical review] 2 (July 1980): 63–72. David Kelley noted the group's activities in eighteenth-century Hangzhou in "Temples and Tribute Fleets: The Luo Sect and Boatmen's Associations in the Eighteenth Century," *Modern China* 8, 3 (July 1982): 361–91. On sectarian religion in late imperial China, see Susan Naquin, *Millenarian Rebellion in China: The Eight Trigrams Uprising of 1813* (New Haven: Yale University Press, 1976); Daniel L. Overmyer, *Folk Buddhist Religion: Dissenting Sects in Late Traditional China* (Cambridge, Mass.: Harvard University Press, 1976); Susan Naquin, "The Transformation of White Lotus Sectarianism in Late Imperial China," in David Johnson, Andrew Nathan, and Evelyn Rawski, eds., *Popular Culture in Late Imperial China* (Berkeley: University of California Press, 1985), 255–91; and, most recently, Philip Kuhn, *The Soulstealers: The Chinese Sorcery Scare of 1768* (Cambridge, Mass.: Harvard University Press, 1990).

15. Wu settled for peace after Yue surrendered the country's most cherished beauty, Xishi. Yue recovered enough of its military might to lay a siege on the Wu capital in 475 B.C., taking the city and annihilating the kingdom in 473 B.C.

16. Quan Hansheng, "Tang Song diguo yu yunhe" [Tang-Song empire and the Grand Canal], originally published in *Zhongyang yanjiu yuan lishi yuyan yanjiu suo zhuankan* [Bulletin of the Institute of History and Philology, Academia Sinica], 1943, reprinted in Quan Hansheng, *Zhongguo jingji shi yanjiu* [Studies in Chinese economic history] (Hong Kong: Xinya yanjiu suo chuban she, 1976), 1:265–395. Quan argued that the vicissitudes of dynastic fortune for the next five centuries after the con-

struction of the Grand Canal should be understood primarily in terms of the shifting balance in regional economy, which had a lot to do with the transportation capacity of the canal. On the Grand Canal as an artificially maintained waterway linking the grain baskets of the Yangzi Delta to China's imperial capitals in the north, see Van Slyke, *Yangtze*, 65–80.

17. Zhang Shicheng began his career as a salt smuggler. He led his followers in uprisings against the Yuan and entered the Yangzi Delta from the north in 1356. At the height of his military power in the late 1350s, Zhang Shicheng crowned himself king of Wu and controlled the rich and populous area bounded by Hangzhou and Shaoxing in the south, Jining (Shandong) in the north, Anhui in the west, and the coast of the East China Sea on the east. See Wu Chenbo (Wu Han), *Zhu Yuanzhang zhuan* [Biography of Zhu Yuanzhang] (reprint Taipei: Guoshi yanjiu shi, 1972), 76–78; John W. Dardess, "Late Yuan Chekiang," in Hok-lam Chan and William Theodore de Bary, eds., *Yuan Thought: Chinese Thought and Religion under the Mongols* (New York: Columbia University Press, 1982), 350.

18. Zhu Yuanzhang's measures succeeded in drastically reducing the presence of eminent households in Zhexi as well as in Zhedong. Wu Han, *Zhu Yuan zhang zhuan*, 112–13. On the tax captain system, see Ray Huang, "Fiscal Administration during the Ming Dynasty," in Charles O. Hucker, ed., *Chinese Government in Ming Times: Seven Studies* (New York: Columbia University Press, 1969), 85–94.

19. Gu Yanwu, *Tianxia junguo libing shu* [On the benefits and ailments of all counties under the heaven] (Shanghai: Erlinzhai shiyin, 1899), 88:1.

20. Ibid.

21. Much has been published on the relationship between the imperial state and gentry society in late imperial China in the past two decades. For summary collections, see Frederic Wakeman, Jr., and Carolyn Grant, eds., *Conflict and Control in Late Imperial China* (Berkeley: University of California Press, 1975), and Esherick and Rankin, *Chinese Local Elites*.

22. Gu Yanwu, *Tianxia junguo libing shu*, ibid.

23. Zhang Xuecheng (courtesy name: Shizhai) (1738–1801), the great Qing historian, was among the first to point out the intellectual affinity between Zhexi and Jiangnan scholarly traditions. He was also the first to describe the differences that separated the intellectual traditions of Zhexi from those of Zhedong, and to identify Gu Yanwu, the classicist, and Huang Zongxi, the historian, as the founding figures of the two respective schools under the Qing. See his chapter "Zhedong xueshu" [Zhedong scholarship] in *Wenshi tongyi* [General treatise on literature and history] (reprint Taipei: Guoshi yanjiu shi, 1972), 51–53. Zhang Xuecheng's classifications continue to inform twentieth-century scholarship on the intellectual history of Qing China. On Zhang Xuecheng, see David Nivison, *The Life and*

Thought of Chang Hsueh-ch'eng (1738–1801) (Stanford: Stanford University Press, 1966). On the twentieth-century development of Zhang Xuecheng's ideas about Zhexi and Zhedong scholarly traditions, see Liang Qichao, "Jindai xuefeng zhi dili fenbu" [Geographical distribution of late imperial Chinese scholarship by style], in *Qinghua xuebao* [Qinghua journal] 1, 1 (June 1924): 26–31, and Liang Qichao, *Zhongguo jin sanbai nian xueshu shi* [History of Chinese scholarship of the past three hundred years] (reprint Shanghai: n.p., 1936), 43–72, passim. For fuller treatment of aspects of Zhexi scholarship during the Qing, see Benjamin Elman, *From Philosophy to Philology: Intellectual and Social Aspects of Change in Late Imperial China* (Cambridge, Mass.: Council on East Asian Studies Publications, Harvard University Press, 1984), and Elman, *Classicism, Politics, and Kinship: The Ch'ang-chou School of New Text Confucianism in Late Imperial China* (Berkeley: University of California Press, 1990). On the Zhedong School, see Lynn Struve, "Chen Que versus Huang Zongxi: Confucianism Faces Modern Times in the 17th-Century," *Journal of Chinese Philosophy* 18, 1 (March 1991): 5–23, and Struve, "The Hsu Brothers and Semiofficial Patronage of Scholars in the K'ang-hsi Period," *Harvard Journal of Asiatic Studies* 42, 1 (June 1982): 231–66, the latter of which treats the first phase of scholarly accommodation to the Qing conquest.

24. Dong Chuping, *Wu Yue wenhua xintan* [New perspectives on Wu-Yue culture] (Xiaoshan: Zhejiang renmin chuban she, 1988), 69–71. Chinese archaeologists working in the ancient marshland of Zhejiang—including Hemudu, Liangzhu, Songze, Majiabang, and Fanshan on both sides of the Qiantang River—have tentatively argued that there were two major complexes of the Neolithic in Zhejiang divided by the Qiantang River. To the south there was Hemudu, "an advanced hunter-gatherer society" "drawing upon many resources from plain and foothill," with its distinct cord-marked pots and usage of querns until the Zhou. To the north there were Majiabang, Songze, and Liangzhu, with smooth-surfaced pottery at an early stage and no querns until the end of the Neolithic period. I am indebted to David Keightley for sharing the information and observations contained in a confidential report that he prepared in 1991 on the Fanshan site.

25. Kwang-chih Chang was the first scholar to develop this thesis by citing the Dapenkeng (Ta-p'en-k'eng) Neolithic site in Taipei County, with its cord-marked pottery dated in the early third millennium B.C., as evidence of a Neolithic culture on the southeast China coast that existed as a "parallel regional development" to the farming cultures on the north China plain. See Kwang-chih Chang, *The Archaeology of Ancient China*, 3d ed. (New Haven: Yale University Press, 1977), 83, 85–91. Chinese historians and archaeologists had been engaged in debates since the 1920s over the issue of singular versus multiple sources of Chinese civilization.

Chang was among the first to present systematic archaeological evidence to substantiate his thesis. His basic thesis, much further developed later on, also became, in the late 1980s, the foundation of popularized cultural theories in Chinese intellectual circles that sought to rediscover in the Chinese past a multiplicity of mutually independent regional traditions.

26. Tian Yuqing, *Dong Jin menfa zhengzhi* [Eastern Jin aristocratic politics] (Beijing: Beijing University Press, 1991), 78–79.

27. On the opening up of Zhedong between the third and sixth centuries, see Liu Shufen, "San zhi liu shiji Zhedong diqu jingji de fazhan" [Economic development in the Zhedong region from the third to the sixth century], *Zhongyang yanjiu yuan lishi yuyan yanjiu suo jikan* [Bulletin of the Institute of History and Philology, Academia Sinica] 58, 3 (September 1987): 485–524.

28. Shiba Yoshinobu argues that Ningbo, by virtue of waterways linking it to Hangzhou via Yuyao, Caoe, and the Zhedong Canal, was in effect the southern terminus of the Grand Canal. Furthermore, owing to shallows and tidal currents in Hangzhou Estuary and at the mouth of the Yangzi, large ocean-going junks from southeastern China were forced to transfer their cargoes at Ningbo either to smaller boats capable of negotiating the canals and other inland waterways or to small luggers, which then sailed for Hangzhou, the Yangzi River ports, and the north China coast. Ningbo was thus very much at the pulse of a national market system, especially during the Southern Song. The *shibo si*, first established in 992, supervised coastal trade and controlled the maritime tribute of Korea and Japan almost without interruption until 1523. See Shiba Yoshinobu, "Ningbo and Its Hinterland," in Skinner, *The City in Late Imperial China*, 392. Scholars estimate that the tonnage of these ships going through the Zhedong ports was often in the hundreds. One of these late Song–early Yuan vessels was raised in August 1973 from the waters of the southern Fujian port of Quanzhou. The rebuilt ship measures 34.55 by 9.90 meters, with a cargo capacity of about 375 tons. See Thomas H. C. Lee, "A Report on the Recently Excavated Sung Ship at Chuan-chou and a Consideration of Its True Capacity," *Sung Studies Newsletter* 11/12 (1975/76): 4–9.

29. Shiba, "Ningbo and Its Hinterland," 396, and idem, *Commerce and Society in Sung China* (Ann Arbor: Center for Chinese Studies, University of Michigan, 1970), 25.

30. Jacques Gernet, *A History of Chinese Civilization*, trans. J. R. Foster (Cambridge: Cambridge University Press, 1982), 328.

31. See, for example, Morris Rossabi, *Khubilai Khan: His Life and Times* (Berkeley: University of California Press, 1988), 153–76, passim. Rossabi's thesis of Yuan religious tolerance and cultural cosmopolitanism stands in sharp contrast to the dominant Chinese view held in the twentieth century

on issues of foreign conquest and alien rule of China, which emphasizes conquest, exploitation, oppression, Mongol cultural inferiority, and Han resistance. See Qian Mu, *Guoshi dagang* [Outline of our nation's history] (reprint Taipei: Commercial Press, 1967), 2:467–73. Note that Qian's highly influential college textbook was composed during the War of Resistance (1937–45) and first published in 1940. John D. Langlois, Jr., citing Joseph Fletcher, sums up Mongol rule in China in terms of phases and transformations. By the time of Khubilai's conquest of Southern Song in the 1270s, according to Langlois, a new form of Mongol rule had emerged as a result of its encounter with Chinese civilization. This he characterizes as "a hybrid form of government, partly bureaucratic, partly colonial and military, partly bent on seizing booty, and partly bent on developing wealth and income in the ruled territories, and never compromising on the principle of Mongol superiority. The monarchy remained Mongolian, despite certain evidences of Chinese influences." It was a stratified system of chronic violence. John D. Langlois, Jr., "Political Thought in Chin-hua under Mongol Rule," in Langlois, ed., *China under Mongol Rule* (Princeton: Princeton University Press, 1981), 139.

32. Jacques Gernet offers this description of the caravan trade: "These merchants, usually of Iranian origin, converts to Islam, familiar with the banking practices of the Moslem world, sometimes entrusted with farming the taxes in China, were in contact with the Mongol aristocracy, which often lent them money at high rates of interest. Thus China, exploited by her new masters, participated through the caravans that travelled the old silk roads and steppe roads in a world economic circuit without receiving any of the profits." Gernet sees an impoverishment of Chinese society under the Yuan, and he links the transfers of Chinese money to the Middle East and Europe to the great shortage of metal experienced by the Ming in the late fourteenth century. Gernet, *History of Chinese Civilization*, 372.

33. Shiba, "Ningbo and Its Hinterland," 396–97.

34. This regional leader was Fang Guozhen (1319/20–1374), a native of Taizhou. Fang built up an armed fleet with several thousands of ships. He headquartered his operations in Qingyuan (Ningbo) and controlled the salt trade and coastal fishing from Ningbo and Wenzhou. Wu Han, *Zhu Yuanzhang zhuan*, 82–83. On the tension between Fang Guozhen and the local community of Confucian reformers, see Dardess, "Late Yuan Chekiang," 352–67, passim.

35. The new government placed strict limits on the export of horses, cattle, weapons, iron, copper, and silk out of China; it also threatened to punish anyone involved with the transportation and loading of such goods on land. Yang Jianxin and Lu Wei, *Sichou zhilu* [The silk road] (Lanzhou: Gansu renmin chuban she, 1988), 364. The founder of the dynasty also

renounced Chinese military actions against Japan, Korea, and Southeast Asia. See Wu Han, *Zhu Yuanzhang zhuan,* 153–54.

36. The Mongols in 1284 made the state the sole agent legally permitted to trade overseas. This Mongol system of controlled maritime trade was converted, in 1371 and in 1390, into a purely tributary trade from foreign nations acknowledging Chinese suzerainty by Zhu Yuanzhang, the founding Ming emperor. This policy was largely abandoned in 1567, but by then it had "caused Chinese overseas and coastal trade to go through a prolonged depression, beginning in the fourteenth century and ending in the sixteenth. During the same period Chinese naval power fell from its position of world pre-eminence to a shadow of its former self." Mark Elvin, *The Pattern of the Chinese Past* (Stanford: Stanford University Press, 1973), 215–25; the quote is from p. 224. For the Zheng He interlude, see Frederic Wakeman, Jr., "Voyages," *American Historical Review* 98, 1 (February 1993): 8–14.

37. John K. Fairbank, ed., *The Cambridge History of China* (Cambridge: Cambridge University Press, 1983), vol. 12, pt. 1, "Republican China, 1912–1949," 16.

38. Piracy on the Zhedong coast in the mid-sixteenth century (1522–66) has often been attributed to Japanese pirates sacking Chinese coastal cities. It was interpreted by scholars as a sign of growing friction between China and Japan in the context of the latter half of a period referred to in Japan as the *sengoku* (warring states). These frictions supposedly led to the Japanese militarist Toyotomi Hideyoshi's decision to invade China by attacking Korea in the late sixteenth century. Many sources, however, including the official dynastic history of Ming, indicate that "Chinese traitors" were the ringleaders in Japanese pirate attacks on Zhedong coastal cities in the mid-sixteenth century. This enables the scholar Kwan-wai So to argue in the 1970s that, contrary to frequent textbook accounts, coastal piracy was dominated by the Chinese rather than by the Japanese. The harsh Ming restrictions on overseas trade collided with a growing foreign demand for Chinese goods to engender what, in the beginning, was coastal smuggling by Chinese traders, which then degenerated into piracy in collaboration with the Japanese. Recent Chinese revisionist scholarship places even greater emphasis on domestic Chinese factors as contributing to the rise of coastal disturbance. "Piracy" is sometimes treated as a form of collective resistance by the society against the state. Chinese scholars stress that there were prominent cases in the sixteenth century involving substantial Zhedong landlords being prosecuted by the state, rather unjustly, for piracy. The accused "pirates" who battled the Ming imperial troops often enjoyed the popular support of coastal landlords and merchants. The conflict was thus a struggle between private Zhedong merchants and the Ming imperial bureaucracy over maritime trade restrictions.

See James Geiss, "The Chia-ching Reign, 1522–1566," in Frederick Mote and Denis Twitchett, eds., *The Cambridge History of China*, vol. 7, pt. 1 (Cambridge: Cambridge University Press, 1988), 490–505. For Kwan-wai So's thesis, see *Japanese Piracy in Ming China during the 16th Century* (East Lansing: Michigan State University Press, 1975); for a review of earlier textbook accounts, see So's bibliographical essay on pp. 203–20. On Hideyoshi's ambition to "extend my conquest to China" and his invasion of Korea, see Mary Elizabeth Berry, *Hideyoshi* (Cambridge, Mass.: Harvard University Press, 1982), 207–17. For recent Chinese scholarship, see Yang and Lu, *Sichou zhilu*, 388. See also John E. Wills, Jr., "Maritime China from Wang Chih to Shih Lang: Themes in Peripheral History," in Jonathan Spence and John E. Wills, eds., *From Ming to Ch'ing: Conquest, Region, and Continuity in Seventeenth-Century China* (New Haven: Yale University Press, 1979), 210–13.

39. John Fairbank was convinced that China's maritime activity, "despite its qualitative superiority to that of Europe as late as the 1430s, was still a minor tradition in the Chinese state and society." This was reflected in Chinese state policy especially after the Tumu Incident of 1449, when the Mongols captured the Ming emperor and besieged Beijing. Fairbank believed that this episode "reconfirmed the dominant agrarian-bureaucratic nature of the Chinese realm." Thereafter "near the Great Wall an armed society developed. The northern frontier became an obsession." This continental preoccupation of the Ming set the stage for European expansion into East Asian waters after 1511. Fairbank, *Cambridge History of China*, 12:16. Fairbank's summaries were based on Frederick Mote's research in "The T'u-mu Incident of 1449," published in Frank A. Kierman, Jr., and John K. Fairbank, eds., *Chinese Ways in Warfare* (Cambridge, Mass.: Harvard University Press, 1974), 243–72. Mote shows that the crisis of 1449 led momentarily to a "righteous revival of Confucian morale and morality" (267), and that the northern border frontier "became the fixation, the virtual obsession of many Chinese statesmen throughout the mid and late Ming times" thereafter (271).

40. G. William Skinner, citing Elvin's *Pattern of the Chinese Past*, notes that "beginning early in the fourteenth century under the Yuan and continuing through the fifteenth century under the Ming, there occurred a basic shift in imperial policy in the direction of reducing foreign contact and foreign trade." The impact of this was "an overall decline and stagnation in interregional as well as foreign trade," and a devolutionary trend in the development of Chinese cities. Skinner believes that in the Chinese case "the levels of urbanization achieved in the most advanced regions were higher in the medieval era than in late imperial times." G. William Skinner, "Introduction: Urban Development in Imperial China," in Skinner, *The City in Late Imperial China*, 27–28.

41. Wills, "Maritime China from Wang Chih to Shih Lang," 220–34.

42. Fairbank, *Cambridge History of China*, 12:22.

43. Jones, "The Ningpo Pang and Financial Power at Shanghai," 76–77.

44. Ibid.

45. Ibid. The southern Fujian port of Amoy in the nineteenth century was the center of an active "coolie trade" in contract labor destined for the Philippines. Wakeman, "Voyages," 4–5.

46. The phrase is Fairbank's, in *Cambridge History of China*, 12:9.

47. Chinese geographers sought to determine the source of the Qiantang in the 1950s, when teams of scholars organized expeditions into the area using as their guide information obtained from aerial photographs. Traditional geographers had long accepted the authority of the *Shuijing* (Water classic) and believed that the Qiantang came out of the Xin'an River of Anhui. Early-twentieth-century geographers revised their view on this matter and saw the Lotus Peak (Lianhua Jian) on the borders of Zhejiang, Jiangxi, and Anhui as the source of the Qiantang. Chinese scholars of the present, however, believe that the river originates with the trickles of water in the cracks of Qingzhidi Jian, a giant limestone peak in the Daqingshan (Great Blue Mountains) range on the borders of Zhejiang, Anhui, and Jiangxi. *Qiantang jiang jixing*, 14.

48. Ibid., 21–22.

49. The river begins with waterways that originate along the provincial borders of Anhui and Zhejiang, where the elevation reaches nearly six thousand feet. Two rivers come southeastward from Anhui and converge at Jiande in Zhejiang. Another two come from the western slopes of the eastern ridges inside Zhejiang, converging at Lanxi to flow northward to join the Anhui rivers at Jiande. From Jiande the water turns east, reaching Tonglu, where it is joined by the Tongxi River from the southern slope of the northern ridges. Ninety li (approximately thirty-two miles) below Tonglu the water reaches Fuyang, where it joins the Puyang River coming down from the hills to the south. After another ninety li the river reaches Hangzhou, the provincial capital, where it becomes known as the Qiantang River. The Qiantang is joined by the Caoe River from the northern slopes of the eastern ridges in Shaoxing. Below Hangzhou the Qiantang River enters the sea. The Qiantang River basin (twelve thousand square miles) represents about one-third of the acreage of Zhejiang (thirty-six thousand square miles). Zhang Qiyun, *Zhejiang sheng shidi jiyao*, 2–3, 104.

50. *Qiantang jiang jixing*, 67.

51. Ibid., 51.

52. Qu Yingguang, "Chi Jinhua daoyin shujun shangjiang yidai shuili wen" [Order issued to the Jinhua circuit intendant to dredge up the waterway along the upper stream], *Qu Xun'an xunshi liang Zhe wengao* (n.p.: preface dated 1915), 2:27a; Qu Yingguang, "Chengbao xuxun Jin Qu

Yan Chu yidai shisuo huishu riqi dian" [Report on the conclusion of my official visit to the Jinhua, Quzhou, Yanzhou and Chuzhou area and upon the determination of a return date to my provincial office], in ibid., 1:36a.

53. Cannon and Jenkins, *Geography of Contemporary China*, 189.

54. *Qiantang jiang jixing*, 230. For a detailed analysis of the Hangzhou Estuary from a geographical point of view, see Chen Jiyu, "Hangzhou wan dixing shuyao" [On the principal geographical characteristics of the Hangzhou Estuary], *Zhejiang xuebao* 1, 2 (December 1947): 85–92.

55. *Qiantang jiang jixing*, 226–27. David Johnson, "The Wu Zixu *Pien-wen* and Its Sources," *Harvard Journal of Asiatic Studies* 40, 1 (June 1980): 93–156 and 40, 2 (December 1980): 465–505.

56. *Qiantang jiang jixing*, 225.

57. Ibid., 4, 228–29.

58. Qu Yingguang, "Xunshi Lanxi xian xuanyan" [Proclamation on the occasion of an official visit to Lanxi], *Qu Xun'an xunshi liang Zhe wengao*, 4:107b. From Hangzhou upriver to Tonglu was 180 li. With steamboats the journey could be made in six to eight hours. From Tonglu upstream to Lanxi, the midpoint in the river system, was another 180 li. With the larger *bochuan* (a riverboat that burned coal) it took one day to go down the river and two days to return. Above Lanxi the rivers were navigable only for junks. From this point on it took several days for a short journey to be made. Upstream through the rapids the boats often had to be pulled from the shores onto the steeply rising mountain slopes. The 170 li up to Chun'an took two and a half days, while it was one and a half days to go downstream. The 220 li from Chun'an further up the mountains into Tunxi (Anhui) required six days, with the journey downstream in three days. Zhang Qiyun, *Zhejiang sheng shidi jiyao*, 3–4.

59. Ye Qianchu, *Lanxi shiyan xian shixi diaocha baogao* [Report about an on-the-job training and investigation experience with the experimental administration of Lanxi County] (Taipei: Chengwen chuban she, 1977), 1:77, 137–38.

60. Other stores featured tobacco, shoes, clothing, socks, fabric, paper, ink, and lacquer. Lanxi xian zhengfu [Lanxi County government], ed., *Zhejiang sheng Lanxi xian xianzheng gaikuang* [County government report on the state of administration in Lanxi County, Zhejiang Province], "Jianshe gaikuang" [Section on construction] (Hangzhou: Lanxi xian zhengfu, 1928), 57–58. Lanxi (literally "valley of orchids") was named after the wild orchids that covered its hills each spring and summer. Wei Songtang, *Zhejiang jingji*, 308–9; Lanxi xian zhengfu, ed., *Zhejiang*, "Cishan gaikuang" [Section on philanthropy], 1. The figures given in this survey indicate a total of 2,600 businesses in Lanxi. This would mean an average of one hundred Lanxi residents for every shop—a rather high level of commercialization.

61. Wei Songtang, *Zhejiang jingji*, 312–13.

62. Dong Zhongsheng, *Lanxi shiyan xian shixi baogao* [Report about an on-the-job training experience with the Lanxi experimental county administration], vol. 2 of Ye Qianchu, *Lanxi*, 77,677.

63. Ye Qianchu, *Lanxi*, 1:77,138–39.

CHAPTER 2: THE IDEA OF A MIDDLE COUNTY

1. Other locales, of course, have been associated with eminent Neo-Confucian masters—Luoyang with the brothers Cheng Hao and Cheng Yi (Northern Song), Nanchang with Lu Xiangshan (Southern Song), Yongjia with Ye Shi (Southern Song), Yuyao with Wang Yangming (Ming), and so forth. Jinhua's importance as a hometown of Neo-Confucianism derived, above all, from the pivotal contribution of the Jinhua School to the formation of late imperial Chinese state ideology (a development discussed later in this chapter). There were many lines of thought within Neo-Confucian moral philosophy. For a succinct discussion of the principal differences in basic philosophical approaches between the two schools that developed out of the intellectual traditions of Cheng-Zhu (Cheng Hao, Cheng Yi, and Zhu Xi) and Lu-Wang (Lu Xiangshan and Wang Yangming), see Wei-ming Tu, *Neo-Confucian Thought in Action: Wang Yang-ming's Youth, 1472–1509* (Berkeley: University of California Press, 1976), 147–76. This division is also referred to as that between the Learning of Reason (*Li xue*) and the Learning of Heart (*Xin xue*). Besides moral philosophy, Neo-Confucian learning also encompassed a pragmatic attention to statecraft (*jingshi*) and a philological interest in the classics (*zhang ju xun gu*). Historically, Neo-Confucian scholarly interest in these three areas—moral philosophy, statecraft, and classics—had risen and fallen following a pattern that resembled the movement of a pendulum. See Ying-shih Yu, "Some Preliminary Observations on the Rise of Ch'ing Confucian Intellectualism," *Tsing Hua Journal of Chinese Studies*, new series, 10, 1–2 (December 1975): 105–46. Over the past three decades much scholarly literature has appeared in English that deals with intellectual biographies and aspects of Neo-Confucian philosophy. It is beyond the scope of this study to present an annotated bibliography on this literature, but readers of Hoyt Cleveland Tillman, *Utilitarian Confucianism: Ch'en Liang's Challenge to Chu Hsi* (Cambridge, Mass.: Council on East Asian Studies Publications, Harvard University Press, 1982), and of the two seminal volumes edited by William Theodore de Bary, *Self and Society in Ming Thought* (New York: Columbia University Press, 1970) and *The Unfolding of Neo-Confucianism* (New York: Columbia University Press, 1975), cannot fail to be impressed with the inner complexities of the Neo-Confucian moral philosophical tradition between the twelfth and the seventeenth centuries.

2. Qu Yingguang, "Chengbao xuxun jiu Jin Qu Yan geshu ji Shao shu zhi Zhuji jiu Chu shu zhi Jinyun, Suichang, Xuanping gexian shisuo wen" [Report on continuing the inspection tour into counties formerly under the jurisdiction of the Jin-Qu-Yan Prefecture, into Zhuji County of Shaoxing Prefecture, into Jinyun, Suichang and Xuanping counties of Chuzhou Prefecture], in Qu Yingguang, *Qu Xun'an xunshi liang Zhe wengao*, 1:43b. In the core-pheriphery scheme developed by Keith Schoppa and based on Skinner's categories, Jinhua is categorized as outer core. Official visitors during the 1990s were escorted through the county's main silk factories that supply the state-owned raw silk distribution centers in Hangzhou and were told by proud county cadres the story of the postsocialist migration of mechanized sericulture, for centuries a hallmark of Zhexi commercialization, into the woods of Jinhua. Interviews conducted at the Jinhua Unified Silk Factories (Jinhua sichou lianying chang), May 31, 1992.

3. "Middle county," as developed in this chapter, draws attention to a way of life that places high value on communal harmony and moral self-cultivation on the basis of an agrarian economy of self-sufficiency. It was more a construction than a reality: despite Jinhua's self-regard as a middle county, there were plenty of signs, as will be discussed later in this book, about hardships and tension within its society. The ideal, nonetheless, was of enormous appeal in late imperial Chinese social imagination, in part because it rested on a Confucian ideological underpinning that found expression in household mottoes such as *geng du chuan jia* (perpetuating a family line by tilling and studying) and *ban geng ban du* (tilling and studying), with equal emphasis on farming and classical learning. On economic matters, the middle-county ideal stressed self-sufficiency as opposed to enrichment, equality in the distribution of wealth as opposed to increase in the production of wealth. With regard to learning, it placed the pursuit of enlightenment above that of utility. It also assumed a moral continuum that linked individual self-cultivation through "family" and "state" to the "pacification of the realm," much as outlined in the Confucian classic *Great Learning*. Because of this Confucian underpinning, the middle-county ideal was of central normative importance in imperial days, especially in the vast areas of China that remained agrarian. This is not to suggest that within the context of Zhejiang Jinhua's importance, whether under the Song or the Qing, surpassed that of Zhexi or Ning-Shao. Jinhua retained its composure despite the superior wealth of Zhexi and Ning-Shao in imperial days, precisely because of its serene cultural confidence in the middle-county ideal.

4. To my knowledge, no history of Jinhua has been written in English. This is not to say that Jinhua has completely escaped scholarly attention. The place surfaces from time to time, as the notes in this chapter will show, in scholarly discussions of Song-Yuan intellectual, political, and social

history. No major effort has been made, however, to capture the characteristics of the locale in its own historical context through centuries.

5. Joseph Levenson, in writing the intellectual biography of Liang
Qichao (Liang Ch'i-ch'ao), divides his chapters into two types. Levenson
states: "In Chapters I, III, and V, I describe what meets the eye, the top of
the iceberg, the public record. Liang, whose life is thus chronicled, could
have done that much himself. He knew what he did. But only others could
know what he was. Self-knowledge is a remarkably elusive thing, for the
self is transformed in the knowing, and Liang, trapped like any man in his
own present, could hardly reveal himself and remain himself. He could not
have written the even-numbered chapters, Chapters II, IV, VI. Had Liang
been able to write them, he could never have been their subject; if a man
had the key to his own prison, he would not stay fixed where he was."
Joseph Levenson, *Liang Ch'i-ch'ao and the Mind of Modern China* (Cambridge, Mass.: Harvard University Press, 1953), vii. The distinction that
Levenson introduces here, between subjective, experienced self-knowledge
and objective, researched scholarly knowledge, remains an important one.
The present chapter, in this sense, is concerned more with the former than
with the latter. While making the distinction, Levenson appears to imply,
however, that the latter occupies a higher order vis-à-vis the former. This
chapter operates with a different assumption: to enter the minds of the past,
it is sometimes necessary to see that past in terms of its own construction,
and to observe subsequent developments accordingly.

6. *Jinhua xianzhi* [Jinhua County gazetteer; hereafter cited as JX],
1894 compilation (first printing 1934; reprint Taipei: Chengwen chuban
she, 1970), 1:119.

7. The North Mountains are a branch of the Dapen Shan (Great Basin
Ridges) that form the northern border of the Jinhua Basin. It runs for about
three hundred li within the boundaries of Jinhua County. Yu Dafu, *Jihen
chuchu* [Footprints far and near] (Shanghai: Tieliu shudian, 1946), 16.

8. JX 1:119.

9. Ibid. The construction of the roads took place at a time of significant
commercial development in the Jin-Qu Basin in the sixteenth century.
Another way of regarding the decline of Jinhua's bureaucratic fortune in
late Ming is to consider the overall context of the rise of a monetary
economy and the subsequent cultural reorientation of Jinhua society,
which became preoccupied with "vanity, superficiality, excessiveness and
indulgence in enjoying life, hastening after wealth and fame." See Chun-
shu Chang and Shelley Hsueh-lun Chang, *Crisis and Transformation in
Seventeenth-Century China: Society, Culture, and Modernity in Li Yu's
World* (Ann Arbor: University of Michigan Press, 1992), 136.

10. JX 4:925.

11. Ibid., 927.

12. Modern-day visitors are permitted access only to the Ice Jar and the Twin Dragons, because over the centuries the water level in Morning Purity has risen, submerging many stones and steles bearing Song inscriptions. Visitors of the 1920s described the caves as cool and dark, with light filtering in through cracks. Today the caves are wired and illuminated by electrical lights with colored bulbs, tour guides regale throngs of visitors with tales of the immortals, and commercial photographers stand by to take pictures for a fee.

13. This is Huang Chuping, generally known as Huang the Immortal (Huang Daxian) and much worshiped these days, especially in Hong Kong. Huang demonstrated his magical power one day by turning rocks into sheep in front of a cave at the foot of Twin Dragon Peak. Cao Juren, *Wo yu wo de shijie* [I and my world] (Hong Kong: Sanyu tushu gongsi, 1972), 15.

14. Yu Dafu, *Jihen chuchu*, 17.

15. About the elites of Southern Song, see Richard L. Davis, *Court and Family in Sung China, 960–1279: Bureaucratic Success and Kinship Fortunes for the Shih of Ming-chou* (Durham, N.C.: Duke University Press, 1986), and Hoyt C. Tillman, "Proto-Nationalism in Twelfth-Century China," *Harvard Journal of Asiatic Studies* 36, 2 (December 1979): 403–28.

16. Archaeologists excavated a burial site in Quzhou in 1983 and dated the dirt tomb to circa 1200 B.C. The tomb contained thirteen pieces of blue porcelain with very fine ornamentation. Yiwu was the site in 1981 of an excavation of a dirt burial mound of the same period containing 114 burial objects, with over 100 pieces of blue porcelain. Chun'an was the site of a 1979 excavation of five burial mounds of a slightly later period that contained several dozen pieces of blue porcelain. The presence of this blue porcelain has been documented extensively in the Yangzi Valley and along the southeastern coast. Dong Chuping, *Wu Yue wenhua xintan*, 243–44.

17. For a succinct outline of the history of Song (960–1279), with attention paid to the rise of a new society with a highly developed commercial economy, bureaucratic rule, and Neo-Confucian philosophy, see James T. C. Liu, *Ou-yang Hsiu: An Eleventh-Century Neo-Confucianist* (Stanford: Stanford University Press, 1967), 7–23.

18. For a scholarly treatment on the subject, see relevant sections in Charles A. Peterson, "First Song Reactions to the Mongol Invasion of the North, 1211–17," in John W. Haeger, ed., *Crisis and Prosperity in Sung China* (Tucson: University of Arizona Press, 1975), 215–52.

19. The historiography on the transition from a medieval oligarchy to these newly emerging local elites is a multifaceted one. See, inter alia: David Johnson, "The Last Years of a Great Clan: The Li Family of Chao Chun in Late T'ang and Early Sung," *Harvard Journal of Asiatic Studies* 37, 1 (June 1977): 5–102; Robert Hartwell, "Demographic, Political, and Social

Transformations of China, 750–1550," *Harvard Journal of Asiatic Studies* 42, 2 (1982): 365–442; Robert Hymes, "Marriage, Descent Groups and the Localist Strategy in Sung and Yuan Fu-chou," in Patricia B. Ebrey and James L. Watson, eds., *Kinship Organization in Late Imperial China, 1000–1940* (Berkeley: University of California Press, 1986); Robert Hymes, *Statesmen and Gentlemen: The Elite of Fu-chou, Chiang-hsi, in Northern and Southern Sung* (Cambridge: Cambridge University Press, 1985); Richard Davis, "Political Success and the Growth of Descent Groups: The Shih of Ming-chou during the Sung," in Ebrey and Watson, *Kinship Organization*, 62–94; and Patricia Ebrey, *Family and Property in Sung China: Yuan Ts'ai's Precepts for Social Life* (Princeton: Princeton University Press, 1984).

20. See Patricia Ebrey, "Conceptions of the Family in the Sung Dynasty," *Journal of Asian Studies* 43, 2 (February 1984): 219–45.

21. Wei-ming Tu, "Reconstituting the Confucian Tradition," *Journal of Asian Studies* 33, 3 (May 1974): 441–53. See also Denis Twitchett's classic piece, "The Fan Clan's Charitable Estate, 1050–1760," in David Nivison and Arthur Wright, eds., *Confucianism in Action* (Stanford: Stanford University Press, 1959), 97–133.

22. For the complex relationship between classical learning and bureaucratic expertise, see Robert Hartwell, "Historical Analogism, Public Policy, and Social Science in Eleventh and Twelfth Century China," *American Historical Review* 76, 3 (June 1971): 690–727. John W. Dardess sees the fourteenth century as a crucial period in the development of local Jinhua Confucian communities, when moral elites of little public fame turned from "doctrinal development" of the classics to "practical implementation of an ideal of social service" and transformed themselves into men of local governance and "world-saving sense of purpose." This transformation, according to Dardess, laid the grass-roots foundation for the political activism of Ming Confucianism, which contributed to the rise and maintenance of Ming imperial autocracy. See Dardess, "Late Yuan Chekiang," 327–74; the quotations are from p. 368. For a fuller explication of this thesis, see Dardess, *Confucianism and Autocracy: Professional Elites in the Founding of the Ming Dynasty* (Berkeley: University of California Press, 1983). John D. Langlois also sees the fourteenth century as a critical period when Jinhua Confucian scholars fused the moral teaching of Zhu Xi with the utilitarianism of Chen Liang, embraced the notion of public service, developed a political philosophy of pragmatic accommodation, and went on to offer their service and expertise to the Ming founder Zhu Yuanzhang in the creation of the new dynasty. Langlois, "Political Thought in Chinhua under Mongol Rule," 137–85.

23. Neo-Confucianism during the Yuan has generally been regarded as the Neo-Confucianism of Zhu Xi as interpreted by Huang Gan. This line

of teaching was transmitted principally through Huang's disciples in Jin-hua. Wing-tsit Chan, "Chu Hsi and Neo-Confucianism," in Chan and de Bary, *Yuan Thought,* 197, 200. This certainly does not mean that Zhu Xi and his disciples were without detractors. See Tillman, *Utilitarian Confucianism,* 115–227. See also James T. C. Liu, "How Did a Neo-Confucian School Become the State Orthodoxy?" *Philosophy East and West* 23, 4 (October 1973): 483–505; Conrad Schirokauer, "Neo-Confucians under Attack: The Condemnation of *Wei-hsueh,*" in Haeger, *Crisis and Prosperity in Sung China,* 163–98; Daniel K. Gardner, *Chu Hsi and the Ta-hsueh: Neo-Confucian Reflection on the Confucian Canon* (Cambridge, Mass.: Harvard University Press, 1986).

24. JX 8:5a.

25. Ibid., 2:408–10.

26. Ibid., 8:3a.

27. The jinshi degree carried much higher honor and prestige during the Song than under previous dynasties, because the Song government relied heavily on the civil service examinations as the most important channel to recruit officials. About one-third of regular bureaucratic positions were filled by successful exam candidates in early Song. Thomas H. C. Lee, "Sung Education before Chu Hsi," in William Theodore de Bary and John W. Chaffee, eds., *Neo-Confucian Education: The Formative Stage* (Berkeley: University of California Press, 1989), 108–9.

28. JX 8:3b.

29. Ibid., 4a.

30. It was common during the Tang for sons of the elite to study in Buddhist monastery schools located in scenic mountains. From the late Tang period (tenth century) onward, a new trend emerged for private families to run their own schools and to build their own library collections for instruction in the Confucian classics. These private schools were modeled on Buddhist temple or monastery schools, but were aimed at the preparation of candidates for the civil service examinations. Lee, "Sung Education before Chu Hsi," 105–8.

31. For a discussion of "molding through ritual" and the teaching of ritualized ways of acting as a critical component of Confucian education in the Song period, see Patricia Ebrey, "Education through Ritual: Efforts to Formulate Family Rituals during the Sung Period," in de Bary and Chaffee, *Neo-Confucian Education,* 277–306. Ebrey observes: "In Chinese families, the basic values of filial piety and deference to seniors and males were taught to children primarily by showing them the behavior patterns to practice. . . . Only after the patterns became part of what they took as 'natural' might they learn the theoretical moral principle underlying these ritualized ways of acting" (277). See also Patricia Ebrey, *Confucianism and Family Rituals in Imperial China: A Social History of Writing about Rites* (Princeton: Princeton University Press, 1991).

32. Qian Mu, *Song-Ming lixue gaishu* [Introduction to Song-Ming Neo-Confucianism] (Taipei: Xuesheng shuju, 1977), 196.

33. Ibid., 196–97.

34. Neo-Confucian teaching links a moral endeavor to rectify one's mind-heart with an effort to bring harmony to the family, order to the political community, and peace to all under heaven. Zhu Xi exhorted his disciples: "Be filial to the parents, thus loyalty can be transferred to the monarch. Be deferential to the elder brothers, thus obedience can be transferred to the official superiors." Kwang-Ching Liu observes that Zhu Xi's position was essentially that of the *Xiaojing* (Classic of filial piety) and of Han orthodoxy. See Kwang-Ching Liu, "Socioethics as Orthodoxy: A Perspective," in Kwang-Ching Liu, ed., *Orthodoxy in Late Imperial China* (Berkeley: University of California Press, 1990), 80.

35. When Wang Shiyu's father died, the family was too poor to afford the luxury of a proper burial. Wang's clansmen therefore planned to have Wang's father cremated, to lower the expenses. Wang Shiyu was overwhelmed by grief and refused food and drink for days. His kinsmen, moved by his grief, managed to come up with enough resources to give his father a proper burial. JX 8:10a.

36. Ibid., 17b.

37. Ebrey shows that Song Neo-Confucian family ritual handbooks had been used both to disseminate information about ritually proper conduct in contemporary family and kinship groups and to combat the popularity of non-Confucian and noncanonical practices, such as the influence of Buddhism and Daoism on death rituals. Ceremonial activities also had significance as markers of social status. Ebrey, "Education through Ritual," 304–6.

38. Qian Mu, *Song-Ming lixue gaishu*, 195.

39. Lineages that achieved comparable success included the Shi (with 12 entries in the *Song Yuan xuean*), the Wang (9), the Pan (9), the He (8), the Qi (8), the Ni (7), the Ye (4), and the Tang (4). JX 8:1a–2b. For close studies of a Jinhua lineage during the Yuan and the Ming dynasties, see John Dardess, "The Cheng Communal Family: Social Organization and Neo-Confucianism in Yuan and Early Ming China," *Harvard Journal of Asian Studies* 34 (1974): 7–52, and John D. Langlois, Jr., "Authority in Family Legislation," in Dieter Eikemeier and Herbert Franke, eds., *State and Law in East Asia: Festschrift Karl Bunger* (Wiesbaden: Harrassowitz, 1981), 272–99.

40. JX 8:9b–10a.

41. In Southern Song "a strong commitment to centralized state power was rarely expressed except in the upper reaches of the bureaucracy itself; but a principled and intellectually elaborated commitment to a specific kinship grouping, the *chia* [*jia*], as the primary focus of loyalties was a position articulated in some detail in several Southern Song works that

survive." Robert Hymes, "Lu Chiu-yuan [Lu Jiuyuan], Academies, and the Problem of the Local Community," in de Bary and Chaffee, *Neo-Confucian Education*, 447. Southern Song Neo-Confucianism often displayed a serious and distinct commitment to the *jia* (family) as the primary institution, which has been referred to by Patricia Ebrey as the "*jia* orientation" of Song Neo-Confucianism. Hymes sees in this "family orientation" not just abstention from social activism, but also, as in the case of Lu Xiangshan (Jiuyuan), "a lack of interest in formalizing outside commitments through the promotion of community institutions" such as the local academy, the communal "pact," the communal granary, and the local altar for deceased luminaries. See Hymes, "Lu Chiu-yuan," 448; Ebrey, "Conceptions of the Family in the Sung Dynasty," 224–29; and also Ebrey, *Family and Property in Sung China*.

42. Qian Mu, *Song-Ming lixue gaishu*, 196; JX 2:404. The brothers Cheng Hao and Cheng Yi were masters of the Luoyang School of Northern Song Neo-Confucianism, while Zhang Zai was the master of the Guanzhong School. Lü Zuqian's thought has been characterized by some scholars as a synthesis of these two Northern Song schools of moral philosophy. See Tillman, *Utilitarian Confucianism*, 60–61.

43. Tillman, *Utilitarian Confucianism*, 62. See, in this respect, James T. C. Liu, "Sung Roots of Chinese Political Conservatism," *Journal of Asian Studies* 26, 3 (May 1967): 457–63.

44. Tillman, *Utilitarian Confucianism*, 59–67.

45. *Shuyuan* (academies) as centers for the teaching of Neo-Confucianism began to appear under the Northern Song and developed into a major type of educational institution under the Southern Song and the Yuan. The academies emerged in response to the spread of printing technology and the institution of the civil service examinations system. The latter was of special importance in leading to a rise in popular demand for an education in the Confucian classics, a demand that the Song system of government schools failed to meet. The creation and maintenance of nongovernment academies supported by landed endowments were important institutional expressions of a certain kind of local activism practiced by the moral elites of the community, who wanted to express community interests larger than those of their respective families and lineages. These academies could also evolve into centers of political opinion, as was frequently the case during the Ming. See Thomas H. C. Lee, "Sung Education before Chu Hsi;" Langlois, "Political Thought in Chin-hua"; and the following chapters in de Bary and Chaffee, *Neo-Confucian Education*: de Bary, "Chu Hsi's Aims as an Educator"; Wing-tsit Chan, "Chu Hsi and the Academies"; Hymes, "Lu Chiu-yuan, Academies, and the Problem of the Local Community."

46. Sun Kekuan, *Yuandai Jinhua xueshu* [Jinhua scholarship during the Yuan dynasty] (Taizhong: Sili Donghai daxue, 1975), 17; Qian Mu, *Song-Ming lixue gaishu*, 202–3.

47. Their descendant Ye Shenyan in the fourteenth century continued his contact with Jinhua scholars of his time. He became educational supervisor of Pujiang and Yiwu, and later the headmaster of the Mingzheng Academy in Quzhou, a prefecture to Jinhua's west. He thus contributed to the spread of the Jinhua School of Learning to southern Zhejiang. JX 2:412.

48. Kwang-Ching Liu, "Socioethics as Orthodoxy," 95–97; William Theodore de Bary, *Neo-Confucian Orthodoxy and the Learning of the Mind-and-Heart* (New York: Columbia University Press, 1981), 45.

49. Chen Rongjie [Wing-tsit Chan], *Zhuzi menren* [Zhu Xi's disciples] (Taipei: Xuesheng shuju, 1982), 1.

50. The rise of private academies and the development of a state-sponsored educational system in conjunction with the institutionalization of the civil service examinations during the Song have received considerable scholarly attention. See, for example, Edward A. Kracke, "The Expansion of Educational Opportunity in the Reign of Hui-tsung of Sung and Its Implications," *Sung Studies Newsletter* 13 (1977): 6–30; Thomas Hong-chi Lee, *Government Education and Examinations in Sung China* (New York: St. Martin's, 1985). See also John W. Chaffee, *The Thorny Gates of Learning in Sung China* (Cambridge: Cambridge University Press, 1985), and Lu Kuang-huan, "The Shu-yuan Institution, a Development by Sung-Ming Philosophers," *Chinese Culture* 9 (September 1968): 98–122. Academies continued to be established during the Ming, especially with the rise of the Neo-Confucianism of Wang Yangming and Zhan Ruoshui. Private academies, however, became places where scholars gathered for philosophical discussions. These were prohibited in a sweeping ban ordered by the imperial government in 1579, although the late Ming witnessed a revival of such institutions. See John Meskill, "Academies and Politics in the Ming Dynasty," in Hucker, *Chinese Government in Ming Times*, 149–74. On the attack on Zhu Xi's teaching by the Southern Song court in the twelfth century, see Schirokauer, "Neo-Confucianism under Attack."

51. Qian Mu, *Song-Ming lixue gaishu*, 199; Sun Kekuan, *Yuandai Jinhua xueshu*, 17.

52. Chang and Chang, *Crisis and Transformation*, 138–39. Lü Zuqian's readiness to accommodate divergent viewpoints could be seen as an "awareness of his own uncertainty." Tillman, *Utilitarian Confucianism*, 60.

53. JX 8:17b–18a.

54. Chen Rongjie [Wing-tsit Chan], *Zhuzi menren*, 1–2. See also Wing-tsit Chan, "Chu Hsi and Neo-Confucianism," 200–18, and Langlois, "Political Thought in Chin-hua," 149–51. He Ji was the teacher of Wang Bo, grandson of Wang Shiyu, who, in turn, was a disciple of Lü Benzhong, Lü Zuqian's grandfather. Wang Bo strongly emphasized self-cultivation and moral practice. He was primarily a scholar who devoted his life to the compilation of the classics and the teachings of Zhu Xi. He was the principal lecturer at the Lize Academy for many years, took many students, and

never served in the bureaucracy. Like so many other scholars taught either by Lü Zuqian or Zhu Xi, he placed emphasis on the concentration of the will and acting with deference and sincerity. JX 2:417; see also the summary in Chang and Chang, *Crisis and Transformation,* 139–40.

55. Denis Twitchett, "Problems of Chinese Biography," in Arthur F. Wright and Denis Twitchett, eds., *Confucian Personalities* (Stanford: Stanford University Press, 1962), 35.

56. JX 4:18b, 20a–b.

57. Wu Lai (1297–1340), a native of Pujiang County, Jinhua Prefecture, was renowned for his mastery of the Confucian classic *Chunqiu* (Spring and autumn annals). Wu Lai regarded the text as a surrogate for ancient legal codes. Confucian rulers, he believed, must be scholars as well as judges. The annals contained words of wisdom on how to be a good judge and thus served as a legal code for Confucian scholars acting as rulers. See John D. Langlois, Jr., "Law, Statecraft, and *The Spring and Autumn Annals* in Yuan Political Thought," in Chan and de Bary, *Yuan Thought,* 128–31.

58. Conrad Schirokauer, "Chu Hsi's Political Career," in Wright and Twichett, *Confucian Personalities,* 165–66. See also Patricia Ebrey's discussion of Chu Xi's *Family Rituals* in Ebrey, "Education through Ritual," 296–306.

59. He Ji spent his lifetime "sitting alone in his study in the middle of a multitude of volumes of books." He declined even to serve as the head of the Lize Academy, the one founded by Lü Zuqian, and lived his entire life in the North Mountains. JX 2:431.

60. Xu Qian, a fifth-generation Jinhua person of Beijing origin, decided that his lifetime work was not officialdom, but classical learning. He studied with Jin Lüxiang, another major figure in the Jinhua area, and then spent the rest of his life in the caves of the Jinhua mountains, followed around by equally dedicated disciples. Ibid., 442–50.

61. Pan Lianggui's nephew and disciple Pan Shi was simultaneously a disciple of Lü Zuqian. When serving as an official, he never took action simply according to the wishes of his superiors, but rather judged by the right and wrong of the matters at hand. He was mindful in particular of socially beneficial acts, such as just jurisprudence, irrigation projects, famine relief, bandit control, school education, and the nurturing of local talent. He considered the people to be the foundation of local government, and local government to be the foundation of the dynasty. He was a kind and sincere man whose son, Pan Youduan, became Zhu Xi's disciple and earned a jinshi degree. Ibid., 401. See Ye Shenyan's biography (ibid., 412–13) for another example of Confucian hagiography.

62. For a discussion of the historical passage of living subjects "from life into museum" and a conception of the museum as "a storehouse of

value and inspiration" that ceases to be involved in daily struggles and judgments, see Joseph Levenson, *Confucian China and Its Modern Fate: A Trilogy* (Berkeley: University of California Press, 1968), 2:76–82. See also Stephen Greenblatt, "Resonance and Wonder," in Ivan Karp and Steven D. Lavine, eds., *Exhibiting Cultures: The Poetics and Politics of Museum Display* (Washington, D.C.: Smithsonian Institution Press, 1991), 42–56.

63. JX 13:3b.

64. See, for comparison, Hilary J. Beattie, *Land and Lineage in China: A Study of T'ung-ch'eng County, Anhwei in the Ming and Ch'ing Dynasties* (Cambridge: Cambridge University Press, 1979). See also Harriet T. Zurndorfer, *Change and Continuity in Chinese Local History: The Development of Hui-chou Prefecture, 800–1800* (Leiden: E. J. Brill, 1989).

65. Jinhua intellectual tradition in the seventeenth century was characterized by its particular strength in three areas: 1) a strong emphasis on moral self-cultivation and personal integrity; 2) utilitarian statecraft and faith in universal kingship; 3) achievement in literary and historical studies (as opposed to textual and philological studies of the Confucian classics). Chang and Chang, *Crisis and Transformation*, 136–44. On intellectual tradition during the Ming, see also the chapters in Kwang-Ching Liu, *Orthodoxy*, by Edward L. Farmer, "Social Regulations of the First Ming Emperor: Orthodoxy as a Function of Authority," 103–24, and Romeyn Taylor, "Official and Popular Religion and the Political Organization of Chinese Society in the Ming," especially 144–48.

66. *Zhejiang sheng nongcun diaocha* [Investigations of Zhejiang villages], ed. Xingzheng yuan nongcun fuxing weiyuan hui (Shanghai: Shangwu yinshu guan, 1934), 235.

67. For a description of similar features of government offices, academies, and shrines, but with a much more substantial commercial sector of shops, guilds, and markets, see Shiba Yoshinobu's description of the Ningbo prefectural seat, in "Ningbo and Its Hinterland," 405–24.

68. JX 7:25a. Public, ceremonial recognition (*jing biao*) of chaste widows and filial sons, along with the honoring of celebrated officials and native worthies in local shrines, often involved "bonded petitions (from neighbors, local gentry, etc.) and checking and rechecking ordered by officials on various levels." This was clearly "a process of red tape that benefited mainly the clerks who handled the matters." The petitions were answered by provincial authorities, although the honor was supposedly bestowed by the imperial court. In all likelihood, only the wealthy and eminent were resourceful enough to initiate such petitions and to cope with the demands of county clerks. Lien-sheng Yang, "Ming Local Administration," in Hucker, *Chinese Government in Ming Times*, 18.

69. JX 7:26b, 27a, 28a–29b.

70. See Mori Masao, "The Gentry in the Ming—An Outline of the Relations between the *Shih-ta-fu* and Local Society," *Acta Asiatica* 38 (1980): 31–53; Mi Chu Wiens, "Lord and Peasant: The Sixteenth to the Eighteenth Century," *Modern China* 6, 1 (January 1980): 3–40.

71. The Chief Censor Archway (*Dujian fang*), on the other hand, was built on the occasion of the retirement of Feng Liang from that position. JX 9:23b–24a.

72. There were two routes for the classically educated under the Ming to move into a bureaucratic career: by advancement from local government schools into the Imperial Academy in the capital on the basis of one's literary accomplishment and moral character, or by successfully passing the various levels of civil service examinations. Tilemann Grimm, "Ming Educational Intendants," in Hucker, *Chinese Government in Ming Times*, 114. On the social history of exams, academies, classical education, and access to bureaucratic power, see the seminal study by Ho, *The Ladder of Success in Imperial China*. For a detailed description of the examination system, see Ichisada Miyazaki, *China's Examination Hell: The Civil Service Examinations of Imperial China*, trans. Conrad Schirokauer (New Haven: Yale University Press, 1976).

73. JX 4:14a, 14b. On Qi Xiong, see ibid., 9:27a–b.

74. Pan Hong, Pan Zhang, Pan Xizeng, Pan Hui. Ibid., 4:14a.

75. Ibid., 14a–b. Social historians have been able to show that Zhejiang was a major center of political power during the Ming. Within the province there was a clear tendency for power to concentrate in particular local areas. Timothy Brook shows that the Yin County of Ningbo, like Jinhua, featured gentry lineages that produced successful examination candidates over generations. This honor was shared among a much larger number of surnames—forty-eight by his count—in Ningbo than in Jinhua. Timothy Brook, "Family Continuity and Cultural Hegemony: The Gentry of Ningbo, 1368–1911," in Esherick and Rankin, *Chinese Local Elites*, 35–36. Pan Guangdan shows that Jiaxing County in Huzhou featured powerful gentry lineages that perpetuated themselves through examination success and intermarriages over a span of nearly six centuries (1368–1911). Jiaxing's achievement appeared to be much more impressive than that of Jinhua, especially during the Qing. Pan Guangdan, *Ming Qing liangdai Jiaxing de wangzu* [Eminent lineages of Jiaxing during the Ming and the Qing] (Shanghai: Shangwu yinshu guan, 1947). But Ming bureaucracy, "erected on a broadly based foundation . . . was remarkably successful in maintaining integrity against pressures which would bend it toward particularistic ends." It was the exception rather than the norm for great gentry lineages to produce multiple members who served in the bureaucracy, and "only a mere handful of these strong clans succeeded in achieving a continuity in power which was of sufficient extent to be worthy of

the term 'dynastic.'" For a study of the geographical patterns of bureaucratic success and clan connections within the Ming government, see James B. Parsons, "The Ming Dynasty Bureaucracy," in Hucker, *Chinese Government in Ming Times*, 181–227; the quotations are from pp. 226–27.

76. Court testimonials of merit to chaste widows began under the Ming. The Ming state also exempted households headed by widows from corvee labor. Susan Mann shows that under the Ming chaste widowhood was primarily a gentry affair. The Qing expanded the reward system to a grand scale, "setting forth aggressive and elaborate procedures for locating, verifying, and recognizing widow chastity, specifically in commoner households." See Susan Mann, "Widows in the Kinship, Class, and Community Structure of Qing Dynasty China," *Journal of Asian Studies* 46, 1 (February 1987): 37–56; the quotation is from p. 38.

77. Also celebrated was a daughter of the Ye lineage who married He Dengyuan. JX 4:14b.

78. Ibid., 18a–b.

79. This is not to suggest, of course, that Southern Song did not have its share of defenders and loyalists who gave their lives in armed resistance against the Mongols. The resistance campaigns led by Zhang Shijie and Wen Tianxiang have been well documented in *Song Shi*, the official dynastic history. Other sources suggest that numerous other Southern Song local defenders fought to their death in a determined resistance against the Mongols. These deeds of resistance, however, had not been duly recorded in the official dynastic history that was compiled under Mongol rule. See Zhao Yi (1736–1820), *Ershier shi zhaji* [Study notes on twenty-two dynastic histories] (reprint Taipei: Shijie shuju, 1967), 356–58. On Zhao Yi's historical scholarship, see Du Weiyun, *Zhao Yi zhuan* [Biography of Zhao Yi] (Taipei: Shibao chuban gongsi, 1983), 202–83.

80. The Mongols supposedly valued practical skills such as record keeping over general learning, and rewarded personal loyalty over moral integrity. They "refused to use the services of Confucian-educated scholars . . . and deliberately excluded members of the Chinese elite in favor of clerks who had not been imbued with Confucian learning." Elizabeth Endicott-West, *Mongolian Rule in China: Local Administration in the Yuan Dynasty* (Cambridge, Mass.: Council on East Asian Studies Publications, Harvard University Press, 1989), 113. But see also Dardess, *Confucianism and Autocracy*, and Langlois, "Political Thought in Chin-hua."

81. JX 9:3a–7a.

82. On Ming martyrdom at the end of the dynasty and on Qing appropriation of this vital symbol of legitimation during the rebellion of the Three Feudatories, see Frederic Wakeman, Jr., "Romantics, Stoics, and Martyrs in Seventeenth-Century China," *Journal of Asian Studies* 43, 4 (August 1984): 647–56.

83. Altogether, the area produced 129 jinshi during the Song, 45 during the Ming, and 16 during the Qing (up to the 1850s). The figures for juren were 144 and 72, respectively, for Ming and Qing. JX 6:2a.

84. Ibid., preface, 14.

85. As late as the 1930s—more than a quarter-century after the custom had been attacked in Zhexi—residues of the tradition of bound feet could still be observed among peasant women who worked Jinhua's fields. *Zhejiang sheng nongcun diaocha*, 236.

86. On the complex division of household women into wives, concubines, adopted daughters, indentured maids, and servants, and on the issue of female dependency under patriarchy in the Pearl River Delta in the first half of the twentieth century, see Rubie S. Watson, "Wives, Concubines, and Maids: Servitude and Kinship in the Hong Kong Region, 1900–1940," in Rubie S. Watson and Patricia Buckley Ebrey, eds., *Marriage and Inequality in Chinese Society* (Berkeley: University of California Press, 1991), 231–55.

87. Vivien Ng shows that by changing the law on sexual violations in 1646, the Qing Code made it virtually impossible for Qing women, as opposed to their Ming predecessors, to present themselves as victims of rape short of struggling vigorously against the assailant throughout the entire ordeal, perhaps to the point of death. All other situations may be judged "illicit intercourse by mutual consent," in which case the woman would be subjected to punishment. See Vivien W. Ng, "Rape Laws in Qing China," *Journal of Asian Studies* 46, 1 (February 1987): 57–70; the quotation is from p. 58.

88. *Zhejiang sheng nongcun diaocha*, 71.

89. Ibid., 71–77.

90. Ibid., 77, 236, 239.

91. Ibid., 10.

92. Ibid., 239.

93. On Fujian "shed people" in the hills of southern Zhejiang, see Yeh, "Renshen zhijian," 76–84. In Zhejiang, shed people could be found in the hills of Jinhua, Ningbo, Wenzhou, Taizhou, and Chuzhou. The majority were able-bodied unmarried men who came not to settle but to grow hemp on the hills. These men also traveled back and forth between Fujian and Zhejiang on a seasonal basis. They tended to be followers of sectarian religion. *Peng min* communities were often reported to be in armed feuds with the local society. Li Wei, governor of Zhejiang under Yongzheng Emperor, described these mountainside cultivators as ignorant, obtuse, litigious, and militant. See ibid., 76. The shed people were also a phenomenon in the hills of Jiangxi and Fujian: for the Jiangxi case, see Duan Congguang, "Ganxi pengmin de kang Qing douzheng" [On the anti-Qing struggles of the shed people of western Jiangxi], *Lishi jiaoxue* (January

1955): 33–36; for the Fujian case, see Fu Yiling, "Ming Qing shidai Fujian diannong fengchao kaozheng" [Tenant riots in Fujian during the Ming and the Qing], in *Ming Qing nongcun shehui jingji* [Village society and economy under the Ming and the Qing] (Beijing: Sanlian chuban she, 1961), 157. On an immigrant community, see also Philip Kuhn, "The Taiping Rebellion," in Twitchett and Fairbank, *Cambridge History of China*, vol. 10: *Late Ch'ing: 1800–1911* (Cambridge: Cambridge University Press, 1978), pt. 1:265.

94. *Zhejiang sheng nongcun diaocha*, 243.

95. For comparison, see the anthropologist Arthur P. Wolf's study of a village on the outskirts of Taipei in the 1960s, in "Gods, Ghosts, and Ancestors," in Arthur P. Wolf, ed., *Religion and Ritual in Chinese Society* (Stanford: Stanford University Press, 1974), 155–59, 169.

96. Qu Yingguang, *Qu Xun'an xunshi liang Zhe wengao*, 1:37a.

CHAPTER 3: PROVINCIAL BACKWATERS

1. There is an extensive secondary literature in English on the Taiping Uprising, sometimes studied as a nineteenth-century precursor to the peasant movement led by the Chinese Communists in the twentieth century. For an authoritative account and a comprehensive bibliographical essay, see Kuhn, "The Taiping Rebellion," 264–317, 603–4. See in particular Philip Kuhn, *Rebellion and Its Enemies in Late Imperial China: Militarization and Social Structure, 1796–1864* (Cambridge, Mass.: Harvard University Press, 1970), and Frederic Wakeman, Jr., *Strangers at the Gate: Social Disorder in South China, 1839–1861* (Berkeley: University of California Press, 1966).

2. This is another subject with wide secondary literature in English. For a succinct statement, see John K. Fairbank's discussion of the rise of Shanghai in "The Creation of the Treaty System," in Twitchett and Fairbank, *Cambridge History of China*, vol. 10, pt. 1:237–43.

3. In May 1855, a Taiping army, led by Fan Rujie, defeated the Zhejiang units stationed at Qimen and Xiuning in southern Anhui. Jinhua prefect Shi Jingfen sped to the provincial border of Anhui-Zhejiang to command the defense. His units were augmented by an additional two thousand men dispatched by Xiang Rong, the imperial field commander in the Jiangnan area. Fan Rujie's Taiping units, however, moved southward into the northeastern territory of Jiangxi Province, where he kept a sizable imperial force occupied along the Anhui border. A second Taiping unit, based in southeastern Jiangxi, then moved northward into southern Zhejiang, entering Changshan County in late March 1855. The Taiping maneuver, however, was part of a larger operation in Anhui and Jiangxi rather than an attack on Zhejiang proper. Later that year the Taipings pulled out of southern Zhejiang after a brief occupation of Kaihua that lasted for nine

days. Xu Heyong, Zheng Yunshan, and Zhao Shipei, *Zhejiang jindai shi* [Modern history of Zhejiang] (Hangzhou: Zhejiang renmin chuban she, 1982), 53–54.

4. Ibid., 55–56; Li Guoqi, *Zhongguo xiandai hua de quyu yanjiu— Min Zhe Tai* [Modernization in China: A regional study of Fujian, Zhejiang, and Taiwan] (Taipei: Zhongyang yanjiu yuan jindai shi yanjiu suo, 1982), 145–46.

5. Li Shoukong, *Zhongguo jindai shi* [History of modern China] (Taipei: Sanmin shuju, 1958), 228; Xu Heyong et al., *Zhejiang jindai shi,* 58–60.

6. Li Shoukong, *Zhongguo jindai shi,* 231; Xu Heyong et al., *Zhejiang jindai shi,* 62–68.

7. Xu Heyong et al., *Zhejiang jindai shi,* 105–6. For a detailed account of warfare in Zhejiang during the Taiping Uprising, see Jian Youwen, *Taiping tianguo quanshi* [Complete history of the Taiping Heavenly Kingdom] (Hong Kong: Jianshi mengjin shuwu, 1962), 3:1,909–2,024, 2,081–2,122.

8. Xu Heyong et al., *Zhejiang jindai shi,* 127; Li Guoqi, *Min Zhe Tai,* 146–47, 149, 152–53. On the effect of depopulation on sericulture, see E-tu Zen Sun, "Sericulture and Silk Textile Production in Ch'ing China," 104.

9. In the early 1920s population density along the upper Qiantang ranged from 50 to 100 per square mile. The average in the middle counties was 250 to 500. Population density in the commercialized north, on the other hand, ran from a low of 1,750 to a high of over 3,700 per square mile. Zhang Qiyun, *Zhejiang sheng shidi jiyao,* 68. Twenty-two Zhejiang counties had a population density of over 657 per square mile in the early 1920s, surpassing the figure obtained in Belgium for the same period. Ibid., 70.

10. Xu Heyong et al., *Zhejiang jindai shi,* 128.

11. Zhang Zhongli, ed., *Jindai Shanghai chengshi yanjiu* [Study of the urban development of modern Shanghai] (Shanghai: Renmin chuban she, 1990), 97, 100.

12. Zheng Yifang, *Shanghai qianzhuang (1843–1937): Zhongguo chuantong jinrong ye de tuibian* [Shanghai native banks, 1843–1937: The transformation of the traditional Chinese credit system] (Taipei: Zhongyang yanjiu yuan sanmin zhuyi yanjiu suo, 1981), 9–10; Andrea Lee McElderry, *Shanghai Old-Style Banks (Ch'ien-chuang), 1800–1935* (Ann Arbor: Center for Chinese Studies, University of Michigan, 1976), 1–82; Linda Cooke Johnson, "Shanghai: An Emerging Jiangnan Port, 1683–1840," in Johnson, ed., *Cities of Jiangnan in Late Imperial China* (Albany: State University of New York Press, 1993), 151–81.

13. Fu Yiling, *Ming Qing shidai shangren ji shangye ziben* [Merchants and mercantile capital under the Ming and the Qing] (Beijing: Renmin chuban she, 1956), 92–106; Paolo Santangelo, "Urban Society in Late

Imperial Suzhou," trans. Adam Victor, in Johnson, *Cities of Jiangnan,* 81–116.

14. Zhang Zhelang, *Qingdai de caoyun* [Shipment of tributary grain during the Qing] (Taipei: Jiaxin shuini gongsi wenhua jijin hui, 1969), 63. See also Antonia Finnane, "Yangzhou: A Central Place in the Qing Empire," in Johnson, *Cities of Jiangnan,* 117–49.

15. Zheng Yifang, *Shanghai qianzhuang,* 9; Zhang Zhelang, *Qingdai de caoyun,* 57–58. Shipping through the Grand Canal was blocked from time to time in the first half of the nineteenth century by Yellow River floods. As a temporary measure, tributary grains collected from Jiangsu were sometimes shipped through Shanghai via seafaring vessels.

16. Zhang Guohui, *Wan Qing qianzhuang he piaohao yanjiu* [Study of late Qing native banks and Shanxi banks] (Beijing: Zhonghua shuju, 1989), 72, 103; Zheng Yifang, *Shanghai qianzhuang,* 15. Within Shanghai itself, there was a concurrent shift in the center of financial gravity away from the old Chinese city (Nanshi) in the south into the International Settlement in the north. McElderry, *Shanghai Old-Style Banks,* 67–68.

17. Zhang Zhelang, *Qingdai de caoyun,* 68. The Qing assessed silver in lieu of rice in provinces that were occupied by the Taipings. See Xia Nai, "Taiping tianguo qianhou Changjiang gesheng zhi tianfu wenti" [Land tax in Yangzi Valley provinces before and after the Taiping Uprising], *Qinghua xuebao* 10, 2 (April 1925): 408–74.

18. The first such enterprise was the Tongjiu Cotton Works, founded in Ningbo in 1887. Li Guoqi, *Min Zhe Tai,* 308. On the tremendous growth of the silk industry in this region in response to trading opportunities centered in Shanghai, see Lillian Li, *China's Silk Trade,* 103–12.

19. Li Guoqi, *Min Zhe Tai,* 308.

20. Yen-p'ing Hao, *The Commercial Revolution in Nineteenth-Century China: The Rise of Sino-Western Mercantile Capitalism* (Berkeley: University of California Press, 1986).

21. Lillian Li, *China's Silk Trade,* 131–38, 154–96; Robert Eng, *Economic Imperialism in China: Silk Production and Exports, 1861–1932* (Berkeley: Institute of East Asian Studies, University of California, 1986), 38–58, 70–136. See also Lynda Schaefer Bell, "Merchants, Peasants, and the State: The Organization and Politics of Chinese Silk Production, Wuxi County, 1870–1937," Ph.D. diss., University of California, Los Angeles, 1985.

22. Lillian Li, *China's Silk Trade,* 160–61. The "elephants"—Liu, Zhang, Pang, Xing, and Yue, actually five in number—were said to be worth more than one million taels each, the "cows" half a million or more, and the "dogs" were supposedly families with three hundred thousand or more. Nanxun was the trading center of raw silk. Huzhou in the late 1850s had been described as one of the most prosperous areas in China. There was

a saying, however, that "all of the wealth of the prefectural city of Hu-chou [Huzhou] could not match half the wealth of the town of Nan-hsun [Nanxun]." Many Huzhou silk merchants invested in salt, pawnshops, and wastepaper business; they were also sizable landowners. Ibid., 131.

23. Li Guoqi, *Min Zhe Tai*, 388–89.

24. For post-Taiping elite activism and the rise of the public sphere, see Mary Backus Rankin, *Elite Activism and Political Transformation in China: Zhejiang Province, 1865–1911* (Stanford: Stanford University Press, 1986), 92–135.

25. Ibid., 136–309; Li Guoqi, *Min Zhe Tai*, 217–18; Susan Mann, *Local Merchants and the Chinese Bureaucracy, 1750–1950* (Stanford: Stanford University Press, 1987), 21–23; Min Tu-ki, in Philip A. Kuhn and Timothy Brook, eds., *National Polity and Local Power: The Transformation of Late Imperial China* (Cambridge, Mass.: Council on East Asian Studies Publications, Harvard University Press, 1989), 137–218.

26. Zhang Zhongli, *Jindai Shanghai*, 88–89; Albert Feuerwerker, *China's Early Industrialization: Sheng Hsuan-huai (1844–1916) and Mandarin Enterprise* (Cambridge, Mass.: Harvard University Press, 1958; reprint New York: Atheneum, 1970), 190–207; Xie Bin, *Zhongguo tiedao shi* [History of Chinese railroads] (Shanghai: Zhonghua shuju, 1929), 357–62.

27. E-tu Zen Sun, *Chinese Railways and British Interests, 1898–1911* (New York: Columbia University, King's Crown Press, 1954); Min, *National Polity*, 191–206.

28. Shang Qiliang, "Zhejiang xingye yinhang xingshuai shi" [Rise and fall of the Zhejiang Industrial Bank], *Zhejiang wenshi ziliao xuanji* 46 (1992): 41–44. The British loan for the construction of a proposed Suzhou-Shanghai-Ningbo railroad was approved by the Throne on October 20, 1907. It immediately touched off several antiloan movements on the part of Zhejiang's gentry. See the detailed discussions about the loan dispute in Min, *National Polity*, 191–216.

29. Paul Cohen, *Between Tradition and Modernity: Wang T'ao and Reform in Late Ch'ing China* (Cambridge, Mass.: Council on East Asian Studies Publications, Harvard University Press, 1974); Leo Ou-fan Lee and Andrew J. Nathan, "The Beginning of Mass Culture: Journalism and Fiction in the Late Ch'ing and Beyond," in David Johnson, Andrew Nathan, and Evelyn Rawski, eds., *Popular Culture in Late Imperial China* (Berkeley: University of California Press, 1985), 361–78.

30. Zhang Qiyun, *Zhejiang sheng shidi jiyao*, 68. The proposal was made against the backdrop of an impending war between the warlords of Zhejiang and Jiangsu, which broke out in August 1924. Qi Xieyuan, military governor of Jiangsu, fought the troops of Lu Yongxiang, military governor of Zhejiang. Qi used up the best of his troops in a hard battle against Lu in Liuhe—only to find that Shanghai and its vicinity, the prize

coveted by all, had already been taken by his erstwhile ally and nominal subordinate, Sun Chuangfang, who had moved his troops up from Fujian through Zhejiang. Lucian W. Pye, *Warlord Politics: Conflict and Coalition in the Modernization of Republican China* (New York: Praeger, 1971), 105–6.

31. John K. Fairbank, *Trade and Diplomacy on the China Coast: The Opening of the Treaty Ports, 1842–1854* (Cambridge, Mass.: Harvard University Press, 1953; paperback ed. Stanford: Stanford University Press, 1969), 329. See also Brook, "Family Continuity and Cultural Hegemony," 27–50.

32. Jones, "The Ningpo Pang," 76–77.

33. For a contemporary testimony on the close links between Shanghai and Ningbo in shipping and the trading in cotton, salt, and tea, see Qu Yingguang, "Xunshi Yuyao xian xuanyan" [Proclamation on an official tour of Yuyao County], in *Qu Xun'an xunshi liang Zhe wengao*, 4:76b. The best known example in this connection was Yu Xiaqing, born in 1867 into a tailor's family in the village of Longshan, Zhenhai. Yu went to Shanghai in 1881 at the age of fourteen. By the time of his death on April 26, 1945, he had served as past chairman of Shanghai's Security Exchange, General Chamber of Commerce, and Ningbo Native Place Association, and was remembered as a leading financier and shipping magnate. Sun Choucheng, Huang Zhenshi, He Guotao, Fan Xuewen, Dai Yufang, "Yu Xiaqing shilue" [Outline of Yu Xiaqing's life], in Zhongguo renmin zhengzhi xieshang huiyi Zhejiang sheng wenshi ziliao yanjiu weiyuan hui, ed., *Zhejiang ji ziben jia de xingqi* [Rise of Zhejiang capitalists] (Hangzhou: Zhejiang renmin chuban she, 1986), 104–28. See the discussion in Marie-Claire Bergère, *The Golden Age of the Chinese Bourgeoisie, 1911–1937*, trans. Janet Lloyd (Cambridge: Cambridge University Press, 1986), 142.

34. See in particular the important works by Jones, "The Ningpo Pang," and Bergère, *Golden Age*, 135–39, 142–45. See also Lu Kang, "Zhejiang bang jinrong jia zai Shanghai" [Zhejiang capitalists in Shanghai], in *Zhejiang ji ziben jia de xingqi*, 193–201; Li Guoqi, *Min Zhe Tai*, 393.

35. See the important chapter by Bergère, "The Shanghai Bankers' Association: 1915–1927: Modernization and the Institutionalization of Local Solidarities," in Frederic Wakeman, Jr., and Wen-hsin Yeh, eds., *Shanghai Sojourners* (Berkeley: Institute of East Asian Studies, University of California, Berkeley, 1992), 15–34.

36. This is not to suggest that there were no prominent businessmen or intellectual figures from Shaoxing. Qiu Jin, the revolutionary martyr, Cai Yuanpei, president of Beijing University in the late 1910s, and Lu Xun, a writer and leading intellectual figure, were all from Shaoxing. Compared with other parts of Zhejiang, the countryside of Shaoxing was noted for

salt smuggling, secret society activity, banditry, village armed feuds over water rights, and the presence of a hereditary *jianmin* (demeaned people), sometimes referred to as *duomin* (lazy people), who constituted a déclassé caste. These traits were especially notable toward the end of the nineteenth century after the Taiping Uprising. See James Cole, *Shaohsing: Competition and Cooperation in Nineteenth-Century China* (Tucson: University of Arizona Press, 1986), 56–72, 155–67.

37. Elizabeth Perry, *Shanghai on Strike: The Politics of Chinese Labor* (Stanford: Stanford University Press, 1993), 186–88.

38. A succinct summary of this view can be found, for example, in Fei Hsiao-tung, *China's Gentry: Essays in Rural-Urban Relations* (Chicago: University of Chicago Press, 1953). This left-wing literature has been opposed by research that tries to show some if not all of the following points: (1) Shanghai was never a colonial city, and foreign communities in Shanghai were "outsiders" to China's society, characterized either by an impenetrable clannishness or by a surprisingly high degree of native shrewdness; (2) Western activities in modern trade and industry did greater benefit than harm to the Chinese economic system; whatever difficulties they caused might have been redressed had the Chinese government known how to act. See, for example, Rhoads Murphey, "The Treaty Ports and China's Modernization," in Elvin and Skinner, *The Chinese City between Two Worlds*, 17–71; and see in John Fairbank and Albert Feuerwerker, eds., *The Cambridge History of China*, vol. 13, pt. 2, "Republican China, 1912–1949," Mary Backus Rankin, John Fairbank, and Albert Feuerwerker, "Introduction: Perspectives on Modern China's History," 11–29, and Ramon Myers, "The Agrarian System," 230–69.

39. By the early years of the twentieth century Zhejiang was once again in heightened social tension. Despite the significant commercial wealth accumulated in towns and cities, peasant households (which in Zhenhai, for example, consumed on the average only 17.2 percent of their produce, sending the remaining 82.8 percent to market) were particularly vulnerable to market fluctuations. The Zhexi and Zhedong areas' high degree of dependency on imported grains assured that in years of recession rice riots were frequent. Part of the price that the enriched counties of Zhexi and Zhedong had to pay for their participation in the spectacular rise of Shanghai was a growing tension between the rich and the poor. See Li Guoqi, *Min Zhe Tai*, 392–93.

40. For a fictional representation of the thorough grip of Shanghai's import-export market on the livelihoods of women and children in Zhexi's silk-producing villages, see Mao Dun [Shen Yanbing], *Chuncan* [Spring silkworm] (Beijing: Foreign Language Press, 1956). For a synthesis of the socialist view, see Fei Hsiao-tung, *China's Gentry*, 91–142. See also Albert Feuerwerker, "China's Modern Economic History in Communist Chinese

Historiography," in Feuerwerker, ed., *History of Communist China* (Cambridge, Mass.: MIT Press, 1968), 232–38.

41. Wenzhou appeared to have a population of well below eighty thousand in the late nineteenth century; by 1921 that figure had more than doubled to 198,300. Li Guoqi, *Min Zhe Tai*, 441. Available population statistics for Zhejiang cities for the early twentieth century, it should be noted, are unreliable and hopelessly confused.

42. Chao Ch'eng Hsin, "An Ecological Study of China from Segmentation to Integration," Ph.D. diss., University of Michigan, 1933, 58; Zhang Guohui, *Wan Qing qianzhuang*, 69.

43. Chao, "Ecological Study of China," 58.

44. Zhang Guohui, *Wan Qing qianzhuang*, 70.

45. Qu Yingguang, "Xunshi Lanxi xian xuanyan," 4:107b.

46. The rest of Lanxi's modern sector of the economy consisted of dozens of factories that were engaged in rice grinding, sausage making, and the production of consumer goods such as socks, towels, soap, rock sugar, dates, and tiles. Lanxi xian zhengfu, ed., *Zhejiang sheng Lanxi xian xianzheng*, section on "Jianshe gaikuang" [Construction projects], 49.

47. Ibid., 59–60.

48. Among the 196 admitted into the poor house in 1929 there were natives of Ningbo and Huizhou, as well as residents of Lanxi and Jinhua. See Lanxi xian zhengfu, ed., *Zhejiang sheng Lanxi xian xianzheng*, section on "Cishan gaikuang" [Charity], 1, 4. The district government raised a total of eight thousand yuan from individual merchants and gentrymen.

49. Hu Qi, "Yiwu de 'qiaotang bang'" [Candy-hawkers of Yiwu], *Zhejiang wenshi ziliao xuanji* 21 (June 1982): 161–63.

50. Ibid., 168.

51. Ibid., 162.

52. Ibid., 164–66.

53. Ibid., 163.

54. Qu Yingguang, *Qu Xun'an xunshi liang Zhe wengao*, 4:115a–b.

55. The smaller villages, such as Gejia (80 square li) and Shouchang (110 square li) to the east, registered 449 and 573 households, respectively, with 2,167 and 3,208 individuals each. Zhejiang sheng juanshui jianli weiyuan hui, ed., *Zhejiang sheng jiu Jinshu gexian xiangzhen diaocha biao* [Investigative report on villages and towns in counties formerly under the Jinhua Prefecture of Zhejiang Province], "Jinhua xian" [Jinhua County] (n.p., n.d.).

56. For Baoan xiang (administrative village) in Wuxian, 1,575 households and 7,004 residents; 1,814 and 8,210 for Wukong xiang in Jiangyin; 2,687 and 12,514 for Yunlin in Wuxi. Philip Huang, *The Peasant Family and Rural Development in the Yangzi Delta, 1350–1988* (Stanford: Stanford University Press, 1990), 59, 61.

57. Qu Yingguang, *Qu Xun'an xunshi liang Zhe wengao*, 4:104b.

58. This is not to imply that Jinhua society was free from armed feuds prior to the twentieth century. The communities of "shed people" in the remote parts of the county, for example, had long been a source of local tension since the early Qing. Nor does this suggest that Jinhua peasants never had their own forms of cult worship and popular entertainment on which the elites frowned. Elite culture in the county seat hardly ever managed to tame popular culture in the countryside. Villagers followed unofficial cults and performed drama viewed as lewd by the elite. As elite cultural confidence eroded in the early twentieth century, elite lamentation over the decay of social customs became all the more strident.

59. Qu Yingguang, *Qu Xun'an xunshi liang Zhe wengao*, 4:105b–106a.

60. Bergère, *Golden Age*, 192.

61. Ibid., 83.

CHAPTER 4: FIRST NORMAL

1. On the May Fourth Movement, consult the standard text in Chow Tse-tsung, *The May Fourth Movement.*

2. Of the remaining, three were published in Shaoxing, two in Huzhou, one in Ningbo, and perhaps two in Yongjia. The place of publication for the remaining two is unclear.

3. Of the total of twenty-six, the publication dates of only seventeen are known. Of these seventeen, ten were published between October 1919 and March 1920.

4. See data in Zhonggong Zhejiang shengwei dangxiao dangshi jiaoyan shi, ed., *Wusi yundong zai Zhejiang* [May Fourth Movement in Zhejiang] (Hangzhou: Zhejiang renmin chuban she, 1979), 96.

5. Between October 1919 and March 1920, First Normal students brought out over half of the more than thirty issues of the journals, under five different titles. They also published forty-odd issues of other student journals, including more than twenty newsletters of the Hangzhou Student Association. Ibid.

6. Zhang Zengyang named the school Zhejiang Higher Normal School (Zhejiang youji shifan xuetang). It was a five-year program that included a one-year preparatory period. The school was renamed the Zhejiang Provincial First Normal School in 1905. *Hangzhoufu zhi* [Hangzhou Prefecture gazetteer] (1922; reprint Taipei: Chengwen chuban she, 1974), 2:488–90.

7. On the New Policies of the first decade, which were a conservative approach to reform proposed by Governor General Zhang Zhidong (Chang Chih-tung), see Daniel H. Bays, *China Enters the Twentieth Century: Chang Chih-tung and the Issues of a New Age, 1895–1909* (Ann Arbor:

University of Michigan Press, 1978), and Douglas Reynolds, *China, 1898–1912: The* Xinzheng *Revolution and Japan* (Cambridge, Mass.: Council on East Asian Studies Publications, Harvard University Press, 1993), which highlights Japanese influence on China during this period.

8. The old examination hall consisted mainly of rows of walled cubicles, which were cells to segregate test-takers from each other. To convert the examination hall to a school, these inner partitions were torn down to create large lecture halls and classrooms. Much of the outer facade of the building, however, was left intact. The old examination hall had a watchtower in each corner of its compound, where the official proctors stationed themselves to maintain surveillance over the examination candidates. These four commanding structures were left intact through the reform and reconstruction, and on the eve of the May Fourth Movement they were still standing to remind passersby of the imperial examination system with all its forbidding majesty, much to the awe and nostalgia of old conservatives.

9. *Zhejiang shengli diyi shifan xuexiao xiaoyou huizhi* [Gazette of friends and associates of Zhejiang First Normal School] (cited hereafter as ZSDS) 3 (summer 1914): 3. The teachers were asked to "change local customs and attitudes" (*yi feng yi su*).

10. The enrollment quota was fixed at six hundred, with two hundred for the senior division, three hundred for the junior division, and another one hundred for those training to become physical education teachers. This number remained unchanged when First Normal later took on the training of secondary and elementary teachers in arts, crafts, and music. Zhejiang sheng zhengxie wenshi ziliao weiyuan hui, eds., *Xinbian Zhejiang bainian dashi ji, 1840–1949* [New chronicle of major events in the past century in Zhejiang, 1840–1949] (Hangzhou: Zhejiang renmin chuban she, 1990), 121.

11. The Zhejiang Provincial Assembly evolved out of the late Qing Zhejiang Provincial Assembly, which was a product of the New Policies and convened for the first time, along with other provincial assemblies, in 1909. See Min, *National Polity.*

12. In the same act of 1913 that created the Zhejiang Provincial First Normal School, the Provincial Assembly also legislated the creation of ten other normal schools, named numerically, at the seats of the ten former prefectures under the Qing administrative division. All eleven normal schools were supposed to be funded by the provincial government, but in 1913, the provincial government was able to find money only for the normal schools in Hangzhou, Ningbo, Shaoxing, Jinhua, Wenzhou, and Chuzhou. The creation of the remaining five (in Jiaxing, Wuxing, Linhai, Quxian, and Jiande) was postponed to 1917. *Jiaoyu zazhi* [Educational review; cited hereafter as JZ] 9, 3 (March 1917): "xueshi yishu" [school news], 22.

13. First Normal had an annual budget of over 42,000 yuan in the mid-1910s. The total enrollment of normal school students in the province was just over one thousand, and the combined annual budget of the eleven schools was 212,000 yuan. Lin Chuanjia, ed., *Da Zhonghua Zhejiang sheng dili zhi* [Geography of Zhejiang province, greater China] (Hangzhou: Zhejiang yinshua gongsi, 1918), 144–46.

14. Ibid., 145. The total annual government contribution to the eleven provincial middle schools on the eve of the May Fourth Movement amounted to over 187,500 yuan. The total enrollment of the eleven middle schools was 3,110.

15. Xia Zhu, "Ruxue shi xunci" [Lecture on the first day of school], ZSDS (fall 1917): 6–7. There were over five hundred applicants for 1915; eighty students were admitted after taking written examinations and verbal interviews. Jing Ziyuan, "Shiye shi xiaozhang xunci" [Principal's speech at the beginning of the term], ZSDS 7 (1915): 3.

16. Yu Heping, ed., *Jing Yuanshan ji* [Collected works by Jing Yuanshan] (Wuhan: Huazhong shifan daxue chuban she, 1988), 408; for Jing Yuanshan's biographical sketch of Jing Wei, see pp. 169–70.

17. Mary Backus Rankin describes Jing Yuanshan as a merchant-philanthropist-reformer and one of the most active welfare managers in Shanghai. See Rankin, *Elite Activism*, 140; see also pp. 144–47, 167, 180–85, 196.

18. Jing Yuanshan published numerous pieces of writings in *Shenbao* in connection with the relief activities of the late 1870s. For samples, see Yu Heping, *Jing Yuanshan*, 1–27; for samples of publicized receipts, see 108–17.

19. Individual contributions in this category were in the range of tens of thousands of taels. See Rankin, *Elite Activism*, 143.

20. Yu Heping, *Jing Yuanshan*, 2–4. Rankin estimates that the four major private relief centers in Shanghai, Hangzhou, Suzhou, and Yangzhou, coordinated by Jing Yuanshan, raised over one million taels in silver between 1878 and 1880. Rankin, *Elite Activism*, 144.

21. On Sheng Xuanhuai, see Feuerwerker, *China's Early Industrialization*. On Li Hongzhang, see Stanley Spector, *Li Hung-chang and the Huai Army: A Study in Nineteenth-Century Chinese Regionalism* (Seattle: University of Washington Press, 1964).

22. Yu Heping, *Jing Yuanshan*, 9–14.

23. Liang Qichao was a disciple of Kang Youwei, the leading radical Confucian reformer of the late Qing. Kang and Liang provided much of the intellectual leadership for the aborted Hundred Days Reform of 1898. Although the reform was cut short by a palace coup and the execution of six progressive figures, it inspired the conservative reform of the New Policies adopted by the Qing court in the 1900s. Several aspects of these

events have been reported in English. Briefly, for an account of Liang Qichao, see Chang Hao, *Liang Ch'i-ch'ao and Intellectual Transition in China, 1890–1907* (Cambridge, Mass.: Harvard University Press, 1971). On the politics of the Hundred Days Reform of 1898, see Luke S. K. Kwong, *A Mosaic of the Hundred Days: Personalities, Politics, and Ideas of 1898* (Cambridge, Mass.: Council on East Asian Studies Publications, Harvard University Press, 1984).

24. Yu Heping, *Jing Yuanshan*, 15. On treaty-port Chinese intellectuals of the middle and late nineteenth century, see Cohen, *Tradition and Modernity*.

25. Yu Heping, *Jing Yuanshan*, 181–82.

26. Ibid., 182–83.

27. Ibid., 198, 203.

28. Sheng Jingying, "Xian weng Jing Yuanshan jianli" [Biographical sketch of my deceased father-in-law Jing Yuanshan]," in Yu Heping, *Jing Yuanshan*, 406.

29. The full text of this telegram appeared in the newspaper *Subao* [Su paper] that day. See reprint in Yu Heping, *Jing Yuanshan*, 309.

30. Ibid., 26, 310–13, 417–18.

31. Ibid., 11–13, 29–34, 269.

32. According to Rankin, "Jing Yuanshan explicitly related patriotic mobilization to elite activism and representational participation in government." See Rankin, *Elite Activism*, 167. See also Yu Heping, *Jing Yuanshan*, 139–50.

33. Cai Yuanpei held the highest civil service examinations degree of jinshi and was a former member of the prestigious Hanlin Academy. Nanyang was a new-style college funded jointly by the central government and the Jiangsu provincial government. It was a school of engineering and management that relied heavily on the use of English-language materials in instruction. The objective of the college was to train engineers and managers for the construction and supervision of China's railroads, telegraphs, shipping, and other communications industries. Like many other new-style schools created at this time to help realize the goal of national self-strengthening in accordance with the formula of "Chinese learning as substance, Western learning for application," Nanyang also placed considerable emphasis on classical studies in its Chinese curriculum.

34. Tao Yinghui, *Cai Yuanpei nianpu* [Chronological biography of Cai Yuanpei] (Taipei: Zhongyang yanjiu yuan jindai shi yanjiu suo, 1976), 105.

35. Wu Jingheng resigned from Nanyang in protest and went to Tokyo, where he joined the Revolutionary Alliance of Sun Yat-sen in 1905.

36. On November 14, 1902, several students left a pot of ink on the chair of their teacher, Guo Zhenying, in a classroom, shortly before Guo was about to begin a class. Guo was a conservative much disliked for his stiff

manner. When he sat down on his chair that morning and broke the pot of ink, students burst out laughing. Guo was furious. Unable to determine who placed the inkpot on his chair, Guo nonetheless accused one particular student and insisted on his immediate expulsion. Some of the students, already antagonized by the earlier dispute with the teacher over the creation of campus political societies, were galvanized into action. They petitioned to the president of Nanyang and demanded the immediate resignation of Guo. The president sided with the teacher and threatened to punish the petitioners. The next day, over two hundred students from six classes issued a statement that contained sentences such as "the teachers have restricted our freedom and treated us as if we were slaves"; "Our president is a foolish and stubborn man; he suppressed our freedom of expression." These students withdrew en masse. Tao Yinghui, *Cai Yuanpei*, 105.

37. On the Chinese Educational Association–Patriotic School–*Subao* connection, see Mary Backus Rankin, *Early Chinese Revolutionaries: Radical Intellectuals in Shanghai and Chekiang, 1902–1911* (Cambridge, Mass.: Harvard University Press, 1971), 78.

38. Ibid., 103, 108–9. See Tao Yinghui, *Cai Yuanpei*, 167, for a chronological account of these events. The membership of the Chinese Educational Association included revolutionaries, such as Xu Xilin, who chose armed uprisings in cooperation with the secret societies, rather than political reform, as the way to oppose the Qing. During the Russo-Japanese War in 1905 Cai Yuanpei organized ninety-five members of the Chinese Educational Association, including senior figures such as Wu Jingheng and Huang Zongyang, to form the Corps of the Righteous and Brave (*Yiyong tuan*). This new group was organized around a nucleus of Patriotic School students. Tao Yinghui, *Cai Yuanpei*, 156, 121.

39. The new school, also located in Shanghai, received funding primarily from private gentry sources. The Patriotic School was perhaps the first new educational institution to organize military-style training for its faculty and students. Among the first class of Patriotic School students were several cadets, formerly of the Jiangnan Military Academy, who had been attracted to the gentry cause of reform and had left their military education to join the Nanyang College protestors. Cai Yuanpei asked them to conduct military drills for their civilian brethren at the Patriotic School. He cut off his own queue and put on a military uniform, lining up to be drilled with the rest of the school members. Tao Yinghui, *Cai Yuanpei*, 167.

40. On the linkages between anarchist influence and egalitarianism, see ibid., 98–99, and Rankin, *Early Chinese Revolutionaries*, 106. See also *Zhendan daxue ershiwu nian xiaoshi* [Twenty-five years of Université L'Aurore] (Shanghai: n.p., 1928), 1–2. On the Russian influence on the

Chinese revolution, see Don C. Price's path-breaking study, *Russia and the Roots of the Chinese Revolution, 1896–1911* (Cambridge, Mass.: Harvard University Press, 1974). The revolutionary group centered on the Patriotic School collapsed later over personal feuds. See Price, *Russia,* 129–30.

41. Jing Ziyuan thereafter managed to support himself and his wife by pawning her jewelry while at the same time writing for journals. Jing Ziyuan, "Liushi shuhuai," 46b; *Wusi yundong zai Zhejiang,* 32.

42. Cao Juren, *Wo yu wo de shijie,* 144–49; Tao Yinghui, *Cai Yuanpei,* 91, 118. Sun Yat-sen had bequeathed to Jing Ziyuan the handwritten draft manuscript of *Jianguo dagang* (Outline of national construction), which Jing Ziyuan in his old age passed on to his son. Jing Ziyuan, "Liushi shuhuai," 44a. Jing Ziyuan's Tokyo sojourn took place at a time when anarchist influence ran high in the community of Chinese revolutionaries. These anarchists were familiar with Russian nihilism and admired Russian political figures such as Mikhail Bakunin and Sophia Perovskaya. While the activists among them understood anarchism as basically a straightforward promotion of violence, and hence felt few qualms in resorting to assassination as a revolutionary tactic, the pamphleteers were mainly attracted to anarchism as a vision of an egalitarian utopia and as a possible postrevolutionary form of nonauthoritarian self-government. Most of the latter were Jing Ziyuan's fellow provincials from Zhedong. Influential among them were the Guangzhou couple Liu Shifu and He Zhen, who formed the Society for the Study of Socialism in Tokyo in 1907. He Zhen, in particular, was featured among modern China's first generation of feminists as well as anarchists. There were no signs, however, that Jing Ziyuan himself was attracted to anarchism. On the anarchists, see Rankin, *Early Chinese Revolutionaries,* 106–7; Peter Zarrow, *Anarchism and Chinese Political Culture* (New York: Columbia University Press, 1990); and Price, *Russia,* 122–28.

43. ZSDS 14/15 (1918): 2.

44. On the Jiangsu Provincial Educational Association and vocational education, see Wen-hsin Yeh, *The Alienated Academy: Culture and Politics in Republican China, 1919–1937* (Cambridge, Mass.: Council on East Asian Studies Publications, Harvard University Press, 1990), 119–21.

45. Jing Ziyuan, "Huanying ge shixiao zhiyuan xuesheng yanshuo ci" [Speech to welcome the staff and students of normal schools assembled for the occasion, March 30], ZSDS 14/15 (1918): 2.

46. Jing Ziyuan, "Shizhou jinian hui kaihui ci" [Speech to note the tenth week of the term], ZSDS 14/15 (1918): 6.

47. Jing Ziyuan, "Wuwu shujia xiuye shi xunci" [Speech delivered at the ceremony to mark the conclusion of the spring term in the year Wuwu (1918)], ZSDS 14/15 (1918): 9–10.

48. Jing Ziyuan, "Xiaoyou hui kaihui ci" [Speech at a meeting of the friends and associates of the school], ZSDS (1917): 3–4.

49. Jing Ziyuan, "Huanying ge shixiao zhiyuan xuesheng yanshuo ci," 2.

50. Benjamin I. Schwartz, In Search of Wealth and Power: Yen Fu and the West (Cambridge, Mass.: Harvard University Press, 1964).

51. Jing Ziyuan, "Huanying ge shixiao zhiyuan xuesheng yanshuo ci," 3.

52. Jing Ziyuan, "Shengdan jinian shi shici" [Speech and resolutions on the birthday of the Sage], October 12, 1917, ZSDS (fall 1917): 5.

53. Jing Ziyuan, "Xiaoyou hui kaihui ci," 3.

54. Jing Ziyuan, "Shengdan jinian shi shici," 5.

55. Schwartz, In Search of Wealth and Power, 17–19.

56. Wusi shiqi de shetuan [Associational organizations of the May Fourth period] (Beijing: Shenghuo, dushu, xinzhi sanlian shudian, 1979), 3:148.

57. ZSDS 13 (fall 1917): 63–64.

58. Zhaomin, "Xiaoxun zhi kuice" [Thoughts on school mottoes], ZSDS 4 (winter 1914): 25.

59. Jing Ziyuan, "Shiye shi xiaozhang xunci," ZSDS (spring 1917): 1.

60. Ibid. 7 (1915): 1.

61. See, for example, He Zuochen, "You hu ji" [Tour on the lake], ZSDS 7 (1915): "wenyuan" [literary garden], 3–4.

62. By the West Lake stood the Zhejiang Provincial Library, which was built on the ruins of Wenlange, one of the seven imperial libraries of the Qing that were destroyed during the Taiping Uprising. The Zhejiang Provincial Library, until its total destruction by the Japanese during the War of Resistance in 1937, held one of the largest collections of rare books in China. Zhejiang's long standing as a central locus of literati culture and scholarly activities of national importance was evidenced not so much by the existence of the library as by the weight of the contribution made by Zhejiang authors to the Imperial Manuscript Collection, when the project was undertaken in the eighteenth century. Nearly one-quarter of the 10,223 titles (172,626 books) was contributed by Zhejiang authors hailing from the five northern prefectures of Hangzhou, Jiaxing, Huzhou, Ningbo, and Shaoxing. In the nineteenth century, Zhejiang led the country in the number of private libraries and of volumes held in its collections. These libraries supported an extended and active network of philological scholarship and created the material condition for the rise of the Han Learning of the Qing. Li Jiefei, Zheshi jiyao [Highlights in Zhejiang history] (Shanghai: n.p., 1948), 86–89.

63. Jing Ziyuan himself told his students in 1915 that "the reputation

of our school rests on our students' ability to compose in Chinese." ZSDS 7 (1915): 2.

64. Shan Pei was also a renowned filial son, performing deeds eulogized in the classic "twenty-four paragons of filial piety." See Cao Juren, *Wo yu wo de shijie*, 167–69.

65. Shan was said to have mastered the Five Confucian Classics, the Twenty-Four Dynastic Histories, and the dozens of texts by Warring States philosophers. The result of this lifetime of learning was a manuscript entitled "A Supplementary Annotation to the 'Supplementary Annotation to the Annotated History of Later Han,'" in the tradition of Han Learning. Shan unfortunately did not live to finish his supplementary annotation. Worse yet for posterity, the manuscript was lost by his illiterate widow. Ibid., 169.

66. *Zhejiang shengli diyi zhongxue tongxue lu, 1923* [Roster of fellow scholars at the Zhejiang Provincial First Middle School, 1923] (Hangzhou: Zhejiang shengli diyi zhongxuexiao, 1923), 1.

67. ZSDS (1915): 1a–2a.

68. It was in this informal extracurricular arena that many of the most accomplished students of Li Shutong, the music and art teacher, had their initiation into becoming cartoonists, poets, and novelists. For biographical information on Li Shutong, see Lin Ziqin, *Hongyi dashi nianpu* [Chronological biography of master Hongyi] (Hong Kong: Honghua yuan, 1944); Feng Zikai, "Fofa yinyuan" [Chance encounter via Buddhism], in Feng Zikai, *Zikai xiaopin ji* [Collection of Zikai's short pieces] (Shanghai: Zhongxuesheng shuju, 1933), 71–93.

69. The "Yiyuan shiji" was compiled in 1936, shortly after Jing's sixtieth birthday.

70. ZSDS 7 (1915): "wenyuan," 1.

71. See Xia Mianzun's complaint about modern student attempts to emulate ancient literati style, in ZSDS 1 (1913): "zalu" [miscellaneous], 1.

72. ZSDS 4 (winter 1914): 50.

73. Jing Ziyuan, "Zhongye shi xunci" [Speech at the end of the term], ZSDS (fall 1917): 1.

74. ZSDS 4 (winter 1914): 40–41; 8 (1915): "wenyuan," 9; 12 (winter 1917): 77; 13 (fall 1917): 63–64. There has been no systematic study to date on youthful mortality, or, for that matter, related issues of disease, death, public health, and medicine during the Republican period. Cursory surveys of contemporary student journals and school publications indicate that such occurrences were not uncommon. There were a few celebrated cases of students committing suicide during the May Fourth Movement. Scholarly attention on Republican suicide has been focused on cases of famous intellectuals—Wang Guowei and Liang Ji, in particular. On Wang

Guowei's death, see Joey Bonner, *Wang Guowei* (Cambridge, Mass.: Harvard University Press, 1986); on Liang Ji's death, see Guy Alitto, *The Last Confucian: Liang Shu-ming and the Chinese Dilemma of Modernity* (Berkeley: University of California Press, 1979), 62–69.

CHAPTER 5: A PROVINCIAL BOYHOOD

1. The best-known First Normal students of Jiangsu origin were the Qu brothers, Qu Sen and Qu Yue, of Wujin, admitted in 1920. The brothers were much better known by their courtesy names Jingbai and Shengbai, respectively. Their eldest brother was the nationally known Qu Qiubai, secretary general of the Chinese Communist Party from 1927 to 1934. The two brothers were classmates with Feng Xuefeng, of Yiwu, Zhejiang. Feng later gained national fame as a literary protégé of Lu Xun and figured prominently in the Hu Feng campaign in the 1950s. *Zhejiang shengli diyi zhongxue tongxue lu*, 1923, 58, 60. About Qu Qiubai, see Paul Pickowicz, *Marxist Literary Thought in China: The Influence of Ch'u Ch'iu-pai* (Berkeley: University of California Press, 1981).

2. First Middle students were admitted after passing examinations on Chinese, mathematics, and English. First Normal students were required only to compose an essay in Chinese and to pass a test in arithmetic. Shi Cuntong, "Huitou kan ershier nian lai de wo" [Retrospective view of myself of the past twenty-two years], "Juewu" [Awakening] section, *Minguo ribao* [Republican daily], September 22, 1920, p. 3; Ruan Yicheng, "Yicheng zizhuan nianpu ji zishu" [Yicheng's autobiographical chronological account], *Zhongshan xueshu wenhua jikan* [Zhongshan scholarship and culture quarterly] 10 (1972): 639.

3. Jing Ziyuan, "Huanying ge shixiao zhiyuan xuesheng yanshuo ci," 2.

4. Of the thirty-nine students admitted in 1911, eight were from Zhexi, thirteen from Ningbo and Shaoxing, twelve from Jinhua Prefecture, six from the Wenzhou-Taizhou area, and three from elsewhere. Of the thirty-one students admitted in 1912, fifteen were from Zhexi, nine from Ningbo and Shaoxing, two from Jinhua, five from Wenzhou-Taizhou. Of the thirty-nine admitted in 1914, nine were from Zhexi, eleven from Shaoxing-Ningbo, fourteen from Jinhua, two from Taizhou. See Zhejiang shengli *diyi shifan xuexiao tongxue lu*, 1915 [Roster of fellow scholars at the Zhejiang Provincial First Normal School, 1915] (Hangzhou: *Zhejiang shengli* diyi shifan xuexiao, 1915). Two Zhedong prefectures, Shaoxing and Jinhua, supplied a sizable contingent of students even though each had its own provincial normal school.

5. These counties as a group fall into the categories of outer core and inner peripheries in Skinner's and Schoppa's constructs.

6. ZSDS (fall 1917): 67–72.

7. Ibid.

8. Wang Huanqing, a native of Xianju, lived in "No. 34, Shangban Lane, Hangzhou"; Fu Xucheng, of Hangzhou, lived in "Number 65, Shi-wukui Lane, Hangzhou." See ibid., 69, 71.

9. *Zhejiang shengli diyi shifan xuexiao tongxue lu, 1922*, 11.

10. Ibid., 53–54.

11. Similar differences in fee structure existed between the Seventh Normal and the Seventh Middle schools of Jinhua Prefecture in the 1910s, with comparable sociological ramifications. Wu Han, who was a student in the Provincial Seventh Middle School in Jinhua in 1919, paid a total of eighty yuan for his education that year. Qian Jiaju, who transferred from Seventh Middle to Seventh Normal in the summer of 1922, spent under forty yuan for his education at the same time. Qian Jiaju, "Wo yu Wu Han" [Wu Han and I], *Zhuanji wenxue* (Taipei) 57, 2 (August 1990): 35–37.

12. When asked by Jing Ziyuan what motivated them to apply to the school, a majority of the approximately five hundred applicants interviewed in 1915 for admissions replied that they were attracted by the lesser expenditures entailed. The principal was dismayed, since he had high hopes about the applicants' commitment to educational enterprises. See ZSDS 7 (1915): 2.

13. Ruan Yicheng, "Yicheng zizhuan nianpu ji zishu," 639; also idem, "Ruan Xingcun," *Zhuanji wenxue* 23, 3 (September 1973): 18–19.

14. Ruan Yicheng, "Yicheng zizhuan nianpu ji zishu," 609–14.

15. Ibid., 639.

16. Ibid., 640.

17. Ibid., 641.

18. Ibid.

19. See student rosters in *Zhejiang shengli diyi shifan xuexiao tongxue lu, 1922*, 1–10, for the native places of the first three classes.

20. "Xiaoyou jinxun" [alumni news], ZSDS 8 (1915): 2.

21. Zhu Jiajin, who taught in his home county of Lanxi, simultaneously held jobs at two schools, one private and one public. At the private higher elementary school he was the math teacher as well as the science and physical education instructor. Together with five colleagues, he ran a school of thirty pupils. At the public, "model" junior elementary school of Lanxi, Zhu taught all of the previously mentioned subjects plus crafts and singing; with four other teachers he taught a total of eighty pupils. "Xiaoyou jinxun," ZSDS 8 (1915): 1–2.

22. Ibid.

23. "Disici biyesheng jinkuang" [News concerning the fourth class of graduates], ZSDS 14/15 (1918): 1.

24. The schools in the area were nearly without exception operated by the lineages. The pupils shared the same surname and came from the same village. Qu Yingguang, "Xunshi Jiangshan xian xuanyan" [Proclamation on a tour of inspection of Jiangshan County], *Qu Xun'an xunshi liang Zhe wengao*, 4:134b.

25. Ibid.

26. Qu Yingguang, "Xunshi Yongkang xian xuanyan" [Proclamation on a tour of inspection of Yongkang County], *Qu Xun'an xunshi liang Zhe wengao* 4:116b.

27. News report entitled "Zhesheng jiaoyuhui lianhe hui" [Association of Zhejiang provincial educational associations], JZ 12, 8 (August 1920): "Jishi" [news], 3.

28. Ibid., and Xianjiang, "Wosheng zhi yi xueqi" [One semester in Wosheng's life], ZSDS 3 (summer 1914): 5.

29. See, for example, Yang Qitao, "Shujia guicheng jilue" [Journal kept during the trip home in the summer], ZSDS (fall 1917): 32–33.

30. Shao Baosan, "Xiaoxia zazhi" [Miscellaneous summer notes], ZSDS (fall 1917): 28.

31. Yang Qitao, "Shujia guicheng jilue," 32.

32. Wei Jinzhi, "Dongri jiagui ji" [Account of my homeward journey in the winter], ZSDS 14/15 (1918): "zazhu" [miscellaneous], 5.

33. Yang Qitao, "Shujia guicheng jilue," 32.

34. Shang Kui, "Shu yu san xian" [Three life-threatening incidents in my life], ZSDS (fall 1917): 33–34.

35. Wei Jinzhi, "Dongri jiagui ji," 4–5.

36. Shao Baosan, "Xiaoxia zazhi," 30.

37. Ibid.

38. For comparison, see Jon L. Saari, *Legacies of Childhood: Growing Up Chinese in a Time of Crisis, 1890–1920* (Cambridge, Mass.: Council on East Asian Studies Publications, Harvard University Press, 1990).

39. The following reconstruction of Shi Cuntong's early life is based on an autobiographical statement written in the summer of 1920, supplemented with materials from the Jinhua local gazetteer and interviews with relatives conducted both in Jinhua (May and June 1992) and in Shi Cuntong's home village, Yecun (June 1992). Shi Cuntong's biographical account was completed in September 1920, when he was studying in Tokyo. Shi by then had had a few months to reflect on his experience during the May Fourth Movement in Zhejiang. He had also been to Beijing and Shanghai, and had gained some distance from his hometown. Compared with memoirs and autobiographies of his contemporaries, Shi's account was unique for its details and directness, which might be related to his sense of liberation as a result of being in Tokyo. Written in the vernacular and

serialized over four issues in the pages of the "Juewu" (Awakening) section of the newspaper *Minguo ribao* (Republican daily), the piece belonged to no established genre. In the context of the history of early Chinese Communism, Shi's memoir, like Qu Qiubai's "Superfluous Words" ("Duo yu de hua") of 1935, was a rare occurrence remarkable for its willingness to reveal. Qu's essay, written in a military prison while the author awaited execution, was confessional. Shi's piece, on the eve of his conversion to Communism, was defiant. To contextualize his autobiography, I visited with Shi's surviving relatives, including four of his second and third cousins, and fellow villagers in Yecun. The interview, on June 1, 1992, took place in the main hall in Shi Cuntong's former residence—the house he built with his wife and father in 1933, and which remained the largest construction in the village. The interviewees, who sat on wooden stools around a large table, all had experience serving as Party secretaries, committee members, and accountants for the village branch of the production brigade. The gathering inside Shi Cuntong's former living room was predominantly male.

40. JX 1 (1970): 140–41.

41. Shi Cuntong, "Huitou kan ershier nian lai de wo," September 20, 1920, p. 1.

42. Interview in Yecun, June 1992. Xu was remembered as "three or four years younger than Changchun," and she died "when the youngest child was still small." Fellow villagers remembered well that Shi Changchun died "the year before the Japanese took Yecun," which was on the eighth day in the fourth month of 1942 on the lunar calendar. Changchun was said to be seventy-two sui (seventy-one years old) at the time of his death.

43. Two eggs were considered the norm, three eggs were sumptuous fare. Interview in Yecun, June 1992.

44. Shi Cuntong, "Huitou," September 20, p. 1.

45. Interview with Shi Changchun's cousin, June 1992.

46. For comparison, see Margery Wolf, "Child Training and the Chinese Family," in Maurice Friedman, ed., *Family and Kinship in Chinese Society* (Stanford: Stanford University Press, 1970), 37–62. See also Wolf's book *Women and the Family in Rural Taiwan* (Stanford: Stanford University Press, 1972) and Ai-li S. Chin, "Family Relations in Modern Chinese Fiction," in Friedman, *Family and Kinship,* 92–93, 108–9.

47. Margery Wolf observes that village children in Taiwan often take revenge on an attacker by reporting him or her to the attacker's parent. The mother of the aggressor then either beats her own child in the presence of the victim or promises to do so when she finds her child. This response is often necessitated by the mother's own sense of insecurity in

her husband's home village. Wolf, "Child Training and the Chinese Family," 55.

48. Shi Cuntong, "Huitou," September 20, p. 1.

49. Interviews in June 1992 in Jinhua, Quzhou, and Yecun.

50. This and the following nine paragraphs are based on Shi Cuntong, "Huitou," September 20, pp. 2–3.

51. Interview in Yecun, June 1992.

52. Shi Cuntong, "Huitou," September 20, p. 2.

53. Ibid., 3.

54. Ibid., September 21, p. 2.

55. Ibid., September 20, p. 2; September 21, p. 2.

56. Xu Ke, *Qing bai lei chao* [Digest of Qing anecdotes, classified] (Shanghai: Shangwu yinshu guan, 1917), book 76:48–49.

57. Hua Yan, *Wuzu Yan Fu de yisheng* [My grandfather Yan Fu] (Taipei: Datong wenhua jijin hui, 1992), 2.

58. Shi Cuntong, "Huitou," September 21, p. 2.

59. Ibid., pp. 2, 3.

60. Ibid.

61. Ibid., 3; interview in Yecun, June 1992.

62. Interview in Yecun, June 1992.

63. Ibid.

64. Spirit possession was one of the defining characteristics of the Boxer Uprising of 1900, and the gods who descended to possess the Boxers often came from the pages of vernacular novels such as *Journey to the West, Romance of the Three Kingdoms, Water Margin,* and so forth. See Joseph Esherick, *The Origins of the Boxer Uprising* (Berkeley: University of California Press, 1987), 294.

65. Shi Cuntong, "Huitou," September 22, p. 1.

66. Ibid. On the activities of the triads in Zhejiang in the 1900s and their connections with the 1911 Revolution see Mary Backus Rankin, "The Revolutionary Movement in Chekiang: A Study in the Tenacity of Tradition," in Mary Wright, ed., *China in Revolution: The First Phase, 1900–1913* (New Haven: Yale University Press, 1968), 321–28.

67. Shi Cuntong, "Huitou," September 22, p. 3.

68. Ibid.

69. Ibid., 2.

70. Ibid.

71. The Xinshe, or Heart Society, originated in 1912 with Liu Shifu in Hong Kong. Liu Shifu was an admirer of Tolstoy. The Heart Society's charter included the following points: no meat, no alcohol, no cigarettes, no servants, no rickshas, no marriage, no official government service; do away with surname, hold no local assembly seats, join no political parties, serve no military units, join no church. See Wending, "Shifu zhuan"

[Biography of Shifu], in Ge Maochun, Jiang Jun, and Li Xingzhi, eds., *Wuzhengfu zhuyi sixiang ziliao xuan* [Selection of source materials on anarchist thought] (Beijing: Beijing daxue chuban she, 1984), 2:924.

72. Shi Cuntong, "Huitou," September 22, pp. 2, 3. *Daoxue* referred specifically to Neo-Confucianism of the Zhu Xi School, of which Jinhua was a main locus of transmission. *Daoxue* adherents during the Song often set themselves apart from their contemporaries by adopting distinctive dress and behavior. They "sat squarely with their backs erect, walked in measured steps looking straight ahead, bowed slowly and deeply to express sincere propriety, spoke in a dignified way with few gestures and carefully made at that." John W. Chaffee, "Chu Hsi in Nan-K'ang: *Tao-hsueh* and the Politics of Education," in de Bary and Chaffee, *Neo-Confucian Education*, 426–31; Liu, "How Did a Neo-Confucian School Become the State Orthodoxy?" 497. See also Ebrey, "Education through Ritual," 277. On twelfth-century *Daoxue (Tao-hsueh)* as a new culture that represented a radical break with the intellectual tradition of the past, see Peter Bol, *"This Culture of Ours": Intellectual Transitions in T'ang and Sung China* (Stanford: Stanford University Press, 1992), 300–342.

73. Shi Cuntong, "Huitou," September 21, p. 3.

CHAPTER 6: THE ASSOCIATION

1. Sally Borthwick, *Education and Social Change in China: The Beginnings of the Modern Era* (Stanford: Hoover Institution Press, 1983), 76, 87.

2. On the financing of elementary education in traditional China, see Evelyn Sakikida Rawski, *Education and Popular Literacy in Ch'ing China* (Ann Arbor: University of Michigan Press, 1979), 24–80.

3. Ibid., 95–96, and Wang Shukuai, "Qingmo Jiangsu difang zizhi fengchao" [Late Qing local riots and self-rule], *Zhongyang yanjiu yuan jindai shi yanjiu suo jikan* 6 (1977): 313–27. Prasenjit Duara argues that "the production of symbolic values" in local communities was often related to "the functional requirements of organizations." A key feature in village cultural nexus was that "authority in local society was a product neither of some Confucian ideal conferred from a higher culture nor of an idealized solitary community. Rather, the local representation of authority emerged from the partial overlap and interplay of sectional, communal, and imperial definitions of popular symbols." A cult like that of Guandi was "the pursuit of these particular symbols by various groups" for a common framework of authority. Conflicts over symbols and rituals almost always involved opposing interests between gentry networks. See Duara, *Culture, Power, and the State: Rural North China, 1900–1942* (Stanford: Stanford University Press, 1988), 35, 40.

4. See Borthwick's detailed discussion in *Education and Social Change* (96), of a case in Guangxi involving a militia leader who brought a lawsuit against local reformers for not respecting the temple of the God of Literature. He was defeated in court and proceeded to slander the new school by saying that its purpose was to spread foreign religion. Borthwick's discussion is based on Li Runren, "Tongmenghui zai Guilin, Pingle de huodong" [Revolutionary alliance activities in Guilin and Pingle], in Wenshi ziliao weiyuan hui, ed., *Xinhai geming huiyi lu* [Recollections of the 1911 revolution] (Beijing: Zhonghua shuju, 1961), 2:454–55. Village temple fairs, Dragon King worship, and temple property maintenance had long been a source of conflict between locals and village converts to Christianity, who disputed their share and role in contributing to the communal worship. See Lü Shiqiang, *Zhongguo guanshen fanjiao de yuanyin* [Causes of Chinese official and gentry opposition to Christianity] (Taipei: Wenjing shuju, 1973), 132–50. See also Paul Cohen, *China and Christianity: The Missionary Movement and the Growth of Chinese Antiforeignism, 1860–1870* (Cambridge, Mass.: Council on East Asian Studies Publications, Harvard University Press, 1963).

5. These regulations were the "Xuebu zouni jiaoyu hui zhangcheng zhe" (Ministry of education memorial to the throne, draft charter of the educational association) and "Jiaoyu hui zhangcheng" (Charter of the educational association), in Shu Xincheng, ed., *Zhongguo jindai jiaoyu shi ziliao* [Sources on the history of modern Chinese education] (Beijing: Renmin jiaoyu chuban she, 1961), 1:361–65.

6. Ibid.

7. Borthwick, *Education and Social Change*, 65–86, and Reynolds, *China, 1898–1912*, 105–6.

8. Ibid.

9. For literature on the late Qing constitutional movement, see, among others, P'eng-yuan Chang, "The Constitutionalists," and John Fincher, "Political Provincialism and the National Revolution," both in Mary Wright, ed., *China in Revolution: The First Phase, 1900–1913* (New Haven: Yale University Press, 1968), 143–83, 185–226; John Fincher, *Chinese Democracy: The Self-Government Movement in Local, Provincial, and National Politics, 1905–1914* (New York: St. Martin's Press, 1981); Min, *National Polity*. On the educators' participation, see Borthwick, *Education and Social Change*. On the local level, gentry management of community projects had been common since at least the nineteenth century. The constitutional movement of 1909 legitimated these practices and spelled out new revenues for local self-government bodies to make further appropriations in case of need. See Philip Kuhn, "Local Taxation and Finance in Republican China," in Susan Mann Jones, ed., *Proceedings of*

the NEH Modern China Project in China from 1850 to the Present, Select Papers from the Center for East Asian Studies, No. 3 (Chicago: University of Chicago Press, 1979). See also Joseph Esherick, *Reform and Revolution in China: The 1911 Revolution in Hunan and Hubei* (Berkeley: University of California Press, 1976), and Rankin, *Elite Activism*.

10. "Jiaoyu bu gongbu jiaoyu hui zhangcheng" [Ministry of education, charter of educational associations] (1912), in Shu Xincheng, *Zhongguo jindai*, 1:365–66.

11. JZ 7, 5:08,672–73 (May 1915) and 8, 1:11,208–12 (August 1916).

12. Shu Xincheng, *Zhongguo jindai*, 1:230–31; Gu Mei, *Xiandai Zhongguo ji qi jiaoyu* [Modern China and its education] (1934; reprint Hong Kong: Longmen shudian, 1975), 2:392–96. The motion was made by the Hunan Provincial Educational Association in 1915.

13. Xu Heyong et al., *Zhejiang jindai shi*, 277–80.

14. Ibid., 280.

15. Chen Gongmao, "Shen Dingyi qiren" [Shen Dingyi the man], *Zhejiang wenshi ziliao xuanji* 21 (1982): 39. On Shen's politics, see R. Keith Schoppa, "Rent Resistance and Rural Reconstruction: Shen Dingyi in Political Opposition, 1921 and 1928," in Roger B. Jeans, ed., *Roads Not Taken: The Struggle of Opposition Parties in Twentieth Century China* (Boulder, Col.: Westview, 1992).

16. Xu Heyong et al., *Zhejiang jindai shi*, 282.

17. In 1917, over 46 percent of the provincial budget was spent on the military and police forces of Zhejiang. See ibid., 286–87.

18. Ibid., 282. When Yuan Shikai died, Li Yuanhong became the president of the Republic. He called back the disbanded National Assembly and restored the provisional constitution. Feng Guozhang, the leader of the Zhili militarists, was elected the Republic's vice president. The Zhili and Anhui cliques thus fought in the National Assembly for their respective political interests. The struggle came to a head over the question of whether China should declare war on Germany. The Anhui militarists, backed by the Japanese and working through assembly members of the Study Society for a Constitutional Government of the Progressive Party, or the former constitutionalists of the 1900s, favored the declaration of war. The Zhili militarists, backed by British and American interests in China and working through the Study Society for a Constitutional Law of the Nationalist Party, or the former revolutionaries of the 1900s, thought otherwise. Ibid., 283.

19. In June 1918, its annual meeting was attended by 171 members. In 1920, at the time of Jing Ziyuan's resignation, membership attendance was 151. See JZ 10, 7 (July 1918): "xueshi yishu," 54, and 12, 8 (August 1920): 17,238.

20. Ibid., 9, 6 (June 1917): "xueshi yishu," 47.

21. The size of the advisory committee increased over the years. In 1920, there were thirty-two members on it representing eleven prefectures. See ibid., 12, 8 (August 1920): 17,238.

22. Ruan Xunbo, who represented Shaoxing Prefecture, for instance, had been an instructor at the Hangzhou Law and Political Science Institute since 1906, a founder of the private Institute for Legal and Political Studies in 1910, and a gentry advisor to the provincial governor on financial matters in 1911. Ruan was the lifetime head of the Yuyao Co-Provincial Association in Hangzhou, and was for fifteen years until his death in 1929 the head of the Zhejiang Bar Association. As a member of the Zhejiang Provincial Assembly Ruan voted for the establishment of a Zhejiang University and organized social and intellectual clubs for educators and local intellectual leaders. See Ruan Yicheng, *Minguo Ruan Xunbo Xiansheng Xingcun nianpu* [Chronological biography of Mr. Ruan Xingcun (Xunbo) of the Republican period] (Taipei: Taiwan Commercial Press, 1979), 25, 27, 31–32, 38, 44–46.

23. *Wusi shiqi qikan jieshao* [Introduction to periodicals of the May Fourth period] (Beijing: Shenghuo, dushu, xinzhi sanlian shudian, 1959; reprint 1979, 2 (pt. 1): 428.

24. JZ 9, 10 (October 1917): "xueshi yishu," 78.

25. Ibid., 9, 5 (May 1917): "xueshi yishu," 38.

26. Ibid.

27. Ibid.

28. Ibid., and 9, 7 (July 1917): "xueshi yishu," 54–55.

29. Ibid., 10, 7 (July 1918): "xueshi yishu," 54.

30. *Wusi shiqi qikan jieshao*, 2 (pt. 1): 428.

31. Ibid., 428.

32. The organizational details of the Youth Corps are no longer available. Contemporary observers remarked that the corps modeled itself on "European, American, German and Japanese youth corps and boy scouts," which is to say that the Youth Corps was non-Chinese in inspiration and open to a wide range of actual organizational possibilities. Ibid., 428, 429, and JZ 11, 5 (May 1919): 15,274–75.

33. *Wusi shiqi qikan jieshao*, 2 (pt. 1): 428.

34. JZ 11, 5 (May 1919): "xueshi yishu," 46–47.

35. *Wusi shiqi qikan jieshao*, 2 (pt. 1): 429–30.

36. The journal began as a weekly newsletter of the Zhejiang Provincial Educational Association. When publication resumed in October 1920, both Jing Ziyuan and Shen Zhongjiu, the editor, had been removed from their posts, and the journal turned conservative. The publication was discontinued in January 1922, after the printing of four more issues. Ibid., 431; 2 (pt. 2): 882–87.

37. Ibid., 2 (pt. 1): 431; "Jiaoyu chao fakan ci" [Inaugural editorial of *Tides in Education*], in ibid., 2 (pt. 2): 582–86.

38. "Jiaoyu chao fakan ci," in ibid., 2 (pt. 2): 583.

39. Ibid., 585.

40. Ibid., 585–86.

41. The rest of the journal consisted of gazette-style news coverage of educational events inside and outside of the province. Ibid., 882.

42. Ibid., 883–84.

43. Ibid., 882–87.

44. Fu Binran, "Huiyi Zhejiang xinchao she" [Recollections of the Zhejiang New Tide Society], *Wusi shiqi de shetuan*, 3:148.

45. JZ 9, 4 (April 1917): "dashiji" [chronicle of major events], 27, and 9, 6 (June 1917): 42–43.

46. Ibid., 11, 11 (November 1919): "xueshi yishu," 108–9, and 9, 10 (October 1917): "xueshi yishu," 72.

47. Ibid., 10, 1 (January 1918): "xueshi yishu," 6–7; 11, 5 (May 1919): "xueshi yishu," 46–47; 9, 11 (November 1917): "tebie jishi" [note on special events], 110; 10, 12 (December 1918): "zhuanjian" [special column], 4.

48. Ibid., 9, 11 (November 1917): "xueshi yishu," 84.

49. Ibid., 9, 10 (October 1917): "xueshi yishu," 74–75.

50. Ibid., 10, 1 (January 1918): "xueshi yishu," 7.

51. Ibid., 9, 12 (December 1917): "xueshi yishu," 91–92.

52. Ibid., 10, 8 (August 1918): "xueshi yishu," 64–65.

53. Ibid., 10, 3 (March 1918): "xueshi yishu," 22, and 10, 8 (August 1918): "xueshi yishu," 64–65.

54. Ibid., 9, 4 (April 1917): "xueshi yishu," 30–31.

55. Ibid., 10, 8 (August 1918): "xueshi yishu," 64–65.

56. Ibid., 11, 2 (February 1918): "dashiji," 14–15.

57. Ibid., 11, 5 (May 1919): "dashiji," 40–43; 10, 12 (December 1918): "zhuanjian," 4; 11, 7 (July 1919): "xueshi yishu," 63; 11, 11 (November 1919): "xueshi yishu," 108–9.

58. See discussion in Chapter 4.

59. JZ 9, 12 (December 1917): "xueshi yishu," 90–91.

60. Schoppa, *Chinese Elites and Political Change*, 169–71.

61. Ibid., 171–72.

62. Ibid.

63. Ruan Yicheng, *Minguo Ruan Xunbo Xiansheng Xingcun nianpu* [Chronological biography of Mr. Ruan Xingcun (Xunbo) of the Republican period] (Taipei: Taiwan Commercial Press, 1979), 39.

64. In the early 1920s Jing Ziyuan emerged as a senior member in the left wing of the Nationalist Party that was sympathetic to the socialist tendencies represented by Liao Zhongkai and opposed to the right-wing

military clique centered on fellow Zhejiang provincial Chiang Kai-shek. Jing Ziyuan's daughter later married Liao Zhongkai's son, Liao Chengzhi. In the Nanchang Uprising of 1927, Jing Ziyuan's name appeared on Tan Pingshan's list of "Guomindang Revolutionary Committee" members along with the names of Communist leaders Zhou Enlai, Zhang Guotao, and Li Lisan. See Shen Yunlong, "Cong Wuhan fen gong dao Guangzhou baodong" [From the Wuhan purge of Communists to the Guangzhou Commune], *Zhuanji wenxue* 33, 6 (December 1978): 24. Jing was a delegate to the Expanded Nationalist Party Conference (Guomindang kuoda huiyi) of 1928 organized by Wang Jingwei and held in Beijing. This Party congress was a prelude to civil war against Chiang Kai-shek's forces in Nanjing. See Shen Yunlong, "Kuoda huiyi zhi youlai ji jingguo" [Origin and proceeding of the Expanded Conference], *Zhuanji wenxue* 33, 4 (October 1978): 16. In the early 1930s Jing Ziyuan was a member on the Guomindang Central Executive Committee. See Shen Yunlong, "Guangzhou feichang huiyi de fenlie yu Ning Yue Hu siguan dahui de hezuo" [Schism of the Guangzhou Conference and the collaboration among Nanjing, Guangzhou and Shanghai delegates during the Fourth Party Congress], ibid. 35, 3 (September 1979): 24.

65. JZ 10, 6 (June 1918): 43–44.

66. Ibid., 11, 11 (November 1919): "xueshi yishu," 101–2.

67. Ibid.

68. *Wusi shiqi de shetuan*, 3:149.

69. Ruan Yicheng, *Minguo Ruan Xunbo*, 45.

70. See the letter from the Provincial Assembly to the provincial governor of Zhejiang in December 1919, in which the assembly also demanded a thorough investigation of the Zhejiang New Tide Society. Fu Binran, "Huiyi Zhejiang xinchao she," 146.

CHAPTER 7: THE MAY FOURTH MOVEMENT IN HANGZHOU

1. Other slogans were: "Return our Qingdao!" "Wake up, Countrymen!" "Death to the Traitors!" and "The Wealth and Power of the Nation Are Every Commoner's Responsibility!"

2. Four days later and after much discussion, the Provincial Assembly cabled the president of the Republic, albeit in a much moderated tone of voice, to report on the public's indignation and to request that the three ministers be dismissed. See Zhongguo shehui kexue yuan jindai shi yanjiu suo and Zhongguo dier lishi dang'an guan shiliao bianji bu, eds., *Wusi aiguo yundong dang'an ziliao* [Archival source materials concerning the May Fourth patriotic movement] (Beijing: Zhongguo shehui kexue chuban she, 1980), 210.

3. Zhonggong Zhejiang, *Wusi yundong zai Zhejiang*, 2. Outside Hangzhou, similar meetings and street demonstrations took place in major county centers of northern Zhejiang, as secondary and normal students of Jiaxing, Ningbo, Huzhou, and Shaoxing announced the formation of their organizations. Later, following the examples set in Hangzhou, these students also formed themselves into teams of ten, as the May Fourth Movement reached its next stage of active boycotting against Japanese goods.

4. Ruan Yicheng, "Yicheng zizhuan nianpu ji zishu," 66; Xia Yan, "Dang wusi langchao chong dao Zhejiang de shihou" [When the tide of May Fourth reached Zhejiang], in Zhongguo shehui kexue yuan jindai shi yanjiu suo, ed., *Wusi yundong huiyi lu* [Recollections of the May Fourth Movement] (Beijing: Zhongguo shehui kexue chuban she, 1979), 730.

5. On mobilization in Shanghai, see Joseph T. Chen, *The May Fourth Movement in Shanghai: The Making of a Social Movement in Modern China* (Leiden: E. J. Brill, 1971).

6. Zhongguo shehui kexue yuan jindai shi yanjiu suo et al., *Wusi aiguo yundong dang'an ziliao*, 214–15. During the following week students of Jiaxing, Ningbo, Shaoxing, Taizhou, and Wenzhou announced their strike. See Zhonggong Zhejiang, *Wusi yundong zai Zhejiang*, 4–5.

7. See relevant archival materials printed in the collection *Wusi aiguo yundong dang'an ziliao*, especially 218, 231, 235–38.

8. Ibid., 238–39, 240–42.

9. Zhonggong Zhejiang, *Wusi yundong zai Zhejiang*, 5–6.

10. Ibid., 4–5; *Wusi shiqi de shetuan*, 3:128; Ruan Yicheng, "Yicheng zizhuan nianpu ji zishu," 69–70.

11. [Shen] Xuanlu, "Zhejiang xuechao de yipie" [Student unrest in Zhejiang: A glimpse], *Xingqi pinglun* [Weekend review] 1 (June 8, 1919): 2–3.

12. *Xingqi pinglun* 26 (November 30, 1919): 4.

13. [Shen] Xuanlu, "Zhejiang xuechao de yipie."

14. Shi Cuntong, "Huitou," September 23, p. 1.

15. Of the three, Xia Mianzun had been with the First Normal School since 1912 as a proctor. His appointment as the Chinese teacher began in fall 1919.

16. The novel first appeared in 1887 in Italian under the title *Cuore: A cura di Ettore Barelli;* an English translation, from the 224th Italian edition, appeared in 1899 titled *The Heart of a Boy: A Schoolboy's Journal.*

17. For an introductory summary of *Cuore,* see Ye Shengtao and Zhu Ziqing, *Guowen luedu zhidao* [Guide to preliminary studies of national literature] (Hong Kong: Chuangken chuban she, 1955), 219–40.

18. Ibid., 222.

19. Selections from *Cuore* were used—along with a chapter of *Mencius*, excerpts from the *Record from the Grand Historian (Shiji)*, Tang poetry, Hu Shi's essays, and Lu Xun's short stories—by Zhu Ziqing and Ye Shengtao in their secondary school textbook, *Guowen luedu zhidao*.

20. Hangzhou still is about four hours by train from Shanghai in the 1990s.

21. Xia Mianzun and Ye Shengtao, *Wenxin* [The heart of literature] (Shanghai: Kaiming shudian, 1933), 53, 54, 57. Author's translation.

22. Liu Dabai's writings later appeared in two major collections: *Baiwu wenhua* [Reflections on literature in a white chamber] (Shanghai: Shijie shuju, 1929) and *Baiwu shuoshi* [Reflections on poetry in a white chamber] (Shanghai: Kaiming shudian, 1929).

23. Liu Dabai, "Tongcheng pai guihua wen he bagu wen de guanxi" [Relationship between the eight-legged essays and the language of the dead of the Tongcheng School], in Liu Dabai, *Baiwu wenhua*, 39. See also the preface by Tan Ming in Liu Dabai, *Liu Dabai xuanji* [Selected works of Liu Dabai] (Hong Kong: Xianggang wenxue yanjiu she, n.d.), 4.

24. Liu Dabai, "Jianshu huanyi fa de guihua wen zuofa mijue" [Secret methods for the composition of essays in dead languages: The use of references and the substitution of characters], in Liu Dabai, *Baiwu wenhua*, 41–50. Since Liu regarded linguistic positions as political strategies, he was ready to hail the victory of the Northern Expedition of the Guomindang in 1927 as a victory of the New Culture Movement, which he thought the Nationalists had more or less championed after May Fourth. See his "Wenqiang geming he guomin geming de guanxi" [Relationship between literary and national revolutions], in *Baiwu wenhua*, 149–65.

25. Dabai [Liu Dabai], "Sixiang de jianyu" [Prisonhouse of thought], *Xingqi pinglun* 6 (July 13, 1919): 3–4.

26. Liu's vernacular poems were later printed in two anthologies, entitled *Jiumeng* (Faded dreams) and *Youwen* (Mailing kisses). Liu Dabai and He Fuxia were later divorced.

27. Preface by Liu Dabai to a collection of his own poems entitled *Shuqing xiaoshi* (Casual poems of feeling), quoted in Cao Juren, *Wo yu wo de shijie*, 191, 194.

28. Dabai, "Sixiang de jianyu," 3–4.

29. Cao Juren, *Wo yu wo de shijie*, 162.

30. Ni Weixiong, "Zhejiang xinchao de huiyi" [Recollections of the Zhejiang New Tide Society], in Zhongguo shehui, *Wusi yundong huiyi lu*, 2:738–39.

31. Shen Xuanlu was the leading landowner in his home county Xiaoshan, Zhejiang. He was drawn to the social and economic issues of his region shortly after the 1911 Revolution, and had long associated himself with the left wing of the Nationalist Party. His socialist sympathies culminated in

his involvement with the Marxism Study Society and the founding of the Chinese Communist Party in Shanghai in 1921. Shen Xuanlu's political leanings earned him the ire of fellow landlords of the area, to which some commentators have attributed Shen's death in 1928 at the hands of an assailant. But Shen Xuanlu had abandoned his left-wing position after 1927 and become a staunch supporter of the Nationalist attempt to purge the Party of Communist members. Cao Juren, *Wo yu wo de shijie,* 162–63.

32. Liu Dabai, *Xuanji,* 60–61. See also Cao Juren, *Wo yu wo de shijie,* 177.

33. Liu Dabai became Jiang Menglin's chief secretary in 1927, when Jiang was appointed the head of Zhejiang's provincial bureau of education by the new Nationalist government. Jiang Menglin later became minister of education in Nanjing, and Liu Dabai was named to become his deputy minister of education. Liu resigned in 1930 on grounds of poor health; he died in 1931. See the biographical sketch of Liu Dabai written by Zhu Bangda in a volume edited by the ministry of education, *Diyi ci Zhong-guo jiaoyu nianjian* [Yearbook of Chinese education, first compilation] (Shanghai: Kaiming shudian, 1934), section wu, 412. On his denunciation by the Communists as a heartless enemy of the people, see Lou Shiyi, "Huainian Xia Mianzun xiansheng" [Remembering Mr. Xia Mianzun], *Renwu shuangyue kan* [People bimonthly] 4 (1981): 152–59.

34. See "Chen Wangdao tongzhi luezhuan" [Biographical sketch of comrade Chen Wangdao], in Fudan daxue yuyan yanjiu shi, ed., *Chen Wangdao wenji* [Collected works of Chen Wangdao] (Shanghai: Renmin chuban she, 1979), 1:11.

35. Cao Juren, *Wo yu wo de shijie,* 164.

36. Chen Wangdao, in Fudan daxue, *Chen Wangdao wenji,* "pinglun" [commentary], 4.

37. *Laodong jie* was a Shanghai-based weekly published between August 1920 and January 1921. Twenty-three issues were printed.

38. "Luezhuan," in *Chen Wangdao wenji,* 12, 17.

39. Between 1920 and 1949 Chen Wangdao served at different times as department chairman, dean of the College of Letters, and acting dean of academic affairs at Fudan University; he was appointed president in the early 1950s. Ibid.

40. The Beijing intellectuals of the New Culture Movement had by then become divided over political issues. Liberal intellectuals such as Hu Shi debated socialist activists such as Li Dazhao on whether a socialist revolution represented China's best course of action in the hope of achieving national rejuvenation. The debates were touched off by the publication of Hu Shi's article "More Study of Problems, Less Talk of 'Isms,'" in the pages of *Meizhou pinglun* [Weekly commentary] (July 20, 1919). See Chow Tse-tsung, *The May Fourth Movement,* 218–53, and Maurice Meis-

ner, *Li Ta-chao and the Origins of Chinese Marxism* (Cambridge, Mass.: Harvard University Press, 1967), 105–14.

41. Some accounts gave the names of Shi Cuntong and Yu Xiusong as members of the original seven who formed the core organization under Chen Duxiu of the Chinese Communist Party. Yu Xiusong was active in the Shanghai labor movement in the mid-1920s. He later worked as a Comintern representative in Xinjiang and married a younger sister of Sheng Shicai, the warlord of Xinjiang. He was secretly executed by his brother-in-law, who had launched a purge against the Communists. See An Zhijie, "Sheng Shicai pohai meifu Yu Xiusong jingguo" [How Sheng Shicai persecuted his brother-in-law Yu Xiusong] *Zhuanji wenxue* (Taipei) 53, 2 (August 1988): 25–29.

42. He Zhongying, "Baihua wen jiaoshou wenti" [Problems in the teaching of the vernacular], JZ 12, 2 (February 1920): 16,450–54.

43. Ni Weixiong, "Zhejiang xinchao," 2:737; Shi Fuliang [Cuntong], "Wusi zai Hangzhou" [The May Fourth Movement in Hangzhou], in Zhongguo shehui, *Wusi yundong huiyi lu,* 2:754.

44. Shi Fuliang, "*Wusi zai Hangzhou,*" and Shi Cuntong, "Huitou," September 23, 1920, p. 1.

45. [Shen] Xuanlu, "Xuexiao zizhi de shenghuo" [Self-rule by students], *Xingqi pinglun* 22 (November 2, 1919): 1.

46. "Zhejiang xuechao de dongji" [Rise of student unrest in Zhejiang], *Xingqi pinglun* 39 (February 29, 1920): 3.

47. Shi Cuntong, "Huitou," September 22, p. 3.

48. Cao Juren, *Wo yu wo de shijie,* 220, 223. In the late Qing political satire *Guanchang xianxing ji* (Officials revealing their true forms), Grand Councillor Wang Wenshao, a native of Hangzhou, was depicted as a man who rose to high offices mainly by his willingness to bend to imperial wishes and to keep his mouth shut (*duo ketou, shao shuohua*—many kowtows, few words). The term *liuli dan* was affixed to him to suggest his politically slippery, nonstick quality.

49. *Wusi shiqi de shetuan,* 3:149.

50. Cao Juren, *Wo yu wo de shijie,* 220, 223. On fox maiden, see the fictional rendering by the Qing novelist Pu Songling (1640–1715) in Judith Zeitlin, *Historian of the Strange: Pu Songling and the Classical Chinese Tale* (Stanford: Stanford University Press, 1993), 174–81, 211–16.

51. Ruan Yicheng, "Yicheng zizhuan nianpu ji zishu," 648.

52. Ibid., 648–49.

53. Pan Guangdan, *Ming Qing liangdai Jiaxing de wangzu,* table 1. The Zha lineage produced six individuals holding offices in Ming times, which made it one of the forty-four lineages in the province of such splendid bureaucratic achievement. See table 29, "Politically Powerful Clans," in Parsons, "The Ming Dynasty Bureaucracy," 209.

54. Ruan Yicheng, "Yicheng Zizhuan nianpu ji zishu," 647.

55. Ibid., 648.

56. The seven students were Zhu Baoshi, Wang Jun (Yuquan), Huang Xingqiu, Cai Jingming, Shen Naixi (Duanxian), Sun Jinwen (Zeping), and Ni Weixiong (Shendu). Ibid., 649.

57. Ibid.

58. Ibid.; Cao Juren, *Wo yu wo de shijie*, 141; Perry Link, *Mandarin Ducks and Butterflies: Urban Popular Fiction in Twentieth Century Chinese Cities* (Berkeley: University of California Press, 1980).

59. Ruan Yicheng, "Yicheng zizhuan nianpu ji zishu," 651.

60. The following discussion of *Double Ten* is based on material in ibid., 650–51.

61. Ibid. and Xia Yan, "Dang wusi langchao," 731.

62. Xia Yan, "Dang wusi langchao," 731–32; Ni Weixiong, "Zhejiang xinchao de huiyi," 2:737–38.

63. Ruan Yicheng, "Yicheng zizhuan nianpu ji zishu," 653. The radicalization of the reorganized weekly under the influence of the First Normal students was evident first in the very choice of the title. In 1903, a group of Zhejiang revolutionaries, including Sun Yizhong, Jiang Zhiyou, and Jiang Fangzhen, founded the *Zhejiang chao* (Zhejiang tide) in Tokyo to promote revolution. The Zhejiang New Tide Society was named consciously after that revolutionary journal. See ibid., 651.

64. Shi Cuntong, "Huitou," September 24, p. 2. Several sources, including Ruan Yicheng's autobiography, give Huang Zongzheng's name as Huang Zongfan. Huang Zongzheng, however, was the name that appeared on the journal as its correspondent.

65. Ruan Yicheng, "Yicheng zizhuan nianpu ji zishu," 653.

66. Ibid., 652.

67. This editorial appeared in the first issue of *Zhejiang New Tide* (November 1, 1919) and is reprinted in *Wusi shiqi de shetuan*, 3:124–27.

68. Ibid., 125.

69. For a discussion of the Mencian concept of *liangzhi* (mind) in Neo-Confucian philosophy, see Thomas A. Metzger, *Escape from Predicament: Neo-Confucianism and China's Evolving Political Culture* (New York: Columbia University Press, 1977), especially 82–134, 214–35. Metzger discusses "the good cosmic force as a given" in Neo-Confucianism—a beneficient, transcendent cosmic force that was seen to impinge on the naturally given mind and organically shape the world outside. On linkages between this cosmic optimism and Chinese anarchism, see Zarrow, *Anarchism and Chinese Political Culture*, 71.

70. *Wusi shiqi de shetuan*, 3:125.

71. Xia Mianzun, "Duile Milai de 'Wanzhong'" [Reflections on the 'Evening Bell' by Millet], in Xia Mianzun, *Pingwu zawen* [Miscellaneous

writings of the Pingwu] (Shanghai: Kaiming shudian, 1935), 71–81. *The Gleaners* is now at the Museé d'Orsay, Paris. See also Liana Vardi, "Constructing the Harvest: Gleaners, Farmers, and Officials in Early Modern France," *American Historical Review* 98, 5 (December 1993): 1,424–47.

72. *Wusi shiqi de shetuan*, 3:126.

73. Ibid., 127.

74. Ibid. Other articles printed in the first issue of the *Zhejiang New Tide Weekly* along with the inaugural editorial included a feature article by Fu Binran, which discussed the future direction of the student movement; "A Letter to the Editors of *Zhejiang Daily, Quanzhe Daily* and *Zhejiang People*" by Wang Yuquan, which attacked the conservative editorial position of these major newspapers; a brief comment by Xia Yan, under the pen name Zaibai, which echoed Wang's attack; "Thoughts on the Birthday of the Sage" by Xikang, which criticized the hypocrisy of the Confucian rite; and another brief piece by Xia Yan entitled "Does Printed Material Require Official Supervision?" See *Wusi shiqi qikan jieshao*, 2 (pt. 2): 888.

75. Zarrow, *Anarchism and Chinese Political Culture*, 77–81.

76. Ibid., 83–99. Liu Shipei believed that when compared with the West, Chinese political culture and tradition contained elements that lent themselves readily to the realization of the anarchist ideal. He also believed that communal ownership of property was realized in the days of the Yellow Emperor and the Three Dynasties. See [He] Zhen and [Liu] Shenshu (courtesy name: Shipei), "Lun zhongzu geming yu wuzhengfu geming zhi deshi" [On the pros and cons of ethnic revolution vis-à-vis anarchist revolution], *Tianyi bao* (Natural justice), vols. 6–7, September 1 and 15, 1907, reprinted in Ge Maochun, Jiang Jun, Li Xingzhi, eds., *Wuzhengfu zhuyi sixiang ziliao xuan* [Selection of source materials on anarchist thought] (Beijing: Beijing daxue chuban she, 1984), 1:97–98; and "Lun gongchan zhi yixing yu Zhongguo" [On the feasibility of communism in China], *Hengbao* 2 (May 8, 1908), reprinted in Ge Maochun et al., *Wuzhengfu*, 139–41.

77. Ruan Yicheng, "Yicheng zizhuan nianpu ji zishu," 653. The controversy stirred up by the printing of Shi Cuntong's article "Fei Xiao" (Decry filial piety!), in the second issue of the *Zhejiang New Tide*, attracted the attention of Beida students and inspired critical examination of traditional familial values, as seen in discussions contained in Yi Jiayue and Luo Dunwei, *Zhongguo jiating wenti* [Problems with Chinese families] (Shanghai: Taidong shuju, 1924); for the authors' acknowledgment of the influence of Shi Cuntong, see pp. 145–46.

78. N.a., "Zhejiang zhi wenhua yundong" [The cultural movement in Zhejiang], *Shishi xinbao* [Current affairs] (Shanghai), October 27, 1919; reprinted in *Wusi shiqi de shetuan*, 3:128.

79. Ibid., 129.

80. See Shi Cuntong's letter to the editors of *Xinchao* and the response by Luo Jialun, in *Xinchao* (reprint Taipei: Dongfang wenhua shuju, 1972) 2, 2:368–71.

81. Fu Binran, "Huiyi Zhejiang xinchao she," 3:149–50; and idem, "Wusi qianhou" [Before and after May Fourth], in *Zhongguo shehui, Wusi yundong huiyi lu*, (pt. 2), 2:751. On the Marxism Study Society in Shanghai, see Dirlik, *Origins of Chinese Communism*, 160–63.

82. *Xiaojing* [Book of filial piety] (reprint Shanghai: Hanfenlou, 1922), 12a.

83. Changsha's reputation for radicalism rested largely on the publication of *Xiangjiang pinglun* (Xiang River review), edited by Mao Zedong. The fame of Mao's journal was "second only to that of Shi Cuntong's Zhejiang New Tide," in the words of Zhang Guotao, the Beijing University Marxist who chaired the First Party Congress of the Chinese Communist Party in July 1921, and who later turned against the Party and assisted the Nationalists in anti-Communist campaigns. See excerpts of Zhang Guotao's memoirs, reprinted in Zhonggong Guangdong shengwei dangshi yanjiu weiyuan hui bangong shi and Guangdong sheng dang'an guan, eds., *Yida qianhou de Guangdong dang zuzhi* [Party organization in Guangdong before and after the First Congress] (Dongguan: Guangdong sheng dang'an guan, 1981), 73.

CHAPTER 8: "DECRY FILIAL PIETY!"

1. [Shen] Xuanlu, "Hunjia wenti" [On marriages], *Xingqi pinglun* 27 (December 7, 1919): 2.

2. *Wusi shiqi de shetuan*, 3:134–35.

3. Ibid.

4. *Daoxue* scholars believed in the moral value of ritualized behavior and were often seen by others as mannered and arrogant. See note 72 in chapter 5.

5. Cao Juren, *Wo yu wo de shijie*, 156.

6. Chen Duxiu published several essays in 1916 and 1917 to refute Kang Youwei's attempt to turn Confucianism into a "state religion" of China. These pieces included "Bo Kang Youwei zhi zongtong zongli shu" [Refutation of Kang Youwei's letter to the president and the prime minister], *Xin qingnian* [New youth] 2, 2 (October 1916); "Xianfa yu Kong jiao" [The constitution and Confucianism], *New Youth* 2, 3 (November 1916); "Kongzi zhi dao yu xiandai shenghuo" [Confucian teaching and modern life], *New Youth* 2, 4 (December 1916); and "Jiu sixiang yu guoti wenti" [Old thoughts and problems with national polity], *New Youth* 3, 3 (May 1917). Other important pieces on Confucianism in the pages of *New Youth* included Yi Baisha, "Kongzi pingyi" [A fair evaluation of Confucius]

(February and September 1916); Wu Yu, "Jiazu zhidu wei zhuanzhi zhuyi zhi genju lun" [Familism as the basis of authoritarianism] (February 1917); Lu Xun, "Kuang ren riji" [Diary of a madman] (May 1918); and Wu Yu, "Chiren yu lijiao" [Men-eating and ritual teaching] (November 1919).

7. Zhang Xun, the military governor of Anhui, led his troops into Beijing in the summer of 1917—at the urging of Kang Youwei—and hoped to restore the Qing dynasty. Kang had sought to promote Confucianism as a state religion. Chen attacked Confucianism by showing its link to the autocratic structure of the Chinese family. He undermined Kang's position by citing the philological scholarship of classicists of the School of Han Learning, especially the work of Zhang Binglin, a leading master from Zhejiang. Kang Youwei's position on Confucianism was attacked, in other words, both as an authoritarian system of values and as the result of poor classical scholarship. See discussions in Lee Feigon, *Chen Duxiu: Founder of the Chinese Communist Party* (Princeton: Princeton University Press, 1983), 121–22.

8. Lee Feigon sees 1916 as a turning point in the debate between the conservatives and the progressives over the issue of Confucianism as a state religion. Prior to 1916, the Confucian establishment, though under attack and sounding defensive, nevertheless felt confident about its power and authority. After 1916, with the downfall of Yuan Shikai's monarchy, the Confucian principles on which Yuan had based his government were discredited, and the conservative government lost its authority. Chen Duxiu, who had been attacking Confucianism and arguing that history was on his side, was increasingly regarded as the authoritative voice in his capacity as the dean of a government university. Feigon, *Chen Duxiu*, 118–19.

9. Shi Cuntong, "Huitou," September 22, p. 3.

10. Ibid.

11. On Yan Fu's translation work and intellectual influence, see Schwartz's classic study, *In Search of Wealth and Power.*

12. Shi Cuntong, "Huitou," September 22, p. 3, and September 23, p. 3.

13. Ibid., September 23, p. 3; Fu Binran, "Wusi qianhou," 2:745–46; Ge Maochun et al., *Wuzhengfu,* 2:953.

14. "Cock-crow" is a somewhat awkward translation of *huiming,* a term alluding to two lines in the Confucian classic *Shi jing* (Classic of odes): *feng yu ru* hui, *ji* ming *bu yi.* These lines are rendered variously as "All's dark amid the wind and rain, ceaselessly the cock's clear voice" (James Legge) and "The wind and rain make it like darkness, the cocks crow unceasingly" (Bernhard Karlgren). *Hui* refers to the darkness amid the wind and rain; *ming* refers to the cock's crow. *Huiming* is thus no mere "cock-crow," but a crowing cock at a stormy daybreak. See *Shih Ching* [The book of poetry], trans. James Legge (New York: Paragon Book

Reprint, 1967), 99, and Bernhard Karlgren, *The Book of Odes: Chinese Text, Transcription, and Translation* (Stockholm: Museum of Far Eastern Antiquities, 1950), 58.

15. On Liu Shifu (Sifu), see Edward S. Krebs, "Liu Ssu-fu and Chinese Anarchism, 1905–1915," Ph.D. diss., University of Wisconsin, 1977; Arif Dirlik, *Anarchism in the Chinese Revolution* (Berkeley: University of California Press, 1991), 124–33; Zarrow, *Anarchism and Chinese Political Culture*, 212–17.

16. Ge Maochun et al., *Wuzhengfu*, 2:950; Dirlik, *Anarchism*, 174.

17. Ge Maochun et al., *Wuzhengfu*, 2:952–53; Dirlik, *Anarchism*, 175.

18. Dirlik, *Anarchism*, 117. See also Chapter 7 herein.

19. For a classic explication on the interconnectedness between political beliefs and familial ethics, see Benjamin Schwartz, "Some Polarities in Confucian Thought," in Nivison and Wright, *Confucianism in Action*.

20. On filial piety as the critical linkage between familial values and national construction among modern Chinese revolutionaries at the turn of the century, see Don C. Price's thought-provoking piece, "Revolution for the Ancestors: National Identity in Experience and Rhetoric," paper presented at the Annual Meeting of the Association for Asian Studies, Los Angeles, March 27, 1993.

21. Dirlik, *Anarchism*, 155.

22. Shi Cuntong, "Huitou," September 22, p. 3.

23. Ibid.

24. Ibid.

25. *Wusi shiqi de shetuan*, 3:135.

26. Shi Cuntong, "Huitou," September 23, p. 3.

27. Ibid.

28. Ibid.

29. Ludwig Wittgenstein, *The Blue and Brown Books* (New York: Harper and Row, 1958), 6.

30. Karl Marx, *A Contribution to the Critique of Political Economy* (1859) (New York: International Publishers, 1970), 207, 206. See discussions in W. J. T. Mitchell, *Iconology: Image, Text, Ideology* (Chicago: University of Chicago Press, 1986), 160–61.

31. Shi Cuntong, "Huitou," September 23, p. 3.

32. Zhongguo shehui kexue yuan jindai shi yanjiu suo et al., *Wusi aiguo yundong dang'an ziliao*, 631–32.

33. Ibid., 633. To ensure the effectiveness of the censorship measures, Qi Yaoshan also wrote to the governor of Jiangsu on November 27 with a request for cooperation. See *Wusi shiqi de shetuan*, 3:143.

34. Shi Cuntong, "Huitou," September 23, p. 3.

35. Ni Weixiong, "Zhejiang xinchao de huiyi," 738–39; Ruan Yicheng, "Yicheng zizhuan nianpu ji zishu," 653.

36. Shen Ziqian et al., *Zhejiang yishi fengchao* [Disturbance at the Zhejiang First Normal] (Hangzhou: Zhejiang daxue chuban she, 1990), 117, 124.

37. Ruan Yicheng, "Yicheng zizhuan nianpu ji zishu," 654.

38. *Wusi shiqi de shetuan*, 3:143.

39. Ruan Yicheng, "Yicheng zizhuan nianpu ji zishu," 655.

40. For student efforts to persuade Jing to stay and Jing's response, see Cao Juren, *Wo yu wo de shijie*, 218–20.

41. Shen Ziqian et al., *Zhejiang yishi fengchao*, 118, 123. Jing phrased the issue as a difference between *ying ruhe jiaoren* (what a person ought to be taught) versus *ren ying ruhe jiao* (how a person ought to be taught).

42. Ibid., 121, 196.

43. Ibid., 118–21, 131–32.

44. Ibid., 122–23.

45. Ibid., 147–49, 224–26.

46. Ibid., 149, 217–18, 229–30, 232–33.

47. Ibid., 151–52, 261, 268, 270, 299. See also Jiang Danshu, "Feixiao yu Zhejiang diyi shifan de fan fengjian douzheng" [Critique of the concept of filial piety and the antifeudal struggle at Zhejiang First Normal], in Zhongguo shehui, *Wusi yundong huiyi lu*, 2:760–61.

48. Shen Ziqian et al., *Zhejiang yishi fengchao*, 155–56, 295–96.

49. Ibid., 156–57, 237–38.

50. Ibid., 159–60; see also the reprint there of reports by *Shenbao*, Shanghai's leading daily news, on pp. 237–41, by *Minguo ribao* on pp. 304–6, and by *Shishi xinbao* on pp. 307–09.

51. Ibid., 160, 240. Jiang Qi assumed his post as the new principal of First Normal School sometime later in the month. His took office after Jiang Menglin, the acting president of Beijing University, gave a speech in support of Jiang. Jiang Qi promised not to reverse Jing Ziyuan's liberal measures. Jiang Danshu, "Feixiao yu Zhejiang diyi shifan," 761–62.

52. First Normal School was staggered by a major tragedy on the evening of March 10, 1923. Poisoned rice was served to the students in the dining hall. Within an hour after dinner 24 students died, and 213 others fell critically ill. Although the chef and two students were later sent to the gallows, the case was never satisfactorily resolved. Zhejiang shengli diyi shifan xuexiao, ed., *Zhejiang shengli diyi shifan xuexiao du'an jishi* [A truthful record of the poison case at Zhejiang Provincial First Normal School] (Hangzhou: n.p., 1923), 1–2. The former student activist hanged in this case was Yu Zhangfa, one of the dozen or so activists visible in the petitioning and rallying activities in February–March 1920. The case drew wide attention from Shanghai and Beijing intellectuals.

53. Ruan Yicheng, "Yicheng zizhuan nianpu ji zishu," 656.

54. Ibid.

55. Shu Xincheng, *Wo he jiaoyu* [Education and I] (Taipei: Longwen chuban she, 1990), 166–67. Mao had published in 1919 an article contrasting Marx and Kropotkin. In the summer of 1920 he threw himself into the Hunan autonomy movement, attacking the old order as incapable of reforming itself. See Stuart Schram, *The Thought of Mao Tse-Tung* (Cambridge: Cambridge University Press, 1989), 20–26.

56. Xia personally served as Kaiming's chief editor. He was joined by his former First Normal student Fu Binran on the editorial staff. Cao Juren, *Wo yu wo de shijie*, 181–86; "Kaiming Shudian gudong mingce" [Roster of registered shareholders, Kaiming Bookstore], Ministry of Economics Archives, Institute of Modern History, Academia Sinica, Taipei, 17-23/ 25-(2).

57. Chen Yi was later executed by Chiang Kai-shek. On the February 28 Incident, see Chen Chongguang, Ye Mingxun, Lai Zehan, *Er er ba shijian yanjiu baogao* [Investigative report on the February 28 Incident] (Taipei: Shibao wenhua chuban qiye youxian gongsi, 1994). On Shen Zhongjiu's appointment to the committee, see p. 3.

58. Ge Maochun et al., *Wuzhengfu*, 2:761.

59. On Liu's later career, see Chapter 7.

60. "Chen Wangdao tongzhi luezhuan," 12.

61. Fu Binran, "Wusi qianhou," 749, and Shi Cuntong, "Huitou," September 24, pp. 2–3.

CHAPTER 9: UPROOTED PROVINCIALS

1. Wang Guangqi, "Gong du huzhu tuan" [Work-Study Corps], in Qinghua daxue Zhonggong dangshi jiaoyan zu, ed., *Fu Fa qingong jianxue yundong shiliao* [Historical sources on the Chinese diligent-work frugal-study movement in France] (Beijing: Beijing chuban she, 1979), 278.

2. (Shi) Cuntong to Zhiqian, "Juewu" section, *Minguo ribao*, April 16, 1920.

3. Shi Cuntong, "Huitou," September 24, 1920, p. 3.

4. Ibid.

5. Shortly after Shi and Yu moved in with the editors, Shen Xuanlu's daughter-in-law, Yang Zhihua, visited from Hangzhou. She found ten people, including the two senior editors, living under the same roof. Yang Zhihua, "Yang Zhihua de huiyi" [Yang Zhihua's recollections], in Zhongguo shehui kexue yuan jindai shi yanjiu shi and Zhongguo geming bowu guan dangshi yanjiu shi, eds., *Yida qianhou: Zhongguo Gongchandang diyi ci daibiao dahui qianhou ziliao xuanbian* [Before and after the First Party Congress: Selected edition of materials on the First Party Congress of the Chinese Communist Party] (Beijing: Renmin chuban she, 1980), 2:23, 25. Yang listed Chen Wangdao, Li Hanjun, Shen Xuanlu, Dai Jitao,

Shao Lizi, Liu Dabai, Shen Zhongjiu, Yu Xiusong, Shi Cuntong, and Ding Baolin.

6. Lü Fangshang, *Geming zhi zaiqi: Zhongguo Guomindang gaizu qian dui xin sichao de huiying, 1914–1924* [(Original English title) Rekindle the Revolution: The Kuomintang's Response to New Thought before the Reorganization, 1914–1924] (Taipei: Zhongyang yanjiu yuan jindai shi yanjiu suo, 1989), 43.

7. The law faculty in Japan's leading universities at this time was heavily under the influence of socialism and social legislatures. See Irwin Scheiner and Peter Duus, "Socialism, Liberalism, and Marxism, 1901–1931," in *The Cambridge History of Japan*, vol. 6, *The Twentieth Century*, ed. Peter Duus. (Cambridge: Cambridge University Press, 1988), 654–710.

8. Shao Lizi, "Dang chengli qianhou de yixie qingkuang" [Conditions before and after the founding of the Party], in Zhongguo shehui kexue yuan, *Yida qianhou*, 2:61.

9. See the chapters by Elizabeth Perry, Emily Honig, and Bryna Goodman in Frederic Wakeman, Jr., and Wen-hsin Yeh, eds., *Shanghai Sojourners* (Berkeley: Institute of East Asian Studies, University of California, Berkeley, 1992); and Emily Honig, *Creating Chinese Ethnicity: Subei People in Shanghai, 1850–1980* (New Haven: Yale University Press, 1992).

10. Shi Cuntong, "Gongdu huzhu tuan de shiyan he jiaoxun" [Experiment of and lessons from the Work-Study Corps], *Xingqi pinglun* 48 (May 1, 1920): 7.

11. Shi Cuntong spoke of "a style of life suitable for the dignity of men" in an open letter to a friend in the pages of the *Republican Daily*. See Zhemin's letter to Cuntong, "Juewu" section, *Minguo ribao*, April 10, 1920. Yu Xiusong spoke of the necessity to adopt "radical means" (*jijin de fangfa*) to restructure an urban society that was "capitalist" and exploitative. See "Yu Xiusong gei Luo Zhixiang de xin" [Yu Xiusong's letter to Luo Zhixiang], April 4, 1920, held in the First Party Congress Museum, reprinted in Zhonggong zhongyang dangshi ziliao zhengji weiyuan hui, ed., *Gongchan zhuyi xiaozu* [Communist small groups] (Beijing: Zhonggong dangshi ziliao chuban she, 1987), pt. 1, 63.

12. "Yu Xiusong gei Luo Zhixiang de xin," 64.

13. Shi Cuntong's letter to Zhiqian, *Minguo ribao*, April 16, 1920.

14. Shi Cuntong to Zhemin, "Juewu" section, *Minguo ribao*, April 11, 1920.

15. "Yu Xiusong gei Luo Zhixiang de xin," 63.

16. As early as the mid-1900s, Zhu Zhixin and Liao Zhongkai, members of the Revolutionary Alliance in Tokyo, were already engaged in reading and writing about social democracy. Liao Zhongkai was the translator, in 1906, of Henry George's *Progress and Poverty*, which appeared in *Minbao* (People's journal), the organ of the Revolutionary Alliance based in Tokyo.

Zhu Zhixin was credited as the first person to introduce socialism to a Chinese readership. Zhu and Liao wrote mainly about social democracy and showed sympathy for anarchism. They lost interest in the subject around 1907. See Martin Bernal's pioneering work, *Chinese Socialism to 1907* (Ithaca: Cornell University Press, 1976), 114, 222–23. Both Zhu Zhixin and Liao Zhongkai were identified with the left wing of of the Guomindang and died in Guangzhou at the hands of assassins.

17. Zhang Dongsun, editor of the Shanghai newspaper *Shishi xinbao*, was quoted as saying in late 1919 that "before the conclusion of the World War, not one person in China spoke of socialism; since the war ended, everyone spoke of socialism." Dirlik has pointed out that while there was merit to the second half of Zhang's statement, the first half was historically inaccurate. Zhang's remark nonetheless conveyed his impression of an outburst of interest on socialist issues in the wake of the May Fourth Movement. Dirlik, *Origins of Chinese Communism*, 60; see also ibid., 60–73, and Bernal, *Chinese Socialism.* So many discussions were over such vaguely articulated concepts, however, that the term *socialism* lost much of its descriptive specificity. It prompted Yang Duanliu, the American-trained economist, to complain: "Even those who have absolutely nothing to do with socialism try to invoke the term!" Yang Duanliu, "Guiguo zagan" [Miscellaneous thoughts on returning to my home country], *Taiping yang* [Pacific Ocean] 3, 6 (August 1920): 1–8.

18. *Dongfang zazhi* [Eastern miscellany] 18, 1 and 22 (1921).

19. The articles featured in the May 1919 (vol. 6, no. 5) issue of *New Youth* were Gu Zhaoxiong, "Makesi xueshuo" [Marx's teaching]; Huang Lingshuang, "Makesi xueshuo piping" [Critique of Marx's teaching]; Liu Binglin, "Makesi luezhuan" [Biographical sketch of Marx]; and the first half of Li Dazhao's two-part essay "Wo de Makesi zhuyi guan" [My views on Marxism]. Huang Lingshuang was a leading anarchist in Beijing at this time. The same issue of *New Youth* also carried the second half of Qiming's translation of an essay by Angelo S. Rapport that had appeared originally in the July 1917 issue of the *Edinburgh Review.* The translated piece was titled "Eguo geming de zhexue jichu" [Philosophical foundation of the Russian revolution]. The essay discussed the Decemberists and Aleksandr Herzen. Another essay, by Keshui, contained a biographical sketch of Bakunin.

20. (Dai) Jitao, "Eguo liang zhengfu de duihua zhengce" [China policies of two Russian governments], *Xingqi pinglun* 15 (September 14, 1919): 2.

21. Dai Jitao's piece appeared in the November 1919 issue of *Jianshe* (Construction), a Guomindang journal. In a second essay that appeared in April 1920, Dai hailed the Karakhan Manifesto as "unprecedented in history and unsurpassed in spiritual nobility." Echoing the *Communist*

Manifesto, Dai called on "all the plundered and oppressed" of this world to unite. To facilitate that process, he gave considerable space in the pages of both *Weekend Review* and *Construction* to the coverage of conditions in the new Russia. See (Dai) Jitao, "Eguo laonong zhengfu tonggao de zhenyi" [True meaning of the proclamation of the Russian labor-peasant government], *Xingqi pinglun* 45 (April 1, 1920): 2.

22. On Chen Duxiu as the founder of the Chinese Communist Party, see Feigon, *Chen Duxiu,* 137–65. According to Party historian Chen Shaokang, the founding of the Party can be traced to a critical conversation that took place between Chen Duxiu and Li Dazhao in January 1920 aboard a mule cart en route from Beijing to Tianjin, just before Chen's departure by ship for the south. During this trip the two men pledged to launch Party organizations in Beijing and Shanghai, respectively. Chen Shaokang, "Shanghai gongchan zhuyi xiaozu zongshu" [General account of the Shanghai Communist small groups], in Zhonggong zhongyang dangshi ziliao, *Gongchan zhuyi xiaozu,* 1:24. The phrase that is sometimes used is *Nan Chen bei Li, xiang yue jian dang* (Chen in the south and Li in the north joined together to create the Party); see ibid., 1:12. Chen Shaokang's presentation runs counter to a Western view that attributes the organizational launch of the Chinese Communist Party to a visit by Gregory Voitinsky, chief of the Far Eastern bureau of the Comintern in Irkutsk, with Li Dazhao in March 1920. See Dirlik, *Origins of Chinese Communism,* 149–50, but see also 195.

23. There has been a lack of consensus on the dates for the formation of the Marxism Study Societies in Shanghai and Beijing. The two dates most commonly given for Beijing are March and October 1920; those given for Shanghai are May and August 1920. The issue at stake is whether Beijing or Shanghai could claim the formation of the first proto-Communist organization in China. This dating attempt is difficult, of course, because the 1920 "organizations" were informal and erratic.

24. Chen Wangdao, "Huiyi dang chengli shiqi de yixie qingkuang" [Recollections of the founding days of the Party], in Zhongguo shehui kexue yuan, *Yida qianhou,* 21:20, 23.

25. Chen Shaokang, "Shanghai gongchan zhuyi," 24. Several of Dai Jitao's contemporaries recalled how he agonized over the choice between the Guomindang and the Marxism Study Society and even shed tears. Zhang Dongsun was firm about his membership in the Progressive Party and his loyalty to Liang Qichao, for which he was later denounced by the Communists and declared one of their top enemies.

26. Prior to this, the Wuhan organization had developed along two separate tracks. One involved the activities of Dong Biwu at the private Wuhan Middle School, which taught ideas of social reform and communal property. Another centered on Yun Daiying's Mutual Aid Society and a

bimonthly journal entitled *New Voice (Xin sheng),* which devoted space to the discussion of the Russian Revolution. See Dong Biwu, "Sili Wuhan zhongxue jianji" [Brief account of the private Wuhan middle school], in Zhonggong zhongyang dangshi ziliao, *Gongchan zhuyi xiaozu,* 1:435; see also "Wuhan gongchan zhuyi xiaozu zongshu" [General account of the Wuhan Communist small groups], in ibid., 349–55. Dirlik presents a more detailed but somewhat different account of the Hubei group in *Origins of Chinese Communism,* 166–68.

27. Zhonggong Hunan shengwei dangshi ziliao zhengji yanjiu weiyuan hui, ed., "Changsha gongchan zhuyi xiaozu zongshu" [General account of the Communist small groups in Changsha], in Zhonggong zhongyang dangshi ziliao, *Gongchan zhuyi xiaozu,* 2:474.

28. The Jinan Communist organization grew out of Chen Duxiu's acquaintance with Wang Leping, a member of the Shandong Provincial Assembly and owner of the Qilu Bookstore that distributed *New Youth* in Jinan. The Guangzhou Communist organization was formed by Chen Duxiu on his arrival in the city in late 1920. Chen Shaokang, "Shanghai gongchan," 46.

29. Yue Jiwei, *Xun zong mi ji* (Shanghai: Fanyi chuban gongsi, 1991), 23.

30. Principal Yang Mingzhai, a Shandong native who had returned from Russia, had presented himself and Gregory Voitinsky of the Comintern to Chen Duxiu earlier in the spring, having first met Li Dazhao in Beijing. On the staff at the school, see ibid., 25; *Gongchandang* [The Communist] 6 (July 7, 1921): 62.

31. Yue Jiwei, *Xun zong mi ji,* 25; Cao Jinghua, "Cao Jinghua de huiyi" [Cao Jinghua's recollections], in Zhonggong zhongyang dangshi ziliao, *Gongchan zhuyi xiaozu,* 1:202.

32. Cao Jinghua, "Cao Jinghua de huiyi," 1:202.

33. Yue Jiwei, *Xun zong mi ji,* 24.

34. Xu Zhizhen, "Guanyu xin Yuyangli liuhao de huodong qingxing" [About activities at the new Number 6 Yuyangli address], in Zhonggong zhongyang dangshi ziliao, *Gongchan zhuyi xiaozu,* 1:197. An ordinary day at the school included half a day of classroom attendance and half a day of study on one's own.

35. Ibid., 198; Bao Huiseng, "Huiyi Yuyangli liuhao he Zhongguo laodong zuhe shuji bu" [Recollections of Number 6 Yuyangli and the secretariat of the Chinese Labor Federation], in Zhongguo shehui kexue yuan, *Yida qianhou,* 2:352. Li Qihan was the founder of the mechanics' and printers' unions, the first labor organizations formed under Communist sponsorship. Elizabeth Perry sees it as "probably not coincidental," given the dominance of the Zhejiang presence in the early Chinese Communist Party in Shanghai, that "this breakthrough occurred in the trades of

metalworking and printing, which were dominated by artisans from Zhejiang." Perry, *Shanghai on Strike*, 73–74.

36. Xu Zhizhen, "Guanyu xin Yuyangli," 198.

37. Liu Shaoqi, for instance, appeared to have shared quarters with Anhuiese as well as Hunanese. He had also maintained multiple addresses at the same time. Ibid., 198.

38. Yue Jiwei, *Xun zong mi ji*, 25.

39. Shanghai Municipal Police files, no. 4,131.

40. Xu Zhizhen, "Guanyu xin Yuyangli," 198.

41. The First Party Congress commenced on July 23, 1921. When delegates to the congress were engaged in the third day of their discussion, a stranger broke into Li Hanjun's living room on Wangzhi Road where the meeting was being held, which prompted the delegates to disperse instantly through the back door. Li Hanjun and Chen Gongbo stayed behind. Moments later, French police arrived to conduct a careful search and close questioning. Before departing the police lectured the two men on how the Russian system was unsuitable for China. Chen Tanqiu, "Dixi ci daibiao dahui de huiyi" [Recollections of the First Party Congress], in Zhongguo shehui kexue yuan, *Yida qianhou*, 2:288. Because of the underground nature of the early Chinese Communist Party, few documents survived from the First Party Congress, and none of the participants was able to reconstruct the exact dates of the First Party Congress. When the Party commenced a tradition in Yan'an in the 1940s to celebrate its own founding, it picked July 1 as the first day of the Party congress. July 23 was later determined to be the actual date for the opening of the congress. See Shao Weizheng, "Yida zhaokai riqi he chuxi renshu de kaozheng" [Empirical inquiry into the conference dates and number of participants of the First Party Congress], in *Yida huiyi lu* [First Party Congress memoirs] (Beijing: Zhishi chuban she, 1980), 130–58.

42. Chen Duxiu left Guangzhou on September 10 for Shanghai. He had been elected the secretary general of the Chinese Communist Party on the final day of the First Party Congress (July 30), which by then had been moved to a boat on the South Lake (Nanhu) in Jiaxing, Zhejiang. *Yida huiyi lu*, 69.

43. *Minguo ribao*, October 22, 1921.

44. Shao Lizi, "Shehui zhuyi yu gongqi" [Socialism and communal sharing of women], *Minguo ribao*, October 21, 1921.

45. *Minguo ribao*, October 6, 1921; October 20, 1921; and October 26, 1921. Maring, the Comintern representative, was believed to have worked hard to secure Chen Duxiu's release. He was also believed to have contributed to the payment of the fine as well as the initial bail for Chen's wife and another comrade, who were arrested together with Chen. Maring's efforts in this connection helped to relax his relationship with Chen Duxiu,

which had been strained only two weeks earlier by Chen Duxiu's displeasure over Maring's selection of Zhang Tailei, Maring's Chinese interpreter, to go to Japan as a Comintern representative on liaison mission without prior consultation with Chen Duxiu. See Ishikawa Yoshihiro, "Waka ki hi no Shi Zuntou" [Young man Shi Cuntong], *Toyo shi kenkyu* (September 1994): 302.

46. *Minguo ribao*, October 20, 1921.

47. "Beijing Gongchan zhuyi zuzhi de baogao" [Report by the Communist cell organization in Beijing], in Zhongyang dang'an guan, *Zhongguo Gongchandang diyi ci daibiao dahui dang'an ziliao zeng ding ben*, 21.

48. In addition to Shanghai, Beijing, and Guangzhou, Communist cell organizations were created in Wuhan, Changsha, Jinan, and Sichuan in 1920. About the Sichuan organization, which went unrepresented at the First Party Congress and was little known until the publication of files formerly belonging to the liaison office of the Chinese Communist Party at the Comintern, see "Sichuan sheng Chongqing gongchan zhuyi zuzhi de baogao" [Report by the Communist organization of Chongqing, Sichuan Province], in ibid., 27–32. Van de Ven used this material in his discussion of the early Communists, in *From Friend to Comrade*, 73–75.

49. Luo Zhanglong, "Huiyi Beijing daxue Makesi xueshuo yanjiu hui" [Recollections of the Marxism Study Society at Beijing University], in Zhonggong zhongyang dangshi ziliao, *Gongchan zhuyi xiaozu*, 1:319.

50. Cai Yuanpei delivered brief remarks and posed for photographs with the society's members on this occasion. See ibid., 311.

51. Ibid., 311–12.

52. This information is based on Zhang Guotao's recollection. See *Gongchan zhuyi xiaozu*, 1:335.

53. "Beijing Gongchan zhuyi zuzhi de baogao," 17.

54. Liu Renjing, "Beijing Makesi zhuyi yanjiu hui de qingkuang" [About the Marxism Study Society in Beijing], in Zhonggong zhongyang dangshi ziliao, *Gongchan zhuyi xiaozu*, 1:321–22.

55. "Beijing Gongchan zhuyi zuzhi de baogao," 15–19.

56. David Strand shows that contrary to the stereotypical images presented by the young Communists, the ricksha men, at least by the late 1920s, had "met, petitioned, marched, protested, fought, and finally rioted in a continuous fashion until they were among the most politically active groups in the city." See Strand's ground-breaking work, *Rickshaw Beijing: City People and Politics in the 1920s* (Berkeley: University of California Press, 1989), 243–51. The quotation is from pp. 242–43.

57. "Beijing Gongchan zhuyi zuzhi de baogao," 16.

58. Ibid., 17; Cai Hesen, "Wo dang chansheng de beijing ji qi lishi shiming" [Background for the birth of our Party and our Party's historical

mission], in Zhongyang dang'an guan, *Zhongguo Gongchandang diyi ci daibiao*, 64.

59. "Guangzhou gongchandang de baogao" [Report by the Communist Party of Guangzhou], in ibid., 23.

60. "Shanghai, Guangzhou, Wuhan, Changsha ying jinxing zhi gong-zuo" [Activities to be carried out in Shanghai, Guangzhou, Wuhan, Chang-sha], in ibid., 36.

61. Maring, "Report of Comrade H. Maring to the Executive," July 11, 1922. This document is held in the Sneevliet Archive in Amsterdam. For a reprint of the German original with an English translation, see Tony Saich, *The Origins of the First United Front in China: The Role of Sneevliet (Alias Maring)* (Leiden: E. J. Brill, 1991), 1:286–325. The reference to the Guangzhou Seamen's Union is on p. 322.

62. "Gei Guoji Gongchan de baogao" [Report to the Comintern], June 30, 1922, in Zhongyang dang'an guan, *Zhongguo Gongchandang diyi ci daibiao*, 38.

63. Maring, "Report," 97–98. Saich, *Origins of the First United Front,* 1:317–23. Maring left Shanghai on April 24, 1922, "after some discussions with leaders of the Communist Organization and with members of the KMT (Guomindang) Central Committee there. I suggested to our comrades that they give up their exclusive attitude towards the KMT and that they begin to develop activities within the KMT, through which one can gain access much more easily to the workers and soldiers in the South" (Saich, 1:323).

64. Maring, "Report," 93; Saich, *Origins of the First United Front,* 1:308.

65. "Shanghai, Guangzhou, Wuhan, Changsha ying jinxing de gong-zuo," 34–35.

66. (Dai) Jitao, "Guojia zhuyi zhi pochan yu shehui de geming [Bank-ruptcy of nation-states and the social revolution]," *Xingqi pinglun* 47 (April 25, 1920): 1–4.

67. "Laodong ri jinian" [Commemoration on Labor Day], *Xingqi pinglun* 48 (May 1, 1920): 1.

68. Benshe tongren, "Xingqi pinglun kanxing zhongzhi de xuanyan" [Declaration on the discontinuation of publication of *Weekend Review*] *Xingqi pinglun* 53 (June 6, 1920): 4.

69. Shi Cuntong was questioned by the foreign affairs department of the Japanese police on June 17, 1921, about the nature of his stay and the sources of his support. He replied that he came as a student with the help of Dai Jitao (Tianchou), who had arranged for him to contact Miyazaki; that he had been "studying English in the morning and Japanese and economics in the afternoon" ever since his arrival in Japan, and that his goal was to enroll in the Economics Department of Keio University. He claimed that

he was fully supported by his family, which sent him one hundred yuan every month. Miyazaki told the police, however, that Shi Cuntong had been supported by Dai Jitao, who sent him a stipend of fifty yuan every month. Ishikawa, "Waka ki hi no Shi Zuntou," 299.

70. Ibid., 295. The exact address of the house was Takada Mura 1556 Banchi, Mitsu Zakikan. This is the address printed in the anarchist journal *Ziyou* (Freedom) that alerted the Japanese police to Shi Cuntong's whereabouts in Tokyo. On the Miyazaki family, see Marius B. Jansen, *The Japanese and Sun Yat-sen* (Cambridge, Mass.: Harvard University Press, 1967).

71. Shi Cuntong, "Zhongguo Gongchandang chengli shiqi de jige wenti" [A few problems at the time of the founding of the Chinese Communist Party], in Zhongguo shehui kexue yuan, *Yida qianhou*, 2:34–35; Hu Juewen, Hu Zi'ang, Sun Xiaocun, Zhou Shiguan, Feng Hefa. "Minzhu geming shiqi de yingyong zhanshi Shi Fuliang tongzhi" [Comrade Shi Fuliang, brave warrior during the phase of democratic revolution], *People's Daily*, June 17, 1982. Shi Cuntong (Fuliang) was listed, along with Chen Duxiu, Li Hanjun, Chen Wangdao, Li Da, Yu Xiusong, Chen Gongpei, Shen Xuanlu as among the eight founders of the first Marxism Study Society that led to the creation of the Chinese Communist Party in 1921. The appearance of this essay in *People's Daily* in 1982 signaled a new openness in official Chinese historiography on the question of the origins of Chinese Communism, which until then had been much obfuscated by constructions of Party history strictly from a perspective based on the activities of Mao. On Yamakawa Hitoshi, Sakai Toshihiko, and Takabatake Motoyuki in the context of Taisho socialism, see Germaine Hoston, *Marxism and the Crisis of Development in Prewar Japan* (Princeton: Princeton University Press, 1986), 3–75. On Kawakami Hajime, see Gail Lee Bernstein, *Japanese Marxist: A Portrait of Kawakami Hajime, 1879–1946* (Cambridge, Mass.: Harvard University Press, 1976).

72. Karl Korsch, *Marxism and Philosophy* (London: NLB, 1970), 136. See also Franz Mehring, *Karl Marx: The Story of His Life* (New York: Covici, Friede, 1935), 538.

73. Ishikawa, "Waka ki ho no Shi Zuntou," 301. "Lenin and the Bolsheviks found in . . . Marx's *Critique of the Gotha Programme* (Marx and Engels, 1875–1891) the justification of their revolutionary and insurrectionary tactics." David L. Sills, ed., *International Encyclopaedia of the Social Sciences* (New York: Macmillan and Free Press, 1968), 14:508.

74. Shi Cuntong's edited volumes in the early 1920s included *Laodong yundong shi* (History of the labor movement) and *Makesi xueshuo gaiyao* (Succint summary of Marxism), both based on Takabatake Motoyuki, *Makesi zhuyi yu weiwu shiguan* (Marxism and historical materialism), which included the writings of Kawakami Hajime, and a series in social and

economic theories featuring Shi's commentaries and translations of Kawakami and Yamakawa Hitoshi. Ishikawa Yoshihiro, "Marukusu shugi no denha to Chukoku Kyosanto no ketsusei" [Spread of Marxism and the development of the Chinese Communist Party], *Chukoku kokumin kakumei no kenkyū* [Studies on the Chinese revolution] (Kyoto: Kyoto University Press, 1992), 424, 427, 435, 437, 443–51.

75. The first piece, entitled "Makesi de gongchan zhuyi," was published in *Xin qingnian* 9, 4 (August 1, 1921). The second piece, "Weiwu shiguan zai Zhongguo de yingyong," was completed on August 27, 1921, and appeared in the "Awakening" section of Shanghai's *Minguo ribao* on September 8, 1921. Both pieces were selected for reprint in Zhongguo shehui kexue yuan, *Yida qianhou* (1:327–45).

76. Ishikawa, "Waka ki hi no Shi Zuntou," 301.

77. Xin qingnian she bianji bu, ed., *Shehui zhuyi taolun ji* [Discussions on socialism: An anthology] (Guangzhou: Xin qingnian she, 1922). This volume is a selection of twenty-five essays, including five pieces by Shi Cuntong, and amounts to a compilation of early Party canons. It is telling that few of the essays in the 1922 anthology made their way into *Liu da yiqian—Dang de lishi cailiao* [Before the Sixth Party Congress: Historical materials on the Party] (Yan'an, 1942; reprint Beijing: Renmin chuban she, 1980), an authorized collection issued by the Central Secretariat of the Chinese Communist Party in 1942 at Yan'an. The essays have reappeared in recent editions released in the 1980s such as Zhongguo shehui kexue yuan, *Yida qianhou*.

78. See Zhou Fohai's letter to Shi Cuntong, dated April 19, 1921, in Ishikawa, "Waka ki hi no Shi Zuntou," 298.

79. Shi Fuliang, "*Zhongguo Gongchandang chengli.*" On Peng Pai, see Roy Hofheinz, Jr., *The Broken Wave: The Chinese Communist Peasant Movement, 1922–1928* (Cambridge, Mass.: Harvard University Press, 1977).

80. Ishikawa "Waka ki hi no Shi Zuntou," 298–99; Shi Fuliang, "Zhongguo Gongchandang chengli," 2:34–35.

81. This account is based on the research of Ishikawa Yoshihiro, who consulted the archival collections on foreign affairs at the Japanese foreign ministry, especially the collections on radicalism and Chinese students in Japan. Ishikawa also examined a photocopy of Shi Cuntong's depositions taken at the Tokyo municipal court on December 23, 1921, prepared by the court clerk, with the defense lawyer's comments written in the margin. See Ishikawa, "Waka ki hi no Shi Zuntou," 308–9. The information in the next four paragraphs is from ibid., 295–96, 299–300.

82. On the hiatus in the development of the Japanese socialist movement between the Meiji and the Taisho reigns, see Scheiner and Duus, "Socialism, Liberalism, and Marxism," and Hoston, *Marxism in Prewar*

Japan, 19. The "winter period" was inaugurated with the execution in 1911 of the anarchist Kotoku Shusui, who was convicted on charges of high treason.

83. The Comintern Far Eastern Bureau in Shanghai was the "communications hub" and the center of "a series of high-grade spy rings around the world" in the late 1920s and 1930s. For a succint explanation on how the bureau operated, see Frederic Wakeman, Jr., *Policing Shanghai 1927–1937* (Berkeley: University of California Press, 1994), 146.

84. Ishikawa, "Waka ki hi no Shi Zuntou," 302.

85. Ibid., 304.

86. George M. Beckmann and Okubo Genji, *The Japanese Communist Party, 1922–1945* (Stanford: Stanford University Press, 1969), 30–35; Hu Juewen et al., "Shi Fuliang."

87. Ishikawa, "Waka ki hi no Shi Zuntou," 304–5.

88. Ibid., 305.

89. Writers with a national reputation commanded high payments. As soon as Chen Duxiu arrived in Shanghai he was offered by Commercial Press, Shanghai's largest publishing house, an honorary advisory position on its editorial board, which came with a monthly stipend of three hundred yuan. Some writers, such as Li Da and Li Hanjun, were paid a high rate of five yuan per one thousand characters for their translations of Japanese Marxism. See Mao Dun, *Wo zouguo de daolu* [The path that I have taken] (Hong Kong: Sanlian shudian, 1981), 155. Most others, however, had to struggle for the acceptance of their submissions, and the rate was often determined at the discretion of the editors.

90. Chen Gongbo, "Guangdong Gongchandang de baogao" [Report by the Guangdong Communist Party], in Zhonggong Guangdong sheng wei dangshi yanjiu weiyuan hui bangong shi and Guangdong sheng dang'an guan, eds., *Yida qianhou de Guangdong dang zuzhi*, [Party organization in Guangdong before and after the First Congress] (Dongguan: Guangdong sheng dang'an guan, 1981), 1.

91. Shi Fuliang, "Zhongguo Gongchandang chengli," 2:37; Shi Fuliang, "Zhongguo shehui zhuyi qingnian tuan chengli qianhou de yixie qingkuang" [Conditions before and after the formation of the Chinese Socialist Youth Corps], in Zhongguo shehui kexue yuan, *Yida qianhou*, 2:73.

92. Shi Fuliang, "Zhongguo shehui zhuyi," 2:73.

93. Tan Pingshan, "Zhi Guochang xiansheng" [Letter to Guochang (Shi Cuntong)], in Zhonggong Guangdong, *Yida qianhou de Guangdong*, 6; Chunmu [Zhang Tailei], "Zhi Wenliang xiong" [To Wenliang], in Zhonggong Guangdong, *Yida qianhou de Guangdong*, 10. Existing sources on the early Chinese Communist movement provide little information as to how the Party financed its activities. There was little indication, based on the

fragments of information that have survived, that the Party attempted careful maintenance of its own financial records.

94. Chunmu (Zhang Tailei), "Zhi Hesen, Xiusong, Guochang" [Letter to Cai Hesen, Yu Xiusong, Shi Cuntong], in Zhonggong Guangdong, *Yida qianhou de Guangdong*, 8. The Guangzhou branch had attempted to finance itself by asking its members to contribute 10 percent of their income. It achieved uneven success trying to collect this contribution. See Yuan, "Zhi Xiusong xiong" [Letter to Yu Xiusong], in Zhonggong Guangdong, *Yida qianhou de Guangdong*, 13; Chen Gongbo, "Guangdong gongchandang de baogao," 1.

95. Shi Fuliang, "Zhongguo Gongchandang chengli," 2:37. Li Dazhao secured Shi Cuntong's release on this occasion.

96. Shi Fuliang, "Zhongguo shehui zhuyi," 2:75. The corps elected Yun Daiying along with Zhang Tailei to take responsibility.

CHAPTER 10: SHANGHAI SPRING

1. Qin Yingjun and Zhang Zhanbin, eds., *Da lang tao sha: Zhonggong yida renwu zhuan* [Waves washing away the beach sand: Individual biographies of the First Party Congress of the Chinese Communist Party] (Beijing: Hongqi chuban she, 1991), 271–72.

2. Chen Gongbo, "Wo yu Gongchandang" [I and the Communist Party], in Zhishi chuban she, *Yida huiyi lu*, 73–75.

3. Zhang Guotao, "Changxindian gongren faqi laodong buxi xuexiao" [Changxindian workers initiated the labor adult school], *Laodong jie* 15 (November 21, 1920), reprinted in Sheng Renxue, ed., *Zhang Guotao nianpu ji yanlun* [Zhang Guotao: Chronological biography and writings] (Beijing: Jiefangjun chuban she, 1985), 99–101.

4. "Beijing Gongchan zhuyi zuzhi de baogao," 18–21.

5. These meetings took place in Shanghai. Zhang Guotao was accompanied by Zhang Tailei. Sheng Renxue, *Zhang Guotao nianpu*, 6.

6. Ibid.

7. Van de Ven refers to Li Hanjun and his close associates Chen Wangdao and Shen Xuanlu, both from Zhejiang, as a group of "intellectualist" Party members. See Van de Ven, *From Friend to Comrade*, 63–64.

8. Cai Hesen, "Wo dang chansheng," 65–70.

9. Ibid.

10. Qin Yingjun and Zhang Zhanbin, *Da lang tao sha*, 277.

11. Chen Gongbo, "Wo yu Gongchandang," 73–74.

12. Qin Yingjun and Zhang Zhanbin, *Da lang tao sha*, 284.

13. See Bao Huiseng's quotation of Li Hanjun's own remarks in Bao Huiseng, "Huainian Li Hanjun xiansheng" [Remembering Mr. Li Hanjun], *Dangshi ziliao congkan*, no. 2, 1980.

14. Qin Yingjun and Zhang Zhanbin, *Da lang tao sha*, 284.

15. Cai Hesen, "Wo dang chansheng," 69. Neither did Li Hanjun's disassociation with the Communist Party disqualify him as a Communist in the minds of non-Communists. During the height of the White Terror in Wuchang in 1927 he was arrested and then shot, on December 17, by the soldiers of the Guangxi warlord Hu Zongyi. In August 1952 Mao Zedong awarded Li Hanjun the honor of being a "comrade" and a "martyr," on behalf of the Party that had expelled Li and in ultimate recognition of Li's unassailable credentials as a Communist. See Qin Yingjun and Zhang Zhanbin, *Da lang tao sha*, 291.

16. Cai Hesen, "Wo dang chansheng," 67.

17. Shi Cuntong, "Women yao zenmeyang gan shehui geming," *The Communist* 5 (July 1921): 10–32. The essay was completed on May 16, 1921. Subsequent page references to the article appear in parentheses in the text.

18. *Wuchan jieji*, or propertyless class, is the ambiguous translation of *proletariat* into Chinese.

19. Shi Cuntong's understanding of Social Darwinism was most likely mediated by Yan Fu's influential translation of Thomas Huxley's 1893 Romanes Lectures titled "Evolution and Ethics," which appeared in Chinese in 1898 under the title *Tianyan lun* (On evolution). See Schwartz, *In Search of Wealth and Power*, 98–112.

20. The state of Guomindang finance at this time remains poorly understood. According to Lin Nengshi, although Guangdong was China's second richest province in the late Qing, its provincial finances deteriorated drastically in the 1910s. This financial stress helped to account for Sun Yat-sen's forced departure from Guangzhou in May 1918. Besides using provincial revenue, Sun had recourse to financial contributions from overseas Chinese in Southeast Asia. Japanese consular reports from Guangzhou suggested that he was also receiving Comintern financial support in the mid-1920s. See Lin Nengshi, "Diyi ci hufa yundong de jingfei wenti, 1917–1918" [Budgetary questions during the first campaign to uphold the constitution, 1917–1918], paper presented at the Centennial Symposium on Sun Yat-sen's Founding of the Guomindang for Revolution, Taipei, November 19–23, 1994. See also V. Usov, "Soviet Aid to China in Training Party and Revolutionary Cadres," *Far Eastern Affairs* 6 (1987): 74–81.

21. Despite the Guomindang Historical Commission's recent policy to open up archival collections from this period, it remains difficult for scholars to gain direct access to these primary sources. Only recently were some sources made available in published volumes edited by archival authorities. Because of the importance of the subject, however, there has been no dearth of published scholarly works that pertain to the history of this period, most of which focus attention on the role of the Comintern. A partial list includes

C. Martin Wilbur and Julie Lien-ying How, eds., *Documents on Communism, Nationalism, and Soviet Advisers in China, 1918–1927* (New York: Columbia University Press, 1956); Wilbur and How, *Missionaries of Revolution: Soviet Advisers and Nationalist China, 1920–1927* (Cambridge, Mass.: Harvard University Press, 1989); Allen S. Whiting, *Soviet Policies in China, 1917–1924* (Stanford: Stanford University Press, 1953); Robert C. North, *Moscow and Chinese Communists* (Stanford: Stanford University Press, 1963); Jane L. Price, *Cadres, Commanders, and Commissars: The Training of the Chinese Communist Leadership, 1920–1945* (Boulder, Col.: Westview, 1976); and Saich, *Origins of the First United Front.*

22. For a discussion of Shanghai University, see Yeh, *Alienated Academy,* chap. 4. The meeting on December 28 was attended by Yu Youren, Liao Zhongkai, Zhang Qiubai, Peng Jianren, Xie Chi, Ye Chucang, Lin Yeming, Sun Jing, and the Guomindang's top fundraiser, Zhang Ji; Wang Jingwei, a committee member, was absent. Guomindang dangshi yanjiu hui, [Archives of the Historical Commission of the Chinese Nationalist Party] Huanlonglu dang, 0-2/1, file no. 11.

23. Yeh, *Alienated Academy,* 141–42.

24. Ibid., 147–48.

25. Ding Ling, "Wo suo renshi de Qu Qiubai tongzhi" [Comrade Qu Qiubai as I knew him], in Yi Qiubai bianji xiaozhu, ed., *Yi Qiubai* [Remembering (Qu) Qiubai] (Beijing: Renmin wenxue chuban she, 1981), 132–40.

26. Wang Yizhi, "Zou xiang geming—wusi huiyi" [Marching toward revolution—remembering May Fourth], in Zhongguo shehui kexue yuan jindai shi yanjiu suo, ed., *Wusi yundong huiyi lu* [May Fourth memoirs] (Beijing: Zhongguo shehui kexue chuban she, 1979), 1:508. The following six paragraphs on Wang Yizhi are from ibid., 510–15. The quotations are from 511–13.

27. Shi Fuliang, *Rensheng wenti wujiang: Zuoren, zuoshi, ji nannü wenti* [Five lectures on problems in our lives: Integrity, career, and men-women relationships] (Shanghai: Xinlu shudian, 1947), 82.

28. Shanghai zhoubao she, ed., *Dangdai shisheng* [Contemporary historical gazette] (Shanghai: Shanghai zhoubao she, 1933), 324, 332–34.

29. Hu Juewen et al., "Shi Fuliang." Zhong Fuguang remained Shi Cuntong's loyal companion for the rest of his life. My own experience speaking with colleagues in China is that, with the exception of Party-history specialists, few people recognize the name Shi Cuntong, whereas many more have heard of Shi Fuliang and his activities in the 1940s. Shi is also much better known not by his own works but by the accomplishment of his eldest son, Shi Guanglan, a composer who acquired national fame for many highly popular lyrics.

30. Minutes of District Branch Party Delegate Meeting, Shanghai, December 12, 1923. Goumindang Historical Archives, Huanlonglu, 0-2/1, no. 1.

31. Ibid.

32. Party affairs in southern China (Guangdong, Guangxi, and Yunnan) were reported directly to the Central Committee in Guangzhou. Ibid., nos. 1, 3.

33. The organizational chart of the Shanghai Executive Committee on February 25, 1924, showed that there were three standing members of the secretariat: Hu Hanmin, Ye Chucang, Wang Jingwei. The most important department under their direction was the Department of Organization, which was headed by Hu Hanmin and staffed by Mao Zedong as its executive secretary. Shi Cuntong worked under Wang Jingwei as Director of Propaganda. Ibid., 0-2/5, no. 1.

34. Ibid., 0-2/1, no. 3.

35. Ibid., no. 1. Ye Chucang, Shen Dingyi, Lin Boqu, and Guan Nan were appointed.

36. The point of this chapter is not to highlight Mao Zedong's participation in the Shanghai Party organization during the First United Front, but research conducted in the Huanlonglu files held at the Archives of the Guomindang Historical Commission shows that Mao was a key participant in the headquarters of the Shanghai Executive Committee between February and April 1924. He was present at four important meetings—on February 25, February 28, March 6, March 20—that laid down the organizational plan and mobilizational campaign of the Party in Shanghai during the First United Front. On February 25, the main organizational plan (*zuzhi zhangcheng*) and full roster of the Shanghai Executive Committee were drafted and adopted. On February 28, the operating procedures (*banshi tongze*) of the committee were discussed and adopted. On March 6, the committee voted to organize a unit to promote commoners' education. It also decided to structure the Party's Shanghai local membership by workplace. On March 20, the committee voted to create a course on current events at Shanghai University for propaganda purposes. It also summoned the heads of the Guomindang's Shanghai districts to discuss interpretations of the Party's platforms and charters. In conjunction with the campaign to promote the commoners' schools, the committee laid down detailed organizational plans for the departments of workers, peasants, women, and students. This last meeting was chaired by Hu Hanmin; Mao was the note-taker. This is the earliest document known to the scholarly world with Mao wielding the brush in his own hand. See ibid., 0-2/5, 0-2/6. Mao was also the author, on March 31, 1924, of a memo from the Organization Department of the Shanghai Executive Committee to a "Comrade Shouyuan" of the fifth subdistrict of the third district of the

Party in Shanghai. The third district corresponded to the French Concession. A high proportion of the members there were Guomindang veterans
unhappy with the reorganization of the party under the United Front. Ibid.,
no. 9,722. I am grateful to Stuart Schram for sharing thoughts on the
significance of these documents with me. Note that *Mao Zedong nianpu*
(Chronological biography of Mao Zedong) does not mention the February
28, 1924, meeting. The biography also omits the motion on the Party's local
organization in its entry under March 6, 1924.

37. Guomindang Historical Archives, Huanlonglu, 0-2/1, nos. 2, 7.

38. Ibid., no. 5.

39. Ibid., no. 9,631.

40. Ibid., no. 9,643.

41. Ibid., no. 9,631.

42. Ibid., nos. 9,643, 9,574; Honig, *Creating Chinese Ethnicity*, 44–53.

43. Guomindang Historical Archives, Huanlonglu, nos. 9,578, 9,573,
9,577, 9,578, 9,704.

44. Ibid., nos. 9,713, 9,728. File no. 9,717 supplied evidence for a comparable case with the Number 17 subdistrict in the French Concession.

45. Ibid., nos. 9,966, 9,585, 9,593, and 9,794.

46. Ibid., no. 9,794.

47. Ibid., 0-2/1, no. 11.

48. "Shanghai zhixing bu zhiwei huiyi jilu, February 25, 1924," in ibid.,
0-2/5, nos. 1, 4.

49. For the Commoners' School, the Party paid a total bill of 164 yuan
for the procurement of desks, chairs, stools, blackboards, electric lights, and
so forth, plus another 22 yuan for rent. It also budgeted a monthly operating cost of 80 yuan thereafter, which included a stipend of 30 yuan for
the school's director. Ibid., nos. 9,697, 11,124.

50. Ibid., no. 11,088; "Qingnian dang wu weiyuan hui jilu" [Minutes
of meeting, youth committee], in ibid., no. 0-2/8.

51. Ibid., no. 0-2/8.

52. Nicholas R. Clifford, *Shanghai, 1925: Urban Nationalism and the
Defense of Foreign Privilege* (Ann Arbor: Center for Chinese Studies,
University of Michigan, 1979); Perry, *Shanghai on Strike*, 77, 81–87.

53. Chen Gongbo, "Jinhou de Guomindang" [The Nationalist Party
hereafter], *Geming pinglun* [Revolutionary commentary] 1 (May 1928):
4, 8.

54. Shi Cuntong's principal ideas in this period are contained in "Huifu
shisan nian gaizu jingshen" [Revive the spirit of reorganization of 1924],
Geming pinglun 5 (June 1928): 10–19; "Chengshi xiao zichan jieji yu
minzhu geming" [Urban petit bourgeoisie and democratic revolution],
Geming pinglun 9 (July 1928): 11–16; "Zhongguo geming yu xuesheng

yundong" [Chinese revolution and the student movement], *Geming pinglun* 18 (September 1928): 7–11.

55. On the left wing of the Guomindang—especially the Reorganization Faction led by Wang Jingwei—between 1924 and 1930, see Yamada Tatsuo's important study, *Chūgoku kokumintō saha no kenkyū* [Study of the left wing of the Chinese Nationalist Party] (Tokyo: Keio University Press, 1980). Wang Shuixiang, Chen Liejiong, and Wang Zuhan, "Aiguo minzhu yingyong zhanshi Shi Fuliang" [Patriotic, democratic, brave warrior Shi Fuliang], *Zhejiang wenshi ziliao xuanji* 41 (1989): 94–95.

56. Gu Mei's book is entitled *Xiandai Zhongguo jiqi jiaoyu* (Modern China and its education). Li Gongpu's ideas can be found in the Shanghai-based biweekly, *Dushu shenghuo* (Learning and living), which he edited. The journal was inaugurated in November 1934, and besides Li's own writings, it featured those of Liu Ti, Ai Siqi, and Xia Zimei (Zhengnong).

57. Shi Cuntong, *Zhongguo xiandai jingji shi* [History of modern Chinese economy] (Shanghai: Liangyou tushu yinshua gongsi, 1932), preface, 368–404; also Hu Juewen et al., "Shi Fuliang."

58. Hu Juewen et al., "Shi Fuliang"; Xu Yaofang, "Shi Fuliang de baobei" [Shi Fuliang's treasure], *Jinhua ribao*, July 6, 1992.

59. Xu Yaofang, "Shi Fuliang de baobei"; interview in Yecun, June 1992. The Confucian motto, *ban geng ban du*, was still visible when I visited the house in June 1992.

60. Hu Juewen et al., "Shi Fuliang"; Wang Shuixiang, et al., "Aiguo minzhu," 99–101.

61. Wang Shuixiang et al., "Aiguo minzhu," 102–5.

62. Hu Juewen et al., "Shi Fuliang"; Wang Shuixiang et al., "Aiguo minzhu," 108.

Bibliography

Alitto, Guy. *The Last Confucian: Liang Shu-ming and the Chinese Dilemma of Modernity.* Berkeley: University of California Press, 1979.

An Zhijie [Sheng Shitong]. "Sheng Shicai pohai meifu Yu Xiusong jingguo" [How Sheng Shicai persecuted his brother-in-law Yu Xiusong]. *Zhuanji wenxue* (Taipei) 53, 2 (August 1988):25–29.

Averill, Stephen C. "Local Elites and Communist Revolution in the Jiangxi Hill County." In *Chinese Local Elites and Patterns of Dominance,* edited by Joseph W. Esherick and Mary Backus Rankin. Berkeley: University of California Press, 1990.

Bao Huiseng. "Huainian Li Hanjun xiansheng" [Remembering Mr. Li Hanjun]. *Dangshi ziliao congkan,* no. 2, 1980.

———. "Huiyi Yuyangli liuhao he Zhongguo laodong zuhe shuji bu" [Recollections of Number 6 Yuyangli and the secretariat of the Chinese Labor Federation]. In *Yida qianhou: Zhongguo Gongchandang diyi ci daibiao dahui qianhou ziliao xuanbian* [Before and after the First Party Congress: Selected edition of materials on the First Party Congress of the Chinese Communist Party], edited by Zhongguo shehui kexue yuan xiandai shi yanjiu shi and Zhongguo geming bowu guan dangshi yanjiu shi. Vol. 2. Beijing: Renmin chuban she, 1980.

Barkan, Lenore. "Patterns of Power: Forty Years of Elite Politics in a Chinese County." In *Chinese Local Elites and Patterns of Dominance,* edited by Joseph W. Esherick and Mary Backus Rankin. Berkeley: University of California Press, 1990.

Bays, Daniel H. *China Enters the Twentieth Century: Chang Chih-tung and the Issues of a New Age, 1895–1909.* Ann Arbor: University of Michigan Press, 1978.

Beattie, Hilary J. *Land and Lineage in China: A Study of T'ung-ch'eng County, Anhwei in the Ming and Ch'ing Dynasties.* Cambridge: Cambridge University Press, 1979.

Beckmann, George M., and Okubo Genji. *The Japanese Communist Party, 1922–1945.* Stanford: Stanford University Press, 1969.

"Beijing Gongchan zhuyi zuzhi de baogao" [Report by the Communist cell organization in Beijing]. In *Zhongguo Gongchandang diyi ci daibiao dahui dang'an ziliao zeng ding ben* [Expanded edition, Archival materials on the First Party Congress of the Chinese Communist Party], edited by Zhongyang dang'an guan [Central Party Archives]. Beijing: Renmin chuban she, 1984.

Bell, Lynda Schaefer. "Merchants, Peasants, and the State: The Organization and Politics of Chinese Silk Production, Wuxi County, 1870–1937." Ph.D. dissertation, University of California, Los Angeles, 1985.

Benshe tongren. "Xingqi pinglun kanxing zhongzhi de xuanyan" [Declaration on the discontinuation of publication of *Weekend Review*]. *Xingqi pinglun* 53 (June 6, 1920): 4.

Bergère, Marie-Claire. *The Golden Age of the Chinese Bourgeoisie, 1911–1937*. Trans. Janet Lloyd. Cambridge: Cambridge University Press, 1986.

————. "The Shanghai Bankers' Association, 1915–1927: Modernization and the Institutionalization of Local Solidarities." In *Shanghai Sojourners*, edited by Frederic Wakeman, Jr., and Wen-hsin Yeh. Berkeley: Institute of East Asian Studies, University of California, Berkeley, 1992.

Bernal, Martin. *Chinese Socialism to 1907*. Ithaca: Cornell University Press, 1976.

Bernstein, Gail Lee. *Japanese Marxist: A Portrait of Kawakami Hajime, 1879–1946*. Cambridge, Mass.: Harvard University Press, 1976.

Berry, Mary Elizabeth. *Hideyoshi*. Cambridge, Mass.: Harvard University Press, 1982.

Bingbing. "Yige Makesi xueshuo de shumu" [Bibliographical list of works on Marxism]. *Zhongguo qingnian* 24 (March 29, 1924): 3–11.

Bo Yibo. *Ruogan zhongda juece yu shijian de huigu* [Major policies and events revisited]. 2 vols. Beijing: Zhonggong zhongyang dangxiao chuban she, 1991.

Bol, Peter. "Chu Hsi's Redefinition of Literati Learning." In *Neo-Confucian Education: The Formative Stage*, edited by W. Theodore de Bary and John W. Chaffee. Berkeley: University of California Press, 1989.

————. "This Culture of Ours": Intellectual Transitions in T'ang and Sung China. Stanford: Stanford University Press, 1992.

Bonner, Joey. *Wang Guowei*. Cambridge, Mass.: Harvard University Press, 1986.

Borthwick, Sally. *Education and Social Change in China: The Beginnings of the Modern Era*. Standford: Hoover Institution Press, 1983.

Braudel, Fernand. *The Identity of France*. Vol. 1. Trans. Sian Reynolds. New York: Harper and Row, 1990.

Brook, Timothy. "Family Continuity and Cultural Hegemony: The Gentry of Ningbo, 1368–1911." In *Chinese Local Elites and Patterns of Dominance*, edited by Joseph Esherick and Mary Backus Rankin. Berkeley: University of California Press, 1990.

Cai Hesen. "Wo dang chansheng de beijing ji qi lishi shiming" [Background for the birth of our Party and our Party's historical mission]. In

Zhongguo Gongchandang diyi ci daibiao dahui dang'an ziliao zeng ding ben [Expanded edition, Archival materials on the First Party Congress of the Chinese Communist Party], edited by Zhongyang dang'an guan [Central Party Archives]. Beijing: Renmin chuban she, 1984.

Cannon, Terry, and Alan Jenkins, eds. *The Geography of Contemporary China: The Impact of Deng Xiaoping's Decade.* London: Routledge, 1990.

Cao Jinghua. "Cao Jinghua de huiyi" [Cao Jinghua's recollections]. In *Gongchan zhuyi xiaozu* [Communist small groups], edited by Zhonggong zhongyang dangshi ziliao zhengji weiyuan hui. Beijing: Zhonggong dangshi ziliao chuban she, 1987, vol. 1.

Cao Juren. *Wo yu wo de shijie* [I and my world]. Hong Kong: Sanyu tushu gongsi, 1972.

Chaffee, John W. "Chu Hsi in Nan-K'ang: *Tao-hsueh* and the Politics of Education." In *Neo-Confucian Education: The Formative Stage,* edited by W. Theodore de Bary and John W. Chaffee. Berkeley: University of California Press, 1989.

———. *The Thorny Gates of Learning in Sung China.* Cambridge: Cambridge University Press, 1985.

Chan, Hok-lam, and William Theodore de Bary, eds. *Yuan Thought: Chinese Thought and Religion under the Mongols.* New York: Columbia University Press, 1982.

Chan, Wing-tsit. "Chu Hsi and the Academies." In *Neo-Confucian Education: The Formative Stage,* edited by W. Theodore de Bary and John W. Chaffee. Berkeley: University of California Press, 1989.

———. "Chu Hsi and Neo-Confucianism." In *Yuan Thought: Chinese Thought and Religion under the Mongols,* edited by Hok-lam Chan and William Theodore de Bary. New York: Columbia University Press, 1982.

Chang, Chun-shu, and Shelley Hsueh-lun Chang. *Crisis and Transformation in Seventeenth-Century China: Society, Culture, and Modernity in Li Yu's World.* Ann Arbor: University of Michigan Press, 1992.

Chang, Hao. *Liang Ch'i-ch'ao and Intellectual Transition in China, 1890–1907.* Cambridge, Mass.: Harvard University Press, 1971.

Chang, Kwang-chih. *The Archaeology of Ancient China.* 3d ed. New Haven: Yale University Press, 1977.

Chang, P'eng-yuan. "The Constitutionalists." In *China in Revolution: The First Phase, 1900–1913,* edited by Mary Wright. New Haven: Yale University Press, 1968.

Chao Ch'eng Hsin. "An Ecological Study of China from Segmentation to Integration." Ph.D. thesis. University of Michigan, 1933.

Chen Chongguang, Ye Mingxun, Lai Zehan. *Er er ba shijian yanjiu baogao* [Investigative report on the February 28 Incident]. Taipei: Shibao wenhua chuban qiye youxian gongsi, 1994.

Chen Duxiu. "Bo Kang Youwei zhi zongtong zongli shu" [Refutation of Kang Youwei's letter to the president and the prime minister]. *Xin qingnian* 2, 2 (October 1916): 1–4.

———. "Jiu sixiang yu guoti wenti" [Old thoughts and problems with national polity]. *Xin qingnian* 3, 3 (May 1917): 1–3.

———. "Kongzi zhi dao yu xiandai shenghuo" [Confucian teaching and modern life]. *Xin qingnian* 2, 4 (December 1916): 1–7.

———. "Xianfa yu Kong jiao" [The constitution and Confucianism]. *Xin qingnian* 2, 3 (November 1916): 1–5.

Chen Gongbo. "Guangdong Gongchandang de baogao" [Report by Guangdong Communists]. In *Yida qianhou de Guangdong dang zuzhi* [Party organization in Guangdong before and after the First Congress], edited by Zhonggong Guangdong shengwei dangshi yanjiu weiyuan hui bangong shi and Guangdong sheng dang'an guan. Dongguan: Guangdong sheng dang'an guan, 1981.

———. "Jinhou de Guomindang" [The Nationalist Party hereafter]. *Geming pinglun* [Revolutionary commentary] 1 (May 1928): 1–15.

———. "Wo yu Gongchandang" [I and the Communist Party]. In *Yida huiyi lu* [First Party Congress memoirs], edited by Zhishi chuban she. Shanghai: Zhishi chuban she, 1980.

Chen Gongmao. "Shen Dingyi qiren" [Sheng Dingyi the man]. *Zhejiang wenshi ziliao xuanji* 21 (1982): 36–47.

Chen Jiyu. "Hangzhou wan dixing shuyao" [On the principle geographical characteristics of the Hangzhou Estuary]. *Zhejiang xuebao* 1, 2 (December 1947): 85–92.

Chen, Joseph T. *The May Fourth Movement in Shanghai: The Making of a Social Movement in Modern China.* Leiden: E. J. Brill, 1971.

Chen Rongjie [Wing-tsit Chan]. *Zhuzi menren* [Zhu Xi's disciples]. Taipei: Xuesheng shuju, 1982.

Chen Shaokang. "Shanghai gongchan zhuyi xiaozu zongshu" [General account of the Shanghai Communist small groups]. In *Gongchan zhuyi xiaozu* [Communist small groups], edited by Zhonggong zhongyang dangshi zhengji weiyuan hui. Beijing: Zhonggong dangshi ziliao chuban she, 1987, vol. 1.

Chen Tanqiu. "Diyi ci daibiao dahui de huiyi" [Recollections of the First Party Congress]. In *Yida qianhou: Zhongguo Gongchandang diyi ci daibiao dahui qianhou ziliao xuanbian* [Before and after the First Party Congress: Selected edition of materials on the First Party Congress of the Chinese Communist Party], edited by Zhongguo shehui kexue yuan xiandai shi yanjiu shi and Zhongguo geming bowu guan dangshi yanjiu shi. Beijing: Renmin chuban she, 1980, vol. 2.

Chen Wangdao. "Huiyi dang chengli shiqi de yixie qingkuang" [Recollections of the founding days of the Party]. In *Yida qianhou: Zhongguo Gongchandang diyi ci daibiao dahui qianhou ziliao xuanbian* [Before and after the First Party Congress: Selected edition of materials on the First Party Congress of the Chinese Communist Party], edited by Zhongguo shehui kexue yuan xiandai shi yanjiu shi and Zhongguo geming bowu guan dangshi yanjiu shi. Beijing: Renmin chuban she, 1980, vol. 2.

"Chen Wangdao tongzhi luezhuan" [Biographical sketch of comrade Chen Wangdao]. In *Chen Wangdao wenji* [Collected works of Chen Wangdao], edited by Fudan daxue yuyan yanjiu shi. Shanghai: Renmin chuban she, 1979.

Chin, Ai-li S. "Family Relations in Modern Chinese Fiction." In *Family and Kinship in Chinese Society*, edited by Maurice Friedman. Stanford: Stanford University Press, 1970.

Chow Tse-tsung. *The May Fourth Movement: Intellectual Revolution in Modern China*. Cambridge, Mass.: Harvard University Press, 1960.

Chu, Ron-Guey. "Chu Hsi and Public Instruction." In *Neo-Confucian Education: The Formative Stage*, edited by W. Theodore de Bary and John W. Chaffee. Berkeley: University of California Press, 1989.

Chunmu [Zhang Tailei]. "Zhi Hesen, Xiusong, Guochang" [Letter to Cai Hesen, Yu Xiusong, Shi Cuntong]. In *Yida qianhou de Guangdong dang zuzhi* [Party organization in Guangdong before and after the First Congress], edited by Zhonggong Guangdong shengwei dangshi yanjiu weiyuan hui bangong shi and Guangdong sheng dang'an guan. Dongguan: Guangdong sheng dang'an guan, 1981.

———. "Zhi Wenliang xiong" [To Wenliang]. In *Yida qianhou de Guangdong dang zuzhi* [Party organization in Guangdong before and after the First Congress], edited by Zhonggong Guangdong shengwei dangshi yanjiu weiyuan hui bangong shi and Guangdong sheng dang'an guan. Dongguan: Guangdong sheng dang'an guan, 1981.

Clifford, Nicholas R. *Shanghai, 1925: Urban Nationalism and the Defense of Foreign Privilege*. Ann Arbor: Center for Chinese Studies, University of Michigan, 1979.

Cohen, Paul. *China and Christianity: The Missionary Movement and the Growth of Chinese Antiforeignism, 1860–1870*. Cambridge, Mass.: Council on East Asian Studies Publications, Harvard University Press, 1963.

———. *Between Tradition and Modernity: Wang T'ao and Reform in Late Ch'ing China*. Cambridge, Mass.: Council on East Asian Studies Publications, Harvard University Press, 1974.

Cole, James. *Shaohsing: Competition and Cooperation in Nineteenth-Century China*. Tucson: University of Arizona Press, 1986.

Dabai [Liu Dabai]. "Sixiang de jianyu" [Prisonhouse of thought]. *Xingqi pinglun* 6 (July 13, 1919): 3–4.

Dardess, John W. "The Cheng Communal Family: Social Organization and Neo-Confucianism in Yuan and Early Ming China." *Harvard Journal of Asian Studies* 34 (1974): 7–52.

————. *Confucianism and Autocracy: Professional Elites in the Founding of the Ming Dynasty.* Berkeley: University of California Press, 1983.

————. "Late Yuan Chekiang." In *Yuan Thought: Chinese Thought and Religion under the Mongols,* edited by Hok-lam Chan and William Theodore de Bary. New York: Columbia University Press, 1982.

Davis, Richard L. *Court and Family in Sung China, 960–1279: Bureaucratic Success and Kinship Fortunes for the Shih of Ming-chou.* Durham, N.C.: Duke University Press, 1986.

————. "Political Success and the Growth of Descent Groups: The Shih of Ming-chou during the Sung." In *Kinship Organization in Late Imperial China, 1000–1940,* edited by Patricia B. Ebrey and James L. Watson. Berkeley: University of California Press, 1986.

de Amicis, Edmondo. *The Heart of a Boy (Cuore): A Schoolboy's Journey.* Trans. from the 224th Italian edition by G. Mantellini. Chicago: Laird and Lee, 1899.

de Bary, William Theodore. "Chu Hsi's Aims as an Educator." In *Neo-Confucian Education: The Formative Stage,* edited by W. Theodore de Bary and John W. Chaffee. Berkeley: University of California Press, 1989.

————. *Neo-Confucian Orthodoxy and the Learning of the Mind-and-Heart.* New York: Columbia University Press, 1981.

————, ed. *Self and Society in Ming Thought.* New York: Columbia University Press, 1970.

————, ed. *The Unfolding of Neo-Confucianism.* New York: Columbia University Press, 1975.

————, and John W. Chaffee, eds. *Neo-Confucian Education: The Formative Stage.* Berkeley: University of California Press, 1989.

————, and Hok-lam Chan, eds. *Yuan Thought: Chinese Thought and Religion under the Mongols.* New York: Columbia University Press, 1982.

Ding Ling. "Wo suo renshi de Qu Qiubai tongzhi" [Comrade Qu Qiubai as I knew him]. In *Yi Qiubai* [Remembering (Qu) Qiubai], edited by Yi Qiubai bianji xiaozhu. Beijing: Renmin wenxue chuban she, 1981.

Dirlik, Arif. *Anarchism in the Chinese Revolution.* Berkeley: University of California Press, 1991.

————. *The Origins of Chinese Communism.* New York: Oxford University Press, 1989.

Dong Biwu. "Sili Wuhan zhongxue jianji" [Brief account of the private

Wuhan middle school]. In *Gongchan zhuyi xiaozu* [Communist small groups], edited by Zhonggong zhongyang dangshi zhengji weiyuan hui. Beijing: Zhonggong dangshi ziliao chuban she, 1987, vol. 1.

Dong Chuping. *Wu Yue wenhua xintan* [New perspectives on Wu-Yue culture]. Xiaoshan: Zhejiang renmin chuban she, 1988.

Dong Zhongsheng. *Lanxi shiyan xian shixi baogao* [Report about an on-the-job training experience with the Lanxi experimental county administration]. Vol. 1 of *Lanxi shiyan xian shixi diaocha baogao*, compiled by Ye Qianchu. Taipei: Chengwen chuban she, 1977.

Dongfang zazhi [Eastern miscellany]. Shanghai.

Du Weiyun. *Zhao Yi zhuan* [Biography of Zhao Yi]. Taipei: Shibao chuban gongsi, 1983.

Duan Congguang. "Ganxi pengmin de kang Qing douzheng" [On the anti-Qing struggles of the shed people of western Jiangxi]. *Lishi jiaoxue* (January 1955): 33–36.

Duara, Prasenjit. *Culture, Power, and the State: Rural North China, 1900–1942*. Stanford: Stanford University Press, 1988.

Dushu shenghuo [Learning and living]. Shanghai.

Ebrey, Patricia. "Conceptions of the Family in the Sung Dynasty." *Journal of Asian Studies* 43, 2 (February 1984): 219–45.

———. *Confucianism and Family Rituals in Imperial China: A Social History of Writing about Rites*. Princeton: Princeton University Press, 1991.

———. "Education through Ritual: Efforts to Formulate Family Rituals during the Sung Period." In *Neo-Confucian Education: The Formative Stage*, edited by W. Theodore de Bary and John W. Chaffee. Berkeley: University of California Press, 1989.

———. *Family and Property in Sung China: Yuan Ts'ai's Precepts for Social Life*. Princeton: Princeton University Press, 1984.

Eikemeier, Dieter, and Herbert Franke, eds. *State and Law in East Asia: Festschrift Karl Bunger*. Wiesbaden: Harrassowitz, 1981.

Elman, Benjamin. *Classicism, Politics, and Kinship: The Ch'ang-chou School of New Text Confucianism in Late Imperial China*. Berkeley: University of California Press, 1990.

———. *From Philosophy to Philology: Intellectual and Social Aspects of Change in Late Imperial China*. Cambridge, Mass.: Council on East Asian Studies Publications, Harvard University Press, 1984.

Elvin, Mark. *The Pattern of the Chinese Past*. Stanford: Stanford University Press, 1973.

———, and G. William Skinner, eds. *The Chinese City between Two Worlds*. Stanford: Stanford University Press, 1974.

Endicott-West, Elizabeth. *Mongolian Rule in China: Local Administration in the Yuan Dynasty*. Cambridge, Mass.: Council on East Asian Studies Publications, Harvard University Press, 1989.

Eng, Robert. *Economic Imperialism in China: Silk Production and Exports, 1861–1932*. Berkeley: Institute of East Asian Studies, University of California, 1986.

Erda he Sanda: Zhongguo Gongchandang dier, disan ci daibiao dahui ziliao xuanbian [Second and third Party congresses: Selection of materials on the second and third Party congresses of the Chinese Communist Party]. Edited by Zhongguo shehui kexue yuan jindai shi yanjiu suo. Beijing: Zhongguo shehui kexue chuban she, 1985.

Esherick, Joseph W. *The Origins of the Boxer Uprising*. Berkeley: University of California Press, 1987.

———. *Reform and Revolution in China: The 1911 Revolution in Hunan and Hubei*. Berkeley: University of California Press, 1976.

———, and Mary Backus Rankin, eds. *Chinese Local Elites and Patterns of Dominance*. Berkeley: University of California Press, 1990.

Fairbank, John K. "The Creation of the Treaty System." In *The Cambridge History of China*, vol. 10, pt. 1, edited by Denis Twitchett and John K. Fairbank. Cambridge: Cambridge University Press, 1988.

———. *Trade and Diplomacy on the China Coast: The Opening of the Treaty Ports, 1842–1854*. Cambridge, Mass.: Harvard University Press, 1953; paperback edition, Stanford: Stanford University Press, 1969.

———, ed. *The Cambridge History of China*. Vol. 12, pt. 1, "Republican China, 1912–1949." Cambridge: Cambridge University Press, 1983.

———, and Albert Feuerwerker, eds. *The Cambridge History of China*. Vol. 13, pt. 2, "Republican China, 1912–1949." Cambridge: Cambridge University Press, 1986.

Faligot, Roger, and Remi Kauffer. *The Chinese Secret Service*. Trans. Christine Donougher. London: Headline Book Publishing, 1989.

Farmer, Edward L. "Social Regulations of the First Ming Emperor: Orthodoxy as a Function of Authority." In *Orthodoxy in Late Imperial China*, edited by Kwang-Ching Liu. Berkeley: University of California Press, 1990.

Fei, Hsiao-tung. *China's Gentry: Essays in Rural-Urban Relations*. Chicago: University of Chicago Press, 1953.

Feigon, Lee. *Chen Duxiu: Founder of the Chinese Communist Party*. Princeton: Princeton University Press, 1983.

Feng Airan. "Yi Pan Tianshou" [Remembering Pan Tianshou]. *Zhejiang wenshi ziliao xuanji* 21 (1982): 24–31.

Feng Huazhan. "Huazuo chunni geng huhua—huainian wode fuqin Feng Zikai" [Into the spring earth that nurtures the blossoms—memory of my father Feng Zikai]. *Xin wanbao* (Hong Kong), April 24, 1979; reprinted in *Huiyi yigu wenxuejia, shixuejia, yishujia ziliaoji* [In memory of deceased writers, historians, and artists: A collection of sources]. Hong Kong: Zhishi chuban she, 1979.

Feng Zikai. *Zikai xiaopin ji* [Collection of Zikai's short pieces]. Shanghai: Zhongxuesheng shuju, 1933.

Feuerwerker, Albert. *China's Early Industrialization: Sheng Hsuan-huai (1844–1916) and Mandarin Enterprise*. Cambridge, Mass.: Harvard University Press, 1958; reprint New York: Atheneum, 1970.

———. "China's Modern Economic History in Communist Chinese Historiography." In *History of Communist China*, edited by Albert Feuerwerker. Cambridge, Mass.: MIT Press, 1968.

———, ed. *History in Communist China*. Cambridge, Mass.: MIT Press, 1968.

Fincher, John. *Chinese Democracy: The Self-Government Movement in Local, Provincial, and National Politics, 1905–1914*. New York: St. Martin's Press, 1981.

———. "Political Provincialism and the National Revolution." In *China in Revolution: The First Phase, 1900–1913*, edited by Mary Wright. New Haven: Yale University Press, 1968.

Finnane, Antonia. "Yangzhou: A Central Place in the Qing Empire." In *Cities of Jiangnan in Late Imperial China*, edited by Linda Cooke Johnson. Albany: State University of New York Press, 1993.

Fogel, Joshua. *Ai Ssu-ch'i's Contribution to the Development of Chinese Marxism*. Cambridge, Mass.: Council on East Asian Studies Publications, Harvard University Press, 1987.

Fu Binran. "Huiyi Zhejiang xinchao she" [Recollections of the Zhejiang New Tide Society]. In *Wusi shiqi de shetuan* [Associational organizations of the May Fourth period]. Beijing: Shenghuo, dushu, xinzhi sanlian shudian, 1959; reprint 1979, vol. 3.

———. "Wusi qianhou" [Before and after May Fourth]. In *Wusi yundong huiyi lu* [Recollections on the May Fourth Movement], edited by Zhongguo shehui kexue yuan jindai shi yanjiu suo. Beijing: Zhongguo shehui kexue chuban she, 1979, vol. 2.

Fu Yiling. "Ming Qing shidai Fujian diannong fengchao kaozheng" [Tenant riots in Fujian during the Ming and the Qing]. In *Ming Qing nongcun shehui jingji* [Village society and economy under the Ming and the Qing]. Beijing: Sanlian chuban she, 1961.

———. *Ming Qing shidai shangren ji shangye ziben* [Merchants and mercantile capital under the Ming and the Qing]. Beijing: Renmin chuban she, 1956.

———. *Mingdai Jiangnan shimin jingji shitan* [Preliminary research on urban economy in Jiangnan under the Ming]. Shanghai: Renmin chuban she, 1957.

Fudan daxue yuyan yanjiu shi, ed. *Chen Wangdao wenji* [Collected works of Chen Wangdao]. 2 vols. Shanghai: Renmin chuban she, 1979.

Furth, Charlotte. *The Limits of Change: Essays on Conservative Alternatives in Republican China.* Cambridge, Mass.: Harvard University Press, 1976.

Gan Yang. "Bashi niandai wenhua taolun de jige wenti" [A few problems in the cultural discussions of the 1980s]. In *Zhongguo dangdai wenhua yishi* [Contemporary Chinese cultural consciousness], edited by Gan Yang. Taipei: Fengyun shidai chuban gongsi, 1990.

Gardner, Daniel K. *Chu Hsi and the Ta-hsueh: Neo-Confucian Reflection on the Confucian Canon.* Cambridge, Mass.: Harvard University Press, 1986.

Geiss, James. "The Chia-ching reign, 1522–1566." In *The Cambridge History of China,* vol. 7, pt. 1, edited by Frederick Mote and Denis Twitchett. Cambridge: Cambridge University Press, 1988.

George, Henry. "Progress and Poverty." Trans. Liao Zhongkai, in *Minbao* [People's journal] (Tokyo) 1 (November 1906): 122–30.

Gernet, Jacques. *Daily Life in China on the Eve of the Mongol Invasion, 1250–1276.* Trans. H. M. Wright. New York: Macmillan, 1962.

———. *A History of Chinese Civilization.* Trans. J. R. Foster. Cambridge: Cambridge University Press, 1982.

Giddens, Anthony. *Central Problems in Social Theory: Action, Structure and Contradiction in Social Analysis.* Berkeley: University of California Press, 1979.

Golas, Peter J. "Early Ch'ing Guilds." In *The City in Late Imperial China,* edited by G. William Skinner. Stanford: Stanford University Press, 1977.

Gongchan guoji youguan Zhongguo geming de wenxian ziliao, 1919–1928; diyi ji [Comintern documentary sources pertaining to the Chinese revolution, 1919–1928, part I]. 2 vols. Edited by Zhongguo shehui kexue yuan jindai shi yanjiu suo fanyi she. Beijing: Zhongguo shehui kexue yuan chuban she, 1980.

Gongchan zhuyi xiaozu [Communist small groups]. Edited by Zhonggong zhongyang dangshi ziliao zhengji weiyuan hui. 2 vols. Beijing: Zhonggong dangshi ziliao chuban she, 1987.

Gongchandang [The Communist]. Shanghai.

Goodman, Bryna. "New Culture, Old Habits: Native-Place Organization and the May Fourth Movement." In *Shanghai Sojourners,* edited by Frederic Wakeman, Jr., and Wen-hsin Yeh. Berkeley: Institute of East Asian Studies, University of California, 1992.

Greenblatt, Stephen. "Resonance and Wonder." In *Exhibiting Cultures: The Poetics and Politics of Museum Display*, edited by Ivan Karp and Steven D. Lavine. Washington, D.C.: Smithsonian Institution Press, 1991.

Grimm, Tilemann. "Ming Educational Intendants." In *Chinese Government in Ming Times*, edited by Charles O. Hucker. New York: Columbia University Press, 1969.

Gu Mei. *Xiandai Zhongguo ji qi jiaoyu* [Modern China and its education]. 2 vols, 1934. Reprint Hong Kong: Longmen shudian, 1975.

Gu Yanwu. *Tianxia junguo libing shu* [On the benefits and ailments of all counties under the heaven]. 120 vols. Shanghai: Erlinzhai shiyin, 1899.

Gu Zhaoxiong. "Makesi xueshuo" [Marx's teaching]. *Xin qingnian* 6, 5 (May 1919).

Guomindang dangshi yanjiu hui [Archives of the Historical Commission of the Chinese Nationalist Party]. Huanlonglu dang. Taipei, Taiwan.

Haeger, John W., ed. *Crisis and Prosperity in Sung China*. Tucson: University of Arizona Press, 1975.

Hangzhoufu zhi [Hangzhou Prefecture gazetteer]. 1922. Reprint Taipei: Chengwen chuban she, 1974.

Hao, Yen-p'ing. *The Commercial Revolution in Nineteenth Century China: The Rise of Sino-Western Mercantile Capitalism*. Berkeley: University of California Press, 1986.

Harbsmeier, Christoph. *The Cartoonist Feng Zikai: Social Realism with a Buddhist Face*. Oslo: Universitetsforlaget; Irvington-on-Hudson, N.Y.; distributed by Columbia University Press, 1984.

Hartwell, Robert. "Demographic, Political, and Social Transformations of China, 750–1550." *Harvard Journal of Asiatic Studies* 42, 2 (December 1982): 365–442.

———. "Historical Analogism, Public Policy, and Social Science in Eleventh and Twelfth Century China." *American Historical Review* 76, 3 (June 1971): 690–727.

[He] Zhen and [Liu] Shenshu [courtesy name: Shipei]. "Lun zhongzu geming yu wuzhengfu geming zhi deshi" [On the pros and cons of ethnic revolution vis-à-vis anarchist revolution]. *Tianyi bao* [Natural justice], vols. 6–7, September 1 and 15, 1907; reprinted in *Wuzhengfu zhuyi sixiang ziliao xuan* [Selection of sources on anarchist thought], edited by Ge Maochun, Jiang Jun, and Li Xingzhi. Beijing: Beijing daxue chuban she, 1984, vol. 1.

He Zhongying. "Baihua wen jiaoshou wenti" [Problems in the teaching of the vernacular]. *Jiaoyu zazhi* 12, 2 (February 1920): 16,450–54.

He Zuochen. "You hu ji" [Tour on the lake]. *Zhejiang diyi shifan xuexiao xiaoyou huizhi* 7 (1915): "wenyuan" [literary garden], 3–4.

Ho, Ping-ti. *The Ladder of Success in Imperial China: Aspects of Social Mobility, 1368–1911.* New York: Columbia University Press, 1962.

———. [He Bingdi]. *Zhongguo huiguan shilun* [Historical essay on Chinese *Landsmannschaften*]. Taipei: Xuesheng shuju, 1966.

Hofheinz, Roy, Jr. *The Broken Wave: The Chinese Communist Peasant Movement, 1922–1928.* Cambridge, Mass.: Harvard University Press, 1977.

Honig, Emily. *Creating Chinese Ethnicity: Subei People in Shanghai, 1850–1980.* New Haven: Yale University Press, 1992.

———. "Migrant Culture in Shanghai: In Search of a Subei Identity." In *Shanghai Sojourners,* edited by Frederic Wakeman, Jr., and Wen-hsin Yeh. Berkeley: Institute of East Asian Studies, University of California, 1992.

Hoston, Germaine. *Marxism and the Crisis of Development in Prewar Japan.* Princeton: Princeton University Press, 1986.

Hu Juewen, Hu Zi'ang, Sun Xiaocun, Zhou Shiguan, Feng Hefa. "Minzhu geming shiqi de yingyong zhanshi Shi Fuliang tongzhi" [Comrade Shi Fuliang, brave warrior during the phase of democratic revolution]. *People's Daily,* June 17, 1982.

Hu Qi. "Yiwu de 'qiaotang bang'" [Candy-hawkers of Yiwu]. *Zhejiang wenshi ziliao xuanji* 21 (June 1982): 161–76.

Hu Shi. "More Study of Problems, Less Talk of 'Isms.'" *Meizhou pinglun* [Weekly commentary] (July 20, 1919): 1.

Hua Yan. *Wuzu Yan Fu de yisheng* [My grandfather Yan Fu]. Taipei: Datong wenhua jijin hui, 1992.

Huang Lingshuang. "Makesi xueshuo piping" [Critique of Marx's teaching]. *Xin qingnian* 6, 5 (May 1919).

Huang Meizhen, Shi Yuanhua, and Zhang Yun, eds. *Shanghai daxue shiliao* [Historical materials on Shanghai University]. Shanghai: Fudan daxue chuban she, 1984.

Huang, Philip. *The Peasant Family and Rural Development in the Yangzi Delta, 1350–1988.* Stanford: Stanford University Press, 1990.

Huang, Ray. "Fiscal Administration during the Ming Dynasty." In *Chinese Government in Ming Times: Seven Studies,* edited by Charles O. Hucker. New York: Columbia University Press, 1969.

Hucker, Charles O., ed. *Chinese Government in Ming Times: Seven Studies.* New York: Columbia University Press, 1969.

Hymes, Robert. "Lu Chiu-yuan, Academies, and the Problem of the Local Community." In *Neo-Confucian Education: The Formative Stage,* edited by W. Theodore de Bary and John W. Chaffee. Berkeley: University of California Press, 1989.

———. "Marriage, Descent Groups and the Localist Strategy in Sung and Yuan Fu-chou." In *Kinship Organization in Late Imperial China, 1000–*

1940, edited by Patricia B. Ebrey and James L. Watson. Berkeley: University of California Press, 1986.

—. *Statesmen and Gentlemen: The Elite of Fu-chou, Chiang-hsi, in Northern and Southern Sung*. Cambridge: Cambridge University Press, 1985.

Interview by the author with Shi Changchun's cousin. June 1, 1992.

Ishikawa Yoshihiro. "Marukusu shugi no denha to Chukoku Kyosanto no ketsusei" [Spread of Marxism and the development of the Chinese Communist Party]. In *Chukoku kokumin kakumei no kenkyū* [Studies on the Chinese revolution]. Kyoto: Kyoto University Press, 1992.

—. "Waka ki hi no Shi Zuntou" [Young man Shi Cuntong]. *Toyo shi kenkyu* (September 1994): 284–315.

Jansen, Marius B. *The Japanese and Sun Yat-sen*. Cambridge, Mass.: Harvard University Press, 1967.

Jeans, Roger B. *Roads Not Taken: The Struggle of Opposition Parties in Twentieth Century China*. Boulder, Col.: Westview, 1992.

Jian Youwen. *Taiping tianguo quanshi* [Complete history of the Taiping Heavenly Kingdom]. Vol. 3. Hong Kong: Jianshi mengjin shuwu, 1962.

Jiang Danshu. "Feixiao yu Zhejiang diyi shifan de fan fengjian douzheng" [Critique of the concept of filial piety and the antifeudal struggle at Zhejiang First Normal]. In *Wusi yundong huiyi lu*, edited by Zhongguo shehui kexue yuan jindai shi yanjiu suo. Beijing: Zhongguo shehui kexue chuban she, 1979, vol. 2.

Jiaoyu zazhi [Educational review]. 1909–27. Reprint Taipei: Commercial Press, 1975.

Jing, Hengyi [Ziyuan]. "Huanying ge shixiao zhiyuan xuesheng yanshuo ci" [Speech to welcome the staff and students of normal schools assembled for the occasion, March 30]. *Zhejiang shengli diyi shifan xuexiao xiaoyou huizhi* 14/15 (1918): 2–4.

—. "Liushi shuhuai" [Thoughts on turning sixty]. In "Yiyuan shiji" [Yiyuan poetry collection]. Unpublished manuscript.

—. "Shengdan jinian shi shici" [Speech and resolutions on the birthday of the Sage]. *Zhejiang shengli diyi shifan xuexiao xiaoyou huizhi* (fall 1917): 5–6.

—. "Shiye shi xiaozhang xunci" [Principal's speech at the beginning of the term]. *Zhejiang shengli diyi shifan xuexiao huizhi* 7 (1915): 1–3; (1917): 1.

—. "Shizhou jinian hui kaihui ci" [Speech to note the tenth week of the term]. *Zhejiang shengli diyi shifan xuexiao xiaoyou huizhi* 14/15 (1918): 6.

—. "Wuwu shujia xiuye shi xunci" [Speech delivered at the ceremony to mark the conclusion of the spring term in the year Wuwu (1918)]. *Zhejiang shengli diyi shifan xuexiao xiaoyou huizhi* 14/15 (1918): 9–10.

———. "Xiaoyou hui kaihui ci" [Speech at a meeting of the friends and associates of the school]. *Zhejiang shengli diyi shifan xuexiao xiaoyou huizhi* (spring 1917): 3–4.

Jinhua Unified Silk Factories [Jinhua sichou lianying chang] employees. Interview with the author May 31, 1992.

Jinhua xianzhi [Jinhua County gazetteer]. 1894 compilation. 1934. Reprint Taipei: Chengwen chuban she, 1970.

Jitao [Dai Jitao]. "Eguo laonong zhengfu tonggao de zhenyi" [True meaning of the proclamation of the Russian labor-peasant government]. *Xingqi pinglun* 45 (April 11, 1920): 1–2.

———. "Eguo liang zhengfu de duihua zhengce" [China policies of two Russian governments]. *Xingqi pinglun* 15 (September 14, 1919): 2–3.

———. "Guojia zhuyi zhi pochan yu shehui de geming" [Bankruptcy of nation-states and the social revolution]. *Xingqi pinglun* 47 (April 25, 1920): 1–3.

Johnson, David. "The Last Years of a Great Clan: The Li Family of Chao Chun in Late T'ang and Early Sung." *Harvard Journal of Asiatic Studies* 37, 1 (June 1977): 5–102.

———. "The Wu Zixu *Pien-wen* and Its Sources." *Harvard Journal of Asiatic Studies* 40, 1 (June 1980): 93–156; 40, 2 (December 1980): 465–505.

———, Andrew Nathan, and Evelyn Rawski, eds. *Popular Culture in Late Imperial China*. Berkeley: University of California Press, 1985.

Johnson, Linda Cooke. "Shanghai: An Emerging Jiangnan Port, 1683–1840." In *Cities of Jiangnan in Late Imperial China*, edited by Linda Cooke Johnson. Albany: State University of New York Press, 1993.

———, ed. *Cities of Jiangnan in Late Imperial China*. Albany: State University of New York Press, 1993.

Jones, Susan Mann. "The Ningpo Pang and Financial Power at Shanghai." In *The Chinese City between Two Worlds*, edited by Mark Elvin and G. William Skinner. Stanford: Stanford University Press, 1974.

———, ed. *Proceedings of the NEH Modern China Project in China from 1850 to the Present*. Select Papers from the Center for East Asian Studies, No. 3. Chicago: University of Chicago Press, 1979.

Karlgren, Bernhard. *The Book of Odes: Chinese Text, Transcription, and Translation*. Stockholm: Museum of Far Eastern Antiquities, 1950.

Karp, Ivan, and Steven D. Lavine, eds. *Exhibiting Cultures: The Poetics and Politics of Museum Display*. Washington, D.C.: Smithsonian Institution Press, 1991.

Keightley, David. Confidential report to the American Council of Learned Societies on the Fanshan archeological site. 1991.

Kelleher, M. Theresa. "Back to Basics: Chu Hsi's Elementary Learning (*Hsiao-hsueh*)." In *Neo-Confucian Education: The Formative Stage*, edited by W. Theodore de Bary and John W. Chaffee. Berkeley: University of California Press, 1989.

Kelley, David. "Temples and Tribute Fleets: The Luo Sect and Boatmen's Associations in the Eighteenth Century." *Modern China* 8, 3 (July 1982): 361–91.

Kierman, Frank A., Jr., and John K. Fairbank, eds. *Chinese Ways in Warfare*. Cambridge, Mass.: Harvard University Press, 1974.

Korsch, Karl. *Marxism and Philosophy*. Trans. Fred Halliday. London: NLB, 1970.

Kracke, Edward A. "The Expansion of Educational Opportunity in the Reign of Hui-tsung of Sung and Its Implications." *Sung Studies Newsletter* 13 (1977): 6–30.

Krebs, Edward S. "Liu Ssu-fu and Chinese Anarchism, 1905–1915." Ph.D. dissertation, University of Wisconsin, 1977.

Kuhn, Philip. "Local Taxation and Finance in Republican China." In *Proceedings of the NEH Modern China Project in China from 1850 to the Present*, edited by Susan Mann Jones. Select Papers from the Center for East Asian Studies, No. 3. Chicago: University of Chicago Press, 1979.

———. *Rebellion and Its Enemies in Late Imperial China: Militarization and Social Structure, 1796–1864*. Cambridge, Mass.: Harvard University Press, 1970.

———. *The Soulstealers: The Chinese Sorcery Scare of 1768*. Cambridge, Mass.: Harvard University Press, 1990.

———. "The Taiping Rebellion." In *The Cambridge History of China*, vol. 10, pt. 1, edited by Denis Twitchett and John K. Fairbank. Cambridge: Cambridge University Press, 1978.

———, and Timothy Brook, eds. *National Polity and Local Power: The Transformation of Late Imperial China*. Cambridge, Mass.: Council on East Asian Studies Publications, Harvard University Press, 1989.

Kwong, Luke S. K. *A Mosaic of the Hundred Days: Personalities, Politics, and Ideas of 1898*. Cambridge, Mass.: Council on East Asian Studies Publications, Harvard University Press, 1984.

Langlois, John D., Jr. "Authority in Family Legislation." In *State and Law in East Asia: Festschrift Karl Bunger*, edited by Dieter Eikemeier and Herbert Franke. Wiesbaden: Harrassowitz, 1981.

———. "Law, Statecraft, and *The Spring and Autumn Annals* in Yuan Political Thought." In *Yuan Thought: Chinese Thought and Religion under the Mongols*, edited by Hok-lam Chan and William Theodore de Bary. New York: Columbia University Press, 1982.

———. "Political Thought in Chin-hua under Mongol Rule." In *China under Mongol Rule*, edited by John D. Langlois. Princeton: Princeton University Press, 1981.

Lanxi xian zhengfu, ed. *Zhejiang sheng Lanxi xian xianzheng gaikuang* [County government report about the state of administration in Lanxi County, Zhejiang Province]. Hangzhou: Lanxi xian zhengfu, 1928.

Lee, Leo Ou-fan, and Andrew J. Nathan. "The Beginning of Mass Culture: Journalism and Fiction in the Late Ch'ing and Beyond." In *Popular Culture in Late Imperial China*, edited by David Johnson, Andrew Nathan, and Evelyn Rawski. Berkeley: University of California Press, 1985.

Lee, Thomas Hong-chi. *Government Education and Examinations in Sung China*. New York: St. Martin's, 1985.

———. "A Report on the Recently Excavated Sung Ship at Chuan-chou and a Consideration of Its True Capacity." *Sung Studies Newsletter* 11/12 (1975/76): 4–9.

———. "Sung Education before Chu Hsi." In *Neo-Confucian Education: The Formative Stage*, edited by W. Theodore de Bary and John W. Chaffee. Berkeley: University of California Press, 1989.

Levenson, Joseph. *Confucian China and Its Modern Fate: A Trilogy*. 3d ed. 3 vols. Berkeley: University of California Press, 1968.

———. *Liang Ch'i-ch'ao and the Mind of Modern China*. Cambridge Mass.: Harvard University Press, 1953.

Li Dazhao. "Wo de Makesi zhuyi guan" [My views on Marxism]. *Xin qingnian* 6, 5 (May 1919): 521–37, and 6, 6 (June 1919): 612–24.

Li Guoqi. *Zhongguo xiandai hua de quyu yanjiu—Min Zhe Tai* [Modernization in China: A regional study of Fujian, Zhejiang, and Taiwan]. Taipei: Zhongyang yanjiu yuan jindai shi yanjiu suo, 1982.

Li Jiefei. *Zheshi jiyao* [Highlights in Zhejiang history]. Shanghai: n.p., 1948.

Li, Lillian M. *China's Silk Trade: Traditional Industry in the Modern World, 1842–1937*. Cambridge, Mass.: Harvard University Press, 1981.

Li Lisan. "Dang shi baogao" [Report on Party history]. In *Zhongguo Gongchandang diyi ci daibiao dahui dang'an ziliao zeng ding ben* [Expanded edition, Archival materials on the First Party Congress of the Chinese Communist Party], edited by Zhongyang dang'an guan (Central Archives Bureau). Beijing: Renmin chuban she, 1983.

Li Rui. *Lushan huiyi shili* [Lushan Conference: A truthful record]. Reprint Taipei: Xinru chuban she, 1992.

Li Runren. "Tongmenhui zai Guilin, Pingle de huodong" [Revolutionary Alliance activities in Guilin and Pingle]. In *Xinhai geming huiyi lu* [Recollections of the 1911 revolution], edited by Wenshi ziliao weiyuan hui. Beijing: Zhonghua shuju, 1961, vol. 2.

Li Shoukong. *Zhongguo jindai shi* [History of modern China]. Taipei: Sanmin shuju, 1958.

Li Zehou. *Zhongguo jindai sixiang shilun* [Essays on modern Chinese intellectual history]. Beijing: Renmin chuban she, 1979.

————. *Zou wo ziji de lu* [Following a path of my own]. Taipei: Fengyun shidai chuban gongsi, 1990.

Liang Qichao. "Jindai xuefeng zhi dili fenbu" [Geographical distribution of late imperial Chinese scholarship by style]. *Qinghua xuebao* [Qinghua journal] 1, 1 (June 1924): 26–31.

————. *Zhongguo jin sanbai nian xueshu shi* [History of Chinese scholarship of the past three hundred years]. Reprint Shanghai: n.p., 1936.

Liao Gailong, ed. *Zhonggong dangshi wenzhai niankan* [Annual digest of essays on Chinese Communist Party history]. Beijing: Zhongguo Gongchandang zhonggong dangshi lishi yanjiu yuan, issues 1982–86.

Lin Chuanjia, ed. *Da Zhonghua Zhejiang sheng dili zhi* [Geography of Zhejiang province, greater China]. Hangzhou: Zhejiang yinshua gongsi, 1918.

Lin Nengshi. "Diyi ci hufa yundong de jingfei wenti, 1917–1918" [Budgetary questions during the first campaign to uphold the constitution, 1917–1918]. Paper presented at the Centennial Symposium on Sun Yat-sen's Founding of the Guomindang for Revolution, Taipei, November 19–23, 1994.

Lin Ziqin. *Hongyi dashi nianpu* [Chronological biography of master Hongyi]. Hong Kong: Honghua yuan, 1944.

Link, Perry. *Mandarin Ducks and Butterflies: Urban Popular Fiction in Twentieth Century Chinese Cities.* Berkeley: University of California Press, 1980.

Liu Binglin. "Makesi luezhuan" [Biographical sketch of Marx]. *Xin qingnian* 6, 5 (May 1919).

Liu da yiqian—Dang de lishi cailiao [Before the Sixth Party Congress: Historical materials on the Party]. Yan'an, 1942; reprint Beijing: Renmin chuban she, 1980.

Liu Dabai. *Baiwu shuoshi* [Reflections on poetry in a white chamber]. Shanghai: Kaiming shudian, 1929.

————. *Baiwu wenhua* [Reflections on literature in a white chamber]. Shanghai: Shijie shuju, 1929.

————. *Jiumeng* [Faded dreams]. Shanghai: Shangwu yinshu guan, 1924.

————. *Liu Dabai xuanji* [Selected works of Liu Dabai]. Hong Kong: Xianggang wenxue yanjiu she, n.d.

————. Preface to *Shuqing xiaoshi* [Casual poems of feeling]. Quoted in Cao Juren, *Wo yu wo de shijie* [I and my world], Hong Kong: Sanyu tushu gongsi, 1972.

————. *Youwen* [Mailing kisses]. Shanghai: Kaiming shudian, 1933.

Liu, James T. C. "How Did a Neo-Confucian School Become the State Orthodoxy?" *Philosophy East and West* 23, 4 (October 1973): 483–505.

————. *Ou-yang Hsiu: An Eleventh-Century Neo-Confucianist.* Stanford: Stanford University Press, 1967.

————. "Sung Roots of Chinese Political Conservatism." *Journal of Asian Studies* 26, 3 (May 1967): 457–63.

Liu, Kwang-Ching. "Socioethics as Orthodoxy: A Perspective." In *Orthodoxy in Late Imperial China*, edited by Kwang-Ching Liu. Berkeley: University of California Press, 1990.

Liu, Renjing. "Beijing Makesi zhuyi yanjiu hui de qingkuang" [About the Marxism Study Society in Beijing]. In *Gongchan zhuyi xiaozu*, edited by Zhonggong zhongyang dangshi ziliao zhengji weiyuan hui. Beijing: Zhonggong dangshi ziliao chuban she, 1987, vol. 1.

Liu Shufen. "San zhi liu shiji Zhedong diqu jingji de fazhan" [Economic development in the Zhedong region from the third to the sixth century]. *Zhongyang yanjiu yuan lishi yuyan yanjiu suo jikan* 58, 3 (September 1987): 485–524.

Liu Yongcheng. "Shilun Qingdai Suzhou shougongye hanghui" [Handicraft guilds in Suzhou during the Qing dynasty]. *Lishi yanjiu* 11 (1959): 21–46.

Lo Jung-pang. "The Decline of the Early Ming Navy." *Oriens extremus* 5, 2 (December 1958): 149–68.

————. "The Emergence of China as a Sea Power during the Late Sung and Early Yuan Periods." *Far Eastern Quarterly* 14, 4 (1955): 489–504.

————. "Maritime Commerce and Its Relation to the Sung Navy." *Journal of the Economic and Social History of the Orient* 12, 1 (1969): 57–101.

Lou Shiyi. "Huainian Xia Mianzun xiansheng" [Remembering Mr. Xia Mianzun]. *Renwu shuangyue kan* [People bimonthly] 4 (1981): 152–59.

Lü Fangshang. *Geming zhi zaiqi: Zhongguo Guomindang gaizu qian dui xin sichao de huiying, 1914–1924*. [(Original English title) Rekindle the Revolution: The Kuomintang's Response to New Thought before the Reorganization, 1914–1924]. Taipei: Zhongyang yanjiu yuan jindai shi yanjiu suo, 1989.

Lu Kang. "Zhejiang bang jinrong jia zai Shanghai" [Zhejiang capitalists in Shanghai]. In *Zhejiang ji ziben jia de xingqi* [Rise of capitalism of Zhejiang origin], edited by Wenshi ziliao weiyuan hui. Hangzhou: Zhejiang renmin chuban she, 1986.

Lu Kuang-huan. "The Shu-yuan Institution, a Development by Sung-Ming Philosophers." *Chinese Culture* 9 (September 1968): 98–122.

Lü Shiqiang. *Zhongguo guanshen fanjiao de yuanyin* [Causes of Chinese official and gentry opposition to Christianity]. Taipei: Wenjing shuju, 1973.

Lu Xun. *The Complete Stories of Lu Xun: Call to Arms, Wandering*. Trans. Yang Xianyi and Gladys Yang. Bloomington: Indiana University Press, 1981.

————. "Kuang ren riji" [Diary of a madman]. *Xin qingnian* 4, 5 (May 1918): 414–24.

Luo Zhanglong. "Beijing Gongchan zhuyi xiaozu de qingkuang" [Conditions in the Beijing Communist small groups]. *Gongchan zhuyi xiaozu,* edited by Zhonggong zhongyang dangshi ziliao zhengji weiyuan hui. Beijing: Zhonggong dangshi ziliao chuban she, 1987, vol. 1.

———. "Huiyi Beijing daxue Makesi xueshuo yanjiu hui" [Recollections of the Marxism Study Society at Beijing University]. In *Gongchan zhuyi xiaozu,* edited by Zhonggong zhongyang dangshi ziliao zhengji weiyuan hui. Beijing: Zhonggong dangshi ziliao chuban she, 1987, vol. 1.

Mann, Susan. *Local Merchants and the Chinese Bureaucracy, 1750–1950.* Stanford: Stanford University Press, 1987.

———. "Widows in the Kinship, Class, and Community Structure of Qing Dynasty China." *Journal of Asian Studies* 46, 1 (February 1987): 37–56.

Mao Dun [Shen Yanbing]. *Chuncan* [Spring silkworm]. Beijing: Foreign Language Press, 1956.

———. *Wo zouguo de daolu* [The path that I have taken]. Hong Kong: Sanlian shudian, 1981.

Maring. "Report of Comrade H. Maring to the Executive." July 11, 1922. Trans. in Tony Saich, *The Origins of the First United Front in China: The Role of Sneevliet (Alias Maring).* Leiden: E. J. Brill, 1991, vol. 1.

Marme, Michael. "Heaven on Earth: The Rise of Suzhou, 1127–1550." In *Cities of Jiangnan in Late Imperial China,* edited by Linda Cooke Johnson. Albany: State University of New York Press, 1993.

Marx, Karl. *A Contribution to the Critique of Political Economy* (1859). New York: International Publishers, 1970.

Masao, Mori. "The Gentry in the Ming—An Outline of the Relations between the *Shih-ta-fu* and Local Society." *Acta Asiatica* 38 (1980): 31–53.

McElderry, Andrea Lee. *Shanghai Old-Style Banks (Ch'ien-chuang), 1800–1935.* Ann Arbor: Center for Chinese Studies, University of Michigan, 1976.

Mehring, Franz. *Karl Marx: The Story of His Life.* New York: Covici, Friede, 1935.

Meisner, Maurice. *Li Ta-chao and the Origins of Chinese Marxism.* Cambridge, Mass.: Harvard University Press, 1967.

Meizhou pinglun [Weekly commentary]. Beijing.

Meskill, John. "Academies and Politics in the Ming Dynasty." In *Chinese Government in Ming Times: Seven Studies,* edited by Charles O. Hucker. New York: Columbia University Press, 1969.

Metzger, Thomas A. *Escape from Predicament: Neo-Confucianism and China's Evolving Political Culture.* New York: Columbia University Press, 1977.

Min Tu-ki. *National Polity and Local Power: The Transformation of Late Imperial China,* edited by Philip A. Kuhn and Timothy Brook.

Cambridge, Mass.: Council on East Asian Studies Publications, Harvard University Press, 1989.

Minguo ribao [Republican daily]. Shanghai.

Ministry of Economics Archives, Institute of Modern History, Academia Sinica, Taipei.

Ministry of Education. *Diyi ci Zhongguo jiaoyu nianjian* [Yearbook of Chinese education, first compilation]. Shanghai: Kaiming shudian, 1934.

Mitchell, W. J. T. *Iconology: Image, Text, Ideology.* Chicago: University of Chicago Press, 1986.

Miyazaki, Ichisada. *China's Examination Hell: The Civil Service Examinations of Imperial China.* Trans. Conrad Schirokauer. New Haven: Yale University Press, 1976.

Mote, Frederick. "The T'u-mu Incident of 1449." In *Chinese Ways in Warfare,* edited by Frank A Kierman, Jr., and John K. Fairbank. Cambridge, Mass.: Harvard University Press, 1974.

———, and Denis Twitchett, eds. *The Cambridge History of China,* vol. 7. Cambridge: Cambridge University Press, 1988.

Murphey, Rhoads. "The Treaty Ports and China's Modernization." In *The Chinese City between Two Worlds,* edited by Mark Elvin and G. William Skinner. Stanford: Stanford University Press, 1974.

Muzha Archives, Muzha, Taipei.

Myers, Ramon. "The Agrarian System." In *The Cambridge History of China,* vol. 13, *Republican China,* edited by John K. Fairbank and Albert Feuerwerker. Cambridge: Cambridge University Press, 1983, pt. 2:230–69.

Naquin, Susan. *Millenarian Rebellion in China: The Eight Trigrams Uprising of 1813.* New Haven: Yale University Press, 1976.

———. "The Transformation of White Lotus Sectarianism in Late Imperial China." In *Popular Culture in Late Imperial China,* edited by David Johnson, Andrew Nathan, and Evelyn Rawski. Berkeley: University of California Press, 1985.

———, and Evelyn S. Rawski. *Chinese Society in the Eighteenth Century.* New Haven: Yale University Press, 1987.

Ng, Vivien W. "Rape Laws in Qing China." *Journal of Asian Studies* 46, 1 (February 1987): 57–70.

Ni Weixiong. "Zhejiang xinchao de huiyi" [Recollections of the Zhejiang New Tide Society]. In *Wusi yundong huiyi lu,* edited by Zhongguo shehui kexue yuan jindai shi yanjiu suo. Beijing: Zhongguo shehui kexue chuban she, 1979, 2:737–41.

Nivison, David. *The Life and Thought of Chang Hsueh-ch'eng (1738–1801).* Stanford: Stanford University Press, 1966.

———, and Arthur Wright, eds. *Confucianism in Action.* Stanford: Stanford University Press, 1959.

North, Robert C. *Moscow and Chinese Communists*. Stanford: Stanford University Press, 1963.

Overmyer, Daniel L. *Folk Buddhist Religion: Dissenting Sects in Late Traditional China*. Cambridge, Mass.: Harvard University Press, 1976.

Pan Guangdan. *Ming Qing liangdai Jiaxing de wangzu* [Eminent lineages of Jiaxing during the Ming and the Qing]. Shanghai: Shangwu yinshu guan, 1947.

Pang Dexin [Pong Tak-san]. *Songdai liangjing shimin shenghuo* [Original title in English: Daily Life in the Sung Capitals as Reflected in the *Huaben* of the Sung, Yuan and Ming Periods]. Hong Kong: Longmen shudian, 1974.

Parsons, James B. "The Ming Dynasty Bureaucracy." In *Chinese Government in Ming Times: Seven Studies*. New York: Columbia University Press, 1969.

Perry, Elizabeth. *Shanghai on Strike: The Politics of Chinese Labor*. Stanford: Stanford University Press, 1993.

———. "Strikes among Shanghai Silk Weavers, 1927–1937: The Awakening of a Labor Aristocracy." In *Shanghai Sojourners*, edited by Frederic Wakeman, Jr., and Wen-hsin Yeh. Berkeley: Institute of East Asian Studies, University of California, 1992.

Peterson, Charles A. "First Song Reactions to the Mongol Invasion of the North, 1211–17." In *Crisis and Prosperity in Sung China*, edited by John W. Haeger. Tucson: University of Arizona Press, 1975.

Pickowicz, Paul. *Marxist Literary Thought in China: The Influence of Ch'u Ch'iu-pai*. Berkeley: University of California Press, 1981.

Price, Don C. "Revolution for the Ancestors: National Identity in Experience and Rhetoric." Paper presented at the Annual Meeting of the Association for Asian Studies, Los Angeles, March 27, 1993.

———. *Russia and the Roots of the Chinese Revolution, 1896–1911*. Cambridge, Mass.: Harvard University Press, 1974.

Price, Jane L. *Cadres, Commanders, and Commissars: The Training of the Chinese Communist Leadership, 1920–1945*. Boulder, Col.: Westview, 1976.

Pye, Lucien W. *Warlord Politics: Conflict and Coalition in the Modernization of Republican China*. New York: Praeger, 1971.

Qian Jiaju. "Wo yu Wu Han" [Wu Han and I]. *Zhuanji wenxue* (Taipei) 57, 2 (August 1990): 35–41.

Qian Mu. *Guoshi dagang* [Outline of our nation's history]. Vol. 2. Reprint Taipei: Commercial Press, 1967.

———. *Song-Ming lixue gaishu* [Introduction to Song-Ming Neo-Confucianism]. Taipei: Xuesheng shuju, 1977.

Qiantang jiang jixing bianxie zu. *Qiantang jiang jixing* [Journal along the Qiantang River]. Shanghai: Shanghai jiaoyu chuban she, 1981.

Qin Yingjun and Zhang Zhanbin, eds. *Da lang tao sha: Zhonggong yida renwu zhuan* [Waves washing away the beach sand: Individual biographies of the First Party Congress of the Chinese Communist Party]. Beijing: Hongqi chuban she, 1991.

Qu Qiubai. "Duo yu de hua" [Superfluous words]. 1935. Reprint Hong Kong: Zhongguo xin wenxue ziliao shi, 1975.

Qu Yingguang. "Chengbao xuxun Jin Qu Yan Chu yidai shisuo huishu riqi dian" [Report on the conclusion of my official visit to the Jinhua, Quzhou, Yanzhou and Chuzhou areas and on the determination of a return date to my provincial office]. In Qu Yingguang, *Qu Xun'an xunshi liang Zhe wengao.* N.p., preface dated 1915, vol. 1.

———. "Chengbao xuxun jiu Jin Qu Yan geshu ji Shao shu zhi Zhuji jiu Chu shu zhi Jinyun, Suichang, Xuanping gexian shisuo wen" [Report on continuing the inspection tour into counties formerly under the jurisdiction of the Jin-Qu-Yan Prefecture, into Zhuji County of Shaoxing Prefecture, into Jinyun, Suichang and Xuanping counties of Chuzhou Prefecture]. In Qu Yingguang, *Qu Xun'an xunshi liang Zhe wengao.* N.p., preface dated 1915, vol. 1.

———. "Chi Jinhua daoyin shujun shangjiang yidai shuili wen" [Order issued to the Jinhua circuit intendant to dredge up the waterway along the upper stream]. In Qu Yingguang, *Qu Xun'an xunshi liang Zhe wengao.* N.p., preface dated 1915, vol. 2.

———. *Qu Xun'an xunshi liang Zhe wengao* [Governor Qu's writings during an investigative tour of Zhedong and Zhexi]. 4 vols. N.p., preface dated 1915.

———. "Xunshi Jiangshan xian xuanyan" [Proclamation on a tour of inspection of Jiangshan County]. In Qu Yingguang, *Qu Xun'an xunshi liang Zhe wengao.* N.p., preface dated 1915, vol. 4.

———. "Xunshi Lanxi xian xuanyan" [Proclamation on the occasion of an official visit to Lanxi]. In Qu Yingguang, *Qu Xun'an xunshi liang Zhe wengao.* N.p., preface dated 1915, vol. 4.

———. "Xunshi Yongkang xian xuanyan" [Proclamation on a tour of inspection of Yongkang County]. In Qu Yingguang, *Qu Xun'an xunshi liang Zhe wengao.* N.p., preface dated 1915, vol. 4.

———. "Xunshi Yuyao xian xuanyan" [Proclamation on an official tour of Yuyao County]. In Qu Yingguang, *Qu Xun'an xunshi liang Zhe wengao.* N.p., preface dated 1915, vol. 4.

Quan Hansheng. "Tang Song diguo yu yunhe" [Tang-Song empire and the Grand Canal]. In *Zhongguo jingji shi yanjiu* [Studies in Chinese economic history]. Hong Kong: Xinya yanjiu suo chuban she, 1976, 1:265–395. Originally published in *Zhongyang yanjiu yuan lishi yuyan yanjiu suo zhuankan* [Bulletin of the Institute of History and Philology, Academia Sinica]. Taipei, 1943.

Rankin, Mary Backus. *Early Chinese Revolutionaries: Radical Intellectuals in Shanghai and Chekiang, 1902–1911.* Cambridge, Mass.: Harvard University Press, 1971.

————. *Elite Activism and Political Transformation in China: Zhejiang Province, 1865–1911.* Stanford: Stanford University Press, 1986.

————. "The Revolutionary Movement in Chekiang: A Study in the Tenacity of Tradition." In *China in Revolution: The First Phase, 1900–1913,* edited by Mary Wright. New Haven: Yale University Press, 1968.

————, John Fairbank, and Albert Feuerwerker. "Introduction: Perspectives on Modern China's History." In *The Cambridge History of China,* vol. 13, *Republican China,* edited by John Fairbank and Albert Feuerwerker. Cambridge: Cambridge University Press, 1983.

Rapport, Angelo S. "Eguo geming de zhexue jichu" [Philosophical foundation of the Russian revolution]. Trans. Qiming in *Xin qingnian* 6, 4 (April 1919): 365–71, and 6, 5 (May 1919): 470–78.

Rawski, Evelyn. *Agricultural Change and the Peasant Economy of South China.* Cambridge, Mass.: Harvard University Press, 1972.

————. *Education and Popular Literacy in Ch'ing China.* Ann Arbor: University of Michigan Press, 1979.

Reynolds, Douglas. *China, 1898–1912: The* Xinzheng *Revolution and Japan.* Cambridge, Mass.: Council on East Asian Studies Publications, Harvard University Press, 1993.

Rossabi, Morris. *Khubilai Khan: His Life and Times.* Berkeley: University of California Press, 1988.

Rowe, William. *Hankow: Commerce and Society in a Chinese City, 1796–1889.* Stanford: Stanford University Press, 1984.

————. *Hankow: Conflict and Community in a Chinese City, 1796–1895.* Stanford: Stanford University Press, 1989.

Ruan Yicheng. *Minguo Ruan Xunbo xiansheng Xingcun nianpu* [Chronological biography of Mr. Ruan Xingcun (Xunbo) of the Republican period]. Taipei: Taiwan Commercial Press, 1979.

————. "Ruan Xingcun." *Zhuanji wenxue* 23, 3 (September 1973): 18–19.

————. *San ju buli ben Hang* [My hometown Hangzhou]. Taipei: Zhengzhong shuju, 1974.

————. "Yicheng zizhuan nianpu ji zishu" [Yicheng's autobiographical chronological account]. *Zhongshan xueshu wenhua jikan* [Zhongshan scholarship and culture quarterly] 10 (1972): 581–730.

Ruxin. "Yuanzu hui zhi pangren guan" [Hiking trip as seen by a bystander]. *Zhejiang shengli diyi shifan xuexiao xiaoyu huizhi* 2 (1914).

Saari, Jon L. *Legacies of Childhood: Growing Up Chinese in a Time of Crisis, 1890–1920.* Cambridge, Mass.: Council on East Asian Studies Publications, Harvard University Press, 1990.

Saich, Tony. *The Origins of the First United Front in China: The Role of Sneevliet (Alias Maring).* 2 vols. Leiden: E. J. Brill, 1991.

Santangelo, Paolo. "Urban Society in Late Imperial Suzhou." Trans. Adam Victor. In *Cities of Jiangnan in Late Imperial China*, edited by Linda Cooke Johnson. Albany: State University of New York Press, 1993.

Scheiner, Irwin, and Peter Duus. "Socialism, Liberalism, and Marxism, 1901–1931." In *The Cambridge History of Japan*, vol. 6, *The Twentieth Century*, edited by Peter Duus. Cambridge: Cambridge University Press, 1988.

Schirokauer, Conrad. "Chu Hsi's Political Career." In *Confucian Personalities*, edited by Arthur F. Wright and Denis Twitchett. Stanford: Stanford University Press, 1962.

———. "Neo-Confucians under Attack: The Condemnation of *Wei-hsueh*." In *Crisis and Prosperity in Sung China*, edited by John Winthrop Haeger. Tucson: University of Arizona Press, 1975.

Schoppa, R. Keith. *Chinese Elites and Political Change: Zhejiang Province in the Early Twentieth Century*. Cambridge, Mass.: Council on East Asian Studies Publications, Harvard University Press, 1982.

———. "Contours of Revolutionary Change in a Chinese County, 1900–1950." *Journal of Asian Studies* 51, 4 (November 1992): 770–96.

———. "Rent Resistance and Rural Reconstruction: Shen Dingyi in Political Opposition, 1921 and 1928." In *Roads Not Taken: The Struggle of Opposition Parties in Twentieth Century China*, edited by Roger B. Jeans. Boulder, Col.: Westview, 1992.

Schram, Stuart. *The Thought of Mao Tse-tung*. Cambridge: Cambridge University Press, 1989.

Schwarcz, Vera. *The Chinese Enlightenment: Intellectuals and the Legacy of the May Fourth Movement of 1919*. Berkeley: University of California Press, 1986.

Schwartz, Benjamin I. *In Search of Wealth and Power: Yen Fu and the West*. Cambridge, Mass.: Harvard University Press, 1964.

———. "Some Polarities in Confucian Thought." In *Confucianism in Action*, edited by David S. Nivison and Arthur Wright. Stanford: Stanford University Press, 1959.

———, ed. *Reflections on the May Fourth Movement: A Symposium*. Cambridge, Mass.: Council on East Asian Studies Publications, Harvard University Press, 1972.

Shang Kui. "Shu yu san xian" [Three life-threatening incidents in my life]. *Zhejiang shengli diyi shifan xuexiao xiaoyou huizhi* (fall 1917): 33–34.

Shang Qiliang. "Zhejiang xingye yinhang xingshuai shi" [Rise and fall of the Zhejiang Industrial Bank]. *Zhejiang wenshi ziliao xuanji* 46 (1992): 41–44.

Shanghai Municipal Police files.

Shanghai shi dang'an guan, ed. *Shanghai gongren sanci wuzhuang qiyi* [Three armed uprisings by Shanghai's workers]. Shanghai: Renmin chuban she, 1983.

Shanghai zhoubao she, ed. *Dangdai shisheng* [Contemporary historical gazette]. Shanghai: Shanghai zhoubao she, 1933.

Shao Baosan. "Xiaoxia zazhi" [Miscellaneous summer notes]. *Zhejiang shengli diyi shifan xuexiao xiaoyou huizhi* (fall 1917): 28–31.

Shao Lizi. "Dang chengli qianhou de yixie qingkuang" [Conditions before and after the founding of the Party]. In *Yida qianhou: Zhongguo Gongchandang diyi ci daibiao dahui qianhou ziliao xuanbian* [Before and after the First Party Congress: Selected edition of materials on the First Party Congress of the Chinese Communist Party], edited by Zhongguo shehui kexue yuan xiandai shi yanjiu shi and Zhongguo geming bowu guan dangshi yanjiu shi. Beijing: Renmin chuban she, 1980, vol. 2.

————. "Shehui zhuyi yu gongqi" [Socialism and communal sharing of women]. *Minguo ribao*, October 21, 1921.

Shao Weizheng. "Yida zhaokai riqi he chuxi renshu de kaozheng" [Empirical inquiry into the conference dates and number of participants of the First Party Congress]. In *Yida huiyi lu* [First Party Congress memoirs]. Beijing: Zhishi chuban she, 1980.

[Shen] Xuanlu. "Hunjia wenti" [On marriages]. *Xingqi pinglun* 27 (December 7, 1919): 2.

————. "Xuexiao zizhi de shenghuo" [Self-rule by students]. *Xingqi pinglun* 22 (November 2, 1919): 3.

————. "Zhejiang xuechao de yipie" [Student unrest in Zhejiang: A glimpse]. *Xingqi pinglun* 1 (June 8, 1919): 2–3.

Shen Yunlong. "Cong Wuhan fen gong dao Guangzhou baodong" [From the Wuhan purge of Communists to the Guangzhou Commune]. *Zhuanji wenxue* 33, 6 (December 1978): 21–34.

————. "Guangzhou feichang huiyi de fenlie yu Ning Yue Hu siquan dahui de hezuo" [Schism of the Guangzhou Conference and the collaboration among Nanjing, Guangzhou and Shanghai delegates during the Fourth Party Congress]. *Zhuanji wenxue* 35, 3 (September 1979): 15–26.

————. "Kuoda huiyi zhi youlai ji jingguo" [Origin and proceeding of the Expanded Conference]. *Zhuanji wenxue* 33, 4 (October 1978): 11–20.

Shen Ziqian, Zhao Zijie, Xu Bonian, and Huang Meiying. *Zhejiang yishi fengchao* [Disturbance at the Zhejiang First Normal]. Hangzhou: Zhejiang daxue chuban she, 1990.

Sheng Jingying. "Xian weng Jing Yuanshan jianli" [Biographical sketch of my deceased father-in-law Jing Yuanshan]. In *Jing Yuanshan ji* [Collected works by Jing Yuanshan], edited by Yu Heping. Wuhan: Huazhong shifan daxue chuban she, 1988.

Sheng Renxue, ed. *Zhang Guotao nianpu ji yanlun* [Zhang Guotao: Chronological biography and writings]. Beijing: Jiefangjun chuban she, 1985.

Shi Cuntong [Fuliang]. "Chengshi xiao zichan jieji yu minzhu geming" [Urban petite bourgeoisie and democratic revolution]. *Geming pinglun* 9 (July 1928): 11–16.

———. "Fei xiao" [Decry filial piety!]. *Zhejiang xinchao* 2 (November 1919).

———. "Gongdu huzhu tuan de shiyan he jiaoxun" [Experiment of and lessons from the Work-Study Corps]. *Xingqi pinglun* 48 (May 1, 1920): 7.

———. "Huifu shisan nian gaizu jingshen" [Revive the spirit of reorganization of 1924]. *Geming pinglun* 5 (June 1928): 10–19.

———. "Huitou kan ershier nian lai de wo" [Retrospective view of myself of the past twenty-two years]. *Minguo ribao* [Republican daily], pts. 1–5. September 20–24, 1920, "Juewu" [Awakening] section.

———. "Women yao zenmeyang gan shehui geming" [How we make a social revolution]. *Gongchandang* [*The Communist*] 5 (July 1921): 10–32.

———. "Zhongguo geming yu xuesheng yundong" [Chinese revolution and the student movement]. *Geming pinglun* 18 (September 1928): 7–11.

———. , trans. *Makesi xueshuo gaiyao* [Succinct summary of Marxism]. Shanghai: Shangwu yinshu guan, 1922.

Shi Fuliang [Cuntong]. *Rensheng wenti wujiang: Zuoren, zuoshi, ji nannü wenti* [Five lectures on problems in our lives: Integrity, career, and men-women relationships]. Shanghai: Xinlu shudian, 1947.

———. "Wusi zai Hangzhou" [The May Fourth Movement in Hangzhou]. In *Wusi yundong huiyi lu* [Recollections on the May Fourth Movement], edited by Zhongguo shehui kexue yuan jindai shi yanjiu suo. Beijing: Zhongguo shehui kexue chuban she, 1979, vol. 2.

———. "Zhongguo Gongchandang chengli shiqi de jige wenti" [A few problems at the time of the founding of the Chinese Communist Party]. In *Yida qianhou: Zhongguo Gongchandang diyi ci daibiao dahui qianhou ziliao xuanbian* [Before and after the First Party Congress: Selected edition of materials on the First Party Congress of the Chinese Communist Party], edited by Zhongguo shehui kexue yuan xiandai shi yanjiu shi and Zhongguo geming bowu guan danshi yanjiu shi. Beijing: Renmin chuban she, 1980, vol. 2.

———. "Zhongguo shehui zhuyi qingnian tuan chengli qianhou de yixie qingkuang" [Conditions before and after the formation of the Chinese Socialist Youth Corps]. In *Yida qianhou: Zhongguo Gongchandang diyi ci daibiao dahui qianhou ziliao xuanbian* [Before and after the First Party Congress: Selected edition of materials on the First Party Congress of the Chinese Communist Party], edited by Zhongguo shehui kexue yuan xiandai shi yanjiu shi and Zhongguo geming bowu guan dangshi yanjiu shi. Beijing: Renmin chuban she, 1980, vol. 2.

———. *Zhongguo xiandai jingji shi* [History of modern Chinese economy]. Shanghai: Liangyou tushu yinshua gongsi, 1932.

Shiba Yoshinobu. *Commerce and Society in Sung China.* Ann Arbor: Center for Chinese Studies, University of Michigan, 1970.

———. "Ningbo and Its Hinterland." In *The City in Late Imperial China,* edited by G. William Skinner. Stanford: Stanford University Press, 1977.

Shih Ching [The book of poetry]. Chinese text with English trans. by James Legge. New York: Paragon Book Reprint, 1967.

Shu Xincheng. *Wo he jiaoyu* [Education and I]. Taipei: Longmen chuban she, 1990.

———, ed. *Zhongguo jindai jiaoyu shi ziliao* [Sources on the history of modern Chinese education]. 3 vols. Beijing: Renmin jiaoyu chuban she, 1961.

"Sichuan sheng Chongqing gongchan zhuyi zuzhi de baogao" [Report by the Communist organization of Chongqing, Sichuan Province]. In *Zhongguo Gongchandang diyi ci daibiao dahui dang'an ziliao zeng ding ben* [Expanded edition, Archival materials on the First Party Congress of the Chinese Communist Party], edited by Zhongyang dang'an guan [Central Party Archives]. Beijing: Renmin chuban she, 1984.

Sills, David L., ed. *International Encyclopaedia of the Social Sciences.* 19 vols. New York: Macmillan and Free Press, 1968–1991.

Skinner, G. William. "Introduction: Urban Development in Imperial China." In *The City in Late Imperial China.* Stanford: Stanford University Press, 1977.

———. "Introduction: Urban Social Structure in Ch'ing China." In *The City in Late Imperial China.* Stanford: Stanford University Press, 1977.

———, ed. *The City in Late Imperial China.* Stanford: Stanford University Press, 1977.

So, Kwan-wai. *Japanese Piracy in Ming China during the 16th Century.* East Lansing: Michigan State University Press, 1975.

Spector, Stanley. *Li Hung-chang and the Huai Army: A Study in Nineteenth-Century Chinese Regionalism.* Seattle: University of Washington Press, 1964.

Spence, Jonathan D. *Ts'ao Yin and the K'ang-hsi Emperor: Bondservant and Master.* New Haven: Yale University Press, 1966.

———, and John E. Wills, eds. *From Ming to Ch'ing: Conquest, Region, and Continuity in Seventeenth-Century China.* New Haven: Yale University Press, 1979.

Strand, David. *Rickshaw Beijing: City People and Politics in the 1920s.* Berkeley: University of California Press, 1989.

Struve, Lynn. "Chen Que Versus Huang Zongxi: Confucianism Faces Modern Times in the 17th-century." *Journal of Chinese Philosophy* 18, 1 (March 1991): 5–23.

———. "The Hsu Brothers and Semiofficial Patronage of Scholars in the K'ang-hsi Period." *Harvard Journal of Asiatic Studies* 42, 1 (June 1982): 231–66.

Sun Choucheng, Huang Zhenshi, He Guotao, Fan Xuewen, and Dai Yu-fang. "Yu Xiaqing shilue" [Outline of Yu Xiaqing's life]. In *Zhejiang ji ziben jia de xingqi* [Rise of Zhejiang capitalists], edited by Zhongguo renmin zhengzhi xieshang huiyi: Zhejiang sheng wenshi ziliao yanjiu weiyuan hui. Hangzhou: Zhejiang renmin chuban she, 1986.

Sun, E-tu Zen. *Chinese Railways and British Interests, 1898–1911*. New York: Columbia University, King's Crown Press, 1954.

———. "Sericulture and Silk Textile Production in Ch'ing China." In *Economic Organization in Chinese Society*, edited by W. E. Willmott. Stanford: Stanford University Press, 1972.

Sun Kekuan. *Yuandai Jinhua xueshu* [Jinhua scholarship during the Yuan dynasty]. Taizhong: Sili Donghai daxue, 1975.

Tan Ming. Preface. In Liu Dabai, *Liu Dabai xuanji* [Selected works of Liu Dabai]. Hong Kong: Xianggang wenxue yanjiu she, n.d.

Tan Pingshan. "Zhi Guochang xiansheng" [Letter to Guochang (Shi Cuntong)]. In *Yida qianhou de Guangdong dang zuzhi* [Party organization in Guangdong before and after the First Congress], edited by Zhonggong Guangdong shengwei dangshi yanjiu weiyuan hui bangong shi and Guangdong sheng dang'an guan. Dongguan: Guangdong sheng dang'an guan, 1981.

Tao Yinghui. *Cai Yuanpei nianpu* [Chronological biography of Cai Yuanpei]. Taipei: Zhongyang yanjiu yuan jindai shi yanjiu suo, 1976.

Taylor, Romeyn. "Official and Popular Religion and the Political Organization of Chinese Society in the Ming." In *Orthodoxy in Late Imperial China*, edited by Kwang-Ching Liu. Berkeley: University of California Press, 1990.

Tian Yuqing. *Dong Jin menfa zhengzhi* [Eastern Jin aristocratic politics]. Beijing: Beijing University Press, 1991.

Tillman, Hoyt C. "Proto-Nationalism in Twelfth-Century China." *Harvard Journal of Asiatic Studies* 36, 2 (December 1979): 403–28.

———. *Utilitarian Confucianism: Ch'en Liang's Challenge to Chu Hsi*. Cambridge, Mass.: Council on East Asian Studies Publications, Harvard University Press, 1982.

Tu, Wei-ming. *Neo-Confucian Thought in Action: Wang Yang-ming's Youth, 1472–1509*. Berkeley: University of California Press, 1976.

———. "Reconstituting the Confucian Tradition." *Journal of Asian Studies* 33, 3 (May 1974): 441–53.

———. "The Sung Confucian Idea of Education: A Background Understanding." In *Neo-Confucian Education: The Formative Stage*, edited by W. Theodore de Bary and John W. Chaffee. Berkeley: University of California Press, 1989.

Twitchett, Denis. "The Fan Clan's Charitable Estate, 1050–1760." In *Confucianism in Action*, edited by David Nivison and Arthur Wright. Stanford: Stanford University Press, 1959.

———. "Problems of Chinese Biography." In *Confucian Personalities*, edited by Arthur F. Wright and Denis Twitchett. Stanford: Stanford University Press, 1962.

Usov, V. "Soviet Aid to China in Training Party and Revolutionary Cadres." *Far Eastern Affairs* 6 (1987): 74–81.

Van de Ven, Hans. *From Friend to Comrade: The Founding of the Chinese Communist Party, 1920–1927*. Berkeley: University of California Press, 1991.

Van Slyke, Lyman P. *Yangtze: Nature, History, and the River*. Menlo Park, Calif.: Addison-Wesley, 1988.

Vardi, Liana. "Constructing the Harvest: Gleaners, Farmers, and Officials in Early Modern France." *American Historical Review* 98, 5 (December 1993): 1,424–47.

Wakeman, Frederic, Jr. *Policing Shanghai 1927–1937*. Berkeley: University of California Press, 1994.

———. "Romantics, Stoics, and Martyrs in Seventeenth-Century China." *Journal of Asian Studies* 43, 4 (August 1984): 631–66.

———. *Strangers at the Gate: Social Disorder in South China, 1839–1861*. Berkeley: University of California Press, 1966.

———. "Voyages." *American Historical Review* 98, 1 (February 1993): 1–17.

———, and Carolyn Grant, eds. *Conflict and Control in Late Imperial China*. Berkeley: University of California Press, 1975.

———, and Wen-hsin Yeh, eds. *Shanghai Sojourners*. Berkeley: Institute of East Asian Studies, University of California, Berkeley, 1992.

Wang Guangqi. "Gong du huzhu tuan" [Work-Study Mutual Aid Corps]. In *Fu Fa qingong jianxue yundong shiliao* [Historical sources on the Chinese diligent-work frugal-study movement in France], edited by Qinghua daxue Zhonggong dangshi jiaoyan zu. Beijing: Beijing chuban she, 1979.

Wang Gungwu. "The Nanhai Trade." *Journal of the Malayan Branch of the Royal Asiatic Society* 31 (1958), pt. 2: 1–135.

Wang Shoudao. Preface. In *Zhonggong dangshi yanjiu lunwen xuan*, edited by Zhu Chengjia. Changsha: Hunan renmin chuban she, 1983, 1: i–xi.

Wang Shuixiang, Chen Liejiong, and Wang Zuhan. "Aiguo minzhu yingyong zhanshi Shi Fuliang" [Patriotic, democratic, brave warrior Shi Fuliang]. *Zhejiang wenshi ziliao xuanji* 41 (1989): 93–108.

Wang Shukuai. "Qingmo Jiangsu difang zizhi fengchao" [Late Qing local riots and self-rule]. *Zhongyang yanjiu yuan jindai shi yanjiu suo jikan* 6 (1977): 313–27.

Wang Yizhi. "Zou xiang geming—wusi huiyi" [Marching toward revolution—remembering May Fourth]. In *Wusi yundong huiyi lu* [May Fourth memoirs], edited by Zhongguo shehui kexue yuan jindai shi yanjiu suo. Beijing: Zhongguo shehui kexue chuban she, 1979, vol. 1.

Watson, Rubie S. "Wives, Concubines, and Maids: Servitude and Kinship in the Hong Kong Region, 1900–1940." In *Marriage and Inequality in Chinese Society*, edited by Rubie S. Watson and Patricia Buckley Ebrey. Berkeley: University of California Press, 1991.

Wei Jinzhi. "Dongri jiagui ji" [Account of my homeward journey in the winter]. *Zhejiang shengli diyi shifan xuexiao xiaoyou huizhi* 14/15 (1918): "zazhu" [miscellaneous], 4–5.

Wei Songtang, ed. *Zhejiang jingji jilue* [Outline of Zhejiang economic geography]. Shanghai: n.p., 1929.

Wending. "Shifu zhuan" [Biography of Shifu]. In *Wuzhengfu zhuyi sixiang ziliao xuan* [Selection of source materials on anarchist thought], edited by Ge Maochun, Jiang Jun, and Li Xinzhi. Beijing: Beijing daxue chuban she, 1984, vol. 2.

Whiting, Allen S. *Soviet Policies in China, 1917–1924*. Stanford: Stanford University Press, 1953.

Widmer, Ellen, and David Der-wei Wang, eds. *From May Fourth to June Fourth: Fiction and Film in Twentieth Century China*. Cambridge, Mass.: Harvard University Press, 1993.

Wiens, Mi Chu. "Lord and Peasant: The Sixteenth to the Eighteenth Century." *Modern China* 6, 1 (January 1980): 3–40.

Wilbur, C. Martin, and Julie Lien-ying How. *Missionaries of Revolution: Soviet Advisers and Nationalist China, 1920–1927*. Cambridge, Mass.: Harvard University Press, 1989.

———, eds. *Documents on Communism, Nationalism, and Soviet Advisers in China, 1918–1927; Papers Seized in the 1927 Peking Raid*. New York: Columbia University Press, 1956.

Willmott, W. E., ed. *Economic Organization in Chinese Society*. Stanford: Stanford University Press, 1972.

Wills, John E., Jr. "Maritime China from Wang Chih to Shih Lang: Themes in Peripheral History." In *From Ming to Ch'ing: Conquest, Region, and Continuity in Seventeenth-Century China*, edited by Jonathan Spence and John E. Wills. New Haven: Yale University Press, 1979.

Wittgenstein, Ludwig. *The Blue and Brown Books*. New York: Harper and Row, 1958.

Wolf, Arthur P. "Gods, Ghosts, and Ancestors." In *Religion and Ritual in Chinese Society*, edited by Arthur P. Wolf. Stanford: Stanford University Press, 1974.

———, ed. *Religion and Ritual in Chinese Society*. Stanford: Stanford University Press, 1974.

Wolf, Margery. "Child Training and the Chinese Family." In *Family and Kinship in Chinese Society*, edited by Maurice Friedman. Stanford: Stanford University Press, 1970.

―――. *Women and the Family in Rural Taiwan*. Stanford: Stanford University Press, 1972.

Wright, Arthur F., and Denis Twitchett, eds. *Confucian Personalities*. Stanford: Stanford University Press, 1962.

Wright, Mary. *China in Revolution: The First Phase, 1900–1913*. New Haven: Yale University Press, 1968.

Wu Chenbo [Wu Han]. *Zhu Yuanzhang zhuan* [Biography of Zhu Yuanzhang]. Reprint Taipei: Guoshi yanjiu shi, 1972.

Wu Yu. "Chiren yu lijiao" [Men-eating and ritual teaching]. *Xin qingnian* 6, 6 (November 1919): 578–80.

―――. "Jiazu zhidu wei zhuanzhi zhuyi zhi genju lun" [Familism as the basis of authoritarianism]. *Xin qingnian* 2, 6 (February 1917): 1–4.

Wusi aiguo yundong dang'an ziliao [Archival source materials concerning the May Fourth patriotic movement]. Edited by Zhongguo shehui kexue yuan jindai shi yanjiu suo. Beijing: Zhongguo shehui kexue chuban she, 1980.

Wusi shiqi de shetuan [Associational organizations of the May Fourth period]. Edited by Zhang Yunhou, Yin Xuyi, Hong Qingxiang, and Wang Yunkai. 4 vols. Beijing: Shenghuo, dushu, xinzhi sanlian shudian, 1959; reprint 1979.

Wusi shiqi qikan jieshao [Introduction to periodicals of the May Fourth period]. Edited by Zhonggong zhongyang Makesi, Engesi, Liening, Sidalin zhuzuo bianyi ju yanjiu shi. 6 vols. Beijing: Shenghuo, dushu, xinzhi sanlian shudian, 1978.

Wusi yundong huiyi lu [Recollections of the May Fourth Movement]. Edited by Zhongguo shehui kexue yuan jindai shi yanjiu suo. 3 vols. Beijing: Zhongguo shehui kexue chuban she, 1979.

Wusi yundong zai Zhejiang [May Fourth Movement in Zhejiang]. Edited by Zhonggong Zhejiang shengwei dangxiao dangshi jiaoyan shi. Hangzhou: Zhejiang renmin chuban she, 1979.

Wuzhengfu zhuyi sixiang ziliao xuan [Selection of source materials on anarchist thought]. Edited by Ge Maochun, Jiang Jun, and Li Xingzhi. 2 vols. Beijing: Beijing daxue chuban she, 1984.

Xia Mianzun. "Duile Milai de 'Wanzhong'" [Reflections on the 'Evening Bell' by Millet]. In *Pingwu zawen* [Miscellaneous writings of the Pingwu]. Shanghai: Kaiming shudian, 1935.

―――. "Zikai manhua xu" [Preface to the cartoon collection by (Feng) Zikai]. In *Pingwu zawen* [Miscellaneous writings of the Pingwu]. Shanghai: Kaiming shudian, 1935.

―――, and Ye Shengtao. *Wenxin* [The heart of literature]. Shanghai: Kaiming shudian, 1933.

Xia Nai. "Taiping tianguo qianhou Changjiang gesheng zhi tianfu wenti" [Land tax in Yangzi Valley provinces before and after the Taiping Uprising]. *Qinghua xuebao* 10, 2 (April 1925): 408–74.

Xia Yan. "Dang wusi langchao chong dao Zhejiang de shihou" [When the tide of May Fourth reached Zhejiang]. In *Wusi yundong huiyi lu* [Recollections of the May Fourth Movement], edited by Zhongguo shehui kexue yuan jindai shi yanjiu suo. Beijing: Zhongguo shehui kexue chuban she, 1979.

Xia Zhu. "Ruxue shi xunci" [Lecture on the first day of school]. *Zhejiang diyi shifan xiaoyou huizhi* (fall 1917): 6–7.

Xianjiang. "Wosheng zhi yi xueqi" [One semester in Wosheng's life]. *Zhejiang shengli diyi shifan xuexiao xiaoyou huizhi* 3 (summer 1914): 5.

Xiaojing [Book of filial piety]. Reprint Shanghai: Hanfenlou, 1922.

Xie Bin. *Zhongguo tiedao shi* [History of Chinese railroads]. Shanghai: Zhonghua shuju, 1929.

Xin qingnian she bianji bu, ed. *Shehui zhuyi taolun ji* [Discussions on socialism: An anthology]. Guangzhou: Xin qingnian she, 1922.

Xinbian Zhejiang bainian dashi ji, 1840–1949 [New chronicle of major events in the past century in Zhejiang, 1840–1949]. Edited by Zhejiang sheng zhengzhi xieshang hui wenshi ziliao weiyuan hui. Hangzhou: Zhejiang renmin chuban she, 1990.

Xinchao [Original English title, *The Renaissance*]. Reprint Taipei: Dong-fang wenhua shuju, 1972.

Xingqi pinglun [Weekend review]. Shanghai.

Xu Heyong, Zheng Yunshan, and Zhao Shipei. *Zhejiang jindai shi* [Modern history of Zhejiang]. Hangzhou: Zhejiang renmin chuban she, 1982.

Xu Ke. *Qing bai lei chao* [Digest of Qing anecdotes, classified]. Shanghai: Shangwu yinshu guan, 1917.

Xu Yaofang. "Shi Fuliang de baobei" [Shi Fuliang's treasure]. *Jinhua ribao* [Jinhua daily], July 6, 1992.

Xu Zhizhen. "Guangyu xin Yuyangli liuhao de huodong qingxing" [About activities at the new Number 6 Yuyangli address]. In *Gongchan zhuyi xiaozu* [Communist small groups], edited by Zhonggong zhongyang dangshi ziliao zhengji weiyuan hui. Beijing: Zhonggong dangshi ziliao chuban she, 1987, vol. 1.

Yamada Tatsuo. *Chūkoku kokumintō saha no kenkyū* [Study of the left wing of the Chinese Nationalist Party]. Tokyo: Keio University Press, 1980.

Yang Duanliu. "Guiguo zagan" [Miscellaneous thoughts on returning to my home country]. *Taiping yang* [Pacific Ocean] 3, 6 (August 1920): 1–8.

Yang Jianxin and Lu Wei. *Sichou zhilu* [The silk road]. Lanzhou: Gansu renmin chuban she, 1988.

Yang, Lien-sheng. "Ming Local Administration." In *Chinese Government in Ming Times: Seven Studies*, edited by Charles O. Hucker. New York: Columbia University Press, 1969.

Yang Qitao. "Shujia guicheng jilue" [Journal kept during the trip home in the summer]. In *Zhejiang shengli diyi shifan xuexiao xiaoyou hui zhi* (fall 1917): 32–33.

Yang Zhihua. "Yang Zhihua de huiyi" [Yang Zhihua's recollections]. In *Yida qianhou: Zhongguo Gongchandang diyi ci daibiao dahui qianhou ziliao xuanbian* [Before and after the First Party Congress: Selected edition of materials on the First Party Congress of the Chinese Communist Party], edited by Zhongguo shehui kexue yuan jindai shi yanjiu shi and Zhongguo geming bowu guan dangshi yanjiu shi. Beijing: Renmin chuban she, 1980, vol. 2.

Ye Qianchu. *Lanxi shiyan xian shixi diaocha baogao* [Report about an on-the-job training and investigation experience with the experimental administration of Lanxi County]. Taipei: Chengwen chuban she, 1977.

Ye Shengtao and Zhu Ziqing. *Guowen luedu zhidao* [Guide to preliminary studies of national literature]. Hong Kong: Chuangken chuban she, 1955.

Ye Xian'en. *Ming Qing Huizhou nongcun shehui yu dianpuzhi* [Rural society and the system of tenant servants in Huizhou under the Ming and the Qing]. Anhui: Renmin chuban she, 1983.

Yeh, Wen-hsin. *The Alienated Academy: Culture and Politics in Republican China, 1919–1937*. Cambridge, Mass.: Council on East Asian Studies Publications, Harvard University Press, 1990.

———. "Renshen zhijian: Qianlun shiba shiji de Luojiao" [Mortals and immortals: On the Luo Sect in the eighteenth century]. *Shixue pinglun* 2 (July 1980): 45–84.

Yi Baisha. "Kongzi pingyi" [A fair evaluation of Confucius]. *Xin qingnian* 1, 6 (February 1916): 1–6, and 2, 1 (September 1916): 1–6.

Yi Jiayue and Luo Dunwei. *Zhongguo jiating wenti* [Problems with Chinese families]. Shanghai: Taidong shuju, 1924.

Yida huiyi lu [First Party Congress memoirs]. Edited by Zhishi chuban she. Beijing: Zhishi chuban she, 1980.

Yida qianhou: Zhongguo Gongchandang diyi ci daibiao dahui qianhou ziliao xuanbian [Before and after the First Party Congress: Selected edition of materials on the First Party Congress of the Chinese Communist Party]. Edited by Zhongguo shehui kexue yuan jindai shi yanjiu shi and Zhongguo geming bowu guan dangshi yanjiu shi. 2 vols. Beijing: Renmin chuban she, 1980.

Yida qianhou de Guangdong dang zuzhi [Party organization in Guangdong before and after the First Congress]. Edited by Zhonggong Guangdong

shengwei dangshi yanjiu weiyuan hui bangong shi and Guangdong
sheng dang'an guan. Dongguan: Guangdong sheng dang'an guan, 1981.
Yu Dafu. *Jihen chuchu* [Footprints far and near]. Shanghai: Tieliu shudian,
1946.
Yu Heping, ed. *Jing Yuanshan ji* [Collected works by Jing Yuanshan].
Wuhan: Huazhong shifan daxue chuban she, 1988.
Yu Xiusong. "Yu Xiusong gei Luo Zhixiang de xin" [Yu Xiusong's letter
to Luo Zhixiang], April 4, 1920. Held in the First Party Congress
Museum. Reprinted in Zhonggong zhongyang dangshi zhengji weiyuan
hui, ed., *Gongchan zhuyi xiaozu* [Communist small groups]. Beijing:
Zhonggong dangshi ziliao chuban she, 1987, vol. 1.
Yu Ying-shih [Yu Yingshi]. "Some Preliminary Observations on the Rise
of Ch'ing Confucian Intellectualism." *Tsing Hua Journal of Chinese
Studies*, new series 10, 1–2 (December 1975): 105–46.
———. "Wusi—yige wei wancheng de wenhua yundong" [May
Fourth—an unfinished cultural movement]. In *Wenhua pinglun yu
Zhongguo qinghuai* [Cultural commentary and Chinese attachments],
edited by Yu Ying-shih. Taipei: Yunchen, 1988.
Yue Jiwei. *Xun zong mi ji*. Shanghai: Fanyi chuban gongsi, 1991.
Zarrow, Peter. *Anarchism and Chinese Political Culture*. New York: Co-
lumbia University Press, 1990.
Zeitlin, Judith T. *Historian of the Strange: Pu Songling and the Classical
Chinese Tale*. Stanford: Stanford University Press, 1993.
Zhang Guohui. *Wan Qing qianzhuang he piaohao yanjiu* [Study of late
Qing native banks and Shanxi banks]. Beijing: Zhonghua shuju, 1989.
Zhang Guotao. "Changxindian gongren faqi ladong buxi xuexiao"
[Changxindian workers initiated the labor adult school]. In *Laodong jie*
15 (November 21, 1920), reprinted in *Zhang Guotao nianpu ji yanlun*
[Zhang Guotao: Chronological biography and writings], edited by Sheng
Renxue. Beijing: Jiefangjun chuban she, 1985.
Zhang Qiyun. *Zhejiang sheng shidi jiyao* [Historical geography of the
province of Zhejiang]. Shanghai: Commercial Press, 1925.
Zhang Tinghao. "Huiyi Guomindang Shanghai zhixingbu" [Recollections
of the Shanghai Executive Committee of the Guomindang]. *Dangshi
ziliao* 18 (1984): 114–18.
Zhang Xuecheng [Shizhai]. "Zhedong xueshu" [Zhedong scholarship]. In
Wenshi tongyi [General treatise on literature and history]. Reprint
Taipei: Guoshi yanjiu shi, 1972.
Zhang Zhelang. *Qingdai de caoyun* [Shipment of tributary grain during
the Qing]. Taipei: Jiaxin shuini gongsi wenhua jijin hui, 1969.
Zhang Zhongli, ed. *Jindai Shanghai chengshi yanjiu* [Study of the urban
development of modern Shanghai]. Shanghai: Renmin chuban she,
1990.

Zhanhuan. "Liening de zhuzuo yi lan biao" [List of Lenin's writings]. *Gongchandang* 1 (November 7, 1920).

Zhao Yi. *Ershier shi zhaji* [Study notes on twenty-two dynastic histories]. Reprint Taipei: Shijie shuju, 1967.

Zhaomin. "Xiaoxun zhi kuice" [Thoughts on school mottoes]. *Zhejiang shengli diyi shifan xuexiao xiaoyou huizhi* 13 (fall 1917): 63–64.

Zhejiang ji ziben jia de xingqi [Rise of Zhejiang capitalists]. Edited by Zhongguo renmin zhengzhi xieshang huiyi Zhejiang sheng wenshi ziliao yanjiu weiyuan hui. Hangzhou: Zhejiang renmin chuban she, 1986.

Zhejiang sheng jiu Jinshu gexian xiangzhen diaocha biao [Investigative report on villages and towns in counties formerly under the Jinhua Prefecture of Zhejiang Province]. Edited by Zhejiang sheng juanshui jianli weiyuan hui. N.p., n.d.

Zhejiang sheng nongcun diaocha [Investigations of Zhejiang villages]. Edited by Xingzheng yuan nongcun fuxing weiyuan hui. Shanghai: Shangwu yinshu guan, 1934.

Zhejiang shengli diyi shifan xuexiao du'an jishi [A truthful record of the poison case at Zhejiang Provincial First Normal School]. Edited by Zhejiang shengli diyi xuexiao. Hangzhou: n.p., 1923.

Zhejiang shengli diyi shifan xuexiao tongxue lu, 1915, 1922. [Roster of fellow scholars at the Zhejiang Provincial First Normal School, 1915, 1922]. Hangzhou: Zhejiang shengli diyi shifan xuexiao, 1915, 1922.

Zhejiang shengli diyi shifan xuexiao xiaoyou huizhi [Gazette of friends and associates of Zhejiang First Normal School]. Hangzhou: Zhejiang diyi shifan xuexiao, 1914–18.

Zhejiang shengli diyi zhongxue tongxue lu, 1923 [Roster of fellow scholars at the Zhejiang Provincial First Middle School, 1923]. Hangzhou: Zhejiang shengli diyi zhongxuexiao, 1923.

Zhemin. Letter to Shi Cuntong, "Juewu" section, *Minguo ribao*, April 10, 1920.

Zhen [He Zhen] and Shen [Liu Shipei]. "Lun gongchan zhi yixing yu Zhongguo" [On the feasibility of Communism in China]. In *Hengbao* 1, 2 (May 8, 1908). Reprinted in *Wuzhengfu zhuyi sixiang ziliao xuan* [Selection of sources on anarchist thought], edited by Ge Maochun, Jiang Jun, and Li Xingzhi. Beijing: Beijing daxue chuban she, 1984, vol. 1.

———. "Lun zhongzu geming yu wuzhengfu geming zhi deshi" [On the pros and cons of ethnic revolution vis-à-vis anarchist revolution]. In *Tianyi bao* [Natural justice], vols. 6–7, 1907. Reprinted in *Wuzhengfu zhuyi sixiang ziliao xuan* [Selection of sources on anarchist thought], edited by Ge Maochun, Jiang Jun, and Li Xingzhi. Beijing: Beijing daxue chuban she, 1984, vol. 1.

Zhendan daxue ershiwu nian xiaoshi [Twenty-five years of Université L'Aurore]. Shanghai: n.p., 1928.

Zheng Yifang. *Shanghai qianzhuang (1834–1937): Zhongguo chuantong jinrong ye de tuibian* [Shanghai native banks, 1843–1937: The transformation of the traditional Chinese credit system]. Taipei: Zhongyang yanjiu yuan sanmin zhuyi yanjiu suo, 1981.

Zhonggong Hunan shengwei dangshi ziliao zhengji yanjiu weiyuan hui. "Changsha gongchan zhuyi xiaozu zongshu" [General account of the Communist small groups in Changsha]. In *Gongchan zhuyi xiaozu* [Communist small groups], edited by Zhonggong zhongyang dangshi ziliao zhengji weiyuan hui. Beijing: Zhonggong dangshi ziliao chuban she, 1987, vol. 2.

Zhongguo Gongchandang diyi ci daibiao dahui dang'an ziliao zeng ding ben [Expanded edition, Archival materials on the First Party Congress of the Chinese Communist Party]. Edited by Zhongyang dang'an guan. Beijing: Renmin chuban she, 1984.

"Zhongguo Gongchandang laodong zuhe shuji bu xuanyan" [Declaration by the labor secretariat of the Chinese Communist Party]. *Gongchandang* 6 (July 7, 1921): 21–22.

Zhongguo Gongchandang lishi [History of the Chinese Communist Party]. Edited by Zhonggong zhongyang dangshi yanjiu shi. Beijing: Renmin chuban she, 1991.

Zhongguo Guomindang diyi ci quanguo daibiao dahui shiliao zhuanji [Historical materials on the First Party Congress of the Chinese Nationalist Party: A special collection]. Edited by Zhonghua minguo shiliao yanjiu zhongxin. Taipei: Zhonghua minguo shiliao yanjiu zhongxin, 1984.

Zhongguo Guomindang diyi, er ci quanguo daibiao dahui huiyi shiliao [Historical materials on the First and Second Party Congresses of the Chinese Nationalist Party]. Edited by Zhongguo dier lishi dang'an guan. 2 vols. Nanjing: Jiangsu guji chuban she, 1986.

Zhou Fohai. "Wang yi ji" [Notes on bygone days]. In *Yida huiyi lu* [First Party Congress memoirs]. Shanghai: Zhishi chuban she, 1980.

Zhu Bangda, ed. *Diyi ci Zhongguo jiaoyu nianjian* [Yearbook of Chinese education, first compilation]. Shanghai: Kaiming shudian, 1934.

Zhu Chengjia, ed. *Zhonggong dangshi yanjiu lunwen xuan* [Selections of essays on the history of the Chinese Communist Party]. 3 vols. Changsha: Hunan renmin chuban she, 1983.

Zurndorfer, Harriet T. *Change and Continuity in Chinese Local History: The Development of Hui-chou Prefecture, 800–1800*. Leiden: E. J. Brill, 1989.

Index

Designer: Ina Clausen
Compositor: Braun-Brumfield, Inc.
Text: 10/13 Aldus
Display: Aldus
Printer: Braun-Brumfield, Inc.
Binder: Braun-Brumfield, Inc.